w

THE INFIRM GLORY

The author and his mother in 1938. *Photo: E. J. Mason*

The Infirm Glory

GODFREY WINN

Volume I of his autobiography

'Because I do not hope to know again
The infirm glory of the positive hour.'
              T. S. ELIOT
              Ash Wednesday

London
MICHAEL JOSEPH

First published in Great Britain by
MICHAEL JOSEPH LTD
26 *Bloomsbury Street*
London, W.C.1
1967

WIN
434518

ISBN N0015 77530

Set and printed in Great Britain by Tonbridge Printers Ltd,
Peach Hall Works, Tonbridge, Kent, in Garamond eleven on
twelve point, and bound by James Burn at Esher, Surrey

FOR JOANNA

in deep affection and gratitude
for so many things

Contents

Illustrations

Part One
The Green Years

THE MATRIARCHAL figure next to me in the row of cathedral seats reserved for the Bishop's own guests on that occasion of consecration and re-birth wore a plain, far-from-new, green skirt and tweed jacket, and an uncompromising felt hat on her grey hair. Her profile was a noble one, however, as though etched on an ancient coin. I only noticed what my neighbour was wearing because I recognized it as a kind of uniform, and as we all waited expectantly for the Queen's arrival, with the posse of previous High Sheriffs of Warwickshire in their far more dashing insignia, seated just in front of us, I could not help my mind wandering back to another visit to the city, just after the first of the massive blitzes that was to introduce a new word into our language. To coventrate.

This was May 1962, and that had been November 1941. Twenty-one years between. A coming-of-age, perhaps, for this was as much a service of forgiveness as of re-dedication, I reminded myself, living again in my memory every incident of that dark winter's day. In the early morning, I had woken to find the features editor of *The Sunday Express* who only a few hours before I had watched with his usual skill putting my weekly page to bed, now standing like a well-fed apparition at the end of my own bed.

I started up full of apprehension and foreboding. 'What is it, Harold? What is the matter?' Editors don't pay social calls at that time in the morning, and editors, I have learnt from long experience, usually bring difficult tidings.

'Your telephone's off, and John has an extra assignment for you this week. He wants you to go to Coventry. Apparently there's been one hell of a raid, much the worst yet, and no one was allowed into the city yesterday except the essential services. But the King is going today.'

'Go to Coventry?' I repeated, the irony of the phrase escaping us both at that moment. 'How shall I get in?' I added doubtfully,

13

longing to disappear under the bedclothes. 'It was announced on
the wireless last night that no trains were running into the city,
and I've got practically no petrol left.'

'We've seen to that. I've found a taxi that is prepared to take
you there and back. A bit of luck.' For the paper, not me, I
thought. Harold Keeble, with whom I had only just started working but who was to prove the most inspiring of allies across the
years, continued urbanely, 'As a matter of fact, he brought me
here, and is waiting at the door. How soon can you start? You'll
have to find a telephone that works somewhere on the way back,
to give us the story.'

I crawled out of bed, not feeling in the least like a gallant war
reporter. The story, the story, the front page story. That's all
they cared about. But of course, they were right, that was what
newspapers were in business for, and of all editors John Gordon,
I had to admit to myself, had the most attentive ear for the big
news story. The knowledge was a kind of comfort, and as soon
as I had climbed into the cab I began to feel a little more confident. For my driver behaved as though his fare was on the way
to catch a train, and there was plenty of time. I wish I had recorded his name so that I could thank him now. All the same,
even his Olympian chariot could not get me right to my destination. I had to walk the last few miles into the city, because all
the mains had burst and the roads were impassable with débris
of one kind and another.

As I drew near the Council House, drawn in that direction by
the sound of scattered cheering, it was to find a grave, slight
figure, isolated on the steps, almost anonymous in his army great-
coat. Ashes from the grey sky fell on to his shoulders. Everyone
was silent now. Later, I walked in the party behind him, noting
automatically that he never faltered at the sound of a time bomb
exploding unpleasantly near. At one moment I almost stumbled
myself over what I mistook for a charred log of wood, until it was
explained that this was all that was left of the body of a warden
– one of the 'Essential Services' – that had just been dug
out.

So the hours passed, the sort of day in one's education that
seems in retrospect so infinitely more important than the whole
sum of your schooldays. Towards evening, when the royal party
had gone, I found myself suddenly alone in the square beside

the gutted cathedral. Now I felt more like a ghost than a reporter, with the stench of the ashes choking my nostrils. While there above the acrid fumes in the molten skies, at this moment when all the munition workers, like myriad ants, were preparing to trudge on foot, their bicycles discarded because of the broken roads, to clock-in at the factories for the night shifts, I saw a wide banner, with a message it seemed specially for them, for us all, floating in the sky. IT ALL DEPENDS ON ME.

Afterwards, I was to discover that the banner was pinned to the side of the church next to the cathedral. But in that mood of confusion and oblivion, what was left of the bricks and mortar was hidden, only the banner floated surprisingly across the line of one's vision.

I have never been able quite to erase the moment from my consciousness, or the tableau that subsequently took place a few yards away. A woman approached, hopelessly weeping, saying over and over again, between her sobs, as though any explanation was needed, that she had never missed a Sunday service in the cathedral for the last thirty years. Beside her, a fair youth in Royal Air Force uniform tried to comfort her, repeating in his turn the same words with a desperate reiteration. 'Never mind, Mum. We will avenge you.'

His battle-cry had not seemed inappropriate at the time, but so archaic now, and barbaric, too, I thought (twenty-one years later), glancing again at Stella Reading, reading the order of the service, next to me in the rebuilt cathedral. But I saw not her, but the two members of her army in the same civilian uniform, no difference outwardly in any way between themselves and their leader. They were pushing a trolley and on it steaming cups of tea. They gave one to each of us, asking no questions. The W.V.S. One of the truly essential services, in peace as in war. Not wasting time talking about revenge, nor in weeping. Just getting on with the job in hand. As women always do. And I thought then of my mother, and at the same time of something that Cuthbert Bardsley, Bishop of Coventry, with the carved head of a crusader, had said to me the first time he took me round his cathedral, the day that the Graham Sutherland tapestry of Christ had been put in place above the high altar. 'Look at the feet,' my guide had told me in the kind of voice that you would like to hear beside you if you were very ill. 'They are the feet of a man who has walked many, many miles, doing his job.' He might have put it in more ecclesiastical language, 'pursuing his mission, spreading the Word of God.' But he didn't, and the impact was stronger in consequence. Somehow, all the controversy about the merits or demerits of the artist's conception passed over my head after that first appraisal. I remained only aware of the implications of these deliberately un-godlike feet, with the tiny figure of the man silhouetted between them, everyman, who could have been one of the night-shift workers that I had passed on my way out of the coventrated city.

Now we were standing up in duty and respect, for another procession was about to pass us up the nave, so different in mood and colouring and composition from twenty-one years before. All the grey had vanished, here was the gold, the panoply and the authentic gold. The Queen, and behind her, her younger sister with her husband, followed by the Lord Lieutenant of Warwickshire, with whom I had stayed the previous evening, and his wife, Rachel Willoughby de Broke, looking so very English, so exactly right; and behind them again, the High Sheriff for the year, a tall man with very dark eyes and hair, the colour of tar in a cauldron, and at his side, in turn, his lady, wearing the kind of dignity that so many Englishwomen always manage to bring forth when the occasion demands.

Maybe I was prejudiced on this occasion by old, half-forgotten fidelities, because as they passed me on their way to their seats at the front, I had an absurd impulse to clutch at their sleeves, to call out their Christian names, Audrey, John. To prove to myself that all this, all my life for that matter, was not an insubstantial dream; that the man in the ceremonial dress of the High Sheriff, and the woman at his side in the blue dress and fur cape, I really had played with as children, half a century before, when they had been simply a boy and a girl who lived in neighbouring lanes in the Worcestershire village where I spent the earlier years of my childhood.

This unexpected confrontation, in such circumstances, inevitably made my mind tingle as though a fresh battery had that instant been attached to it. Audrey Charles and John Challen. In those days, my elder brother Rodger and I always called Audrey's mother 'Auntie Bee', though she was actually no relation. But my mother had been a bridesmaid at Audrey's own mother's wedding, and I always suspected there was a secret hope between the two mothers that Audrey and I would one day marry. Instead, we eyed each other warily, dancing with each other reluctantly at birthday parties, and it was only later when Audrey, in her teens, became eager to play in county tennis tournaments, that she acknowledged my usefulness as a partner, and a new basis for a close relationship was created, which, this time, proved a lasting success.

'Open the door.' From behind us, outside the great doors of the cathedral, the voice of the bishop could be heard, demanding entry into his own church. The final cue for the service to commence, but I am afraid the exhortation, spoken though it was in that crusader's voice, fell in my case on deaf ears. Or rather, it was another door which was opening, and by the time the Archbishop had begun his rather pedestrian address from the pulpit, my attention had begun to wander again, back to the house on top of the hill, in that village a few miles from Birmingham, where I was born.

'Your Brummagem accent isn't right. It isn't nearly nasal enough,' I had the temerity to remark in her dressing-room to the leading lady of Terence Rattigan's play, *Variations on a Theme,* when it was being tried out in Brighton, the nearest town to my writing retreat under the South Downs, in that other Sussex village where I have finally dropped my anchor.

Whereupon, Margaret Leighton had gently but firmly put me in my place, retorting, 'Nonsense, Godfrey. I ought to know what the accent is like. I was brought up with it. I was born in the vicinity.'

'You were?' I echoed unbelievingly, for how could her frail physique, her orchid-like personality, have survived the winter cold of the Midlands. Compare those conditions with the Russian Run, the ice and blackness of the Barentz Sea, and there really wasn't much difference.

'I was born and brought up in what is now almost a suburb of Birmingham called Barnt Green,' she reiterated.

'I simply don't believe it,' I exclaimed.

'Why don't you believe it?'

'Because from the age of one year old till I was nearly ten, I lived in Barnt Green myself.'

Maggie looked at me reflectively. 'Then you must have left

about the time I appeared on the scene. There simply wasn't room for both of us.'

'I still don't believe it,' I repeated stubbornly, not to be diverted.

'All right then, I'll prove it. We lived at the top of Twatling Road, near the Lickey Memorial, and at the bottom of the hill . . .'

'You mean, opposite Doctor Ambrose's house?'

'Yes, there was the pillar box, with a sort of surround of grass round it, and then the hill ran on down to the left to the station. . . .'

'Actually, there were four roads branching off there, and the sharpest one to the left led to our house. It was called Cherrycroft in our days, because it was at the top of Cherry Hill, which was perfect for tobogganing in the winter. And do you remember the bluebells, in the spring, in the woods that stretched up to the Lickey Hills?'

But another visitor had come into the leading lady's dressing-room. ('Oh, you really liked my performance? I am so glad.') However, the persistent train of coincidence was under way, for a few weeks later, in London, on meeting the very handsome young actor who was playing the juvenile lead opposite Margaret Leighton, it was almost inevitable that I should tell him the story of how I had been properly squashed. To which I received an unexpected reply: 'What did you say was the name of the village where you both came from?' Jeremy Brett asked. When I repeated the name, he exclaimed, 'Barnt Green. Why, how extraordinary. You see, my mother came from there, too.'

'Your mother?' I stammered.

'Yes, her name before she was married was Butler. There were two sisters. Do you remember them?'

'Of course. Christine and Betty Butler.'

Jeremy's mother was to reintroduce herself to me at her son's wedding soon afterwards to Anna Massey, over which the Bishop of Coventry presided. When Jeremy's mother, dressed with matronly suitability as Audrey Challen had been, remarked to me, 'Of course, I must have been much nearer your brother's age, because I only remember you as a tiny boy', I had the same sensation that I had that day in the cathedral of all time, all the years being transported in a giant kaleidoscope and everything put together again in a fresh pattern, with a new meaning that I had never understood or appreciated before.

Along the same road as the Butlers' home was The Pump House, which was my favourite in the neighbourhood because you went down some steps as soon as you entered the front door, and the rooms were all book-lined with low ceilings, and reminded me of a setting for one of Beatrix Potter's stories. Here the Beesly family lived; Helen, with the gentle air of a gazelle, was always full of concern, and never ignored me because I was so much smaller than the others (so perhaps it was appropriate that later she should marry a doctor), and Marion who was dark as Helen was fair; Richard, the same age as myself, so splendid an athlete, who was to row for Cambridge, and yet was to die too soon; Patrick, and finally Spencer, the family leader, who was even senior to my elder brother, which made him very old, in my eyes. In those days, I always seemed to be tagging along behind Rodger, and hoping to be noticed. And behaving, it must be confessed, in an exhibitionist manner until I was.

At least, that probability was planted in my mind not long ago when I found myself seated next at lunch to Elizabeth Pakenham, now Lady Longford, at one of Lady Pamela Berry's glittering lunch parties. In her dining-room in Westminster, behind her seat, hangs a superb Lepine. I sometimes wonder how many of the politicians and the leaders from different worlds notice the quality of the picture, so rapt are they in the table conversation. I first set eyes on my hostess when she was still a school-girl, sitting demurely beside the tennis courts at Charlton, her family home outside Oxford, while her brother's week-end guests indulged in yet another of the matches which her father, the first Lord Birkenhead, had himself enjoyed so much. On that occasion Pam wore a plain white frieze-cloth coat that enhanced her gipsy-black hair, the pallor of her skin and the luminous dark eyes that were already commanding. Instinctively, I was reminded of one of the illustrations for Rossetti's *The Blessed Damozel*, an impression very remote from her authority as, perhaps, the most important political hostess of the day. Her great strength, I would say, is that she is on equally good terms with the front ranks of all three parties. A position that she has entirely made for herself. For her mother is a most accomplished artist, her sister Eleanor was a novelist, her brother is one of the best biographers of our time. It was left to Pam, in her own way, to keep alight her father's torch.

I myself am right outside the world of politics, so at lunch that day I was wondering how to break the ice with my neighbour, who I knew was married to a politician, a member of the Labour Cabinet, when my fellow-guest, who despite the labours of bringing up seven children has surprised the world by producing by far the best Life of Queen Victoria yet, surprised me in quite a different way.

'The first time I set eyes on you, Mr Winn, was at a tea-party at the Beeslys at Barnt Green. I was staying with Helen, who is my cousin. You crawled under the table and started taking off the girls' shoes.'

'A kind of fetish, do you think, Lady Pakenham? Surely very early to start.'

'No, I just imagine you wanted to be noticed.'

I had no recollection of myself, scrambling on the floor, in the tent-like darkness of the tablecloth, no memory, either, of Elizabeth Harmer as she then was, in the days when in her school holidays, or at half term, she would also go to stay at Bampton Manor, with another of her Chamberlain aunts, and often find there my Aunt Edith, my father's sister who never married.

After I discovered the unexpected links we had from the past, I became too intent on my companion to throw any more appreciative glances in the direction of the Lepine, and I feel I shall always be in the debt of my hostess for that encounter. Today, Frank and Elizabeth Longford are Sussex neighbours of mine, and it is always a pleasure for me to visit them in their home in Hurst Green, where the slightly faded air of the drawing-room chintzes creates more of an Edwardian than a Fabian atmosphere.

'You just wanted to be noticed.'

A variation on this theme was also imprinted on my mind when I was engaged in writing *The Younger Sister*, and I asked Princess Margaret what was the first thing in her life she remembered, and she replied, 'Oh, falling out of my pram,' adding, 'I suspect I just wanted to be noticed.'

Perhaps. But had she really remembered the fall? Or had the incident been retold so often by her royal Nannie that in the end she came to believe that she actually remembered it happening, the fuss and the consternation, and the soothing noises?

I am always rather dubious when friends relate to me

incidents from their childhood in which they participated at the stage when they were only learning to say 'Mama' and 'Dada'. I am supposed to possess a photographic memory, I never make any notes during an interview; I can clearly visualize the leather belt with the strong buckle that my governess, Miss Jefferies, wore, and the scent of her blue serge skirt, as though she was standing in the room at this moment; yet, the first experience of my childhood that I can recall in absolute detail did not happen till I was four.

That April afternoon there was a tennis party in progress on the lawn at the back of Cherrycroft. I was running around, eager, no doubt, to be noticed, when my father returned home from his office in Birmingham on the afternoon train. He would have been wearing a bow tie, dark-blue probably with small white spots on it, and a dark-blue suit to match, and his shirt would still seem very clean despite the grime of the city. That was my outstanding memory of him in those days, how clean he always looked behind his glasses, and how clean he smelt when he stooped to kiss me.

He always appeared to be stooping, even then. Perhaps because he was so tall, while my mother was tiny, five-foot at the most. Or perhaps, again, because he took no part in outdoor pursuits. His hobby was photography, he took pictures of a professional standard, he was for ever posing his family in artistic groups. It was his only outlet for self-expression at that time, his safety valve from the long hours he dutifully spent over columns of figures, in his working life, as a chartered accountant. There was no inkling yet of what was to come.

Usually he would have felt shy, and out of place, among the tennis-players, but today he was a messenger from burning Troy. He spoke first to the players sitting round the tea-table, on the top bank, and their cups were suspended in mid-air by his tidings, frozen like a frieze in Pompeii. Swiftly the other players on the court were drawn into the revelation of horror. The guest about to serve dropped his racquet, as though his arm was suddenly numb. I had been looking for a ball that had escaped over the netting into a flower-bed. Like a puppy, I now came trotting back, and crouched down beside my mother's wicker chair. Protectively, her hand went down to touch my hair, as my father continued the narrative that today would have been given in full on the one o'clock news on the radio. There was no more tennis, and the party broke up awkwardly, and in silence, before the refreshing jugs of cider cup were brought out by the parlour-maid.

My parents were left alone. The sense of doom was even stronger now. 'Collect the balls, darling,' my mother said to me, and there was a note of hopeless sadness in her voice that I had never heard before, and it made me frightened, though I did not know why, since I was not yet involved myself. April the fifteenth, 1912. And the news that my father had brought as a messenger, not from Troy but from Birmingham, was of the sinking of the ship that was the new glory of the White Star Line, out to snatch the record for the Atlantic crossing, *Titanic*.

That afternoon I had my first inculcation into the menacing insecurity of life. The sun had been shining with the promise of the summer ahead, everyone had seemed so carefree and happy, and then suddenly this awful thing had happened. I did not, of course, understand the full implications of my father's story, but it was only too clear, even to my childish vision, that something vast and unpredictable had occurred which made even my omnipotent parents seem lost and bewildered, and worst of all, shrink before my eyes.

Nothing in my early childhood left such a mark on me as the sudden drop in temperature of that spring afternoon, and, in contrast, I have no personal sense of participation in the Sunday afternoon when my mother panicked for the first and last time in her life.

It was after lunch, in the drawing-room. As in doubtless many other Barnt Green households, peace reigned. My father snoozed, I was absorbed as always in a picture book, my mother appreciatively drank her second cup of coffee, the best in Barnt Green – at least she had drunk no better – and all due to not being mean with the heaped spoonfuls, and not forgetting the pinch of mustard that her American mother had taught her to add.

At that moment, I must have opened my mouth wide, in her direction, because my mother seized me abruptly and started to peer into the cavity exposed. There appeared to be nothing but a dark brown tunnel. Whereupon a terrible maternal fear took possession of her. I had no roof to my mouth. That was why I was so backward in talking. I was not mentally retarded, but physically so.

'Wake up, Ernest, wake up ... look at the child's mouth.'
Before my father could collect his Sunday afternoon thoughts,
or argue, he found himself pushing me in my go-cart up the hill,
towards where at a later date Margaret Leighton was first to see
the light of day, and the Challens' house – no social call this –
to ring the bell at the doctor's surgery.

No doubt the poor man was disturbed from his own Sunday
afternoon siesta. But he showed no signs of grumpiness. Instead,
there was a twinkle in his eye, as having made his examination he
was able swiftly to disperse my mother's fears. 'Dear lady, your
son has a roof, a perfectly good roof to his mouth, but at the
moment it is concealed by a thick layer of unmasticated chocolate.'

I have no recollection of my father being testy on the home-
ward journey. In those early days, I never heard my parents
quarrel or say bitter things to each other. Instead, the alarum and
excursion must have jolted something in my own metabolism,
for the very next day, according to family legend, I started to talk.
And, I am afraid, have been making up for lost time ever since.

Usually on Sundays we all gathered, the whole family, under
my paternal grandfather's roof, a patriarchic setting at The
Uplands, Selly Oak. My grandfather, Charles Winn, had been
born in 1829 at Church Street, Birmingham, near the cathedral.
His own father had house property in Church Street, and a *papier-
mâché* factory. All this, however, was to be destroyed by fire, and
the shock of the loss, uncovered by insurance of any sort, was to
kill him. So my grandfather's early life had been an extremely
hard struggle, for he had entirely to support himself and his sister
Phoebe, who was later to enter the nursing profession and then
marry one of the most notable Harley Street throat specialists,
Dr Greville MacDonald, himself the son of the celebrated Victorian writer, George MacDonald.

By the time I came on the scene, my grandfather had long
since built up a most flourishing engineering works in Charles
Street, and lived in considerable splendour in a large Victorian
mansion, very awe-inspiring to a small child, because it stood
on a plateau and was approached by a wide, stone staircase.
Actually, there were two grey-stone houses, placed side by side,
and separated by a courtyard. On one side, at the top of their
balustraded approach, lived the Webley family, who were to give

their name to the most famous revolver of the day. The two families were closely related, as one of the Webley sisters had married my grandfather in Old Edgbaston Church, where my parents in their turn had exchanged their vows at the turn of the century. On these Sunday reunions, when all the grandchildren put in an attendance, I remember Granny Winn as a gentle, delicate-looking woman, with beautiful bone structure – inherited by my Aunt Edith – a lace cap on her soft, white hair. She never opened her mouth when her husband was in the room. The truth was that everyone, including his four sons – Philip who helped to run the business, Herbert, my godfather, who bequeathed to me the second of my Christian names, Reginald who escaped to Paris, and Ernest, my father, the youngest of the quartet – was secretly frightened of him.

But no one was as scared as I was, principally because of his nose. In the portrait by John Pettie, that still hangs in the board-room of Charles Winn & Company, he looks a handsome man, with a high forehead, but in his later years his nose was to dis-integrate into an over-large, over-ripe raspberry. What caused this I have no idea, but the moment I was old enough to absorb firm instructions it was impressed upon me that I must never point at Grandad's nose, or draw attention to the phenomenon in any way. Because, if I did, I would never again be given a single one of Grandad's grapes, and we usually went home with at least a bunch. Superb black and white muscatels they were, with a bloom and an aroma that I soon discovered to be intoxicating, when, on a Sunday afternoon, I would slip away from the endless chatter of the grown-ups and play hide-and-seek with myself in the subaqueous avenues of the hot-houses.

Of course, I was absolutely aware that I must not touch any of the bunches, ripe or otherwise. Thus the sense of compulsive guilt lay heavy on me, since I could not resist picking one from here and one from there, hoping and praying that on Monday morning none of the gardeners would discover my vandalism. Fortunately, I was never caught in the act for I shudder even today at the contemplation of what would have happened to me had Grandfather Winn's full wrath descended upon me. The rumbles of distant thunder were enough.

Surprisingly, considering what a man of steel he was, my grandfather was a keen horticulturist and something of a patron

of the arts. Among his letters I have found several from Charles
Sims, an eminent academician of his day, thanking my grandfather for gifts of grapes, which seemed always to have arrived,
unlike the posts today, in 'perfect condition', while among the
pictures that eventually came down to me, through my Aunt
Edith, are two enchanting small John Ruskin water-colours, inscribed to my grandfather on the back.

The Midlands in those days, and the environs of Birmingham
especially, were full of men of brass. That was the admired thing
to be. Not so much a man of property, with many acres to your
name, as a man of brass. Make your pile, and then indulge in
such fancy pursuits as winning prizes for your grapes at horti-
cultural shows, or naming the orchids in your hot-houses after
each new addition to the family. But you had to be sure of the
brass first. While the fact that almost every bathroom in every
new house built in the suburbs of Birmingham had at that time
the label 'Charles Winn & Co.' inscribed upon its taps, was in
no way a handicap to social grace. On the contrary.

The Cadburys, the Nettlefolds, the Kenricks and the Cham-
berlains were the leading lights of the local social horizon, and
my grandparents had many friendly links, particularly with the
Chamberlain family. Indeed, the orchid that Joe Chamberlain
would sport in his buttonhole in the House of Commons often
came from The Uplands' preserves, and years later, whenever I
encountered Mrs Neville Chamberlain, even at the time when her
husband was Prime Minister, she would always ask after my
Aunt Edith, as though we were all still living cosily together in
the smaller parishes of Edgbaston, where I was born in Woodbourne Road, and Selly Oak.

Aunt Edith was considered to be the delicate member of the
family, but like so many other creaking doors, she was to astonish
everyone by outlasting all her brothers and her two sisters, living
right into her ninetieth year. Therefore, to escape from the
rigours of the Midland winters, she used to be dispatched in the
company of another of Grandfather's painter friends, James
MacWhirter, and his wife to Italy. Following in the footsteps
of Elizabeth Browning. In later years it gave her, in consequence,
a kind of magical aura in my eyes, enhanced by the pleasure that
I would receive from gazing at the olive groves and the Italian
skies in the delightful MacWhirter water-colours that she had

brought back and which now hung in the drawing-room at The Uplands. In the dining-room, by contrast, there were huge seascapes by Moore and a recent effusion by Watts.

What was left of this collection of pictures came to me at my godmother's death, and hang mostly in my Sussex home today. The last time that I visited her she was an invalid once more, looked after by my cousin Joan, in a little eighteenth-century house with a most attractive façade, on one of the seven hills surrounding Bath. It was an appropriate setting, I thought, for someone whose whole nature had deplored ugliness in any form.

'The view from Beechen Cliff is the one Jane Austen describes in "Northanger Abbey",' she had written to me in a typical reference that linked with her instinctive liking for living in the past. But though I had been prepared for a view, this one astonished me as I walked along the path overhanging the cliff and found all Bath spread below me in the valley. The delicate tracery of the Abbey was silhouetted in the pale, winter afternoon sunlight.

Time to stand and stare, time in which to appreciate the created beauties of the universe. That is what Aunt Edith had taught me as a boy, before all else, I decided, as I rang the bell. She had not only given me my first awareness of beauty, she had made tangible, she had given a meaning to my instinctive gropings towards an aesthetic standard of appreciation.

A Spode bowl of smooth, grey-green texture which she had just acquired, she would hold in her hands, as though it possessed a life of its own. She would compel me to see it through her eyes. Or a Della Robbia plaque, with its serene pure blue that is the authentic mirror of Southern skies, and which she had brought back from Florence.

'Some day you will go there yourself, and see the Fra Angelicos,' she used to tell me. It was more than a promise, it was a command; a secret revelation between us. And now every time that I do return to revisit the monks' cells (where each occupant was allowed to choose one Fra Angelico mural for solitary contemplation during the rest of his time on earth) I think of the spinster aunt who made me first and lastingly aware that there is so much more to human experience than the eternal struggle to keep one's feet in the race. There is the quickening life of the imagination, too. Moreover, if a child's imagination is not awakened early, so often it never is.

That afternoon, as I stood beside her bed in Prospect House, with a bunch of grape hyacinths in my hands, which used to grow in such profusion along the borders of The Uplands, I had a great longing to try and put into words all my gratitude for her help and understanding in my childhood.

But we were both silent at first because we knew that this would be our last meeting. At last, she said: 'You have grown to look like your grandfather's portrait by John Pettie.'

'Have I?' I exclaimed, full of self-consciousness, only able to think of Grandfather's nose as it was at the end, until suddenly the tug that blood ties have for all of us, however indifferent we may pretend to be to them, enveloped me. I sat down on the side of the bed and took her cold, thin hand in mine. Now all barriers were down between us, and her mind cleared, as sometimes happens just before the end, after a brain has been clouded for a time. She spoke of my father, her brother, without flinching or shying away with excuses from all that had happened, and I could sense the relief it was to be rid of so many family skeletons. By the time we were finished, the last of the day had faded from her room, but I did not put on the lamp beside her bed because the lights in the city below were coming out like stars, one by one. 'At this moment, each day as I lie here, I often think that Bath resembles Florence. Looking down from Fiesole,' she added in explanation.

I got up reluctantly to kiss her goodbye and drive back to London, but she had one thing left to say. 'I have left Rodger Grandfather's silver, but I want you to have all the pictures. At least, those that are left. They are stored in the vaults in Birmingham.'

'Oh, Aunt Edith,' I exclaimed with an instinctive note of urgency in my voice, 'is the picture of you and Aunt Jessie there, the one that used to hang in the dining-room at The Uplands? You remember, you and Jessie were dressed alike, in dark coats and fur hats and scarlet scarves of chiffon at your throat. It was my favourite of all the pictures at The Uplands. I don't know who it was painted by, but it was like an early Renoir.'

'It was painted by an R.A. of the day, John Pettie, and given to Grandfather as a present from the artist, but I am afraid it was sold after Grandfather's death. It was much too large for my flat in Newhall Street. No, I have no idea where it went to. It only fetched a few pounds. Nearly all the canvasses were too big for modern homes, or out of fashion. I only kept the smaller pictures, but I have some of grandfather's books for you, and all the autographed copies of George MacDonald. He was your great, great uncle, you know.'

Alas, not a blood relation. So I could not suggest that any literary talent I possessed came from the author of *Phantastes* and *The Diary of an Old Soul*. As far as I can discover, there has never been a professional author on either side of my family or, for that matter, any member of the legal profession either to stand as a signpost for my brother's eminence today. Though on my mother's side there was a strolling player – her paternal grandfather – who had journeyed from town to town, setting up his tent to perform to whoever might turn up, in the company of the great Macready. And is there not supposed to be an affinity between the Theatre and the Bar?

My passion for collecting pictures, inherited directly from my own paternal grandfather, is easier to explain, and after my godmother's death, when the moment came to unpack the cases from the warehouse, although I was delighted to resume acquaintance with the Ruskins and the MacWhirters, I still found myself hankering after, yearning for the portrait of the aunts, as teenagers of the day. So much so that it became almost an obsession with me, a source of bitter regret. Without this picture in my possession, somehow I felt the most important link with my Winn ancestry had been broken. It was absurd to argue like that, but we are all inclined to have superstitious hunches, and for me this was one of them. And then one evening, a very strange thing happened, which made me more than ever a convinced believer that the pattern of our lives, together with its supports, its signs and omens, is meticulously arranged with other hands than our own.

I was playing bridge with some friends, and as my hostess dealt a fresh hand she casually remarked, 'I went to Sothebys today to a sale of Victorian pictures. We were disposing of a couple of family relics we haven't room for any more, and in the list there was a most attractive portrait of two girls. I was so struck by it that I looked in the catalogue to see who they were.

The Misses Winn. That was all it said. You don't suppose, Godfrey, they could have been any relation of yours? After all, spelt that way, the name is rather an uncommon one . . .'

A shiver touched my spine. It was as though somewhere a trumpet was sounding and I was being summoned. I am afraid I played my cards poorly that evening. My thoughts were elsewhere. I was a boy again, in the cool, shadowy drawing-room at The Uplands, with the sunblinds always drawn outside, full of quiet muted shades – none of the bright chintzes that my mother loved – with Aunt Edith, lying on the sofa beside the window after lunch, with a soft fawn rug over her legs, and a Liberty necklace of large beads round her throat. Resting.

I had never seen my mother put her feet up for a moment. She was always on the go. Working in the garden, training her beloved roses over yet another pergola, getting up amateur theatricals in the Badminton Club, taking part herself in the local pierrot troupe, always busy, perhaps not in the kitchen, because in those days you could engage an excellent cook for twenty pounds a year and a parlour-maid for even less. But always busy, especially at pleasing my father.

But Aunt Edith was different. She existed in a more rarefied atmosphere. Whereas I was a quicksilver child, never walking, always running, full of some unquenchable, inexhaustible store of energy, my batteries re-charged during the night. The only time I was willing to be still was when I was given an exercise book and a pencil and allowed to scribble to my heart's delight. Not pictures – I had no aptitude of any kind for drawing – but words that I could not spell but had heard the grown-ups use. I was a secret tape-recorder of all their conversations I overheard, it was my pre-training for a journalistic career. The reason why I enjoyed the company of my Aunt Edith so much and was prepared to keep quiet in her presence, on the rug beside her couch, was that she treated and talked to me like a grown-up.

Even the way that she handled the cardboard container of chocolates on her knees was so different from how my governess grudgingly doled out from her store of boiled sweets, after lunch: 'there's one for you, and one for your brother.'

'I took your cousin Muriel into Kunzle's last week, when I bought these,' Aunt Edith announced confidentially, as though it was something very important. 'I thought it would be a treat for her, but all she said as we came out again was "Drat that mat. I *always* trip over it." '

It was a very special kind of treat for me to be invited by my godmother to spend the day as her guest at The Uplands. It could only have happened when my elder brother was a hundred miles away, a boarder at his preparatory school, The Glebe House at Hunstanton on the Norfolk Wash, where we rented a bungalow called Sandy Lodge, near the golf course on the old beach every June. While I was still at the Barnt Green Kindergarten, Tanglewood, of which I have no recollections at all, though Rowena Goodrick Clarke, who lived half-way down Cherry Hill with her parents, and is now in her married state another neighbour of mine in Sussex, tells me that when my brother was first brought back after his attack of infantile paralysis, in the middle of that sun-cursed summer term of 1911, I was taken in as a temporary boarder at the house in the Plymouth Road, to make room for the nurses who had to be installed at Cherrycroft.

'You had all the more fuss made of you then. As though it had happened to you, and it was *you* who needed all the sympathy,' my hostess exclaimed, as we sat one evening over our coffee, reminiscing indulgently after a most pleasant reunion dinner. 'Looking back, it's extraordinary, Godfrey, how you always managed to worm your way into the centre of things, especially any kind of drama. After all, you were so much more of an infant than the Ambrose brothers, or Bay Reynolds, whose elder brother was an officer in the Guards and we were never allowed to forget it – do you remember? – or even John Challen, who was so shy he never spoke a word at parties, but look how well he has done. Yet despite being the youngest, you always seemed to turn up everywhere, and no one appeared to mind, or shoo you away.

'For instance, my father who really only lived for his fishing and shooting, had a very soft spot in his heart for you. Do you remember how you used to call him Me Kark – the nearest I suppose you could get to Mr Clarke – and trot down the hill almost every morning, escaping from Miss Jefferies, to have another breakfast with him? One day there was a terrible to-do on the telephone, because you returned home triumphantly and announced you had been plied with port, of all things. Apparently your father had been dining with mine a few evenings previously, and you heard him speaking the next day with relish of the vintage port they had consumed. So you had to turn the trout my father had caught into port!'

I shook my head, bewildered and defenceless, and only too aware at that moment of the depressing total of all the egregious tales that are produced about other people's infancy, of which the central characters themselves have only the dimmest recollection; thinking, too, how bewildering it was in quite a different way that some of us should have survived the big events and the small anecdotes while others of our contemporaries, with whom we shared our school holidays, and who at the time seemed so much stronger and more confident than ourselves, such as Richard Beesly, with the looks of a young Viking, had already gone. Together with both the doctor's sons, though John Ambrose, in my hero-worshipping eyes, had appeared such a tremendous buck.

'But you simply must remember the tobogganing down Cherry Hill, between your house and ours,' Rowena was saying, her hair white now, but her all-embracing smile unfaded, so I could still recognize why I had translated her once upon a time into one of Walter Scott's heroines. 'What fun it was. Indeed, I have always told Harry – isn't he a lamb to do the washing-up – that I never enjoyed winter sports in Switzerland later, and the nursery slopes, nearly as much as our own Cresta Run, down Cherry Hill.

'I remember particularly one winter when you were given a toboggan of your own, as a Christmas present. It had a wicked curved front to it, to make it go faster, a sort of racing model, and I was thrilled to bits when you graciously invited me to be your passenger, instead of Audrey Charles or Beatrice Cohen. I felt absurdly proud, though I was years older than you were. I suppose it was the maternal instinct coming out in me already.

'We were lucky, too, because there was lots of snow that Christmas holidays. We used to start our runs directly after breakfast, and go on as long as the light lasted. We had such energy in those days. Now I tell Harry I'm not going to risk driving the car in London any more.' My hostess put down her coffee cup and refilled her guest's brandy glass. 'And then one afternoon,' she continued, with almost a puzzled note in her voice now, 'after I came up the hill again after lunch, your mother greeted me with the announcement at the gates of Cherrycroft, like the latest bulletin from number 10 Downing Street,

"Godfrey won't be coming out this afternoon, but he says you can have his toboggan. He's retired upstairs to the boys' den, he's reading."

'I was absurdly disappointed. Besides, I couldn't understand. You had a passion for tobogganing, almost as much as for tennis. You seemed to have no nerves, however fast you went. I can hear you shouting out now with excitement and sheer joy. And you were so possessive, too, about your toboggan.'

She had touched a spring at last. It all came flooding back with a rush. 'I was in the middle of *A Tale of Two Cities*. I had chosen it as another of my Christmas presents, at Hudson's bookshop in Birmingham's New Street. *That's* still there. It was my introduction to Dickens.'

My voice trailed awkwardly away into silence. For that was only part of the explanation, the lesser part; strangely, though, the other major part had already been uppermost in my thoughts, as I drove over from my present writing retreat, at Falmer, to Uckfield, a short journey by road (but how much further we were travelling in our joint memories) and then I had pushed it away again, closing the door, telling myself that it would only embarrass, it would seem ludicrous to Rowena and Harry Saxton if bang in the middle of supper I pompously announced, 'I must tell you about the afternoon when I made up my mind what I wanted to be in life. The afternoon when I decided once and for always what my rôle was going to be.'

Yet now, surprisingly, this companion of my childhood had spoken of it first. At that moment, when she was standing at the gate of Cherrycroft, talking to my mother, she had been utterly unaware of the real significance of my not being there, while I lay curled up on the old sofa covered in green rep, in the attic, settling down for a long reading session. Even so, at first I was restless, unable to shut out completely the beckoning cries of the tobogganers which still reached me dimly through the clouded windows. Nor had I discarded my outdoor school sweater and my thickest stockings and boots, as though even now I might easily change my mind and join the crowd again, after all. Because half of me tinglingly wanted to be there, rushing down the hill, with Rowena as my passenger, king-pin of the course. While the other half was revelling in the solitude of the den under the eaves, that I ordinarily shared as the junior partner

Grandfather Winn, in portrait by John Pettie, RA. *Photo: H. J. Whitlock & Sons*

Captain Jack Rodgers, my sea-going grandfather

Mrs James Rodgers (my Irish great grandmother)

Left Miss Mollie Foulkes, my American grandmother.
Right Grannie Winn

with my brother; revelling, too, in the absence of the senior partner, and in the complete stillness, as outside the winter sun began to sink and blue shadows deepened mysteriously across the snow-banked grass.

A moment of revelation of the spirit that has often returned to me and will stay with me always now. Suddenly, without any warning, without any premise, I was shown the future, my personal future. All my days I would enjoy taking part in extrovert activities – though of course, that expression from the psychiatrist's phrase book was still unknown to me – but all the time, tugging at me, pulling me back, for some over-ruling reason I could not yet be expected to understand, would be the insistent, compelling pressure of the other side to my character and disposition, the contemplative rôle, as spectator and student, eternally standing on the sidelines, analysing, recording. I would always be alone, behind the inconsequential chatter, and unable to share the burden of my loneliness. Nor was there any hope for me to find any real basis for happiness until I learnt to live with myself, and on my own. In the years to come, I would have to be self-sufficient, or perish.

The last of the light faded from the outside sky, the tobogganers were making for home, their exhortations no longer reached me. I lit the gas and stretched full length on the sofa, utterly absorbed now in my book. My soliloquy was over, and brutally direct though it had been, I was not in the least apprehensive, but instead, a sense of peace spread over me. I had taken my decision, or been made aware, rather, of what my decision later would have to be. However, I had imagined that no one else was equally aware of that afternoon, as the first turning-point in my life. For I hoarded and hugged the experience to myself. Until this unexpected sequel, when Rowena, who had been so instinctively protective towards me in those days, and who typified the kind of woman I should have married, had I not always, through some fatal sense of inadequacy, drawn back at the brink, announced as her own summing up:

'How extraordinary to realize that that afternoon should have meant so much to us both, in different ways. It must have done, because I can recall every moment of it, too. And yet, neither of us at the time realized its importance to the other. I wonder if that happens often to two people?'

'Yes, I am sure it does, except that they seldom meet again, as we have done, years later, and have the chance to be so honest with each other. How old do you think I was, that Christmas?'

'I don't know. Seven or eight, I suppose. I never thought of you being any age. Of course, you were the smallest of our Barnt Green lot, but you talked and behaved in such a curious, adult manner. So much so, that sometimes you appeared to be the oldest of any of us, even our parents; I suppose to some people you must have seemed spoilt and tiresomely precocious. But at the same time, you were disarming because you were always so natural and unself-conscious,' Rowena added, with her customary kindness.

'I don't like the sound of myself very much,' I said ruefully, and went to bed.

It can be a shock to one's vanity to see oneself as a child, through an onlooker's eyes, from outside one's family circle; just as it is a shock when the secret memories that you have never divulged before and having long since been hidden away in your subconsciousness implacably swim to the surface again, like some limb of a naked, murdered body. What meaning does one attach to them now? Why should this particular incident or that have stayed buried but not obliterated by succeeding tides, where so much else has completely faded?

I cannot tell you what colour were the walls of the classroom at Tanglewood (even if it mattered) but I can describe for myself exactly the coalman sitting with his feet dangling from the back of his cart. He wore the face of a blackamoor, and the corduroy trousers to match, knotted at the knees, and grinned at me invitingly that afternoon when I was out on my donkey. How very white were his teeth in contrast to the coal smears on his cheeks, as he beckoned me to join him, for a ride. A ride to where?

Certainly a much faster ride than on Joseph with his maddening habit of hugging the hedgerows so that my left leg was perpetually in the brambles, however hard Miss Jefferies tugged at his reins. And now our progress was jeopardised by all the commotion of the passing cart. So that it was not surprising that I should be unable to resist Pied Piper's call. To the amazement of my governess I slid off the back of stupid, stubborn Joseph, and

started to run after the cart, whose own driver had induced his
nag into a trot. 'Come back, come back at once,' wailed Miss
Jefferies. Fortunately, she was saved from further threat of my
abduction by the cart disappearing round the corner; whereupon I came to a disappointed standstill in the middle of the
road.

The spell was broken, but for a long time afterwards I was to
daydream about the cart and the coalman in black corduroys.
Don't take sweets from a stranger, only take them from Aunt
Edith. But all I had been offered was a smile, and a friendly wave
of the hand, an all-embracing wave, which had seemed to say,
'Come with us. Get as dirty as you like, and live a free life, far
beyond the end of the lane, and the red pillar-box at the corner,
that symbol of suburban respectability.'

The most I could do in revolt was to turn the woods at the
back of our garden into a kind of private kingdom. Belonging
at that time to the Plymouth family, they were only domesticated
woods, but they seemed utterly vast to me, and in the spring the
bluebells grew in untrammelled profusion, while the bracken
rose higher than a man's head. It was easy for a small boy to
make a cavern for himself. Here I could escape and take off all my
clothes. It must have been damp and slimy, even in summer, the
touch of the ferns against my bare skin, but I was enveloped in
the warmth and satisfaction of behaving in a manner which I
would not be allowed to do in the presence of grownups. I held
long conversations with myself, playing all the parts in a play,
imitating their voices, full of glee and emancipation. Only
brought back to reality, to the boundaries of a governess-ridden
existence, when I heard the garden boy, William, hollering for
me. Time for lunch, time for tea, time to eat up what is on your
plate and be grateful for it. Think of all the little boys
in India who would be only too thankful for that nice tapioca
pudding.

Who knows, perhaps that is why I have so far left India out
of my travels. A childhood connection, an instinctive allergy?
En route for Hong Kong a year ago, I found myself deposited
in the transit lounge of Delhi Airport at two o'clock in the morning. If there is any less attractive transit lounge, so different from
Rangoon the next morning, with the fountains playing in the
flower-carpeted courtyard, I have yet to discover it. A huge poster

on the bare wall proclaimed that the Bank of India welcomed all travellers. Not me, I decided, not me.

* * *

'If you had put up the ace on the first round of trumps, and returned my original lead straight away, I would have got a ruff,' my hostess was saying in the same reproving voice that Aunt Edith had used over Muriel and the mat outside Kunzle's shop, in New Street, Brum.

'I am so sorry, Jean,' I muttered, shaking myself, as you do when you are only half-aware of your surroundings, surprised to notice that we were conventionally dressed and that I was wearing a dinner jacket. It was my American grandmother who had lit the spark in me, who had first given me my passion for bridge – auction bridge in those days – which I suppose will conveniently become one of the solaces, the time-killers, of my old age. However, as a child of six, one does not look beyond the immediate horizon; the sense of excitement and importance combined that it would give me to be allowed to squat ('so long as you don't utter a word') beside her chair at the bridge-afternoons my mother would arrange when her widowed parent paid one of her periodic visits from the States. On the other hand, Grandfather Winn, and in consequence Granny Winn, did not approve of card playing, especially on Sundays. So Aunt Edith had no similar solace for her later years, when one by one her old friends died and her brothers, and her sister Dorothy who married a Westmacott, and went to live with Uncle Jack on a sheep station in Australia, and Jessie Peacock, whose husband, with a considerable reputation as an architect, built both the house in Woodbourne Road, Edgbaston, where I was born, and the other house at Barnt Green where I had my first growing pains.

I was fond enough of Aunt Jessie in a remote sort of way, and of Aunt Dorothy, too, who after the break-up of her brother's marriage to my mother visited me at school at Eastbourne, and I suppose to try and comfort me, or compensate her family conscience, gave me a slap-up lunch at the Grand Hotel, making me feel like a prince for a day, because The Grand was a kind of Mecca for all the boys at St Christopher's. But it was my Aunt Edith whom I truly loved and with whom I still feel an affinity of flesh and blood, so that the moment I thought Sothebys would be open the next morning, after that bridge party, and the sale of a Victorian picture inscribed *The Misses Winn*, I put through a call to the office of Peter Wilson, who presides over the auctions with a skill and dignity that have made him the doyen of his particular world.

To Peter's secretary I described one of the pictures, *the* picture to me, that had been sold yesterday. Could she discover who was the purchaser, and what was the price paid? I hung on, at my end, my heart beating uncomfortably. Surely it was too great a coincidence, I told myself, the kind of one chance in a thousand that only happens in a book. Supposing I had dined with Jean a week later, she would have forgotten all about the sale, she would never have mentioned the picture, I would not be telephoning now, scarcely daring to hope, yet seeing this as a very special kind of portent in my life.

A moment later, the voice from the other end was giving me the address of a gallery that was unknown to me, situated off the Fulham Road. And the price? Forty pounds . . .

In half-an-hour I was there, blurting out my mission to the gallery's owner. At once she took me down a staircase into a cellar, and there propped up against the wall, exactly as I remembered the picture in every detail, was the portrait of the two sisters in the springtime of their life, painted nearly a century ago.

'Why did you buy the canvas?' I asked curiously.

'I thought my father would like it. It's his period. I was going to give it to him as a present.'

So then I explained my own family interest, adding, honestly, 'I know what you paid for it. If you would let me have it instead of your father, what do you feel would be a fair profit to yourself?'

'As it is a family picture, you may certainly have it for fifty pounds.'

I had recaptured this entirely happy link with my childhood, for fifty pounds. One of the few mementoes untouched by pain. I could have embraced the stranger for her gesture, since, after all, she had taken a fancy to the picture herself, for the mood it evoked, and she need not have parted with it at all. And what a narrow escape Aunt Edith had had from being lost again, this time assuredly for ever, I decided, as carefully we placed the

frame on the back seat of the car and drove back to my home in
Ebury Street, next door to the plaque perpetuating that George
Moore once lived there. Now Aunt Edith was safe for ever from
alien hands, now she and Jessie would look down on me, with
just a faint smile of recognition, every time I sat down at my
writing desk.

On the next occasion that my brother and sister-in-law dined
with me, I announced to them casually at the end of the evening,
as I took them downstairs, 'I've got something to show you in
my work-room.'

Switching on the light, I pointed across the room to where the
portrait hung, and my brother stood there, not speaking; while
unexpectedly, a tide of memories were released for my sister-in-
law of her Sydenham relations in Edgbaston, especially the ones
who had known the Winn sisters and gone to school with them.
'Is The Uplands still there?' she asked. 'Yes, of course it is, because I heard there was some talk of it being turned into a Home
for ex-prisoners, which a lot of the locals don't like the idea of
at all, and I am not surprised.' But my brother continued to say
nothing, his shoulders hunched as one had grown used to them,
his ivory head, his bloodless cheeks with the sharp, down-turning
lines, like a map of a thousand legal battles, showing no emotion,
in the manner that he had schooled himself, in court, across the
years. Never to be caught off-guard. Let justice be done. But
what had justice to do with this? A fortuitous conversation at
a bridge table. It was a capricious act of Fate or Chance, call it
what you like, but the implacable lucidity of his judgments did
not embrace such mumbo-jumbo, and so this reminder of the
past and present blood ties became a moment of communication
with my sister-in-law, a woman of great sensibility, rather than
between the two brothers.

However, in my heart, I had not expected anything else. We
have always found it difficult to talk to each other, except on
impersonal family matters. Such as trusts and covenants. I am
not apportioning the blame. I do not think it is the fault of either
of us. The mixtures of our respective make-ups simply do not
meld. This can happen so often in close family relationships, and
yet the rest of the world remains surprised. Brothers so unlike
each other, sisters so different, isn't it strange?

Very different, but surely not very strange. My brother

possesses a sense of humour which can be painful or pleasant, according to whether one is a participant. At the time when he was created one of Her Majesty's Judges, and had to be concerned with his armorial bearings, he discovered, to his surprise, that far back our family was related to another Winn family, the one whose family seat is at Nostell Priory in Yorkshire. Here once upon a time a man named Chippendale was the estate carpenter, who would run up a few more kitchen or other chairs whenever needed. This has proved something of an asset in the course of time.

The owner of Nostell is Lord St Oswald, and I had always imagined that duplication of so many of the Christian names, in his family and ours, like Charles, Reginald, Edith, had no significance, though from time to time some of the younger members of the branch have jokingly called me 'Cousin Godfrey'. However, I was really put in my right place one evening when some mutual friends brought Lord St Oswald and my brother together at the dinner table. My brother commented on his discovery that there was a far-distant connection between the two families. At that, his neighbour, after pausing to allow the full implications of this piece of information to sink in, replied, 'How interesting. You must come and stay a week-end at Nostell next time you are at Leeds Assizes.' Then the present head of that branch of the family continued more doubtfully, 'But Godfrey Winn. . . .' there was another pause before he added, 'of course, that's no relation. I mean, surely that's just a made-up name.'

To soften the blow to my pride (though there really was no need, since environment and individual character have always seemed to me more important than either the power of ancestry or heredity) my brother also finds his own kind of pleasure in telling another story; this time of what happened on the night when he was invited to reply to the toast of Distinguished Guests at the annual dinner of his old public school, Oundle, where he earned the privilege of being head boy, despite the drawback of not being able to participate in any school sports. A distinction indeed.

As the time for his speech approached, the toastmaster, resplendent in scarlet, and wrapped in a cloak of self-importance, bent over the back of my brother's chair. 'How would you like me to announce you?' 'I don't mind in the least,' Rodger replied, 'so long as you don't call me Judge Winn.'

A few moments later, glancing down at his notes, my brother was somewhat surprised to hear, in stentorian tones, the words: 'And now pray silence for Sir Godfrey Winn.'

Whereupon, rising to his feet, and in his most urbane manner, with a hint of steel beneath, as when tearing to pieces some clearly untenable, fabricated piece of evidence in court, the star guest of the evening commented, 'Improvising for the first time in my life for my younger brother, I will do my best, etc., etc. . . .'

The Law like the Theatre produces its own specialized type of *raconteur*. I am inclined to act any anecdote I produce in private company, whereas my brother prefers a studiedly ironic manner that is equally if not more effective, because it so exactly suits the personality that he is at pains to project. On the several occasions when I have consulted him about crises in my life of which I had felt he had to be acquainted as head of my family, he has pronounced judgment without condescension, and with a practical consideration for my welfare that has made me long passionately that we were able to be at ease in each other's company on more informal, light-hearted occasions. But I realize it is not to be now. Just as I realize, as I grow older, that not to show one's emotions does not necessarily mean that one has no deep feelings hidden beneath a mask of cynical speculation that can become a habit to wear to the world. On the contrary, such undisclosed depths often have far more permanent meaning than the instinctive outpourings of someone who wears his heart upon the sleeve. Our mother taught us both to despise tears. I only saw her weep once, and it left an irremediable mark upon me. In any case, my brother has had the last laugh, since after what seemed a hopelessly crippling handicap at the start, he has achieved his life's ambitions – and how seldom that can be stated with complete conviction – whereas his younger brother still plods – and I have always been a plodder, whether it was a case of trying to re-shape my backhand at tennis, or to learn how to pitch my voice properly into the studio microphone – on the lower slopes, very much aware of how much further apprenticeship there is for me before I can claim the one title that I long to have earned before I die. That of a good craftsman.

The phrase has haunted me ever since one afternoon soon after the Battle of Britain, I stood in the porchway of the hospital at

East Grinstead which was at that time giving to the crashed air-men, rescued from the burning wreckage of their planes, new faces, new hands, new hope. I had just been watching the most distinguished plastic surgeon of the day, later Sir Archibald McIndoe, perform yet another of those delicate grafting opera-tions that were to give him legendary stature among the 'Guinea Pigs'. Carving slices of the flesh from the patient's thigh, as though it were the Sunday joint, he had transplanted it, like a workman smoothing over putty, in the crevices beneath the air-man's eyes, and on his ravaged cheeks. Afterwards, a pipe of human flesh, a super plumber's job this, was built with unfalter-ing skill to join the new skin with the old, the rebirth, with the base upon the thigh. And so the hours passed. I had been warned that I might feel sick, and faint from the overpowering emana-tions of the operating theatre. Instead, I was too intent upon the movements of the white-coated figures, in their masks.

Now the mask had been removed, the surgeon's gown discarded until the next time. The leader of the team that was in the process of making medical history stood beside me, blink-ing a little in the sudden sunshine, arching his tired back. A fine-looking man, who would have stood out in any company, giving forth only reassurance and optimism. On a sudden im-pulse, I asked him, 'Archie, you are doing such amazing things here. It must seem such a perfect climax for you to your great career. Have you any ambitions still unfulfilled?'

My companion did not answer for a moment. Then he looked down at his broad, spatulate hands, spreading the tired fingers wide. 'I want to be a good craftsman,' he said simply.

I have found in the long course of my writing apprenticeship that a single remark often discarded quite casually will illuminate someone's whole character so that it seems almost unnecessary afterwards to add anything to the portrait. Although Archie McIndoe and I remained close friends until his death, I doubt if he had any idea that what he had said actually made such a pro-found impression upon me that almost unconsciously it became the watchword of my own professional life. *I want to be a good craftsman.* Not like a parrot, but rather, I hope, with fresh enthusiasm, I have used the phrase and explained the context, on so many occasions when I have been giving away prizes at a school, or addressing some group like the London Publicity Club, an evening which I mention particularly because it stands out like a signpost of demarcation between all the speech-making that came before and afterwards.

As it happens, I was invited to pay a return visit and address this same club quite recently, but it is the first meeting that will always come back to me, not, I hasten to add, because of any oratorical triumph, but entirely because of the aftermath. Something strange and unanswerable which happened afterwards, when I had stepped down from the platform and found myself surrounded by a wall of friendly faces and voices, guiding me into the lounge at the Aldwych Hotel, offering me a drink.

I needed one. I had made no reference in my hour-long speech concerning how very nearly I had not, at the last moment, been able to keep the date. Or why. How my mother had been lying in a coma for days, in the ultimate stages of the illness that she could not understand because she had never been really incapacitated before, she hated the idea of wasting even a day in bed, and in consequence, how bitterly she had resented every sign of her increasing helplessness.

At six o'clock I had called once again at her flat, where each morning what had become a dreaded ritual took place. My brother and I would wait in her sitting-room, so impregnated with her taste, so empty of flowers now, looking out on to Eaton Square, in silence, waiting for the sound of the door opening into the passage, and the doctor's return to report, 'No change.' For the last two mornings he had not allowed me to go into her room myself; he could face the implacable ravages of the disease, it was his duty, not mine, however devoted I might be. Or was it that as part of his ministrations he wanted to protect his patient from the humiliation, at such a time, of scrutiny by any eyes except impersonal, medical ones? Whatever the reasoning, I shall always be grateful, for he was right; it had become more than I could bear to see her thus. No change. Too much change. As that evening, on my way to the meeting, I stood in the narrow hallway of her final home, the night-nurse confronting me with wary eyes, and the grandfather clock, one of the few things that had been salvaged from the Barnt Green house, still ticking away, but now more ominously, like Eternity, I seemed to hear, too, my mother's voice repeating to me something that she had said at the beginning of her illness, eight months before. I had looked in then to say goodnight, on my way to make yet another speech, this time a layman's talk from a church pulpit, during Lent. 'If, as you tell me, you are going to talk about Tolerance tonight as the most important of the Christian virtues,' she had urged me, 'then you must remind your audience that Tolerance does not mean simply acquiescence, but instead, active participation.'

My hour of active participation was over. I slumped in a chair in the hotel lounge, the wall of goodwill voices enclosing me, but within the wall itself a feeling of being utterly alone, drained of all strength. It was a weight of emptiness such as I had never experienced before, or since. Often at the end of a long speech one feels as though the virtue has gone out of one, but this was something quite different. Although I was aware that my body was still tethered to the chair, my spirits had momentarily escaped into the wasteland. The other guests, no doubt imagining that I was parched and exhausted from standing on my legs for so long, sympathetically went on chattering among themselves, leaving me in my isolation, my sudden, overwhelming sense of loss. It was not until hours later that I discovered that my mother's own spirit had left this earth at the exact moment when the meeting had ended.

Very early the next morning, I was awakened by the telephone ringing beside my bed. It was my brother.

'Mother died last night. I tried to get you, but there was no answer to your phone. I will let you know the time and the details of the funeral.'

There was a click and he had rung off. A sense of isolation enveloped me. Later, the telephone kept on ringing. My sister-in-law, who at all times has done her best to keep the peace between the two brothers, my other relations, my manager, close friends. No, I wanted nothing. There was an article about, of all things, the spirit of Christmas that had to be written. The magazine had been waiting for days for the copy. It was zero hour. I sat down at my desk till it was finished. I looked at my watch; lunch time, but I was not hungry. Besides, there was an errand I must perform, something I had to do.

I went to a florist in Sloane Street and bought a bunch of her favourite flowers, lilies-of-the-valley, and as I bought them I remembered the motto that had ruled her life: Flowers for the living. But surely she would not mind the extravagance of one small bunch, bought though it was out of season, to place on her folded hands in the coffin. My sister-in-law had offered to come with me, but I knew that I must face this alone. And I was buoyed up by a shining hope. I had been assured so often that in death, when all pain is over at last, the wracked features resume a beauty, often a more ethereal beauty than they have possessed in life. To comfort and reassure the mourner, always.

But I was to discover, horribly, that this is a false myth. Was this witch-like creature, whose lips seemed to be twisted into a final, protesting grimace, my mother? I dropped the flowers and fled from the funeral parlour into the street. Now I was blinded with tears, I could no longer hold them back, though she had always said that tears were no use, no use at all. What was it she had whispered to me, the last time she was conscious of my presence beside her bed? 'You have been a good son to me. Pray for the passing of my soul.'

Had I then prayed with insufficient conviction? For if it was true about the soul's immortality, why had she looked so shrivelled in her coffin? Was it easier for my brother, a Humanist? I do not know how long I walked or where, but later, much later I found myself gazing down at the river from the Embankment, with the street lamps shining on the water, and the tears now frozen on my face by the bitter November wind. And in my heart, a kind of death that was an icy anger, too. Not against the fate that had taken away the person who meant most to me in the world, not against my brother for his few curt words to me that morning, but entirely against myself.

It was my fault, not his. I assumed the superior rôle of the sensitive one, and yet right from the start how many times I must have unconsciously taunted him, so that his blind rages, when murder blazed from his eyes, the kind of rages that he had long since mastered in his maturity, were entirely understandable. Children can be extremely cruel and utterly selfish, spoilt brats who have to be taught to show consideration to their fellow human beings, inside or outside their own family, taught by life to expect in return only one iota of what you give out. One iota. I was no exception.

I lived my whole life again during that day I lost from my life, walking like a sleep-walker. With the wind beating against me, on the Embankment, the years rushed by, in reverse, and it was once again the hottest summer of living memory. 1911. The summer that they brought my brother back on a stretcher. My mother went to fetch him from his preparatory school in Norfolk. He had been playing cricket when it happened. One minute he was running about, fielding the ball, the next he had been stricken down with polio. As suddenly as that.

I do not know for certain how long he lay immobile on his back, but I do know, having heard my mother recount the sequel so many times, that the doctors were extremely doubtful if the small boy who had been up to that moment so sturdy, so passionately keen on games, would ever walk again.

'You will walk,' she kept on repeating to my brother, with the kind of undefeatable faith that some women possess, confounding the more exact knowledge of men. Though, in those days, infantile paralysis, which was supposed to germinate in great heat (and there was certainly an exceptionally large outbreak that year) was very much more of a mystery, its causes, its treatment, than a similar attack of polio would be today.

'You *will* walk again, Rodger,' my mother reiterated, adding at the same time a proviso that she felt it was important for him to grow accustomed to at once. 'Of course you won't be able to be a sailor now, like your grandfather was. What would you like to be instead?'

He did not hesitate in his answer. 'I would like to be a judge,' he said.

'Then you shall be a judge,' she replied, not laughing at such an extraordinary notion from the lips of a child of eight, in a family where no one had followed the Law. Actors, engineers, accountants, sailors. But no solicitor, and certainly no barrister. 'But you must start work *now*,' she added, bringing him his school books, standing over him while he studied and studied till the self-discipline acquired at so early a stage, and the concentration, born of solitude, began to bring their own special rewards.

I have always believed that the one law of life that seldom fails is the law of compensation. Certainly it seemed to bear fruit in the case of my brother, because not only did he get up from his bed in due course and walk, but he succeeded in winning a scholarship from his local school at the Lickey, which he subsequently attended as a day-boy, to Oundle, and then in turn he won the highest classical scholarship at Trinity, Cambridge. This was only the beginning. For he was to achieve the added distinction of heading the Law Tripos list, and being chosen later to be sent as a scholar to Harvard and to Yale, for post-graduate courses, in the same manner as the Rhodes Scholars come to this country.

To write down the bare details of such scholarship successes takes only a paragraph, and bears no relation to the unyielding determination he consistently displayed in pursuit of his goal, the casting out of all self-pity. In his final year at Cambridge, when he was President of the Law Society, Norman Birkett was the guest and my brother the host for the night. In the morning, my brother asked his distinguished visitor a question of considerable importance to himself. Having explained that there was a good chance now of his being offered a Fellowship in Law, he was wondering, because of the physical disability that would obviously incline him to tire, standing up in court, whether he should accept. After all, it would mean a secure and far less arduous life ahead.

Whereupon, the man who had himself overcome so many initial handicaps of other kinds to reach his present eminence, brushed aside all my brother's doubts. 'Go into the hurly-burly, you will never regret it,' he counselled. Which my brother did, starting his career in the chambers of a very different but equally prominent Silk of his day, Sir Patrick Hastings.

And so the years passed and the time came when my brother had, like myself, to take his farewell of the woman who had made it all possible. Once she had bent over his sick bed, now the rôles were reversed. 'It is all right,' he was able to tell her, 'I have had the official letter. I am to be Junior Treasury Counsel. That should mean that after five years, I shall be made a judge.'

It was good that my mother should have that final piece of family news to carry with her, on her journey. The clock had come full circle. She could depart in peace, having made so many sacrifices on behalf of both her sons, especially after her marriage to our father crashed in ruins like the long mirror in her bedroom at Cherrycroft. That was the second of the two warnings she was to receive, the kind of prophetic messages in which she implicitly believed, for right until the end of her life she remained extremely superstitious and impressed by soothsayers.

The first warning came very soon after she was married. There was a Unionist Fête in Edgbaston to which my parents had gone, and as usual, my mother made her first call at the fortune-teller's tent. She slipped her wedding ring into her bag, before facing the scrutiny of the gipsy's gaze. She had no doubts for herself. She was so young, so endearingly pretty, so confident.

'What sort of husband shall I have?' she asked provocatively.

'You have already chosen.' It was not a rebuke for deceit, so much as a statement of fact. All the same, the bride of not yet a year's standing, in her powder-blue dress, started to finger the handle of her parasol nervously as the pause lengthened inside that stuffy, cavernous tent, and the Romany gazed into her crystal. 'You will have two sons,' she pronounced at last.

'No daughter?'

'No, two sons, I tell you, and they will both rise high in their chosen line. But your marriage itself will end in disaster, I see great trouble ahead for you, lady, but take heart . . .'

My mother did not wait to hear why she should take heart. Outside in the sunshine, her husband was still waiting. She fumbled in her bag for her wedding ring. Just to put it on again restored her confidence. 'What did she tell you, Joan? Anything exciting?' 'Oh, nothing. A lot of nonsense. You know what these fortune-tellers are like at a fête. But it all makes money for the cause. Let's go and have tea. It's very hot.'

Nevertheless, she often recounted the prophecy in later years, as proof of the extra-sensory powers that she was utterly convinced some people possess. Despite its flattering reference, and accuracy in his case, my brother found the story embarrassing. He would look disdainful at the telling. No doubt, had he been present, as I was, he would have dismissed the other warning as meaningless, too. And yet I have never been able to banish it from my own mind.

Sometimes I was allowed as a great treat, after I had my bath, to go into my mother's room, to watch her putting the finishing touches to her finery, if she and my father were dining with neighbours in the village. That particular night they were due at a dinner party at Barnt Green House, at the bottom of Cherry Hill, where the Margessons lived.

It was the show place of the village, authentic Elizabethan, and very different from the rest of the local architecture which was mostly solid specimens of late Victorian, the kind of houses that prosperous burghers built anywhere, at the beginning of the century. Lady Isabel Margesson, whose husband was agent for the neighbouring estates of the Earl of Plymouth, had herself something of a reputation as an ardent suffragette. Indeed, she was supposed, on one occasion, to have sent a note up the lane to my mother by the gardener's boy, with a warning not to post any letters that afternoon. 'We are thinking of burning the pillar-box down, as a protest.'

I am sure the story was apocryphal, for I never recall the pillar-box not being there. In any case, I worshipped Lady Isabel, because she treated me as though I were a grown-up, and always gave me a part in the pageants which were her other consuming passion, when I was allowed to run about like Puck, in this case putting a girdle round the field and getting in everyone's way. There was a breath of freedom about the pageant-master that was more catching than chicken-pox. I revelled in it. Once again, though, I was too young to be on ordinary play-terms with the children of the family. It was my brother who was the same age as Vere Margesson and, in consequence, they were at that time inseparable friends, while the elder Margesson son, David, was already very much grown up. Indeed, one of my earliest firm memories is of returning one evening on my donkey, up the lane, with my governess, and coming upon David walking hand in hand with the American girl with corn-coloured hair, Frances Leggatt, that he was about to marry. The last of the sun was shining behind their heads, and to me they looked like god-like figures from another world. I did not expect to be noticed, and wasn't, for they were far too absorbed in each other, and yet an unconscious link was forged between us. As often happens without one being aware of it at the time.

During the war, Lady Isabel wrote to me about something of mine she had read – 'I often think of the years when Vere and Rodger helped you over the high hedges' – asking, too, after my mother, for whom she had a great affection, and thus a long silence was broken. We went together, on my next leave, to see the old lady in the flat where she was now living in Victoria Street, making light of the bombing. She was very frail and changed, but her independent spirit still shone forth. Before the end of our visit, her elder son appeared. David had been Conservative Chief Whip, and was now Secretary of State for War. The aura of my childhood remained; he was still a figure of awe to me, with the halo of the sunset gilding his head. We exchanged a few words, and that was that. But after I returned from the wars, rather battered after months in hospital, wondering how I would get back into harness, let alone into the swim, David Margesson performed a most kindly act. As a director of the Rank Organization, he suggested that I should be taken on as an apprentice script-writer. Fortunately, his confidence was to be justified, as I was able to produce the idea that turned *Holiday Camp* into such a money-spinner, and Jack Warner and Kathleen Harrison into stars. However, neither my sponsor nor I was aware of what lay ahead, the afternoon that nervously I was ushered into the presence of Mr Rank himself, and almost before I could utter, I was leaving with a contract of a hundred pounds a week. And all because two families had once lived by chance at the top and the bottom of the same lane in Worcestershire. The whirligig of time, how bitter can be the revenges it brings in its train, but equally how sweet the rewards.

It is surely impossible that half a century already has passed since that evening I stood enthralled, in my dressing-gown and shining clean from my bath, watching my mother take out of her wardrobe the white fox cape that had been a wedding present from her two brothers. Somehow that cape seemed to me, then and now, not so much a symbol of luxury as the ultimate expression of her own distilled femininity, setting her utterly apart from other members of her sex who were close to me at that time, like my governess, Miss Jefferies.

Putting the cape round her shoulders, its wearer stood in front of the long glass, turning this way, and that, her auburn hair piled high, and round her throat the necklace of turquoises and diamonds, that together with her rings she was to pawn when the crash came, but such a different kind of crash from the one that happened now. Suddenly, for no reason that was ever properly explained, the oval mirror standing against the wall came apart from its supports, and fell with a sound like that of ice-floes breaking asunder, an unearthly sound, which once heard is never forgotten.

Just in time my mother jumped aside, pulling me with her.

I buried my head against her trembling heart, as the door into my father's dressing-room opened, and my other parent rushed in, holding in his hand the tie for his dinner jacket that he was about to ask to have fixed for him. When I raised my head again, it was to find them gazing at each other, not speaking, appalled. My mother had always looked so unscarred, so serene, with a bloom like her roses. Now she had in an instant become a dressmaker's model, with a face of wood. She was too scared to weep, too moved, too shocked and wounded in her mind.

Seven years bad luck ... wasn't that what it was supposed to mean?

My brother's illness, out of a blue sky, began the trail, while I did nothing to arrest it, to make things easier, at home. Looking back, looking down at the reflection of my childhood image in the waters of the river, that afternoon on the Embankment, I hated what I saw. I was ashamed. For in those far-off days, was I not for ever boasting of how fast I could run, showing off how fast I could run in and out of the house, up and down the garden, practising my tennis shots against the outside wall of the garage, while inside my brother was incarcerated, a prisoner, in a pair of old grey flannel trousers, shiny from the long hours that he had to spend, holding to the top bar of a wooden contraption built against the wall, with his legs dangling; his good leg and his bad leg side by side, working them up and down, another hundred times, and another and another, to strengthen and equalize them, with the sweat pouring down his cheeks. And I blithely leapt about outside, revelling in the natural freedom of my own limbs, not even offering to fetch him a glass of lemonade.

I should have been his messenger, fetching and carrying, providing practical sympathy in any way I could, turning myself into the equivalent of a fag at school, but in these circumstances a willing one. However, something in his nature, so undemonstrative, so austere already in its tenacity for fighting its own battles and conquering, daunted and alienated me. I took refuge in my own world, hiding in the woods, making up long serials as additions to my story books, always on the leap, as though I were already conscious how fatally easy it is to miss one's chances and I must hurry, hurry to catch up. All the same, how intolerable it must have been for my brother to have to watch me, darting here and there like a dragonfly. It was not my fault, his illness was not my responsibility. Did I think about it like that? No, I did not think at all. As animals turn away from a wounded member of their tribe, so did I instinctively withdraw into my own secret life, which I sometimes surprise myself as living still, too forthgiving and affectionate one moment, too silent and self-absorbed the next.

So much sentimental nonsense is talked and written about the transparently innocent heart of a child. In actual life, the majority of them are devious and barbaric in their instinctive outlook and have to learn, and learn painfully, the laws that govern polite society. Left to themselves, they do worse things than experiment by pulling the wings off flies, when no one who could chastise them for it, or impose sanctions, is looking; they torture each other, following the prehistoric tribal customs regarding the weaker and stronger, if the odds are propitious for getting away with it.

My mother, only too aware of the lack of communication between her two sons, equally loving them both, but unable to break down the barriers of smouldering antagonism between them, decided upon a solution. No doubt my father was consulted, and no doubt as always had acquiesced. One of the boys, for the sake of general peace, must be got out of the house. As Rodger for the time being was immobile, it could only be Godfrey. I must be sent away to boarding school. I sense, too, now, that there was another motivation for her reasoning. She had an uneasy, though as yet scarcely defined, feeling that before it was too late she should try to harden me and play the spartan mother, since although I suffered from no physical handicap to conquer like my brother, Life, where my emotions were involved, would not be easy for me.

Still, I was only six years old, too young surely to be dispatched like a parcel to The Glebe House, Hunstanton, where my brother had been and where my Ludlow cousins, the sons of my mother's elder sister, Ethel, were in force, representing twin branches of the family. Mr Barber the headmaster, and his wife, whom the boys called Madam, and who was reckoned to be far the more formidable of the two since she had acquired the mystique of ruling from a wheeled chair, would in due course make a little man of me. Meanwhile, what was to be done? A happy compromise swiftly presented itself. In the same seaside town on the

Wash there was an admirable dame's school called Lynfield, presided over by a certain Miss Cook. Into her charge I should be entrusted post haste. Surely it would prove to be a home from home?

'And you know how much you always enjoy our month at Sandy Lodge,' my mother kept on reminding me, soothingly, as she sewed the Cash's tapes on to my new winter underclothes. Yes, but that was in June, that was a holiday month, in the bungalow that we shared with our Ludlow cousins, on the old shore, and this was autumn, and the other side of the tracks, this was school.

My vague apprehensions were fully realized. For some reason, I arrived two days late and had to make a too conspicuous entrance into the dining room, at tea time, appraised by forty pairs of curious and critical eyes. My sense of numbness still gripped me when I crawled into my bed in the dormitory allotted to me. In the mercy of the anonymous darkness, I must have started to whimper a little, like a puppy sold to a stranger and finding himself for the first time away from the rest of the litter. Because the boy in the next bed – a farmer's son from the other side of the county, as I afterwards discovered – and in charge of the dormitory, ordered me to get into his bed, where I nestled down beside him, and with his arm thrown round me, my whimpering died away, and I was instantly asleep, in the combined warmth of our still sexless bodies.

That was my baptism into boarding school life, in comparison with which my days at Tanglewood glowed like a fairy tale, and I have often thought since of that spontaneous act of kindness by someone whose name I have long since forgotten but which meant so much to me at the time. However, it was not repeated. It was part of the breaking-in process that I must stand on my own feet from now on, and it may well have been that same dormitory leader who was instrumental in imposing on me the most frightening experience of my life. Far worse, in retrospect, than anything which happened to me in the Second World War.

If you persisted in talking after lights were out, or larking around in any way, you were threatened by your captain with the dire threat that you would put on your dressing-gown and report yourself to Miss Cook. However, it was a threat which rarely had to be implemented, since it conjured up such a scarifying prospect. For the fact that the ruler of our lives was scrupulously fair did not make her less formidable.

Alas, one evening I must have carelessly or rebelliously refused to pipe down, when commanded. Perhaps someone dared me, and you had to accept almost any reasonable challenge, or be scorned. Anyway, what I do recall still with absolute clarity is the awful moment when it happened and I found myself at the top of the front stairs that led down to the hall with Miss Cook's study on the left, and the dining-room on the right.

On ordinary occasions, the pupils never used the front stairs. Our access to the dormitories lay up an uncarpeted staircase at the back of the house, in direct communication with the classrooms. This added strangeness made the episode all the more unnerving. As my feet slowly and reluctantly descended on the soft carpet, I could hear a murmur of voices drifting upstairs from the dining-room. This indicated the staff were at supper. Horror heaped on horror. For that meant, too, that I should have to face them all.

I saw the front door ahead of me, with the flowery curtain across it. Should I make a bolt for it, in my pyjamas? Then some degree of reason must have convinced me of the utter futility of such an attempt to escape, for the next thing I remember was standing in the entrance to the dining-room, and the sudden hush as the grown-up voices died away into an astonished silence.

What must their impression have been of the small boy with the chubby round face, whose original fair curls had now been regimented into a nondescript, mousy thatch, standing there, blinking like a dormouse as he turned instinctively towards the woman at the top of the table?

'Please Miss Cook,' I gulped, closing my eyes altogether now, because it was too unnerving to watch the red flush suffuse her white cheeks, the invariable prelude of a mighty explosion ahead. 'Please,' I began again, imploringly, 'I have been sent to report myself. For ragging, after lights out.'

For the life of me I am not sure what happened next. Was the sequel an instant departure to her study across the way, the caning ruler brought forth, both hands held out? Or was some other lengthier form of punishment imposed upon the morrow? In a way, I had already served a sentence in the minutes, which seemed like eternity, when I walked down the stairs and braced myself for the confrontation to come; just as I still squirm more from embarrassment than actual pain this time, when I relive another memory of that same dining-room, but filled on this occasion, not by the staff but the pupils themselves.

The staff shared the same menus as ourselves, though none of us suffered from the current snobbery among today's boarders of always asserting that the food at their school is so much better than what is put before them in the holidays. I suppose you could call it the final swing of the pendulum. Certainly, if secondary or primary school pupils were subjected to the living conditions still prevalent at most of our public schools, there would be indignant questions asked in Parliament. For example, I was astonished when I was shown the cramped, antediluvian quarters in which the bloods of Eton sleep and study. In reverse, I am always delighted by the luxurious planning of our most modern State schools. The latest heating system from under the floors, the cheerful pastel colourings of the walls, instead of the gloomy dark-brown paint that used to be so ubiquitous, the vast expanse of glass windows, encouraging the sun to shine; above all, the spotless and generous sanitary arrangements; whereas at Lynfield, in my time, there was only one lavatory in commission for the use of the whole school.

That must seem incredible to a new generation of parents reading this, and no doubt conditions are completely different today, but in my day, as soon as breakfast was over, a queue would form that was still unrelieved by the time the bell for school sounded. Inevitably, complications resulted; in my case, for a time, I was the victim of a particularly unpleasant form of incontinence that would take me shamefaced to Matron's room. Fortunately, the instant that I returned home in the holidays, the symptoms vanished because the cause had automatically been removed, so that I never had the embarrassment of having to make a similar confession to my mother, or to explain to her why I dreaded so much going back each term.

Not long ago, I found myself one Saturday evening as a guest on the panel of the television show, BBC 3. Towards the end of the programme, when I had survived a ten-minute duologue with Malcolm Muggeridge, who in real life, I discovered, is not nearly so fierce or autocratic as he makes himself out to be on the screen, but is as benign as an unfrocked bishop, the subject of bed-wetting cropped up. At once the resident members of the panel seized on this, without a trace of embarrassment, as a suitable anvil on which to sharpen their sophisticated wits. I alone sat uncomfortable and silent. I was back again at Lynfield, in the queue.

However, I had few complaints about the food at my first boarding-school. Especially I looked forward to tea-time, because then we were permitted to have our own tuck, pots of jam, a home-baked cake, fruit. Carefully marked by ourselves, the containers were placed beside our plates, and in the silent wait before grace was pronounced by the senior member of the staff present, an elaborate pantomime of gesturing took place as though this had suddenly become a school for deaf mutes. Standing beside our places, ravenous and expectant, we would point at our particular hoard and then nod, either casually or dramatically, according to our temperament, towards anyone we royally wished to favour with a helping from our own riches.

The evening that I came unstuck, a boy at our table had had a windfall, in the shape of a huge basket of strawberries, sent from the nurseries owned by his father. Every envious eye at the table was on the luscious feast. I alone acted. I kept on pointing at the remnants of the pot of raspberry jam in front of me, and then at the strawberry king. He seemed not to notice my invitation; at any rate, he ignored it and as we sat down an uneasy sensation spread over me. Had I made myself too obvious? Indeed, I had. For the basket of fresh fruit was passed round the whole table, with only one exception. I was left out. It was a cruel reaction, for a dislike touched off by my toadying gestures, but though I was overwhelmed with mortification at the time, I have been very grateful since, for that incident indelibly taught me a lesson which has proved of great benefit across the years. Sucking-up, especially when prompted by greed of any kind, seldom pays. While boasting, and trying to cover up your inability to 'produce the goods', with further prevarication, never does.

This is the other lesson, far more than any I learnt in class, which was impressed upon my character by something that happened, too, at the same stage in my development. The lesson of the peewit eggs. This belonged to the other side of my childhood life at Hunstanton, the recurring Junes when the whole family migrated from Barnt Green and we took the train first to Birmingham. Here we joined up with Aunt Ethel and Uncle Ernest —

who in a set of cards for Happy Families would have been perfectly cast in the mould of The Brewers – and their young: Jack, who was to lie about his age and go to Flanders, as a stretcher-bearer, a tragic sacrifice; Donald, who was to follow in his father's footsteps; and Mollie, whose sweetness of disposition was apparent even at so early an age. Together we then proceeded to King's Lynn, picnicking in the train, with a pile of shrimping nets upon the rack. The aroma of ozone clinging to them from other summers was like the scent of incense rising above our heads, as we bounced up and down upon the seats, in mounting excitement. Would the tide be out when we finally reached our destination? If so, we must chance our luck straight away in the pools left behind on the shore, and share our catch for a late tea. I have never tasted such shrimps since.

Then there were the peewit eggs sometimes to be discovered in the sand-dunes beside the golf course, which the grown-ups fancied for their supper, so that the two families of cousins would vie with each other to produce the largest haul. Somehow, I never had any luck. Perhaps I did not concentrate enough. It was certainly slow searching, and one evening, after a solitary expedition, I returned, fed up, my ego deflated by recurring defeat, and announced, 'I have found six eggs.' 'Where are they?' everyone naturally demanded. 'I am keeping them for myself,' was my rather lame retort. 'Show us, show us.' I can hear the persecuting, pursuing chant as I write. Of course, long before bedtime I had to admit that it was all a fantasy, but I was not allowed to forget my foolishness. For the rest of that June, the favourite family joke was 'Godfrey doesn't want any shrimps for tea. He is going to have one of his own eggs.'

How vividly everything comes back to you when you revisit the actual scene of your early habitat, your breathing spaces of long ago. Rather to my surprise, Lynfield had not shrunk. It stood modestly in the same side road, with its neat front garden, exactly as I remembered it. On the other hand, unexpectedly, The Glebe House where I later was transferred seemed considerably larger, and more impressive than I envisaged it, and surely had acquired several new buildings. I had heard that it now had an admirable clerical headmaster, and had taken on an expanding lease of life. The last time I had come in sight of the cluster of school buildings had been from the air, when the Blenheim bomber on a night reconnaissance, in which I was a passenger-observer, had crossed the Norfolk coastline, out to sea, passing over the Wash, and the goal-posts of the playing fields of my old school, by chance the ultimate glimpse of my homeland.

I found myself peering downwards with a curious mixture of emotions. How frozen I had always been, in my passive rôle of goalkeeper, in those notoriously cold Norfolk winters, with the east wind blowing off the North Sea, so inanimate that I usually muffed the ball when at last it was shot in my direction by the opposing forwards. My hands had been all chilblains. In contrast, the electrically-heated gloves that I was wearing, crouched in the plane, were very comforting, and all my usual reactions, the tight, hollow feeling in the pit of my stomach, for the unknown destiny that lay ahead, left me. A mood of thankfulness enveloped me, instead. At least, like the receding coastline, my schooldays were behind me.

On this later occasion, I peered at The Glebe House through the gate, having been driven over by the friends with whom I was spending the week-end at Sheringham. I almost expected to see Madam propelling herself towards me, in her bath-chair, like a pursuing figure in a dream. Instead, a youngish man in a sports jacket came hurrying down the drive. Clearly a member of the staff, going off duty for the rest of the day. I shyly stopped him, and then could think of nothing to say, except lamely to explain that I had been a pupil in the school for a short time in the First World War. 'Really?' he said, for what was Hecuba to him, or he to Hecuba, and passed on quickly to his few hours of freedom before I could detain him further, or blackmail him into showing me round my old dormitory, and the new Houses. He need not have had such fears.

Not surprisingly, the town itself seemed greatly changed, not larger so much as more crowded, with gaudy kiosks and sun pavilions and ice-cream parlours, and strolling groups of American airmen from neighbouring camps. All equally unknown in my day. It was not until I reached the white walls of the coast-guard station on the cliff that something of the former holiday magic returned, and I had a sudden blurred vision of one summer's day that had been truly perfect from dawn to dusk.

The twenty-second of June, 1911. I have attended two coronations in the Abbey, but I was far too immature to attend this one, the Coronation Day of George V, which was celebrated in that corner of Norfolk by a glorious gymkhana. There an infant of three had his first introduction to such delights as coconut shies and egg-and-spoon races, followed by a drill display of the Norfolk Yeomanry, whose martial hats and magnificent uniforms must have impressed him, although the only picture that I can pinpoint with any real assurance was the climax to the day's loyal rejoicings. The whole town migrated then to the cliff top, for hadn't a giant firework display upon the beach been advertised for weeks? That alone is still projected upon the screen of my own mind, all the rest is simply the reiterated accounts of other family spectators.

Once again I can see the last glimmers of light fading from the western sky, the tall pile of the lighthouse buildings behind us, and nothing in front except the vague expanse of the darkening sea. Every moment the crowd of spectators was growing larger, their laughing chatter hushing into expectancy, as the first rocket climbed higher and higher into the heavens, hesitating for one long instant, before it shivered into a thousand brilliant fragments against the wall of night.

It was the first time I had ever seen a display of fireworks on any scale. I had no idea that such beauty as those fantastic columns of golden light, those cascades of foaming silver bubbles existed in the world. I was led away at last to bed, trembling but exultant with joy, and as I walked along the same cliff edge that Sunday afternoon of another June, something of that first ecstasy returned like a pain, warning me, chiding me rather, for the corrosion of the world's slow stain.

Such avenues of thought lead nowhere, I told myself, better concentrate instead on my mission. Which was our holiday bungalow in the straggling row? They all looked the same indeterminate colours now, and rather cramped. How had two families managed to crowd in so happily? Was I foolish to have come in search of something as elusive as the crown jewels which King John was supposed to have relinquished with his heavy baggage in his hasty retreat across the Wash? How we had searched and searched in vain, buoyed up by the surging optimism of the very young. And now fresh gangs of kids each summer would doubtless play the same games of cricket and rounders on those safe, soft sands as we had done, to warm ourselves after our bathe, and would doubtless suffer the same sense of frustration when it rained, when their pocket-money ran out, when the grown-ups went fishing and left them behind, and would experience the same shy longings of desire, if it was only for gathering the wild roses in the lanes behind the shore and presenting small bouquets to an adored one.

Our own most frequent bouts of self-expression took the form of dressing up in bath towels to act charades, and perform the plays we improvised, upon the stage of the bungalow's verandah. The grown-ups had nowhere else to go, so they were on the whole an acquiescent audience until the evening when I gave my first and last solo performance.

For some reason I had returned earlier than the others from the beach and was standing on the verandah by myself, when I suddenly became aware that everything was turning scarlet. The windows, the wooden floor, my own bare arms and legs, everything was now dyed the colour of blood. The transformation delighted and at the same time bewildered me, even as the fireworks had done, so that I had a muddled, precipitate longing to be bright-red all over myself, and swiftly tore off my grey jersey and my shorts. Then, unashamed, I began to dance up and down on the verandah, a naked little savage, worshipping the sunset. After a time, I was far too drunk with the ecstasy to notice the family's approach, or to mind when I was smacked hard and dispatched supperless to bed. However, as I have already related, this did not deter me from following my nature rites among the bracken of the Lickey woods. After all, I had been blooded.

Staying up late for a special occasion, like going to one's first pantomime, in my case, to see Dorothy Ward in *Jack and the Beanstalk* – and where is her equal in tights today? – or being hurried off to bed, in disgrace; inevitably these are the two pivots for the unleashing of our earliest memories, I decided, as once again I listened for the peewit's cry among the sand-dunes. If only one could have the intervening years again ... again ... again ... seemed to be the mournful lament of the birds upon the shore.

Yet I do not nearly so much regret the things that I have done as those I have left undone, the times that I have drawn back upon the brink, too cautious to take the plunge towards an unknown beach. And if I could hold communion with the holiday families that doubtless still rent Sandy Lodge today, I would urge the children never to be afraid of showing their inmost feelings, to undress their minds in public, if need be, whenever their genuine instinct urges, or the day may come when their response to the quickening pulse of life becomes so self-conscious or so stultified that no fireworks of any kind will have the power to reach their heart.

I have to admit, however, that there is no hint of such advice in the dry bones of my school reports, religiously preserved by my mother, including the one at the end of my first year at Lynfield, headed: July the twenty-ninth, 1914.

It seemed strange to read it now, in the light of what occurred less than a week later in the world beyond my own horizons. I note that I was third in my class of eleven, that as regards my favourite subjects, history, reading and recitation – hadn't I been chosen out of the whole school to recite at a concert in Hunstanton Town Hall an impassioned monologue, in my Eton suit, about a rabbit called 'Ragalug' – I registered *'Thoughtful and intelligent, very good and excellent.'* Even my class singing had *'improved'*, my drawing was *'slowly improving'*, while as regards my conduct, there clearly had been no more rebellious outbursts in the dorm, because Miss Cook had written at the bottom of the page in her faultless calligraphy – so much the mirror of her strong, just character – *'Very good. Has worked well.'*

Unfortunately – since this report was considerably better than the two previous ones – my mother was not there to open it at the breakfast table, when it arrived a few days before the Bank Holiday. She was having a holiday herself, in Brussels, revisiting her own old school; the convent where she was fortunate in having been given a faultless French accent that was of far more use to her in later life than the Horatian tags I scrappily acquired. It had all been part of her mother's plan to turn her daughters into accomplished young ladies of fashion, and, as it happened, my American grandmother was accompanying her on this pilgrimage, as she was over from the States for the summer, together with her youngest daughter, my aunt Nanciebel.

The gathering war clouds made no impact on me. My father must have been increasingly anxious about my mother being out of the country, and in Belgium of all places, but life at Cherrycroft was untouched except by the exuberance of another unleashed school holidays. On August Bank Holiday itself, a picnic had been arranged, as a special treat, on the river at Evesham. My father was in charge of us, rowing clumsily, and not dressed in flannels and a blazer because he would have felt ill-at-ease in such an outfit.

Drowsily the hot afternoon passed, in flicking our cherry stones into the water and drifting past the banks of that lush country-side, which in the spring, when acre upon acre of fruit blossom is in full flower, is like an all-enveloping tide of pink foam. I can truthfully assert that I have come across no fairer sight in the whole of my travels. Barnt Green is only a few miles from Evesham, but the expedition had been a source of intense excite-ment to me for days, though of course not quite of the order of the time that my godfather, the mysterious Mr Murray, had arrived unannounced in a high-waisted automobile, and had in-sisted on carrying us all off for a picnic on the Malvern Hills. In those days, a car journey for any distance seemed as great an adventure as setting off for the Himalayas. In consequence, I have an equally vivid recollection of the occasion when another chariot, this time a bright orange affair, snorted up the drive of Cherrycroft, and out of it stepped a woman in a large motoring hat, an elaborate veil, and dressed in a dust coat, although it was again a warm August day. In contrast, my mother was wearing a very simple pink cotton frock, for it was eleven o'clock in the morning and she was cutting off the dead heads in the rose borders that were stretched from the gravel entrance in front of the house, down past the pergolas to the hedges bordering the lane. Ever since I had woken up, I had been in a fever about the Spencers coming to fetch me. Colin Spencer, a rather plump, placid boy was my special chum at Lynfield. Opposites are always supposed to attract each other. I was so volatile and talkative, whereas nothing ever disturbed Colin's phlegmatic calm, and he seemed to enjoy my endless chatter and mimicry, doling out large portions of his generous rations of tuck, endlessly sucking a bulls-eye, and answering in monosyllables.

The Spencers lived on the other side of Birmingham, in the manufacturing belt, and though Colin was not given to self-dramatization, I had the feeling, perhaps because they owned a car, that his family were better-off than ours. Now I was going to stay with them for a week, and ever since breakfast I had been alternately filled with elation at the prospect of all the exciting treats ahead of me, and doubt as to what impression Cherrycroft would make upon my school friend. Uneasily, I found myself hoping that I had not exaggerated the size of the garden. Would the whole set-up seem very simple to Colin's mother, who I gathered lived a very urban life, with frequent trips, too, to London?

I was particularly anxious, because my own parent had refused to make any concession to the drama of the day, not so much my departure, as the meeting of the two mothers. I longed to suggest that she should change out of her old gardening dress into something grander, and more likely to impress the sophisticated Mrs Spencer.

However, I need not have worried. As usual, her instinct was entirely right. As the car came to a standstill outside the front door, and Mrs Spencer graciously descended, smiling at her son's friend in his best grey flannel suit, jumping up and down nervously in the driveway, my mother came up the steps from the rose-garden, with a bunch of her special Betty UpRichard, an exquisite pink damask tea-rose, in her arms, which, as she pushed a strand of her soft hair off her forehead, she handed with a charming smile of welcome to the stranger, emanating a strong scent of perfume, handsome and rouged beneath her motoring veil.

It is curious how some tableaux that would appear to be of trivial importance, nevertheless remain buried in one's consciousness all one's life. Of course, at the time I was completely unaware that I was absorbing a lesson in the natural dignity of human behaviour that would be of enormous benefit when unexpectedly, like so many others, I found myself precipitated into the rough and tumble of barrack-room life and mucking-in on the lower deck in a later war.

To be oneself at all times; never to try and impress the world by assuming a false manner, or dressing up in a way that would be alien to one's nature. No one's image is harmed by being discovered in the equivalent of one's shirt sleeves. Only by overdressing or false party manners. And my mother was never guilty of either solecism.

I can still experience the irradiating burst of relief I felt as the two women, so contrasted in every way, shook hands, and the visitor murmured polite words of admiration for the roses that so exactly matched the donor's dress. So far from being put in the shade by the other's elaborate and elegant *ensemble*, my mother shone against her own background. How proud I was of her at that moment. Equally delighted, too, with the dialogue that followed when Colin's mother started describing with enthusiasm the visit to Birmingham of the sensational and daring Gaby Deslys.

Had my mother been to the Hippodrome, the music hall in Birmingham, to see the French dancer now touring England who wore so many ostrich feathers, and showed so much of her legs and bare shoulders?

'Of course, you need have no fears we would take Colin and Godfrey during his visit. I myself have already been twice. It isn't so much what she wears or doesn't wear, it is the way she does the Bunny Hug so marvellously with her partner, Harry Pilcer.'

To which my mother replied sweetly, 'No, you see, Mrs Spencer, as we have our own family theatre in Birmingham, if I can ever be dragged away from my garden at this time of the year we have our own box at the *Prince of Wales.*'

It was quite true, we had; though the theatre in Broad Street which my great-grandfather, James Rodgers had taken over and owned when he grew tired of barnstorming, was now leased to other hands. In her widowhood, my American grandmother had lost the personal interest in the theatre which had at first absorbed her, and had returned instead to settle down once more in her native Boston. All the same my mother, never given to any kind of showing off, had nevertheless somehow succeeded in making the verbal exchange sound not like a passing reference to the two rival theatres in a provincial town, but rather to an exclusive label such as an entrance badge, with the name Mrs Ernest Winn on it, for the Royal Enclosure at Ascot. In actual fact, I don't believe my mother attended any race meeting of any sort in her whole life. Her younger son certainly hasn't been to one, and I sometimes wonder what I have missed.

However, what I did miss that August Bank Holiday weekend were not the crowds massing in Trafalgar Square and outside Buckingham Palace, but the bowls of flowers that always filled and perfumed the house when my mother was at home.

From her I have inherited the instinctive feeling that a living-room without some modest plant is bereft of warmth, however infallible the heating system, or bright the colour scheme. I remember on one occasion sitting with Lord Beaverbrook in his hotel suite in the South of France, and commenting that the flowers in the vase on the table beside us looked as though they had been dead for days. 'Have they?' replied my host, honouring them with a brief glance, for the first time, and then continuing the discussion. I don't think the man who invariably behaved with such generosity to me, and did everything to further my career, was so much irritated by this interruption as completely indifferent to the spontaneous observation I had made. Afterwards, I quailed at my own temerity. I never lost my healthy awe of my boss, which is as it should be. The remark had slipped out because I could not help myself. Some people like horses, others flowers.

There is surely ample living space for almost every kind of taste and relaxation in the world. What I have never been able to understand is why so many adult, and therefore presumably intelligent human beings, kick up such a fuss and profess to be so shocked by deviations in aesthetic standards or physical leanings from their own.

That evening, when we returned from our boating expedition at Evesham, the joys of the day were not yet over. The titular head of the family had prepared another treat for his two sons. After our supper, as soon as the dining-room table had been cleared, Father produced the sheets of stamps, mostly British colonials, that he had had sent on appro. from Stanley Gibbons' Headquarters in the Strand.

My brother had been encouraged to pursue this hobby, after outdoor sports were denied him, so that he had by now already the nucleus of a collection that was to continue to give him pleasure long after he had been called to the Bar. I, on the other hand, had only just been started off with a scattering of his swops. Therefore to be promoted to sit opposite my brother, with my own album in front of me, while our parent with the tidiness that was part of his make-up, and with the aid of a pair of stamp tweezers, meted out largesse between us equally, filled the cup of my happiness to overflowing.

Rodger had first choice on one page that was turned over, I

My stepfather, Edward Martino

Below left James Rodgers, my great-grandfather, the strolling player. *Right* My American grandmother's house in Edgbaston, with my mother and my Aunt Ethel before their marriages

myself of the next. Scrupulous fairness was displayed, and we, in our turn, were careful not to draw attention to the more expensive items. A three-cornered Cape of Good Hope, for instance, could only be contemplated as a birthday or a Christmas present. On this occasion, the whole ritual resulted in the spending of a pound or two, but it seemed indeed like an outpouring of riches.

Moreover, it was one of the few moments when I felt close to my father, when for a short time we seemed to exist on the same plane. As a partner in a successful firm of accountants, he possessed the reputation of having a brilliant flair for figures, and was also chairman of Webleys, but I could never envisage him holding a revolver in his hand, or performing any of the daring deeds that occur with such dazzling frequency in the heroic library of the very young. It was not his fault. Unfortunately, he possessed none of the surface attributes that any small boy longs for in his father. He never bowled to us on the sands at Hunstanton. He didn't play tennis, a game for which I myself was already showing an almost infant prodigy aptitude. His hair was receding fast, and he wore rimless glasses.

In consequence, I wasn't even frightened of him or of his wrath, as I suspect he was of his own father, and certainly there was no means of turning him into a hero, though he did seem suddenly as powerful as a Mid-Western Sheriff as I watched the dispenser of bounty turning over the loose pages, announcing in the voice of someone accustomed to dealing with balance sheets: 'Now, Godfrey, how is your position as regards British Guiana? Would you, do you think, have room for a specimen of their new issue?'

This teasing preamble was of such exquisite possibilities that my usually quick ears completely failed to detect the approach of horses' hooves up the drive. Then, in an instant, the peaceful interlude in the lamplight was shattered, as the driver of the station fly drew up in the porch, and there was the sound of muffled voices. The next moment, the menfolk of the family were stampeding into the hall to welcome the female influx there, dominated by my Rodgers grandmother, like a frigate in full sail who does not know how to haul down its sails, on entering harbour. Close behind her came Mary, her personal maid, whom she had taken to America and back, a jealous dragon, holding her mistress's hand luggage, as though still among foreigners,

C

then my aunt Nanciebel, a tall, gawky filly, and finally my mother, who even at that moment gave the impression of being so much less bedraggled and travel-soiled than the others. I watched my father bend down from his own considerable height, lifting her right off the ground, in his embrace, with a most unusual abandonment.

Then they all started to talk at once.

'We've lost all our other luggage. We caught the very last boat out of Ostend. There were a thousand passengers on board. I can't think why we didn't sink. We were packed like sardines, on deck. Look how my coat is ripped, right down the side. The stampede to get on board was awful, it is a miracle that we are here at all. There were soldiers everywhere, commandeering all the transport. It all happened so suddenly. Poor little Belgium.'

I had not been allowed to realize until that moment that there had been any real danger attached to my mother's absence on foreign soil. After all, she was in the company of my other grandmother, who compared to meek and gentle Granny Winn wore always an air of supreme aplomb. Mollie Rodgers had arranged to come to Europe this summer, reuniting her three daughters in Brussels, after Nanciebel, the youngest by far, had first been shown the sights of the other capitals, and who had ever heard of anyone interfering with any of Mollie Rodgers' plans before? Only my mother, in a sudden burst of defiance, when she had chosen Ernest Winn as her lawfully-wedded husband, whom her ambitious, matchmaking parent did not consider nearly good enough a party for the undoubted beauty among her daughters.

Of course, I knew nothing about such past clashes of temperament yet, and as for the present, only the strained expression on my mother's face had the power to disturb me. Otherwise, surely all that mattered was that they were safely home again, and I had been invited to the Goodrick Clarkes tomorrow to play in my very first mixed tournament.

I am sure my father's reaction was the same. England was such a different place from Belgium, a pathetic pawn in a game where the stakes were too large for its capabilities. This return of the travellers had its parallel in the blitz and bomb stories which in a later conflagration the besieged were to pour into the ears of the sympathetic though uncomprehending dwellers in safer areas, blessed with unbroken, unmenaced nights. It was not in any way that the others did not wish to take it all in. It was simply that most of us lacked the imagination to do so.

The stamp sheets laid out on the dining-room table, which now had to be cleared once more for a second sitting for supper, how much more real and tangible their message seemed than the repetitive and incoherent accounts that continued far into the night. The one lasting impression for me was the tone of my mother's voice, as she kept on repeating, 'Poor little Belgium.' Events had overwhelmed and destroyed for ever her unquestioning acceptance of life in terms of how it was led in Barnt Green. While on her face persisted the same look that I had surprised that night when the long mirror had mysteriously broken loose and splintered into small fragments at her feet, as she dressed for the Margessons' party. That had begun something, and now how would it end?

I am not being fanciful or over-dramatic, in retrospect. For I have seen the same look on the face of other women when unexpected pressures concerned with their personal involvements have overwhelmed them – and undoubtedly they are the more trusting of the two sexes – with the inevitable consequence that the smooth timetable of their domestic routine has been shattered beyond repair, like the jagged pieces of glass, an unsolvable crossword puzzle, upon the floor of my mother's bedroom.

'*Women are God's flowers.*' Henry Irving had written this quotation in my mother's autograph book, twenty years earlier, and underneath, on the same page, Ellen Terry had added her postscript in a more rounded, feminine hand-writing: '*Yes, men are God's trees, and women God's flowers, says Tennyson.*'

As a girl, my mother had been full of half-expressed longings to go on the stage herself, dressing up as Juliet for a fancy dress ball, and taking part in amateur theatricals whenever the opportunity occurred. This was hardly surprising, since from her earliest childhood she had been allowed the privilege and the enchantment of meeting all the famous players who visited the family theatre, and were entertained at the white-fronted house in Edgbaston, where her parents lived in some style, when they were not at their other home, Tudor House, Broadway.

In those late-Victorian days, this most celebrated of Cotswold villages was still completely unspoilt, though there was something of an artistic colony there, headed by the well-known painter of his day, Byam Shaw, and Mary Anderson, the most beautiful woman my mother used to say that she had ever set eyes on, and far more lovely a creature, in her view, than Lily Langtry, whose signature is also in her autograph book. Mary Anderson, who had discarded her theatrical name by this time to become Madame Novarro, and put her portrayal of Galatea far behind her, lived higher up on the hill from my grandparents, in another of those golden houses of Cotswold stone that seem even more of a pleasure to the eye today when one has been stunned by the excesses of chromium and concrete in our cities. But that utterly English view from the top of Broadway Hill, before the road moves on into Oxfordshire, and from which you are supposed to be able to see a dozen counties, on a clear day, remains still so nobly untrammelled that one sends up a prayer it may always be thus.

After my mother's death I found among the family letters that she had kept, as any schoolgirl would, from the matinée idols of the day: '*Dear Captain Rodgers, it will give me great pleasure to take luncheon with you on Saturday at three o'clock. Please give my kind regards to Mrs Rodgers, sincerely, Johnston Forbes Robertson. October 5, '93.*' and a yellowed cutting, headed, MASON COLLEGE UNION. This turned out to be a report in the local paper of a performance of Hadden Chambers' 'interesting society play', *The Idlers*.

It starts off:

'On Tuesday last the Mason College Dramatic Union gave their twelfth annual performance in the Edgbaston Assembly Rooms, in the presence of a large and influential audience. Indeed, it was the largest gathering we remember to have seen at these pleasant yearly reunions, every seat having been sold already some time ago . . .'

The play? The cast? My eyes skipped on down the column till they came to the paragraph that had been underlined in ink. '*The toilettes of the ladies, especially those of Miss Winifred Heath and Miss Joan B. Rodgers, were exquisite in taste*. Indeed, the Mason Dramatic Union have made a great acquisition in enrolling Miss Joan B. Rodgers. A more exquisite characterization of a young ingénue it would be difficult to match even on the professional stage, and Miss Rodgers must be credited with the most finished and truly natural acting of the evening. Both in looks and in her by-play, Miss Rodgers realized the saucy character of Kate Merrywater to perfection.'

'*The Readiness is all*' wrote another of my mother's theatrical heroes, Lewis Waller, in her treasured album, but though after receiving such notices she was both ready and eager to take to the boards, like her grandfather, her own mother had other adamantine plans.

It is true that Mollie Foulkes had welcomed the idea of taking over the Rodgers theatre, as part of her marriage dowry, which she proceeded to run with far more élan and efficiency than my grandfather. The Captain, as everyone continued to call Jack Rodgers, even after he had been persuaded to drop anchor for good, still walked up Broad Street with the gait of a sailor, and with the sea for ever mirrored in his very blue eyes, and was palpably ill at ease when he was compelled to drive out with his wife, a footman on the box, to impress the leading ladies of Edgbaston, whose duty calls the American in their midst was careful to return.

In due course, my mother, too, exchanged her autograph book, in which the only signature not connected with the theatre is that of Catherine Gladstone, for another kind of album which would have no sale in any stationer's shop today. Bound in plump leather, it is inscribed in fancy lettering *AT HOME.*

An essential part of the equipment of a young bride of the day. And how important, to be sure, that it was filled to over-flowing with suitable names. I see that the first Monday of the month and the first Friday were particularly popular afternoons for receiving.

I wonder if any of the owners of the names so neatly recorded are living today, or at least, their children or grandchildren still dwelling in the same house.

Mrs George Myers, Mrs Sydenham, Mrs Gilbert Smith, Mrs Cecil Crosky, Mrs Dudley (The Elms), Mrs Vaughan (Handsworth) . . . Miss Monckton, Mrs Hamilton Barnsley, Mrs Handley Greenfield, Mrs Millikin Smith, the Misses Chamberlain, Mrs Walter Pinsent, Mrs Douglas Charles . . . and there my own eyes came to a halt, for here, at long last was a familiar name, Auntie Bee, Audrey's mother, living so close to us at Barnt Green, with her own mother even nearer, just across the road, in the large mansion with the impressive lodge and her At Home day (every Wednesday) also inscribed in this young bride's social almanac. How we delighted as children, every time Wednesday came round, asking, 'Are you going to Mrs ShuffleBOTHAM'S for tea today, Mother?' The same kind of childhood joke as 'Please, Miss Jefferies, pass the DAMson jam.'

However, there was nothing to make me produce an indulgent, reminiscent smile in the third souvenir that I discovered among the little hoard of mementoes of the past from which my mother had been unable to part. I could quite understand why she had kept this one as a kind of talisman, a reminder of a period of her life which she had survived without surrender, without breaking, though it left such a stain upon her outlook that she was unable to believe any more that such a state as lasting security existed for anyone in the world.

I could appreciate her attitude better (than in the days I had been armoured by my own youth) when the moment came for me to turn over the pages of a cheap, black exercise book that was such a contrast from the gold-embossed leather of the other two. For I found that I had chanced upon a most carefully compiled list of the cheapest theatrical digs in the kind of towns which are only visited by number 3 touring companies.

BURY. 'Mrs Colgan, 13 Garden Street, no bath, no inside lav., but house opposite has bath.'

BOSTON. 'Stayed Mrs Ryan, 6A Vauxhall Road, Clean but woman very talkative.'

LUDLOW. 'Stayed Golden Lion Temperance Hotel, Old Street. Bed three shillings a night. Clean. Inside lavatory. No bath.'

RADCLIFFE. Palace Theatre. 'Stayed c/o. Mrs Vizard, 114 Strand Lane. Decent, kind people. Very poor bedroom, and also very primitive outside convenience. The girls had good rooms at 19 Mill Town Street. (To be remembered on the next time round.)'

RAWTENSTALL. Palace Theatre. 'Stayed Mrs Pennington, 124 Bank Street.' This wasn't cheap, the lodger admits, for what could she afford from a salary of five pounds a week, but blessed luxury, there was a BATH.

And finally, STOURBRIDGE. 'Mrs Winnall of 53 Hill Street. Very comfortable indeed,' the compiler writes for the benefit of other pros in other companies. Only seventeen shillings. I write 'finally' since there was a kind of finality for me, when I reminded myself that Stourbridge is only a few miles as the crow flies from Barnt Green, and this happened, this metamorphosis, only a few years later in the order of events I am describing from that August of 1914, when her mother and her younger sister Nanciebel installed themselves at Cherrycroft. Not, as it seemed at first, for the duration, though Joan Rodgers, as she was to describe herself once again on the programmes, had no inkling – how could she have? – that at the end of that war, which had only just begun, she was to find herself playing a small part in a fit-up tour of *Paddy the Next Best Thing*.

The next best thing. Surely there was irony enough in the title of the play in which she made her professional début. Indeed, after the crisis came in her matrimonial fortunes, and she had to take whatever she could get, how she must have wished that her mother had allowed her to chance her luck as a girl of twenty, instead of a matron of forty, since it would not have been difficult to join the company of someone playing a season at the *Prince of Wales*, like Arthur Bourchier, or the Martin Harveys, with the full flowering of her youthful talent, like a banner still unfurled.

Instead, her mother had been absolutely determined to launch her daughter in the only career which she considered suitable for any young woman of that period with an upper-middleclass background. It served her right that in the end none of them made the matches that from a worldly point of view their ambitious parent would have wished for them. And yet, buried beneath that well-corsetted superstructure, there must have lurked a romantic fluttering in her bosom, for the account of her own wooing was like a page out of a novel by Ouida.

As it happened, both Captain Jack Rodgers and his father, James, the strolling player, had made runaway marriages. James, the son of an officer in the Scots Greys, who had fought at the Battle of Waterloo, had been born in Birmingham during the Regiment's stay at the barracks at Ashted. He was educated with a view to a military career, but disappeared from home at the age of seventeen, to become a player. Later, he was to become the manager of the *Liver Theatre,* at Liverpool, and other theatres at Ludlow, Hanley, Coventry and Worcester, ending up with his own in Birmingham, where he produced his first pantomime under the title of *Lulia Rookh* a century ago. He was to make his own last professional appearance at the *Prince of Wales,* in Broad Street, as Mercutio, when he invited Mr and Mrs Kendal to stage their own season there.

Long before that happened, though, and while still in the company of Macready, he had crossed the Irish Sea in search of an audience, and found, instead, a bride. She was a young woman of a good Catholic family from Galway, called O'Donovan, and she came night after night to watch James perform. I have no idea as to how they met, whether it was a stage-door encounter in the beginning, but it quickly proceeded to the big scene in the third act when she naturally wanted to present her handsome admirer to her family, who in their turn were utterly and openly appalled at the suggestion of this sheltered, well-brought-up child even knowing a roving actor, let alone marrying him. But their daughter was too in thrall to listen to their entreaties, so enraptured that she could not bear to be parted from her suitor. In the end, she had the courage to slip away from home one evening to take the night packet to Liverpool, and become Mrs James Rodgers.

I hope her family were mollified and reconciled later, when on Sunday morning James would conduct his wife to her church, with the children, three daughters and a son, Jack, and then go on to his, a staunch Scottish Presbyterian like his military father.

I am very grateful to this great-grandmother, for I owe my Irish blood to her, and I used never to tire of hearing about her legendary romance in my own childhood. What I was not told, however, until many years later, was that she, in her turn, was to run away and leave my great-grandfather for another actor. So it was not surprising that before this happened, she should produce another rolling stone in the family, although my Rodgers grandfather, who took to his heels at the age of fourteen to serve before the mast, and was such a poor sailor, in one respect, all his life, that he had to have a bucket beside him on the bridge, did succeed in ending up as the respectable prototype of every bluff sea captain, bringing his ship safely into harbour.

On this occasion, it was Boston Harbour, and leaving the bridge and the Atlantic behind him, and looking a very handsome figure in his best uniform, more becoming than any stage finery, because it has both the essential aura of virility and the true stamp of authority, he sauntered ashore to take in the local sights. What caught and held his eye, at a dance to which he had been invited by his American hosts, was a well-bosomed young woman, with a mass of ash-blonde hair piled high, eyes as blue as his own, and a translucent skin which she kept all her life, to whom he was presented in the course of the evening.

They found that they had much to talk about, much, indeed, in common, for it soon transpired that Mollie Foulkes, chaperoned by her mother, was to be a passenger on his Blue Star liner, on its return voyage. She explained that they would be *en route* for Paris, where she would be choosing her trousseau. He hid his disappointment as best he could at learning the reason for the voyage, doubtless consoling himself with the thought that, placed at his table at meal-times, and with the luck of a fair wind behind them, much progress might be made. Indeed, such progress was made that, by the end of the voyage, my grandmother, whose increasing determination to have her own way in life on all occasions, and rule everyone and everything in sight, was now to manifest itself, had decided, despite her mother's horrified protests, to break off her engagement, and to marry an English sea captain instead. Her poor deserted swain, it is said, never consoled himself with another bride, whereas this Anglo-American union was blessed with five offspring.

There were three daughters and two sons, Douglas and Stead, who early in his career tried to rebel against the matriarchal system that his mother had insisted on introducing from her own country. Still, it wasn't much of a revolt. A few wild oats sown at Oxford, and he was sent down in temporary disgrace and packed off to the New Country, to a land where all men worked and all women ruled the home.

My Aunt Ethel and my mother chose England as their home, the others followed their American blood back across the Atlantic. They might have been two families. Uncle Douglas married a Canadian wife, and having bought a fruit farm, settled down near the Niagara Falls until the First World War brought him back to Europe as a major in the Canadian Expeditionary Force. He was the only member of that side of the family whom I ever saw again, until chance brought me to speak at Harvard, on a lecture tour just after the Second World War had ended. Between catching trains, on a very tight schedule, I just had time to take a cab out to the suburb of Melrose, to call on my great aunt Bessie, Granny Rodgers' sister, and the only member of their generation still alive.

Aunt Bessie Foulkes seemed to know far more about the English side of the family than her great-nephew. To my surprise, I found she had kept every single letter my mother had ever written to her, together with a cardboard box stacked with pictures of myself and my brother, at all ages, many of which I had long since forgotten, and of our cousins, the Ludlow children. Jack, in his uniform of stretcher-bearer, with a doomed look already on his face; Mollie, with her bright-red hair and sweet smile that possessed a beauty of its own; her mother and my mother as teenagers themselves, with tight, tight waists and starched blouses and straw hats, riding demurely in a dog-cart, and despite the faded sepia tints, so radiantly 'with-it', as youngsters of the same age would say today.

It was like meeting my own family all over again, for the first time. A completely fresh appraisal. Indeed, I had almost forgotten what our den at the top of the house at Cherrycroft had looked like until Aunt Bessie started describing in such detail all the places, all the rooms she had never entered except in her loving imagination, as she pored over my father's photographic studies. In one brief hour, she gave me a sense of the links of family destiny, and the power of heredity that cannot be denied. If I had reasoned about it at all till that moment, it had seemed to me that one was what one was, through upbringing and environment alone. The past, the signposts of my family past, had meant nothing to me, only the present and the future. Now I was made to appreciate, and with a rush of acceptance, exactly how big a part my mixed ancestry, the American and Irish blood on my mother's side, the Welsh and Scottish on that of my father, had played in the making of my own character and personality, bubbling over with the unquenchable vitality of my Bostonian grandmother one moment, so withdrawn and anxious at other times.

However, I felt no shyness in the presence of this old lady of nearly ninety, who was perfectly well aware that she had only a few more months to live. That was why our meeting was so important to her, while I felt at ease in her little wood-framed house in a way that had not happened to me since I had landed at Idle-wild Airport a month before, and had been instantly pitchforked into an atmosphere of such luxurious abundance that my austerity-conditioned body and mind revolted. It was as if the war had never happened, until Aunt Bessie spoke of the five years just past, as though she had spent them in blitzed London herself. She even produced the sea books that I had written, sent her by my mother – 'The Captain would have liked them' – now very ear-marked because she had lent them, or rather pressed them upon every neighbour in the street who might be persuaded to send a Bundle for Britain. What an ambassador, what an ally, I thought admiringly, as the years slipped away, and now instead, we were discussing that other conflagration when Europe had gone up in smoke, and so nearly her sister and her niece Nanciebel had got trapped first in Belgium and, later, in England. Just supposing they had been unable to secure a passage back to the States. Why, Nanciebel at the budding stage – eager to burst – might have married an Englishman, like her sisters, and what a difference that would have made to the family tree.

'Mind you, I wouldn't have disapproved of that,' Aunt Bessie remarked perversely, seated in her rocking chair, surrounded protectively by a regiment of photograph frames. 'On the other hand, I have a strong idea your grandmother would have been mad at the idea.' At that sally, we broke into laughter, like childish conspirators, and I started to describe, as though it were yesterday, all that I could remember of that August when my school holidays had been completely transformed by the upheavals, the demands, the exciting, extravagant behaviour of Granny Rodgers. The house at Barnt Green, which in summer was always full of the scent of flowers and beeswax, became not exactly a gaming salon in the west, but, despite its polished, antique furni-ture, and shiny chintzes, was transformed into a rich passenger's suite on a transatlantic liner.

'It must have been awfully trying for Mother, having to cope with the avalanche, but it was wonderful for me, Aunt Bessie. Nanciebel, who I suppose was about twenty, used to knock the ball backwards and forwards to me on the tennis court every morning, and Granny gave me a bridge lesson every afternoon. She used to stay in bed all morning. That seemed awfully dashing to me. Up till then, I imagined everyone got up for breakfast unless they were really ill. After my game with Nanciebel was over, I would knock on Granny's door because she kept a marvellous box of *crème-de-menthe* sweets beside her bed. You know, the very sugary, Turkish delight kind. She always gave me one, *and before lunch*. When I thanked her ecstatically, she invariably made the same remark, "Always remember, you mustn't love food in life, only people." She meant that you mustn't *say* that you loved food. Because she did, didn't she, Aunt Bessie?'

'Mollie certainly did,' Aunt Bessie agreed.

She loved all the good things. All the pleasures. Travelling first-class with her personal maid in attendance, a box at the theatre, vintage wine. Looking back now, I am surprised she did not enjoy smoking a cigar. Barnt Green, that genteel backwater, was turned upside down to provide amusement for the restless prisoner on these shores. The captain's widow visited her old domain, the *Prince of Wales* Theatre in Birmingham, but now the touring companies seemed poor fry beside the royal visits she had been able to command from the leading players of the day. Therefore, she preferred to hold court in the drawing-room at Cherrycroft every afternoon, laying down the law at the bridge table to whoever could be persuaded to play with her, raising their stakes from the usual modest tuppence to at least sixpence a hundred.

For once, utterly silent, I watched, listened, absorbed. My passion for collecting and looking at pictures I was to inherit from one of my Winn grandparents; here was another legacy, coming to me at a very early stage in my development, from the other side of the family. A child of seven was acquiring the rudiments of a skill that would prove a lifelong release from working pressures, and on the threshold of maturity provide another important turning point in his life. Meanwhile, the music teacher at Lynfield, Miss Watson, had written to my mother suggesting that I should be encouraged to 'keep up my enthusiasm' by practising for at least half-an-hour every morning, during the dog days when it would have been so easy for me to forget my scales. Alas, though I religiously obeyed her bidding, it became an exercise of duty, not a labour of love, with the metronome beating out the passing minutes, lost for ever.

I tried to recapture my first flush of enthusiasm for the piano by the example of a neighbour of ours, Beryl Rushton, who must have been about the same age as Nanciebel, though she possessed more of a Burne-Jones silhouette than that of a long-legged flapper of the period. Beryl already showed such promise that she had been accepted as a pupil by one of the leading concert pianists of the day, Irene Scharrer, and sometimes as a great treat she would allow me to sit beside her while she practised in her family drawing-room, at an impressive grand piano. In consequence, today I can never hear a Chopin étude being played by some such master as Malcuzynski without recalling, though more and more faintly now, I admit, that first rapturous glimpse of a world where all things are beautiful.

Equally I recognized, though, that that path of self-fulfilment was not for me. To be conscious of one's limitations and abide by them, to harness one's ambitions to one's talents, instead of the other way round, that surely is a protective wisdom that should be acquired very early in life, and I was fortunate in doing so. An instinctive skill at bridge, a natural eye for all ball games, but particularly on the tennis court, these were natural assets that I began eagerly to cultivate now, though I had no inkling that the combination was later to be the unexpected means of entirely changing my direction, where my ambitions were concerned, and creating the foundation for all the good fortune that has since come my way. It sounds improbable, but that is how it happened, and without any gambling with chips, either.

My grandmother, on the other hand, enjoyed nothing so much as the challenge of an all-night poker session with the 'boys', on her many crossings and re-crossings of the Atlantic. She was truly in her element then, and found it difficult to conjure up even a semblance of the same excitement during her afternoon 'At Homes', in my mother's house. True, Auntie Bee Charles played a strongly masculine game, and was, moreover, the kind of lavish hostess in her own well-run house of which my grandmother thoroughly approved. Auntie Bee was inclined to wear the trousers, too, in her own home, and of that Mollie Rodgers approved with equal wholeheartedness. But most of the other local residents, like the Sheldons and the Rabones, the Smith-Kerrs and the Wenhams and the Thursfields, preferred the more conventional timetable of tending their gardens and croquet or tennis parties, for the long summer afternoons. Which reminds me, that only the other day a Mrs Whitehead, who now lives in nearby Northfield, where the major part of the landscape has been absorbed by the Austin Motor works, wrote to me to describe her family visits to Barnt Green in her own childhood.

'I used to be taken regularly to visit my grandfather, Mr Gregory Goode of Sandhills Road, where I used to watch my aunts play croquet on the lawn until we were called in for china tea and cucumber sandwiches and seed cake. I remember, too, my aunts spelling out the name of a woman (in shocked voices) who actually shopped in the afternoon in Barnt Green. Evidently, in those days it was considered most inelegant to shop after lunch. How very different life is today.'

All the same, I have an idea that my American grandmother, though I came to have inimical feelings towards her in the end, would have adapted herself to the changing scene. Certainly she would have understood the appeal and admired the undoubted talents of The Beatles. Indeed, she would have led the way to book that group for a one-night stand, at her own theatre, with the same satisfaction as she used to welcome the D'Oyly Carte Company, and that spellbinder of his day, Henry Lytton, for a season of packed houses. It was the other side of the family who refused with an almost suicidal stubbornness to move with the times. So that right up till his death in 1916, my grandfather Winn continued to rule his sons and unmarried daughter like a Mr Barrett of Selly Oak.

I was remote from his last illness, although like all the rest of the family my fortunes were inevitably affected by his passing. He only really came alive for me after he was dead. A long time afterwards when I had become someone in my own right, I was invited to pay a visit to the works in Charles Street where now the man who had once been his office boy presided in the founder's chair. On one wall of the board-room the Pettie portrait of my grandfather hung, in which the sitter looked more in his prime than I remembered him with his blemished nose. "You've got the same forehead as your grandfather,' my host pointed out, appraising the two of us in turn. 'The likeness is often remarked upon, when we have a board meeting in this room.' Was it? While I failed to see any trace of it myself, I was surprised to find how flattered I was by the comparison, presumably because with time the tyrant's Victorian virtues had assumed the enviable aura of omnipotence.

As I made my tour of the works, I encountered elderly gaffers, who volunteered that they had been boy apprentices in Mr Charles's day, and how on a Monday morning he would arrive in his carriage, with its back loaded up with fresh vegetables from The Uplands that he would distribute among them, full of the vitamins he felt they needed for another week's labours. In the same way as he distributed his prize flowers and grapes far and wide. Like so many other human beings, he could be generous and forthcoming towards other people's families, whereas with his own children and grandchildren he remained a grudging martinet until the end.

Aunt Edith, with her Liberty scarves and penchant for grey, was making old bones after all, and somehow it didn't fit into the pattern. The snowdrop daughter who faded away, that should have been the legend. Instead, she had to face reality at last. Both her parents died in swift succession, for deprived of the rock-like strength of the head of the family, Granny Winn almost gratefully gave up. Whereupon, from never having to worry about money, Aunt Edith found herself compelled henceforth to starve herself to keep up appearances. Like other unmarried daughters, after a lifetime of unpaid servitude she was left to fend for herself late in life, on a small annuity. However, with a dignity and a gallantry which became her, she transferred her mementoes of Italy, and what pieces of furniture she needed, from the Selly Oak mansion to a flat on the very top storey of a house with many stairs to climb, in the dentists' quarter of the city. At least, Newhall Street was quiet and respectable, and near her lending library, and here she remained, growing thinner and thinner until, under the harsh threats and brutal cachinnations of the bombing raids, her mind, like so many others, protested and finally broke. In her case, she was to retreat into a blessed amnesia for twenty years, from which gently she awoke just before the end of her life to find herself being cared for by her sister Jessie's daughter, Joan, in the charming house on Beechen Cliffs, of which her beloved Jane Austen would undoubtedly have approved. It was then that my godmother sent for me and we were able to have that long farewell talk, completely lucid, utterly candid, which I have already described. I am grateful, for both our sakes, that it was so.

So many families possess the inevitable spinster aunt; some

treat her as a joke, some as an occasional stab to their conscience; but I remember mine with gratitude and pride. As for her brothers, my uncles, I never had the chance to get to know them, because Uncle Herbert, one of my godfathers, declined early from the consumption that was supposed to have threatened his sister, while Uncle Reginald disappeared from the scene abroad, the only one of the family who rebelled against the dominance of his father. It does not seem to have helped him much. He was the youngest to die. Only Uncle Philip remained, the eldest son, and the successor not only by right but by temperament and unceasing diligence as well. Solid, conscientious, prematurely aged from over-work, a reserved but extremely courteous man, who suddenly astonished everyone in his circle, as he had long since been regarded as a confirmed bachelor, by marrying, of all things, an actress. And an unknown small-part player in a touring musical comedy company at that.

If only the family had been more welcoming to the newcomer in their midst, life might have been different for many of us later on. I have a suspicion, too, that my own mother was the worst offender. For the very reason of her own stage associations, she should have been kinder to her sister under the skin. The so-called gentler sex can be worse snobs than men, and on occasion crueller to each other. Devilishly so. Mrs Philip Winn turned out to be a splendid helpmate to her husband, transforming herself into a most capable business woman who had more than won her right to sit on the board of the family business, after her husband's death. Thus, in the end, financially she had all the cards in her hand in the way that my American grandmother liked to have them dealt. But how in the early days Philip's bride must have suffered from the patronage of her in-laws at those interminable Sunday lunches. If in the end she was to have her revenge, and if the unyielding attitude she adopted repercussed on my own innocent head, I in no way blame her for it. In her shoes, I should have acted in exactly the same way.

Fortunately, for the moment, there were no crises, family or otherwise, and indeed, life seemed exceedingly flat after the departure of my American grandmother with Nanciebel in tow. Surprisingly so, considering by comparison the all-pervading repercussions of the second war to end all wars. The first one did not appear to reach Barnt Green, at least not at the eye level of the very young. True, working parties for the making of bandages took the place of bridge parties in the drawing-room, when all the talk concerned the influx of Belgian refugees. There was the pleasure for me of collecting cigarette cards of the allied leaders, whose uniforms bristled with badges, but even the dropping of an unexploded bomb by a zeppelin in a field at Hunstanton impinged less on my mind than the switch in my educational progress from Lynfield to The Glebe House.

I was leaving a dames school for one ruled over by masters. Jack and Donald Ludlow had moved on by this time, while my brother had not been able to return. So I arrived alone, without allies, but to some extent hardened by two years away from home. This was fortunate, as I was exchanging the fiery discipline of the redoubtable Miss Cook for the far more frightening and ubiquitous presence of my new headmaster's wife. Although I never beheld Madam rise up in her wrath, from her bath chair, as Dame May Whitty rose up in fear from hers, in Emlyn Williams' play *Night Must Fall,* it was always at the back of my mind that such a dreadful portent of doom might occur, and that if it did, I would be the pupil to precipitate the final conflagration.

Otherwise, the boys seemed much less hemmed in than at Lynfield. Doubtless, possessing our own playing fields at the back of the school buildings created a more spacious atmosphere. Certainly the elder boys, soon to go to their public schools, appeared far more sophisticated; we small ones became either their admiring slaves, or their victims. There was one fat slug, with the air and dominion of a sultan. I have no idea how he originally attained his corrupt sway; certainly not through physical strength, because I never saw him fight and conquer. Already his reign of terror was at its height when I arrived in the autumn of 1916, and automatically had to produce my tuck for his inspection – and the taking – like all the other juniors. What I witnessed now was not the rise but the fall.

Suddenly, as a wind can change overnight, a dam be breached by an unquenchable flood, so did the humiliated serfs band together in revolt. Like an outsize rugger scrum, we took courage from each other and set upon him, more in despair than in hope of lasting victory. The sultan had always held court, surrounded by toadying lieutenants, warming his bottom against the only radiator in the recreation space. It was there, instinctively, as though the radiator were his throne, that he took his final stand, until he was dragged away, thrown to the floor, battered beneath the tide of anonymous bodies pummelling on top of him. No international team in a Twickenham match had half the fire and fury of that diminutive, untrained pack.

It was my first taste of what can happen when a dictator falls and a mob takes over. The dethroned one was finally rescued, disappeared into the sanatorium, and was never seen again. The revolt and the reasons for it were hushed up, but it was something ugly, obscene, of which I had been a witness, participated in, and it has left a scar on my memory. That and the cold of yet another Norfolk winter, and Madam's overriding disapproval, are all the impressions left of the year that I spent in Mr Barber's academy, except for the reasons and the method of my abrupt midsummer departure. No, I was not expelled. I planned my own escape.

1917 gave the promise of being another hot summer, though not perhaps with the exceptionally high, dry temperatures of 1911. In the Easter holidays, the tennis court at home was already fit for play, but for once I was unenthusiastic, out of sorts and off my food. The doctor who had been so reassuring about the roof of my mouth now diagnosed trouble with my tonsils. At once, my mother, who was suspicious of doctors all her life, decided that she would like another opinion, from a specialist. After all, it would be free. My great-uncle, Greville MacDonald, the son of George MacDonald, still had his consulting chambers in Harley Street. He had examined many eminent throats, including those of crowned heads; now he would look at mine. I was enchanted to be in such august company. Still more, to be paying my first visit to the metropolis.

My parents and I stayed at the Alexandra Hotel, in Knightsbridge (long since pulled down in the name of progress) which seemed like a palace to me at the time. What wouldn't I have to tell my brother when we got home again. Our rooms looked out on to the Park, because Father had insisted on the best ones. That was all part of his new rôle, that of a generous spender with plenty of loose cash in his pockets. I suppose the change had really started with his own father's death. Something was released in him then. Naturally, he did not come into so much capital as his elder brother Philip, but it must have seemed a fortune, the first lump sum of any size he had ever possessed, so different from a yearly salary. In consequence, he began to throw it about, arriving home, after a 'business' trip to London, with some such article of finery as a brocade evening coat for my mother, which she couldn't possibly have any opportunity to wear in wartime. So she put his placating gifts away in her clothes cupboard on the landing, without the least suspicion that they were being paid for by conscience money first, borrowed money later.

'The wife is always the last person to hear,' my mother told me, with some truth, years later. 'When Auntie Bee warned me that your father had been seen being met at Euston by a woman, I still didn't believe it. Not until the night when I saw him myself taking a woman into the Trocadero.'

Which woman? Apparently there had been so many, once he had left his paterfamilias image behind. But I did not like to probe deeply as to the exact circumstances in which she had succeeded in surprising the guilty pair. That would have meant prolonging the unprofitable post mortems. It had happened, it was over, the great bonanza, the huge deceit, and if my mother suffered bitterly for a time, it could be argued that my father was worse off in the end. Exiled, in poor health, suffering the humiliation of being supported by his two sons, he had to exist in a twilight, enduring the bitterest punishment of all, to live too long.

As it happened, the news of his death was brought to me when I was recovering from a coronary thrombosis, in the Woolavington wing of the Middlesex Hospital, ten years ago. I had had such a narrow escape from death, another of my nine lives gone, and now both my parents were dead, within a few months of each other, while outside, the spring sunshine was lighting up the blossom burgeoning in the courtyard. The same returning sun that had shone with such encouragement that other April, almost forty years ago on my first trip to London.

I tried to feel pity, regret, for my father's passing, but having not set eyes on him since the doldrum days of the divorce, I am afraid that I was chiefly conscious that the drain on my financial resources was now at an end. Does such an admission shock? I should be ashamed of my dishonesty, rather, were I to pretend otherwise. In the future, I would be existing myself on borrowed time, the eminent heart specialist had warned me, but surely better that than on borrowed money, to pay an expensive hotel bill, as it turned out that we had been doing on the day of my visit to Harley Street.

I was rather disappointed when Uncle Greville pronounced that my tonsils were not poisoned and did not need instant cutting at the roots, pronouncing instead that I was probably suffering from growing pains. After this hoary bromide, and enquiries concerning the health of Aunt Phoebe, I was allowed to examine the silver photograph frames of his more aristocratic patients, such as Millicent, Duchess of Sutherland, who at that moment was running a convalescent home for our troops in France. I was even more mollified when my father suggested that we would have a celebratory lunch at the Berkeley. Over coffee, like a conjurer, he produced two gangway stalls for the matinée at the Hippodrome. This was for a show called *Zig Zag,* almost as popular as *The Bing Boys* for soldiers on leave, because it starred the American actress, Shirley Kellogg, whose charms, like those of most of her contemporary performers, were so much more pronounced than those of the pop singers of today, such as Cilla Black, who is inclined to move so awkwardly on the stage as though she is lost unless tethered to her microphone. Up till that time, Miss Dorothy Ward and Miss Clarice Mayne, as Prince Charming in *Cinderella* sporting a quiz-glass in the ballroom scene, had shared my adoration, but now, for months afterwards, I was to boast that the leading lady at the Hippodrome, as she pranced down the cake walk suspended over the stalls, had blown a kiss directly at her youngest admirer in the audience, gazing up at her ecstatically from his favoured seat.

'You take the boy, you'll enjoy it, Joan,' my father had said, pushing the envelope across the restaurant table. 'I managed to get the last two tickets in the house by tipping the hall porter at the Alexandra. Hall porters are always the best bet.' He had begun to talk in this man-about-town manner, as though he had been indoctrinated in the jargon of West End life through his new business contacts.

'Why don't you take him, dear?' My mother's voice sounded doubtful. Perhaps she was instinctively counting the cost of the seats. Perhaps she simply feared that such a leg and bosom show was scarcely the right kind of entertainment for a boy of nine.

'Oh, I've got an appointment in the City.' He made it appear that his meeting was with the Governor of the Bank of England. 'I'll see you back at the hotel before dinner. Take a cab back, of course.' He reached in the pocket of his blue suit and took out his case; it was easy to see that it was bulging with notes. Carelessly he extracted one, and gave it across the table to my mother – all part of the new régime, endless cabs and hired motor cars – with the same lordly gesture as on Christmas Day his own father had been wont to take out his gold sovereign case from his waistcoat pocket and hand out largesse in turn to each of his grandchildren.

Unfortunately, Ernest Winn, the youngest of the family, lacked the solid assets of Charles Winn and Company behind him, and now in place of the substantial silhouette of The Uplands, too large any longer for private occupation today, he was subconsciously pitting the appeal of the smart London restaurants, beckoning to head waiters and head porters, to give himself a spurious sense of power. For so long – too long – he had been kept down, talked down by the patriarch of the family, and now having reached the dangerous age for men of the middle forties, he was undergoing a sea-change to his personality of which he was probably unaware himself. It was my mother who was only too painfully conscious of it, the new arrogance, the boastfulness, the absurd extravagances, so alien to her own nature. Bewildered and helpless, she had to accept the reappraisal as best she could, and when on what seemed to me like a triumphant progress from the Berkeley, my father bought a couple of bunches of violets from the flower girl at Piccadilly Circus, and pinned them on to her coat with a flourish of loving attention, she tried to pretend to herself that this was a second honeymoon.

As for myself, jigging on up Shaftesbury Avenue between the two people I loved best in the world, my mood of enchanted expectation was heightened by being allowed to stop and examine the frames of pictures of the players outside each theatre. This was all leading up to the climax, exquisite dallying. And all the time I hugged to myself the talk there had been at lunch about the car – an Overland – which Father had assured us was about to take its place permanently in the garage where at present my brother's exercise board stood in austere possession. Everything was suddenly so exciting, I began to jump about on the pavement, as though I was intoxicated, not with the glass of cider I had been allowed at lunch but with everything that I would have to tell my fellow boarders at The Glebe House. It would be the best summer term ever.

Certainly it was as far as personal drama was concerned, but not in the manner that I had anticipated. Despite the reassurances my parents had received in Harley Street, I did not feel any better on my return to school. On the contrary, if it was growing pains from which I was suffering, they had now spread to my stomach and seldom left me. When I complained to Matron, Madam intervened with the explanation. 'Nonsense, it's simply a touch of flatulence. You bolt your food, boy.' She had a great eye for malingerers, and any potential talent in that direction must be sharply slapped down. I was, I admit, a potential story-teller because, almost as far back as I can remember, the easiest way to keep me quiet and absorbed on a wet afternoon was to produce a pencil and a sheet of paper on which I could scribble to my heart's delight. Nevertheless, I did not have to call upon my imagination the afternoon I found myself in the outfield, bent double as I retched up everything I had eaten for lunch. Greedy guts. But it wasn't that kind of retribution. Giddiness overcame me, and I had to ask my captain for permission to leave the field, something that I loathed doing. When it was reported later how I had escaped to the sanctuary of the sick bay, it was suggested with inevitable sarcasm that had I been on the batting instead of the fielding side, there would have been no complaints from G. H. Winn. In any case, hadn't my temperature been taken and wasn't it normal?

Unless a boy had a temperature, he could not be ill. Q.E.D. But the grumbling discomfiture, the returning waves of nausea, persisted. Sometimes I could feel, or imagined that I could feel, just inside my right thigh, a distinct swelling. Then it disappeared again the moment that the doctor appeared on his rounds. Battle was joined between myself and Madam, who bore her own infirmities with such stoicism and expected others to do likewise, and not behave like cry-babies. It was deadlock, stalemate.

I could not let it rest like that. Throughout my career, whenever I have been confronted with a crisis in my fortunes, my sense of self-preservation has rallied to my aid. This was the first time. Something warned me that such a crisis was at hand, that I was in real danger, and there was no time to be lost. So I conceived a counter-attack. Ahead of my weekly Sunday letter – which had to be left open to be censored – I would pen a secret S.O.S posting it, without a stamp – but presumably it would still reach its destination – on our way down to the beach to bathe. Drawing opposite the pillar box, I would discover that my gym shoe was undone, and lag behind the attendant master. That should give me my chance. And it did.

In the Lynfield days, I had first felt the urge to produce unofficial dispatches, which I would compose under the bedclothes in my dormitory, in the warm, still-light evenings of the summer term, with the scents from the garden floating in through the curtained windows. Dimly I was becoming aware of the transitory, infirm glories that irradiate one's youth, stumblingly I tried to give expression to my sensations. My screeds in pencil were no doubt incoherent and ill-spelt, and taking my mother by surprise, she was nonplussed and made no reference to their arrival in her own letters. I rather suspect now that she was apprehensive, too. Was this a cuckoo child with poetic aspirations? Certainly it wasn't for this that I had been bundled off to a boarding school, so far from home, and at such a tender age. I was doubtful, even at the time, whether she showed these unsolicited epistles to my father across the breakfast table, and that was why I carefully addressed the envelope to him now, regarding him rightly as the softer-hearted, as well as the weaker, of my two parents. Not surprisingly, my *cri d'estomac* was not preserved. A pity. I would have enjoyed re-examining it today. No doubt it was considerably shorter in context, because of the urgency involved, in comparison with my previous clandestine ramblings. Anyway, it did the trick. It saved my life.

My parents were paying a visit that week-end to a country house near Horsham, the property of a city financier whose name was much in the financial columns of that period, because of his considerable interests in the African markets. Mr Latilla had launched many companies, and was in the process of launching more, and my father had been called in as a consultant on that side of Company Law in which he had made himself an expert, the Excess Profits Tax. It was, for my father, all part of his recurring dream, the introduction that would lift him from the obscurity of being a provincial accountant and re-launch him in

London, where he would work and walk with city big-nobs, on equal terms. The invitation for both himself and my mother to this Whitsun house party was surely the sign that he was seeking, the proof that the bridge was about to be crossed.

In the party, too, there happened to be a surgeon whose practice was in Hove. My father showed him my letter, and characteristically put the onus on his fellow guest. The reply that he received was that it might all be a boy's too vivid imagination – 'and you say he is inclined to dramatize everything' – but, on the other hand, the detailed account of the recurring bouts of nausea and stomach pains sounded very much like the symptoms of an angry appendix. At that period – fortunately for me – appendicitis had become the latest fashionable talking-point.

It may have been the serious weight of the medical expertise, or it may have been the desire to behave in a commanding manner in front of his patron, but whatever the motives which urged him on, my father acted. Ringing up my headmaster, he demanded that his younger son should be placed on the train that coming Monday morning to Liverpool Street, where he would meet me himself and bring me back to Horsham, so that I could be examined by 'one of the leading surgeons of the day'. If his report was that there was nothing seriously wrong with me, I would be dispatched back the very next day.

There was considerable and heated remonstration from the other end of the line. Mr Barber quite rightly did not approve of this kind of precedent being established for any of his pupils. However, my father, supported by the professional figure of his fellow guest at his side, was for once obdurate. In consequence, forty-eight hours later I found myself on the London train. In a way, it was a far lonelier journey than going back to school. What had I done? Weighed down by the alarming weight of my headmaster's displeasure, I saw myself branded as the boy who wrote home and whined. There had been an interview in Mr Barber's study that affected me still with another kind of sickness, and when at last I caught sight of my father's tall figure at the end of the platform, and the bobbing top of the grey trilby that he always wore, I started to run towards him with a sense of overwhelming gratitude and relief such as I had never felt in his presence before. At once, however, a savage pain tore warningly at my side, stopping me in my tracks. At lunch in the adjoining

Great Eastern Hotel, before we crossed London to Victoria, I could eat nothing. All I asked for was glass after glass of water.

They were seated on the lawn having tea when we arrived. I was so used to seeing my mother in her pink and blue cotton garden dresses at home, that for a moment she seemed a stranger in her linen skirt and blouse with elaborate attachments of lace. She was shy and worried for me, too, lest a son of hers should be proved to be a softie. Why could I not be as uncomplaining and manly as my brother? I sat on the edge of a wicker chair and hung my head and for once the conversation of the grown-ups did not interest me.

My misery was soon put to an end by the doctor's suggestion that he should take me upstairs and get the examination over. After the glare of the garden, the bed on which I lay was as comforting as his cool hands, and for the first time since I had posted the letter I felt safe and answered his questions, and suffered his gentle, though probing fingers, without fear. At the end of the examination, he said nothing except, 'lie quite still where you are,' and went out of the room. A few minutes later, he returned with my mother, whose manner had now completely changed. Her familiar scent enveloped me as she bent over the bed, stroking my forehead and explaining that the doctor had most kindly agreed to motor us both into Brighton, so that I could be put to sleep in a nice nursing home that he had recommended.

'Sleep' was her euphemism for the chloroform of the operating theatre. The expert had warned her downstairs that no time was to be lost, and proceeded to telephone the nursing home to have everything prepared for an emergency operation within the hour. The last stage of my journey was an extremely painful one. At each jolt of the road the throbbing pain flared ominously, and sometimes it was all I could do not to cry out aloud; but I was determined to make no sound in front of my mother. All the same, by the time we arrived at the terrace house in Hove, where I was to stay for the next month, I was too dizzy to walk up the steps unaided. Soon there was oblivion, from which I awoke, hours later, still conscious of the same pain, but muffled now, as drowsily I blinked at the light, in a strange room, and the equally strange figure of the special night nurse in the corner.

What had happened to me? I was too full of dope to care. Later, it transpired that in their urgent haste to get me on to the operating table, they had foregone the familiar rites of scrubbing the patient or emptying his bowels, and just as well that they did, for my appendix protestingly burst at the moment the surgeon inserted his knife into my abdomen. A delay of two hours even, and I gathered that my chances of survival would have been slight. As it was, for the first two days my mother scarcely left the Home, until the resilience of my healthy youth tipped the scales. Still, it had been a narrow shave; the first of my nine lives gone. There were other narrow squeaks to follow.

On this first occasion when I received a considerable warning of how brief one's mortal span can be, and how extremely important it is that one should waste no time worrying over what nearly happened but didn't, I spent my enforced leisure devouring a book a day. My mother fed me, like a factory conveyer belt, with a series of cheap editions that she bought off the kiosk on the pier. Reading had already become an obsession with me. I scarcely minded what it was, so long as it was printed words upon a page. By the time I was ten, I had consumed the whole of Dickens' works and had started on Walter Scott. Equally, I was a devoted admirer of Baroness Orczy and, I have to confess, of an American authoress called Gene Stratton Porter, whose best-known work was called *Laddie*. Except that it was set in the backwoods, and abounded in nature descriptions, I can't recollect a single twist of the plot, though I have a shrewd suspicion that it was considerably more innocuous for someone of my age than the copies of Nash's Magazine, to which my mother subscribed and which I read from cover to cover as soon as the grown-ups had finished with the current serials by Cosmo Hamilton or Kathleen Norris. In any case, was this kind of indiscriminate gorging more or less harmful to my intellectual emancipation than the present-day irresponsible attitude of allowing small children to sit, with the curtains drawn against the sunshine outside, spellbound in front of the eternal Telly? Whenever I have the temerity to enquire of any of my platoon of god-children as to what books they have read during the holidays, and what kind of books, I find the conversation changes rapidly to a detailed description of Benny Hill's latest series, or the stars of the Sunday Night Palladium show. Then I give up.

Nowadays it seems almost impossible to envisage a sick-room without the presence of a radio set at the head of the bed, and a television set at the bottom of it. Nevertheless, I was blissfully content, surrounded by my growing hoard of books, and supported by the knowledge that for once I was the complete centre of interest to my family. If not a hero, at least I had been exonerated, and rewarded with the promise that I would not have to return to my old school, either this term or next. There had been such an acrimonious correspondence with the Barbers that both my parents were united, for once, on my side.

Instead, in the autumn, I would be moving to an altogether more splendid establishment (than The Glebe House was at that time) situated in Eastbourne, and which my parents had taken the opportunity of inspecting from Brighton. If they were impressed by the lay-out of the buildings, which included an unusually beautiful small chapel, and the setting, high up above the sea, with the South Downs stretching away behind, they were completely captivated by the reassuring manner of the headmaster himself.

The Reverend Lionel Browne did not look like the average cleric at all. He wore no dog collar and felt most comfortable in a well-worn, grey flannel suit. At first sight, with his very broad shoulders, his jutting head and slightly rolling walk, you might have mistaken him for an ex-rowing blue or member of a 'varsity rugger team. Then the moment that he spoke, you became impressed with his civilized attitude to life, and above all, his compassionate regard for the aspirations and the problems of those in his charge.

In Eastbourne there are more schools for boys and girls to the square mile than in any other town in Britain. But among the plethora which included St Cyprian's, where Cecil Beaton and Evelyn Waugh were uncongenial playmates, and St Anthony's, whose teams we particularly relished barging on the football field, for the pleasure of hearing the tinkle of their crosses, as good little Romans, hidden on their chests, none were more celebrated at the end of the First World War than the three situated in a triangle up at Meads, and owned by a trio of brothers. The largest, St Andrew's, was commanded by a monolithic figure, the Reverend Edwin Browne, with a mantle of white hair that conjured up visions of the Old Testament and fire descending from heaven when he preached to us occasionally from the pulpit of our chapel. We were in such awe of him, and the combined prowess of his hundred pupils, that we always received an extra half-holiday if we defeated St Andrew's at any fixture. Next in order of numbers – we had a complement of sixty ourselves – came St Christopher's, where I was to spend, I sometimes think, the three happiest years of my life, while Aldro School brought up the rear, presided over by the Reverend Harold Browne, who always wore a flower in his buttonhole, had a jovial, florid complexion, and, it was rumoured, was a hit with the ladies.

Altogether, it was a remarkable story of how sheer worth and ability can come to the top, for the three brothers were the offspring of a Yorkshire village parson, who had had to bring up seven sons altogether, educate them, and direct them into holy orders like himself – there was a daughter, too – on a stipend that would scarcely pay the rent of a council house today. How did he do it? By faith. It was as simple as that. I still owe my member of that family the kind of debt which one can only repay by keeping faith oneself and never squandering or abusing what small talents one possesses – and in my case they were very small, in the beginning – which he so vigorously encouraged.

I have been very fortunate in my life in regard to the sponsors whom I encountered at a crucial moment in my growth as a human being. First, there was the fortuitous happening of a burst appendix, which necessitated a change of schools and the air I breathed. Then after a chance meeting at the bridge table, soon after my first novel was published, I had the good fortune to come under the literary influence of Somerset Maugham, who impressed upon me the need and the importance of writing regular hours every day, as he did himself. Even so, I got so far, and then stuck, until a young man of twenty-two, newly-appointed features editor of a national newspaper, took a chance and presented me with a whole page each day to fill, although until that time I had never entered a newspaper office in my life. What a risk for him to take, and what an experience it was for me to work with Hugh Cudlipp, today the most famous of another group of brothers, all to achieve success in the street that is paved with the tombstones of the failures. Hugh was even younger than I was when our partnership took place, but he possessed a flair and a technical brilliance that set him apart. Thus

I shall always be grateful for the apprenticeship I served under him, only matched in importance by the maturity I was to attain when I was later brought into close contact with Lord Beaverbrook, who possessed in his time a stronger sense of communication with the public at large – and every writer, whatever his pretensions, must secretly long for that – than anyone I have met inside or outside the street where I have now worked, off and on, for thirty years.

Of course, all that part of my education was still far ahead. As the moment approached for me to leave that nursing home in Hove, little imagining that one day I would put down my anchor for the last time in a village only a few miles away, my one desire was to go anywhere, to be ordered to sit at anyone's feet, so long as I could be saved from the glacial reception which assuredly would be mine from the throne of Madam's wheel chair.

In consequence, once I was completely certain about my entry for St Christopher's, the rest of the summer of 1917 became a timeless dream for me. I picked raspberries for bottling at a penny a pound, I lay on the grass, watching the rest of the gang play tennis. That was the only snag. I had been forbidden to play, myself, because of the threat of adhesions. To keep still at any time was a sort of agony for me. As my long scar, which I was eager to show to anyone, grew paler, merging into my skin, I became increasingly restless, never pausing to think for a moment what it must be like for my brother, never suspecting besides that our mother was preoccupied with her own problem, concealing a very different kind of agony of heart.

I still wonder sometimes how she managed to play her part so well. For the eyes of children can be very sharp. Yet neither of us had an inkling that this was to be the last summer we would spend in the calm backwater of Barnt Green. Between that luxurious Whitsun, spent under the Latillas' roof at Horsham, and August Bank Holiday, the axe had fallen. All the money that had been lavished on a suite at the Metropole at Brighton during my illness had come from an overdraft; all the talk of the new companies that he was about to advise and launch was idle talk. Father was in the hands of the money-lenders, and only saved from bankruptcy by the generous intervention of his eldest brother, Philip, who paid every debt and started him with a clean sheet again, for the sake of the family honour, the good name of Charles Winn and Company; that must be preserved whatever the cost.

It would have been better, my mother always said afterwards, if the crash had been allowed to come. It might have sobered him, brought him to his senses. As it was, his face was temporarily saved, and he was provided with an alibi. Everything would come right again, once he was established in London as a tax consultant. Always London, the Mecca.

My mother insisted on selling her jewellery, and all the best pieces of furniture which belonged to her, and giving the proceeds of the sales as her contribution to her brother-in-law. Her pride made her do that as mine would have done, but how much of the whole story, the emotional mess as well as the financial one, in which deeper and deeper my father was floundering, she was aware of that summer, I never fully discovered even when it came to the period that we could talk freely to each other on an adult level. Hints, suspicions, probably no more at that moment. The divulgence of all the debts piled one on another was sufficient shock for her to bear in silence, the sudden crumbling of the kind of stability that Uncle Philip represented, a character from the *Forsyte Saga*. Out of all the question marks, one unwelcome fact emerged. It would mean a fresh start, and as it turned out, on the smallest scale yet, a furnished semi-detached in a back street of East Sheen.

Did she already envisage the future in such brutal terms, as she went on cutting off the dead heads of the roses, waiting for us to return to school, so that the packing-up could commence? Years later I was to hear my mother asked what she was proudest of in her life, and I rather expected her to make some reference to the battle which she helped her elder son to win. Instead, she replied without hesitation, 'I have made three gardens from virgin soil.' And there was a ring of triumph in her voice that I had never heard before.

The first two had been in Edgbaston, one at the house in Woodbourne Road where I was born, but where I only lived for the first fifteen months of my life. It was called 'Rosemary', though not surprisingly I had no remembrance of it at all. Indeed, on one occasion between television sessions at the Aston Studios, I walked up and down that long and once-upon-a-time residentiallysuperior road for an hour, peering through hedges, and round the corners of drives, with a faded sepia print from my father's art collection in my hand, until I was only finally convinced that I had rediscovered my birthplace when at last I came upon the initials – J. B. W. – Joan Bristow Winn – and E. B. W. – Ernest Burton Winn – optimistically entwined over the porch.

Today 'Rosemary', under another name, is owned by an Irish woman who has made a career for herself running pop groups of performers in the Midlands, and the only traces of my parents' occupancy remain in the substantial mahogany doors and parquet floors, a mirror of the times. As for the blue-grey house at the top of Cherry Hill, to which I never said goodbye, or to the woods at the back where I had played my solitary games of hide-and-seek with myself as a child, when a few months ago I boldly drove up the drive and rang the bell, there was no answer, no answer at all, not even that of a protesting dog; only the echoing reverberations of the bell itself returned from the silent interior to mock me like an unwanted trespassing ghost. Yet, surprisingly, the exterior of the house, which I was prepared to find shrunk with time, and the surrounding garden, seemed far more attractive than in my receding memories, so that at last I was able to appreciate just what a bitter wrench the parting must have been for my mother.

How she succeeded in hiding the bare facts of the coming upheaval from my brother and myself is still a source of astonishment to me. True, she seemed pale and out of sorts as that summer of 1917 wore on, but she explained her listlessness in terms of a tiresome complaint that required her to lie down, with the curtains drawn in her bedroom, every afternoon. We did not understand – how could we? – that she rested thus, at a time when our father was supposedly in his office in Birmingham, primarily because as they lay side by side in the four-poster at night, sleep would no longer come to her.

Like a family of squirrels, oppressively shut up in a cage, her thoughts chased each others' tails. So all her mother's imperious warnings had been justified, after all. Soon she would be compelled to write to Boston, and make up a convincing story to explain our abrupt departure from Barnt Green that would prove water-tight to all the family on that side of the Atlantic. That she wanted to be near to Ethel, her favourite sister, whose husband had recently been transferred to take charge of the Watney Brewery at Mortlake? Would Mollie Rodgers swallow that? Or that Ernest was going to London himself on a tide of success, not fleeing from his debtors and the odours of near-bankruptcy? All the same, wasn't it the duty of a wife to stay beside her husband, in bad times as well as good? For better or for worse . . .

In the defenceless, arid hour before the dawn, the familiar phrase that could be so reassuring, no longer seemed like an incantation. With her burning head against the hot pillow, she shrank away into her corner of the matrimonial bed. How deeply he slept himself, like a child with a completely untroubled conscience. How could he, with all those debts hanging round his neck, and worse revelations now coming to light almost every day, so that she herself had begun to dread the morning post. (Your father never had a bad night's sleep in his life, she was wont to say accusingly, a long time afterwards.) But children were very adaptable, she tried to comfort herself, they were not yet rooted, they did not appreciate the need for keeping up appearances, they would settle down anywhere, as long as it felt like home. And she was a home-maker, no one could deny that. Besides, it would only be during the school holidays that she would have to manage somehow. Rodger was doing so well at his public school, despite his handicap, while Godfrey would be in the good hands now of that splendid Mr Browne. At least, too, they would all be a long distance away from the gossiping tongues of a small, close-knit community, free from the embarrassment of having to fend off the natural curiosity of friends, compelled to glimpse the patronizing pity in their eyes, even worse than the impinging curiosity of chance neighbours, like the Coops next door, whose son had taught Godfrey to ride a bicycle.

No more the quilted little dinner parties at the Charles, or the Reynolds, who were so disarmingly proud of their son in the Guards; no more the tennis parties in summer, the winter badminton; no more the fun of getting up amateur theatricals, for a Good Cause, such as the poor Belgians, with herself invariably called upon to be producer for the children's shows, or compelled by an unanimous vote of the committee to take the leading part in other productions, like the one of *Diplomacy*

My father (Webley & Scott). In back row, in grey trilby

Left Mary Anderson, the great theatrical beauty of her day, a neighbour of my grandparents in Broadway, Worcestershire. *Centre* My mother as Juliet. *Photo: E. B. Mowll. Right* My mother in wedding dress

"Women are God's Flowers."
Hubert
Henry Irving: 1894

"Yes —
men are God's trees, & women are God's Flowers."
Yours Yours   So says, Tennyson
Ellen Terry =

Autographs by Henry Irving and Ellen Terry, from my mother's
autograph book

when the nearby Bromsgrove weekly paper had praised her performance in these words:

'First place in the very capable cast must be awarded to Mrs Ernest Winn, who as the French marquise gave a perfect presentation of the part, her delicate French-like pronunciation of English, as well as her finished style of acting, meeting with great appreciation from the large audience. She displayed a perfect readiness throughout and was always at home in her part.'

The readiness, perhaps too great a readiness, to forgive and excuse – not the peccadilloes of her children about which she could be protectively strict – but rather her husband, who as long as he remained under the connubial roof must still be regarded as the head of the household. Even today, when the practical reality of sex-equality has progressed far beyond being simply a plank in the suffragette movement, some wives can be too accommodating, too uncritical, too submissively loving. My mother at this crisis in her married fortunes played this part to perfection. Unfortunately, my father, in his turn, found that her acquiescent attitude no longer satisfied his emotional needs.

The world has been made only too aware lately of recurring examples of men, at the same age as my father was at this time, with settled positions of esteem in public life, cutting adrift from conventionalities, seeking to satisfy their erotic urges, in surprising deviations from the normal rhythm that we would expect from their customary place in Society. It would appear almost as though they were bent on social suicide. Instead, it has been suggested to me by a leading neurologist that, at every level of the community, the majority of the aspects of these abrupt changes in behaviour, the increasing bouts of drinking and whoring, the almost paranoiac outbursts followed by the moods of melancholy, the ridiculous running after girls half their age, the rebellion from family responsibilities in which they previously took pride, can be accounted for by a straightforward medical fact, no longer disputed. The menopause can affect the metabolism and the mental balance of the male sex to an even more drastic degree than in the case of the female of the species.

Whether this is the real explanation of what happened to the man who was my father (and naturally, it has puzzled me a great deal, looking back), certainly it is true to say that no professional actress has ever given a better performance than the one my

D

mother produced when she met me, at the platform barrier at Victoria, on my return from my first term at St Christopher's.

Of course, her audience was already in a receptive mood. I was naturally excited at the prospect of spending the whole of my Christmas holidays in London. My trunk had been dispatched ahead to the new, temporary address in East Sheen. We took a number 9 bus from Hyde Park Corner, as it had been explained to me that it was far too long a journey for a taxi. Really, there was no need for any such preamble. This was the first bus whose stairs I had ever climbed, and managed to secure a seat at the front. I was in a new world, enthralled, and I have never lost the sense of freedom and pleasure of riding on top of a London bus.

Soon we were passing the Alexandra Hotel, where we had stayed in such luxury in the spring, and somehow Mother, matching my mood of bubbling expectation, made it appear that the month ahead was going to prove one long extension of that idyllic afternoon when we had sat together in the stalls at the Hippodrome. Yes, she had already made out a list from the morning paper of all the special Christmas shows, and their matinée days, and we would be able to go at least two or three times every week, because it would be such fun, wouldn't it, queueing for the pit, after always sitting in the family box for the pantomimes in Birmingham. And the pit, she added, only cost three shillings.

'Then I shall be able to stand you treat out of my Christmas money,' I announced in my most grown-up voice. Moreover, I was able to implement my lordly instinct, because it happened that both Rodger and myself had been sent presents in postal orders from almost everyone that Christmas, a tactful contribution to the household at large. As for Christmas Day itself, we were invited to spend that with our Ludlow cousins at Guildford House, who in their own way kept up the comforting charade, that everything was going to be for the best in a completely new régime, by reiterations that the Boat Race was exactly opposite Uncle Ernest's brewery, so in due course, in the Easter vacation, there would be a grandstand seat for us all. Now that prospect would never have happened had we stayed in Worcestershire, would it?

Their own new home, with its high wall guarding it, although set in scarcely as salubrious a neighbourhood as Barnt Green, seemed more like an official residence provided by the Government, than the local quarters for the brewer in charge;

especially in comparison with our own temporary dwelling place, a mile or two away, one of twenty very small, semi-detached houses in a row, just off the High Street, with no privacy and no garden. But then, who wanted a garden in London, especially in the winter?

In a way everything, though being an extreme contrast from our previous style of existence (waited on at every meal, cosseted by a trim parlourmaid who knew her place, with the mistress writing down orders for the cook each morning on the slate) made it possible to treat the whole metamorphosis, including our landlord's hideous furniture and decorations, in the same mood of adventure as we enjoyed when we occasionally had spent Easter in seaside lodgings at Old Rhos on the North Wales coast, close to Llandudno. We brought the same carefree, uncritical gaze to bear. The knowledge of the real state of affairs, our hand-to-mouth existence from now on, had not yet dropped like a stone to the bottom of the pool, at least as far as the intelligence of the youngest member of the household was concerned.

On the contrary. Somehow, helping my mother to make the beds, drying the dishes for her, after clearing away the luncheon things, running errands to and from the shops, and making many stimulating discoveries en route, all added to the aura of novelty that should perfume any holiday atmosphere.

Besides, didn't Father keep on reiterating that by the time we came back from school again, we should be in our own permanent home, making the hints sound as though he had something very spectacular up his sleeve? Meanwhile, there was high tea at the Corner House, after our theatrical outings, and all the enchantments of *Going Up*, my first Gaiety show, in which there was a tomboyish young girl in her teens with very fair hair and enormous blue eyes, who as far as we were concerned entirely stole the show from the leading lady, Marjorie Gordon, and for whom my mother, the critic of the family, prophesied far greater triumphs to come. And how right her prophecy on this occasion proved to be, since the name of that soubrette was Evelyn Laye.

Equally my father's prophecy came true, to the extent that on breaking-up day, at the end of the Easter term, this time the No. 9 bus conducted us right on to its final stopping place in Richmond, where, in the Queen's Road, a few yards from *The Lass of Richmond Hill,* a lease had been taken on a tall house which looked by no means unimposing from the curved driveway. In actual fact, No. 16 had been divided into three sections, and we were to occupy the centre one. On one side lived a very old lady, as quiet and unobtrusive as a church mouse, on the other, a mixed batch of Belgian refugees were camping out in wartime possession. Following the social custom that seems almost a rule in the metropolitan area, we made no attempt to fraternize with our neighbours, though it was immediately only too clear that the behaviour of the Belgian young, in their strip of garden over the wooden fence from ours, was violently in contrast to the afternoons we used to spend with the Challen or the Ambrose boys once upon a time.

Our garden was the largest of the three, but my mother made no effort to tame its disheartening wildness, except to remove the empty tins thrown over the wall. As the urgency of the spring increased, she still did not seem to care even whether her sons made an effort to cut the grass or trim the edges. I never remember seeing her walk the length of the garden, which though a pocket-one compared with that of Cherrycroft, had possibilities, fringed as it was by the trees of the park, at the far end. I appreciate now that it was her first open admission of impending defeat. There were others to come.

Not that she gave up easily. All her energies now went in housework, in a stubborn determination that whatever else happened, whatever crises might lie ahead, the house should at least be clean, on the day when the bailiffs came in, or the man of the house disappeared for the last time, leaving not a wrack, not a trace behind.

With my mother's instinctive taste in decoration, our part of the house could have been made extremely attractive had there been money and time to spend. There was a delightful feeling of airiness about the high ceilings, the wide staircase, the considerable landing space. Again, the rooms themselves were well-proportioned. On one side of the front door, there was a room clearly destined to be the dining-room, leading into a smaller study, with a balcony overlooking the garden, while on the other side of the hall, a long room with high windows at both ends ran the whole length of the house. This could have made a most charming drawing-room, but for most of our stay in Queen's Road it stood empty, bereft. The few possessions that Mother had rescued from the Barnt Green sale were spaced meagrely, with a few cheap, locally-acquired additions, about the rest of the house. What was already in residence, far more tenacious tenants than ourselves, was an army of cockroaches, deeply entrenched in their battle positions in the camouflaged wainscoting of the basement kitchens.

One evening, turning on the lights as I went down the stairs with a tray of supper dishes, I found myself confronted by the massed cohorts advancing confidently across the linoleum, and retreated hastily, jettisoning my cargo, a reaction of instinctive terror and disgust clutching at my throat. There was something both sepulchral and supernatural about cockroaches. All the same, I don't think my mother, meticulously house-proud though she was, was nearly as shocked by this unexpected apparition as her son. To her it was all part of our changed circumstances, a suitable companion-piece to the apparition of my other parent, arriving home at four o'clock in the afternoon, clearly very much under the weather.

We would all be crowded into the miniature study, economical with its gas fire to heat, and no grate to clean or polish. 'You look as though you have a temperature, Ernest. You'd better go and sleep it off,' she would say wearily, half a cover-up, half an accusation. Whereupon the tall, stooping figure, his weak eyes watering behind their glasses, would lumber away upstairs. But after a time, was it those holidays or the next, or the next, all patience was finally abandoned, and she would cry out sharply, forgetting my presence in the room, desperately anxious instead about the household bills that were overdue for payment, 'You've been drinking again.' To which he always made the same slow, solemn, innocently-protesting reply. 'But look at your watch, Joan. Don't you appreciate this is out of licensing hours. Where would I be able to get a drink?'

Where indeed? In the shadier clubs to which he was now descending, egged on and surrounded by the con men, for whom he was no match, with his original decency gradually corrupted, the respectable prop of his former regular office time-table gone for ever. As his own employer, he became increasingly his own worst enemy. From now on, he sacrificed all sense of pride or shame. He borrowed money, a fiver here, a fiver there, from anyone who would listen to his tales of bad luck in the immediate past, his grandiloquent schemes for recovery, in the future. From his brother-in-law at the brewery, from his sons, without their knowing, the nest egg from their grandfather Winn, of which he was their trustee as minors, from his mother, who was persuaded to get out of her death bed to accompany him to the lawyer, for her vital signature as the other trustee. When moral judgment becomes pickled in alcohol, nothing is any longer safe, nothing sacred.

Finally, he even tried to blackmail his eldest brother into further contributions. Uncle Philip, who had already behaved in the most quixotically generous manner, rightly answered 'Enough'. After all, he had his own family to consider, including his daughter Cecil, who like her aunt Ethel had decided against marriage, finding self-expression instead in becoming an outstanding Chinese and Russian scholar. Her father prepared a family trust from which both Winn grandsons were eventually to benefit, an extremely altruistic act, and farsighted, too, since the capital was tied up in a manner that would be no benefit to our own father's astute, greedy fingers. At the time, in a last, sad meeting with my mother in London, Uncle Philip promised her that when the moment came for me to leave St Christopher's, where Lionel Browne had offered to keep me on, whether the fees could be paid or not (and they could not be), he would be responsible for my further education at Rugby. Unfortunately, he died before this verbal promise was implemented on paper, and his wife, for reasons I have already mentioned, repudiated it.

But for the moment, the chief crisis in our fortunes was the provision of absolute necessities. Children have hungry appetites, so do heating boilers. I would go out on my bicycle early in the morning, scouring the shops for miles, searching for bargains, returning in triumph if I had been able to secure a pot of plum and apple jam at the Home and Colonial Stores for a penny less than the current price for this staple diet of the First World War. That, and offering to do all the washing-up after meals, were my contributions to the easing of my mother's burdens. Looking back, it seems distinctly inadequate. But what else could a boy of ten do to help?

From this downbeat period of my youth, several incidents stand out with implacable clarity. I was shooting up so fast that there was the unavoidable question of a new grey flannel suit for the summer term. It was one more extra that was quite beyond my mother's shrinking purse. Aunt Ethel, a wise and most compassionate counsellor, who was to make an outstanding success of her work as a J.P., especially in the many cases that emerged concerning children, was able to come to her sister's rescue on this occasion with a suit that had long since been discarded by my cousin Donald, many years my senior.

The solution I am afraid I regarded dubiously, for the suit clearly could not be made to fit me. However, I made no protest, reminding myself how long it was since I had seen my mother in anything new. But there was a cloud over the sun that summer, despite the satisfaction of finding myself in the second eleven, as a left-hand bat and wicket-keeper. Every morning when I put on my cast-away suit, it was like a prison garment for me. I suspected, probably quite untruly, that all the other boys, in their well-fitting greys from Harrods or Barkers, were mocking my reach-me-downs behind my back. Today I have far more suits in my wardrobe than I really need, because of that memory which I cannot erase.

Just as I cannot erase the memory of the afternoon that the anonymous man in the bowler hat with the oppressive, over-smooth manner, paid a surprise call on us in Queen's Road. My father was not there, nor was my brother. My mother and I were standing in the empty drawing-room, playing the game that raised our spirits, of how the decorations should be finished off, where the sofa would stand, now that the curtains, the first and most vital sign of domestic respectability and solvency, had been chosen and hung. Already they had been up for several months, and still the rest of the room was bare.

The stranger in the doorway, when I answered the ringing of the bell, said with a slimy smile, 'Sonny, is the lady of the house at home?' If there was one thing I detested it was being addressed as 'Sonny', and I took an instant dislike to the caller, who was swift to follow me, uninvited, across the threshold into the hall.

My mother came out of the door on the right, demanding, with fear in her voice. 'Who are you? What do you want?'

'I am sorry to disturb you, madam, at home, but I am the representative of . . .' He gave the name of the store where, as her

Christmas present from my father, she had chosen the material for the two wide windows.

Instantly she was aware of the reason for his coming. There had recently been other similar visitations. 'Surely your account has been paid long ago,' she began defensively, but there was no conviction in her voice, only a kind of controlled despair.

The stranger with his bowler hat in one hand, and his final demand in the other, shook his head, adding in a falsely deprecatory manner, 'I understand that the account has been sent in to Mr Winn no less than four times, and on the last occasion a cheque sent in reply was returned by the bank,"Return to Drawer". Here it is.'

My mother would not look. She knew it was true. All true. 'I asked him specially and he promised me,' she was whispering to herself. For a second her face crumpled and then she forced herself to regain her composure and her own dignity. 'How much is it exactly?' When he read out the figures, there was a pause. The sum seemed enormous to my childish reckoning, with seven-and-sixpence in the world to my name. Would that help? What was going to happen? To my amazement, she continued, on a colourless note that no longer betrayed anything of what she must be inwardly feeling, 'If you will wait here, I will get you the money straight away.'

Side by side we waited in the hall while my mother went slowly up the stairs to her room. I had unbounded faith in her, but surely it would be a miracle, like the fishes and the bread, if she could suddenly produce almost twenty pounds from her house-keeping purse. Not only was it a fortune to me. It was equally a fortune to her at that moment.

Then my mother came down the stairs again, her head held high, but she did not look at either of us waiting in the hall, but far away over our heads. I had the impression that she was no longer concerned with routing the enemy, but that in the moment of unlocking the drawer in her dressing-table she had come to some decision, an irrevocable decision which was entirely now occupying her mind. To have to use the major part of the money which had arrived that morning, the quarter's payment of her small allowance from her mother, originally intended purely as a dress allowance, for a bill that he had sworn to her that he had paid, more than a Christmas gift, a reconciliation present, for the drawing-room that she so ached to have again with the silver photograph frames set out. To be hounded like this and humiliated on one's own doorstep. Somehow it was far worse than the other hidden infidelities; this was the breaking point.

She held out four very clean five-pound notes, and said quietly, 'Have you change? Will you count it, please, and make out a receipt to me, in my name.'

I wonder who was more astonished by the sequel, myself or the debt collector. He must have been inured to scenes, protestations, doors slamming in his face, rather than the windfall of a complete cash-down discharge. However, having learnt from hard experience, I imagine, to be surprised by nothing, he swiftly masked his expression and wrote out the receipt with a flourish, adding placatingly,

'I do hope you will pay us another visit soon, madam. We have some exclusive spring materials, fresh in stock.'

My mother gave a non-committal nod. 'At this time of the year it is certainly tempting to have some new covers made, and as it happened my son and I were just planning a colour scheme to go with the curtains, when you rang the bell.'

'In that case, we shall most certainly look forward to another visit from you in the near future. The weather is certainly improving every day.'

'Yes, the spring seems to come earlier here than in the Midlands. Everything in the gardens is far more forward than it used to be with us in Worcestershire.'

And then mercifully the door was shut, (at least, we would never see him again), the last lines in the false, platitudinous dialogue, for ever imprisoned in my mind, had been exchanged. The whole interlude had been as fraught with menace as a scene from a Pinter play, and for a long time afterwards I hung back from answering the summons of the front door bell. Though on occasion there had been a very different kind of surprise, a lean figure in khaki, for instance, and again a stranger to me, but not this time to my mother, who left her housework to throw herself into his arms. 'Oh, Douglas, it *is* good to see you. Come in, come in.'

She was oblivious to her scruffy, blue overall, to the untidiness of her hair, her shiny nose. Here was her elder brother, whom she had last heard of with the Canadian troops in France, here was someone to whom she could pour out her heart without embarrassment. Even with her sister Ethel, to whom she was to come closer and closer as the years passed, she was determined to keep up a façade of pretence, and to impress upon her a vow of secrecy. In contrast, with her brother, only passing through London and soon returning to his fruit farm near Niagara Falls, she could enjoy the blessed relief, the unexpected luxury, of being completely honest about her change of fortune.

'I'll take you out to lunch, my dear,' the head of the Rodgers family announced, sizing up the situation swiftly. 'I hear there's quite a decent hotel on the Terrace.' In dismay – it was a long time since she had had a meal in a three-star restaurant – my mother looked down at her reddened, roughened hands.

In the end she capitulated to his urging, and went upstairs to change out of her working clothes. I don't know what our visitor thought of my enquiring eyes, which even at that stage were inclined to fix themselves on an object of interest and remain there, but I myself was extremely impressed with the polish on his brown shoes and Sam Browne belt. He looked more like an older edition of my cousin Donald than like his sister, I decided. It was the first time I had come in contact with someone who had been wounded in France, and I was suitably impressed. 'Will you send me some unused Canadian stamps when you get home, please, Uncle Douglas,' I asked hopefully, and just in time before Mother reappeared, looking as though she had upset a powder bowl over her face. In a panic, she must have poured it on, unable to examine her reflection in the glass with any objectivity, for the blur of emotion, the unshed tears.

Having watched them depart up the hill, I went out into the wilderness behind the house. I did not feel hungry myself because I was choked with conflicting passions. Irrationally jealous of my uncle for being able to squire my mother, from his backlog of pay, but instinctively grateful to him, too, for making her put on the kind of clothes she never troubled to wear any more, so that she had looked again as every son hopes his mother will look, at half-term.

One day I would make my fortune – the dream was becoming a recurring one, now that my father had finally abandoned his family responsibilities – and arrive at the door in a far grander car than the Spencers had possessed. 'I've come to take you out to lunch, Mother, and look what I have brought you.' A fur coat, even more sumptuous than the one Colin's own mother had worn during my visit to my Lynfield school-chum, impressing me vastly by the manner she would drop it off her shoulders with a carelessly voluptuous movement. Had it been a sable coat? Was there anything richer than that? If so, my mother should possess it one day, and no more worrying about the gas account, or hoarding the lights, or substituting margarine for butter. 'Just let me have all your bills, darling. My secretary will settle them.' Were they drinking champagne at this minute? Surely she should have worn her white foxes, as the complement to Uncle Douglas's uniform with the three pips on the shoulders. After all, it was he with Uncle Stead who had given them to her, as a wedding present.

Now we were driving home, in the station fly at Barnt Green, that was always hired to take me to and from a children's party for the under-sixes, in the winter time. The interior had a not unpleasant, musty aroma, which mingled with the lily-of-the-valley scent my mother always wore, and in the darkness, after all the excitements of the games which we had played, and stuffed with birthday cake, and with a captured balloon on my knee, as treasure trove, I would snuggle up against my mother's side, sleepy now in the warmth, enjoying the luminous touch of the white fox stole which had symbolized the bounty that she had imagined would be hers from now on, as she crossed the uncharted frontiers of married life.

So she could never bear to part with her white foxes, even after they came to represent a very different kind of symbol, sported by ladies of the town. Indeed, after the death of her second husband, whom she had not yet met at the time of this soliloquy in the garden of our Richmond home, as a sign that she once again refused to be defeated she brought them out of a cedar box, where they had been hidden for years, and used them as a trimming for a blue velvet evening coat that she used to wear when I proudly took her to first nights in the West End. There amid all the clamour of the celebrities' arrival in the stalls, heads would turn, not to look at what my mother was wearing, but at the beauty of her unblued white hair, her still glowing skin, her infectious air of unspoiled enjoyment. She only grew old when she died.

Backwards and forwards in time, the confused longings and memories that were already part of my being, the mingled expectations and frustrations, overflowed my imagination until I was abruptly brought back to reality and to the present by an old tennis ball dropping and bounding at my feet. Immediately, through a hole in the wooden palings, childish faces peered at me from the Belgian side of the wall. At the same time, shrill cries in an unknown language entreated and enveloped me. I chucked the ball back, longing to follow it, to be included in their game. For I had had no opportunities to make friends with any children of my own age, in the Richmond area, and now that my brother was a senior prefect at his public school, and soon to be the head boy of Oundle, he seemed to be more remote than ever. Inevitably the gap between us grew larger. We hardly spoke to each other, except at mealtimes, and in the holidays he was often away, for with commendable enterprise and producing already a confident impression of authoritative wisdom, he had succeeded in obtaining a post as holiday tutor. This was not simply a relief to the domestic budget at home, it made him virtually self-supporting while still at school. Thus he set me an example which I tried, with less success, to follow.

The nearest I succeeded in making contact with any local inhabitants of any age were the conversations that would start off with my soliciting cigarette cards from the men in hospital blue, who in their wheel chairs had begun to make a frieze upon the terrace, the occupants of the Home that had been opened close to the park gates, on the site of the former Star and Garter Hotel. Soon every bed was filled in the old Home, and later, the new, more spacious one, with the incurably wounded among Servicemen of two world wars, and their aftermath. With always a long waiting list.

Between the two wars, as I reached gun-fodder age myself, I would vociferously assert that it was better to live for one's country than to die for it. Impotently, like so many others, I was to watch my idealistic hopes washed away in the tide of another holocaust, and in my despair that there could never be any certainty of lasting concord between nations, I would return as a kind of penance to the terrace at the top of the hill, where now stood a permanent, rose-brick building of noble proportions, a lasting memorial with an unsurpassed view of the bend of the river that was to give me the title of one of my books. And so much more besides.

On my recurring visits during this, the second uneasy armistice, I would watch the newcomers settle in and be comforted by the old hands, not with words so much as with a kind of wry, un-crushable stoicism, that inevitably seeps into one's own conscious-ness. Used to visitors of one kind and another, they made it clear to me that they did not mind my intrusion. So I did not have to try to explain how much it meant to me to have acquired a *laisser passer,* to drop in on someone like Ben Jonson, who for me repre-sented them all, not so much the old contemptibles, as the unconquerables.

Ben is gone now from the scene, and to his rest, but on my first visit to the interior of the Star and Garter Home, in the thirties, he produced for my inspection the kind of dolls' house, with a perfection of loving detail, that would be a source of supreme delight for any small girl to possess. It remained so much in my visual memory that when I found myself at sea in the long, black, Arctic nights, I would describe this miniature masterpiece over and over again as I used enviously to watch my companions in the dog-watches using their own hands to carve, with equal pre-cision, their ships' models in wood, to carry home in their kit-bag on their next leave.

Ben Jonson had once been a sailor himself. And the first question that I asked him, when we renewed our friendship as soon as I had come home from sea myself, was, 'Do you still make those superb dolls' houses?'

'I never made *dolls'* houses,' he retorted swiftly, and I apologized for my silly mistake. Of course they were real houses, correct in every proportion, but simply cut down to the scale of existence that he could still manage on terms of equality.

We were sitting together in his small room overlooking the river that he had made as snug as a cabin. 'I had to give up build-ing them while you were the relief for my watch on the bridge,' he explained with a twinkle. 'I couldn't get any more scrap wood, even shavings, because of wartime restrictions, and then my hands started to pack up. So I took up stamp collecting instead, and now it's the second most popular hobby in the Home. We've got thirty-two albums filled already.'

In a way, the stamps would bring them glimpses of the world

that they could only gaze at from the eye level of their wheel-chairs. I had long since discarded my own stamp album; never-theless, even when Ben was no longer there any more to greet me and display for my admiration the latest acquisitions to his own collection, my pilgrimages represented a different kind of symbol from my mother's white furs, the salutary reminder of how important it is never to give way to self-pity, but instead to give thanks every day of one's life. Just for being alive.

Soon after Uncle Douglas's visit, the first war ground to an exhausted stop. I was oblivious to the overwhelming mood of relief of that Armistice Day, when the London streets were filled with dancing and cheering crowds, since I was equally delirious myself, but from a high temperature. A violent epidemic of in-fluenza had devastated all the schools in Eastbourne, including St Christopher's, where every dormitory had become an extension of the sick bay. So I was hardly in a suitable frame of mind to ponder about the release from carnage that had come to the civilized world. Still less, as to what repercussions the termination of hostilities might have in regard to my own family life. Or that it would mean, in due course, civilians would be permitted to cross the Atlantic again, with my grandmother in the vanguard of the queue.

Mother had deliberately tried to keep the more depressing details of the break-up of her marriage from her parent, for she still hoped, not so much for a conjugal reconciliation – though my father had been backwards and forwards for brief, abortive periods – as for a practical change of heart on his side, an honouring of his promises of support, through settling down once again in steady employment. Alas, the truth was, he had already gone too far along the road.

It is strange that it is possible to make up one's mind so irrevocably, at such an early stage, where one's ultimate fidelities lie. I suppose it is that children, like puppies, trust their natural instinct in regard to their fellow creatures. Certainly, in this case, the deserted wife put no pressure on either of her sons to take her side. The silence of banishment, stretching onwards now through the tunnel of the years, stemmed rather from some atavistic, inner compulsion. It can happen with any kind of intimate relationship washed up, like flotsam, on the shore. Blood ties are, by no means, the strongest of all.

My father had always been a shadowy figure to me; now he ceased to exist as a real being any more. I tried to excuse him, to myself, as a sick person, and later when he drifted into a state of semi-invalidism and querulous, repetitive self-justification, on paper, I was ready enough to help with his financial support, not for the sake of my conscience, or expecting any thanks, but simply buying amnesia. After a time, one feels no longer any anger because of the betrayal, everything is swallowed up in a kind of numbness, an overriding desire to be left alone, and not subjected to any frontal contact. There is nothing so dead as a perished love, whatever form the bonds of habit or affection may have taken. So it was, I found now, with my own father. The taste of ashes was in my mouth.

My grandmother arrived primed as to how things really were from the guarded account that Uncle Douglas had felt it his family duty to provide. At least, when the matriarch with her maid, Mary, in tow, descended on Queen's Road, and took over my mother's bedroom, as the spare room was inadequately furnished, she could not accuse her daughter of having summoned her or of whining for help. Her immediate, overall solution was that the two boys should be shipped back across the Atlantic to continue their education in the New World, and to be brought up as American citizens. Exhausting discussions took place, ending invariably in stalemate. However, my mother, almost down for the count though she was, succeeded in finding in her reserves sufficient of her customary spirit – and commonsense – to ward off a proposal that was utterly abhorrent to her. The children were English, and would remain so. Rodger showed the promise of obtaining a top scholarship at Cambridge, I had had the good fortune to find a guardian and protector in Bump, the school's affectionate nickname for the head of St Christopher's; therefore, the idea of any mass exodus was not to be tolerated for a moment.

All the same, I was often to wonder during my lecture tours across the States in 1947, and 1948, what kind of life I would have made for myself, say, in the other Birmingham, had my mother been less positive in her reactions at this moment of re-appraisal concerning the future of herself and her offspring. As it was, it must have taken the very last ounce of her strength to beat off the bullying tactics of someone so accustomed to get her own way, in all things. The meagre amount of food, and its poor quality, on which she had been subsisting for some time now, not simply because of wartime rationing, combined with the emotional battering that she had received, had brought her to the end of her resistance. I only became aware that this was actually so on the day that she abandoned herself to tears. It was the first occasion that I had ever seen her cry in front of other people. I was appalled. But my grandmother had goaded her too far, and because I was indirectly involved, and had to stand by helplessly, the scene had a more cataclystic effect on my character and attitude of mind than anything else that happened to me during those formative years.

It wasn't a very big issue that finally broke the barriers of self-control. It seldom is. In this case, a dentist's bill for attention to my teeth, in the holidays. Reluctantly my mother was compelled to pass it over to the female ruler of the household, now the male had gone, and this sparked off yet another lecture about my mother's folly in not taking the advice offered to her about making a 'good' marriage, instead of preferring as she imagined at the time, a 'good' man.

'But look how I've paid for my mistake,' my mother whispered, like a beaten child.

'Maybe, but I have your bills to pay now.'

Driven too far, my mother burst forth:

'If only I could go out and earn my living at something, anything. But I was never taught to do that. You were always so anxious that Ethel and I should be presented to the world as young ladies of fashion. I could have been an actress, I could have made a success on the stage if I had started early enough. But you wouldn't let me. The only career you approved of for a girl was marriage. Yet you had a career yourself, after you were married, running the theatre.'

'I had brains. I still have them,' and at that contemptuous denigration of the person whom I considered not only the most beautiful but the wisest creature in the world, something broke inside me and I rushed at the heavy, corsetted figure, with the smooth, plump cheeks, butting her in the stomach, like a young bull, beating at her body with my fists. It was then that my mother burst into tears, shocked and ashamed for me, and for the pass to which we had all come, so transformed a trio from the days when I used to crouch in ecstasy beside the bridge-players' table in the drawing-room at Cherrycroft. How could family life become so changed, so utterly barbaric?

Mary, hearing the rising hullabaloo above stairs – my grandmother yelling at me in surprised and wounded rage, my mother weeping in her chair in abandonment, no longer caring any more about trying to maintain a gallant front – came rumbling up the stairs from the basement and sorted out the situation like a police sergeant. She had always disliked my precocious cheekiness as much as I disapproved of her general familiarity and lack of respect for my mother. The upshot was that I was banished ignominiously to my bedroom, to cool my heels for the rest of the day.

The light faded from the free world outside. I did not bother to switch on another kind of light. It suited my mood to be swallowed up by the darkness. I was nothing, nobody. If only I were Rodger's age, I could go out tutoring as he did in the holidays. Except that I was already reconciled to the home truth that I would never attain his standard in scholarship. All the same, there must be something I could do. A paper round? Exercising the Pomeranian belonging to the bedridden old lady next door? Something, anything, that would bring me a few shillings I could hand over in triumph to my grandmother, announcing, 'There, that's towards the dentist.' During those hours I spent in solitary confinement, I beheld no vision, instead I recognized a goal, the unwavering goal that has stayed with me ever since, the only ambition that has never fluctuated. Complete and utter independence was the one thing that mattered above all else. To be self-sufficient. To be able to pay your whack. To have to ask for no favours. Never to be beholden. It has been for me ever since the day I watched my mother weep, at once a challenge and a creed.

Sometimes when people have asked me curiously why there was such a specially close bond between us, I have wanted to be able to produce the black notebook, filled with the landladies' addresses for the theatrical number three tours that were soon to commence. For that brutal exchange sparked off by my dentist's bill was not in vain. It galvanized both mother and daughter into a joint campaign of action. They started seeking interviews with the managers, or the sons of the managers, whom my grandmother had entertained in her Edgbaston home, when she had a theatre, not a daughter, at her disposal. Was there an understudy, even a walking-on part, that Joan Rodgers could have?

'Show Mr Harrison your notices, Joan.' Shyly, from out of her bag the yellowing cuttings would come, with the best bits underlined in ink, and Mr Harrison of The Haymarket, or whoever the manager might be whose sanctum Mollie Rodgers had succeeded in penetrating, would start to read and then break off, with the inevitable comment. 'But I see these are notices for *amateur* productions, Miss Rodgers.' At once, with a few more polite phrases, they would be out in the street again. So different from asking simply for complimentary seats, a courtesy that all managers automatically extended to each other. 'Of course, Mrs Rodgers, if you and Miss Rodgers would care to see the matinée this afternoon, I shall be delighted to put a box at your disposal.'

So it went on until the day that a follow-up letter came from the office of Robert Courtneidge, the father of Cicely and Rosalind, one of the most powerful producers of his day, and an old friend of Captain Jack Rodgers. It happened that he was about to send out yet another touring company of the wartime success, *The Man from Toronto,* still doing well on the road, and there was the part of one of the aunts vacant, which might suit. If Miss Rodgers would be prepared to read the part, and rehearse for a few days on approval.

'What would the salary be?' my mother asked timidly.

'Five pounds a week.'

It was less than she had dared to hope. Moreover, she must have had some kind of premonition of what the endless train calls, the back-street lodgings, the rough and ready companionship of the rest of the cast, and the backstage conditions, so utterly removed from the atmosphere of their charity night performances with the auditorium packed with friends, would entail, in its isolation, its demands for compromise, its squalor. For a moment, she panicked, wavering, but even as she hesitated, a secretary came into the room, announcing, like a cue, that Miss So-and-So had arrived and was in the outer office.

'If you don't want the job, she does,' Mr Courtneidge said. He was simply stating the economic facts of stage life, where half the members of Equity, the theatrical trade union, are permanently out of work. Mother gulped, casting aside for ever her erstwhile dream of playing Juliet, epitomized in the jewelled dress she had worn at the Ball. 'Thank you, Mr Courtneidge, for the chance. It is very kind of you.' And it was. For he was a very kind man. She stood up, drawing on her clean gloves, the armour of undefeat, thinking that if she could only manage to save even a pound a week, it would help towards my school clothes. When she described the interview to me briefly, in a letter to school, I read between the lines, to see everything as clearly as though I had been there in the room.

Otherwise, either then or later, my mother would never speak much about what it was really like. Still it isn't difficult to imagine. They even played one-night stands, packing up after the show was over in the drill hall, moving on at midnight on the milk train, sitting on a cold bench in the station waiting-room, until it was light enough to start looking for digs again, in the new town. The mill towns were the friendliest, she did once confide, and fortunately, the company played most of the time in the north. You never expected a lavatory inside the house, and a bathroom was as rare as a week in the same place.

Sometimes they struck lucky with a cathedral city like Lincoln. Then I would receive a coloured postcard at school, as though she was on a visit to an old friend. None of her letters ever mentioned the rest of the cast, and at the top of the sheet from the cheapest pad of paper she could find she would write the name of the theatre and of the town where she would be next Tuesday, for me to address my Sunday letter. Actually, worst of all for her must have been the dates in familiar small towns of which her previous memories had been of such a contrasting kind. Like Leominster, and Malvern, where we had had so many happy picnics on the Roman escarpment, in my godfather's car; or Dudley, no beauty spot perhaps, but only a few miles from Barnt Green. How she must have longed to make contact again with her old friends, like Auntie Bee Charles, to spend just a few hours (best of all, to sleep once again between linen sheets) in an atmosphere of *pot-pourri* in Worcester china bowls, the scent of polished furniture, and above all, an abundance of flowers. Even if she could have afforded them, there was no use in buying a street-vendor's bunch for your back bedroom, if you were moving on the next day. She had burnt her boats, deliberately she was evasive regarding all invitations, any suggestion of a reunion.

Now she would not cross again to the mainland unless she could do so in her own barque, and though, as an understudy to the leading lady she was called upon to play for her at the Victoria Hall – *'Miss Joan Rodgers substituted for Miss Ivy Blow as Mrs Calthorpe, and proved herself thoroughly capable of the part'* – that was scarcely a sufficient triumph for the relaunching. Something else must happen, and in due course it did.

Meanwhile, between tours – later, she was promoted to a number two tour of *Paddy the Next Best Thing,* in which she doubled two parts, one of them a hilarious sketch of a bibulous old Irishwoman in the surgery scene, so that her salary was raised a pound – she would come and spend a few days at St Christopher's, as the headmaster's guest. For the parts she had to play it had been necessary to eliminate the increasing streaks of white from her head, and now her hair was a rich auburn brown that somehow changed her personality during this period. Whether it was all part of her attitude of self-defence, she appeared to have more confidence. A pay packet, however small, cannot fail to have a psychological effect on anyone who has been used to complete dependence. Then there was another factor, too. Her own mother, having done what she felt was her duty, had departed again for America, at least for a time. That may have been a relief, a reason for the lifting of her spirits. It certainly was for mine.

I could sense that her host, Lionel Browne, who was inclined to be abrupt and shy in the presence of women on their own, placed her in a special category, as she did him. I have encountered a few completely dedicated men in my life, like John Winant, the American Ambassador to Britain in the last war, with the deep-set searching, dark eyes and the taut cheek-bones that reminded one instantly of his countryman, Lincoln, and who when I met him for the first time a week after his arrival at the Embassy in Grosvenor Square, was wearing a pair of brown boots which looked incongruous with his neat, diplomatic suit, until he explained, 'I wore them to come over in the bomber, without any luggage, and I have been too busy to go out and buy a pair of black shoes.' Again, there was Ben Gurion, the Israeli Prime Minister, who when I talked with him for hours in his book-lined study in Jerusalem, so far removed from the hut in which he had been born on the Jordanian border, said to me simply,

'All children wherever they are born are the sons of princes.' Adding, 'but if you asked me where I learnt the lesson of steadfastness for our final battle for independence when it came, it was in your own country, when I was an exile in that other war. I used to watch your people emerge from the shelters in the dawn. There was a look in their eyes that gave me the courage for what lay ahead, in my own country.'

Nor must I leave out Yehudi Menuhin, who has given his services for just causes all over the world, a universal ambassador for peace, and a man of such genuine humility that at a dinner party in a friend's house I have watched him insist on going in last into the dining-room in the procession of guests. I saw him first, a grave child, playing the Elgar violin concerto with the composer conducting the orchestra at the Queen's Hall. Elgar was almost blind and clearly near the end of his life. I am sure that every member of the audience that night must have been aware, as I was, that he was passing on the torch, the master and the miraculous pupil, in that special bond of communication which truly great artists can share with one another, something at once mysterious and eternal.

A year or two later, on Menuhin's return to England, and after another performance, this time in an equally packed Albert Hall, I stood, still a youth myself, at the back of the group of admirers, at the Artists' entrance. At last when my turn came for him to autograph my programme, which I still have today, I could not help noticing the beads of sweat standing out on his pale forehead, so that I blurted out, 'Don't you feel awfully tired after giving a performance, like today?' To which he replied, without a second's hesitation. 'No, I only feel tired when I give a bad performance.'

Lionel Browne was like that, too. Some headmasters hold themselves in holy awe and majesty. He was not one of them. He gazed from the eye-level of the youngest member of his flock, he remained a boy himself at heart, without sacrificing an iota of his absolute authority. Sometimes he would explode for a brief moment, louring at the object of his displeasure. Whereupon the echoes of his wrath would reverberate through the classrooms, and after soughing through the tops of the elm trees that bordered the playing fields would sink to a sigh of regret for the ingrained stupidity of each new generation.

Still, he never harked back over past misdemeanours, he always gave his boys the benefit of any possible doubt, and, in consequence, no one was afraid to knock on the door of his study for counsel or to pour out his homesick heart. Only tale-telling as such was never encouraged or acted upon. There was no need. He possessed eyes in the back of his head. Occasionally, he had recourse to the cane. Yet even when this happened, as a last resort, it was usually followed by a piece of chocolate which you left his study munching, with tingling buttocks, but no ill-will on either side.

Mens sana in corpore sano. The stale old Horatian tag truly meant something to our headmaster, and so in the end to us. He had no favourites and he played fair. He did not expect us to have a cold shower without taking one himself. The school was divided into houses, bearing the names of famous admirals and generals, like Drake, Wellington and Howe. There was inevitably a very healthy rivalry to come out top at the end of the term. Marks were awarded for all sorts of other accomplishments than work and games – such as being chosen as a soloist in the choir for the parents' half-term service – for this parson's son held that it is an integral part of the Christian faith to believe that everyone is born with a talent for something, God-given. So this was Lionel Browne's own way of encouraging the burgeoning and the blossoming, and leaving no one out in the cold. He would make this encouraging point again and again in his chapel sermons, which were a model of brevity and clarity. I was fortunate that it was he who prepared me for confirmation. He succeeded in making the mystery of the God-head so bright and real to me that even today, when I find myself, in a mood of sudden despondency, whispering 'Please God, help me', I see in my mind's eye the reassuring picture of the portly Bump. As he used to be, in an old macintosh and no dog collar, stamping on the sidelines, during our annual blood matches with St Andrew's, bellowing more lustily than all our other supporters together, 'Come on St Christopher's . . . come on School . . .'

He did more than umpire our rugger games at the beginning of the Easter term, as a change from the autumn soccer, he would get his own head down in the scrum, showing us how to tackle fearlessly, but never holding up to sarcastic ridicule anyone who faltered. Often, too, he would take us for runs over the Downs.

He himself wore an outsize pair of grey shorts and thick white sweater, like our own regulation kit, without in the least becoming a ludicrous figure. While in the summer, there would be chosen parties in turn who would bicycle with him out to the tea arbours at Wannock Gardens, where we would have scrumptious strawberry feasts, at his expense. Every boy in the school before he left was invited, at least once, and it was the kind of privilege which meant as much to us then as it does for me to be invited nowadays to the Christies' box at Glyndebourne.

In the evening, during term time, his overriding sense of fairness took the form of a ritual that is amusing to look back upon in retrospect. First he would spend half-an-hour, and smoke one pipe, in the sitting-room of his widowed housekeeper, Mrs Evans, then he would tactfully move upstairs and smoke another in the quarters of the matron. The two ladies loathed each other, and this was his best bet for keeping the peace. Miss Gane, the matron, had a blistering tongue, but the kind of heart that has gone on beating so warmly that she has almost marked up her century. What has kept her going in retirement, she always asserts, has been the visits from her old boys, like the Riley brothers, and Longsworth, and Augustine Courtauld who was destined to achieve fame by spending a winter in complete solitude in a hut near the North Pole; and someone else, equally well-known, in another way, who was in his last year at St Christopher's when I myself arrived. He could not help standing out because he was so tall and almost albino fair, as well as for his insolent drawl which I, from a distance, attributed at the time to the fact that he was so soon to pass on to Eton. However, I suspect now that he had been born with the seeds of arrogance in his make-up, for which the Greeks had a word which cannot be bettered. Hubris. To imagine yourself above the power and the wrath of the gods. No one is. Unfortunately, Paul Latham was to grow up believing that there was one law for him and another for the rest of his fellows. There isn't. For all his inherited wealth and title, his seat in the House of Commons, his dazzling blond looks, his marriage to a charming, cultivated girl, his life was to end in disgrace and social ruin, though at the last he sincerely sought expiation by working anonymously for those less fortunate in their own birth and background. Thus to purge oneself.

The tragic lesson of this rise and fall made more impact on

my own adult behaviour than anything I was taught in the class-rooms of St Christopher's, under the tutelage of the classics master, Mr Challen, who invariably sang *The Duke of Plaza-toro* at school concerts, when he would be received with tumultuous applause, not so much for the remnants of a rousing baritone voice as for the aura of glory in having once represented his county at cricket.

Then there was the English master, Mr Pass, with a liverish skin, who, when he was marking my essays, used to comment: 'I should not be surprised to see you ending up a penny-a-liner in the street of Ink.' This sardonic quip was directed as much at himself as at his pupil; since having discovered himself that the pavements of Fleet Street are seldom lined with gold he had eventually settled for the calmer waters of spending his days subbing the efforts of preparatory school children like myself. Mr Petherbridge came of quite a different mould. He had a small moustache, amused eyes and a delightfully deprecatory manner, as though he couldn't imagine what any of us were doing seated opposite him, discussing 'the pen of our aunt', when the sun was shining and beckoning outside. Finally, the only young master on the staff at that time possessed for us the glamour of a pop singer today, because he had been invalided out of the army, he had seen action at the Front. In consequence, there was a hero-worshipping hush in Joe Griffith's classes, not simply in case Bump was on the prowl. All the same, little work was done.

We were kept in much stricter surveillance by the female members of the staff, the temporary replacements whom the Head accepted as an unavoidable substitute for the times, but without any enthusiasm. As in other competitive branches of public life, the females were inclined to declare war on all males. They reported us at the least provocation. And I do not doubt the masters as well. Bump had his time cut out keeping an uneasy truce. There was a love-hate relationship between themselves and the masculine members of the staff, which showed itself only too apparently in tiffs and tossings of the head. If there were flirtatious interludes, too, we did not have the pleasure of witnessing them.

My own favourite among the ladies was Miss Dodsworth, who taught me mathematics, and who never failed with a little coaxing from the class to give a first-class histrionic performance. She was of an indeterminate age and an indeterminate appearance, with the smudged nose and popping eyes of a Pekinese, and a colourless bang of hair across her forehead. She was much given to sudden attacks of swooning in class, and having what in Victorian times would be described as an attack of the vapours. We enjoyed the dramas hugely, and encouraged her by solicitous enquiries as to the exact state of her well-being before each lesson. On the other hand, I doubt if her male colleagues appreciated her apparent fragility, and the fluctuating state of Doddie's health as much as her classes did.

It was about now that I was compelled to appreciate myself the formidable and at the same time subtle weapons that women possess in their armoury. During the second half of the Easter term we used to change over to hockey, on the warm March afternoons when it already seemed as though summer had come to the south coast. Such a different climate from the rigours of the North Sea. Lulled into a state of false superiority, lying on the grass banks and sunning ourselves, at morning break, we were unwise enough to concoct a plan to challenge those of the girls' schools in the neighbourhood where some of our chaps had sisters in residence. Crossing hockey sticks with them was intended to provide something of a lark, a change from the fierceness of rugger scrums, or the nerve required to stand up to a fast bowler. How swiftly, how painfully we were disillusioned. The forerunners of St Trinian's bore down upon us, their gym skirts floating out like sails engendering more speed, their legs encased in pads, their sticks hacking away at our bare ankles, almost before the bully-off was over. They had done us the honour of sending their own first eleven into battle. Girls of sixteen confronting boys of twelve and thirteen. What chance had any man? What hope had we?

On one occasion, on our own ground, but with their sports mistress as referee, we were faced with the humiliation of twelve – nil against us, at half time. We lay in a huddle, sucking our pieces of lemon, licking our wounds, getting back our breath from being bundled over and enveloped in hot mounds of suffocating blue serge. And just look at the way they kicked the ball. If they couldn't get their stick to the ball, they shamelessly used their feet. That was dead against the rules, and something must be done about it, or the second half would be even more of a rout.

'Go on, Godfrey, you'd better tackle the ref. Tell the old girl her side are cheating and she should have given at least a dozen penalties already.' Proud of being chosen as my side's envoy, I scrambled to my feet and trotted over to where the largest amazon of all was about to raise her whistle for the resumption of hostilities. With her hand suspended in mid-air, she started to listen while I explained my mission, gazing down at me from her massive eminence more in patronizing pity than active irritation. At last she spoke and this was her judgment, much chanted round the dormitories that night. 'Young man, you must understand that there are many things that girls can't help doing in life, and kicking the ball at hockey is only one of them.'

There was, however, as far as I was concerned myself, a rather soothing sequel. Our own headmaster, with an enlightenment rare at that time, allowed tennis as an alternative game during the summer term. It was true that we hadn't any courts of our own but we borrowed the use of some from a girls' school almost opposite us; again we had the temerity to challenge them. Perhaps on this occasion they did not field their best side. I was the captain of ours, and for once lived up to the title. I faced my opponents with my newly-acquired imitation of a cannonball service. I aimed my fiercest top spin forehands at their midriffs if they ventured to the net; I was all out to wipe off the slate our ignominious routs at hockey; and I was so elated with this very local success, and in following it up by winning our own school competition, that I decided on the spot to christen my new racquet, the prize, by entering for the South of England Junior Championship, held at the same time as the Senior Tournament, early in September, at Eastbourne.

The greatest event of my life, so far, happened that summer at Devonshire Park, which after Wimbledon has the reputation for nursing the best grass courts in the country. There an exhibition match took place between Suzanne Lenglen, then at the height of her glory, and members of the American and French Davis Cup teams, who for two days had been playing out their tie, on the same centre courts, where a few weeks later I was to find myself, as a very junior adjunct to the senior tournament, appearing in my own very first open final. Had I been aware of what lay ahead of me – the critical gaze of the spectators in the stands – I doubt if I should have been able to have concentrated with such ardour on every shot in the other match.

Devonshire Park sets a catholic standard in entertainment value and sporting facilities unsurpassed in any other seaside town in the country. Of course, it was always a treat to be one of the party from the school allowed to spend an afternoon at Saffrons cricket ground, watching the Ashtons and Eric Gilligan and Maurice Tate taking part in a county fixture, swarming across the grass when stumps were drawn, to collect autographs.

But Devonshire Park was so much more expansive in its offerings. To begin with, there were the indoor swimming baths where I acquired a steady breast-stroke and passed a life-saving test. I have often in my life felt like a fish out of water and in the water I was a poor emulator compared with some of my contemporaries. However, I was determined to persevere because it was the only way that I could secure yet another coveted cap. St Christopher's had a system that permitted variegated and brilliantly designed caps for the equivalent of first-eleven colours. To acquire the lot, legitimately, meant more to us than for a woman to be dressed *carte blanche* by Dior. The transcending height of joy was to be able to cruise down Carlisle Road to the Baths, on our bikes, sporting each time a different cap on the back of our head. Plus the concrete assurance that we had tuppence in our pockets to purchase a still-warm bun from the shop opposite before the long trudge up the hill again.

In addition, there was the Devonshire Park Theatre, barred to us in term time. However in the nearby Pavilion there were regular celebrity concerts which the musically inclined were sometimes allowed to attend. Here I recall a riveting occasion on which Pachmann was holding forth, in more senses than one, because between each Chopin étude the old gentleman with the white flowing locks enjoyed a little talk to himself, beckoning to someone in the audience like a fellow conspirator. We found his clownlike antics even more entrancing than his music-making, of rather a different calibre from the popular hits of the day that Miss Jenkinson used to pound out on the school piano when she arrived to accompany our dancing lessons, in the gym.

Dear Jenkie, with her blond hair, was the height of sophistication for us, for hadn't she her own orchestra at the Grand Hotel, where to lunch at half-term was the summit of social ambition? Only last summer I was speaking one Sunday in the spectacular new Congress Hall which has taken the place of the old Pavilion in Devonshire Park and afterwards, in that moment of emptiness when you are standing in the wings, shaking and utterly spent, through the pass door came an elderly woman, still upright, still with a suggestion of fairness, still with the wide, welcoming smile that used to seem to say encouragingly that as long as you can dance even for a few steps, life is going to be a bowl of cherries. It was Jenkie, bless her heart. In that moment of reunion, she made me feel like a small boy again, while her appreciation of what I had just been trying to express, my fundamental pride in being British, meant more to me than all the applause of the holiday audience still ringing in my ears. She could not know, but for a short time all the corrosions and the defeats of the years between were gone from me and I was sitting again in the stand, that last summer term, with the sun on my face, and a bag of cherries on my knees, watching the incomparable, the already legendary Suzanne bring off miraculous shots and exquisitely delicate angles that I hadn't realized until that moment existed in the game.

She wore a pleated skirt and the bandeau that was her crown. I wasn't close enough to see her face in detail, but her body was as beautifully proportioned as that of a ballerina, whose grace she matched, and she had a ravishing way of lifting one leg off the ground as she flicked a half-volley off the other foot, to speed a winner unerringly through the minute gap left between her opponents' racquets at the net. Each time she lobbed, the ball fell always within an inch of the baseline; when it was her turn to serve the ball hit the chalk first of this line, then of that. Her accuracy was uncanny, her recovery powers fantastic, the sweep of her backhand had a purity of control which was something to marvel over, to admire for ever.

Beside her, the three international players who made up the four seemed of such clumsier clay. They could bring forth their cannon-ball services, their fiercest smashes, but Suzanne stood her ground, and again and again her racquet flashed back a winner. In the years ahead, I was to have the good fortune to see all the greatest players in action, Tilden against Cochet, in that historic match when the American giant was leading by two sets and five-two, and then allowed his self-admiring gaze to wander to the arrival of the King of Spain in the Royal Box, so that his concentration wavered; Crawford, with his cricket shirt buttoned at the wrists, still as deceptively casual as though he was lazing in the Australian outback, at four-all in the fifth set of the final at Wimbledon against Vines, in contrast a typical American go-getter in a hurry; the two Helens locked in deadly-poisoned rivalry, Helen Wills, so boringly phlegmatic, Helen Jacobs, with the golden head of an ancient Greek coin, but always destined to play second fiddle to her superior-faced rival; but no subsequent encounter, however dramatic, however sweatingly, agonizingly close, ever quite stirred me like my first sight of Suzanne Lenglen in effortless action.

I have often been asked, especially in the days when I was commenting on the game for *Country Life,* whom I considered the most supreme of all the women players. Would, for example, Suzanne have been able to withstand the power game of the Americans like Little Mo Connolly, Doris Hart and Alice Marble, who looked like a boy on court, in her brief shorts, and played like a man? To this I have always replied without hesitation that I am convinced that the French champion, with her undoubted genius for the game, would have automatically adjusted her tactics, and if necessary altered her pace, without sacrificing her rhythm or accuracy, to find cracks in her opponents' armour.

For undoubtedly there were such cracks. Helen Wills looked and played like a champion so long as the ball came to her, and she was permitted to dictate her own terms from the baseline. She was very clumsy on her feet, moved sideways like a crab, disliking intensely short-angled, sliding-away shots, which meant having to move forward from her solid base. While most of the others relied too much on their services and their volleying sorties to secure sufficient points in swift succession. But supposing the rallies lengthened out, as presumably they would have done with Suzanne on the other side of the net? That is the question mark which can never be satisfactorily answered by the supporters of other champions. In my view, only Alice Marble, whose all-round game had no weaknesses, and who possessed great mobility about the court, might seriously have threatened had the two players met at the height of their powers. That is the real testing point, the only really worth-while comparison. And that never happened.

It is generally accepted that there is a difference of thirty – that is to say, two whole points – in every game between a first-class man and woman player. Yet Suzanne held her own, on equal terms, with many of those accepted at the time for the coveted men's entry at Wimbledon, and I have been a spectator myself of their encounters on private courts. Simply because her ball control was so unshakeable. Thus, if such big guns could not blast her off the court, how could any woman expect to do so? It is on record that the Frenchwoman met Helen Wills in the first tide of her success and confidence as the up-and-coming champion, in the finals of the Carlton Club tournament, at Cannes, when she herself was ill and nerve-racked, and on the verge of abdication; yet even so, succeeded in preserving her crown. I accept that myself as the final proof.

Towards the end of her life, and after she had completely given up competitive tennis, I came to know Suzanne quite well. She was far more articulate than most sporting stars and would clearly have made a success of whatever she had taken up. Had the cost not been too great. For in regard to the price of all lasting success in life, not simply reaching one's goal, but staying at the top, she recounted two examples from her own experience that made a permanent impression on me.

When she was a child of twelve, her father mapped out one side of the tennis court in large, numbered squares. After which, Papa Lenglen took up his position on the other side of the net and proceeded to hit balls across for his prodigy in the family to return, calling out as he did so, cinq, deux, onze. Then into the precise squares his daughter was supposed to return the shot. 'And what happened if you failed?' She shrugged her shoulders. 'I was punished, beaten,' she replied, without rancour, but a shiver touched my own spine. Indeed I decided that it was not surprising that right from the start, with her father always present on the sidelines, reproaching his daughter audibly for the slightest error, any missed opportunity, even for losing a single game in any set, and between the matches the endless postmortems, the threatening exhortations, it was scarcely surprising if in the end her nerves should become her most substantial opponent.

In fact, to such an extent did these nervous tensions harry her

THE GREEN YEARS 127

waking and sleeping hours that she confessed this to me. During the week before her much-heralded clash with Helen Wills was due, with high bets being laid on both sides of the Atlantic, and recorded in the headlines, she hid herself away every afternoon, when she should have been practising in the Riviera sunshine, in the anonymous darkness of a cinema on the outskirts of Cannes. 'It was the only way I could escape from the reporters,' she explained. Yes, and from your own crescendo of self-doubts, I thought, made aware for the first time just what the pressures of possessing star quality can mount up to in the end. The loneliness and the nightmares which nothing can banish except your own willpower.

After I had been granted that glimpse of absolute perfection – I was head boy now so I had the pick of any special treats that cropped up – I was naturally keener than ever to improve my own game. There was no chance of receiving any special coaching, because Mr Beck, our rubicund sports master, was only interested in cricket. Fortunately, I was blessed with one unspectacular asset; stubborn tenacity, a refusal to give up, whatever the score, which has supported me throughout my life in far more important ways.

Ostensibly, all my energies at that time should have been directed and concentrated on winning a scholarship at a public school, following my brother's impressive example. But I lacked his affinity with the classics, equally his ability for mastering facts at sight and marshalling the stored knowledge later to his own best advantage. I was voluble and volatile, showy characteristics in company, but distinct disadvantages when you are seated alone in a classroom, floundering with trickles of sweat sliding down your neck because the questions in the examination papers in front of you turn out to be so far above your head.

I see from my school reports, which my mother hopefully preserved, that I was top of every class for the whole of my last year at St Christopher's. I suspect that this was achieved by diligent swotting; the extra something that achieves scholarship standard and status was lacking. The unpalatable truth is, I was a plodder. Then and now. Such talents as I possess have been small ones which I have done my best to enlarge by polishing and polishing them, taking care at the same time not to waste precious time and energy on those people who have swept past me to the top with so little apparent effort. Envy becomes in the end a sin against yourself.

First that summer term I sat for a scholarship for Rugby, where I had been entered in more affluent times. Long before the letter came back from the school authorities, I was resigned to failure, miserable and ashamed, not so much for myself as for my self-appointed guardian who so patently believed that I would never let him down. In his own letter to my mother in which he had so generously assumed responsibility for my school fees, he had stressed that he was certain I would repay the gesture by always being a credit to the school. While he in his turn had become for me the father figure, for which after my own father's departure into limbo, I had been unconsciously searching all my life. Lionel Browne was the first in the line which in due course was to include two such utterly opposed personalities as Somerset Maugham, my literary mentor, and Lord Beaverbrook, my journalistic one.

Therefore, at my headmaster's suggestion that I should sit again, this time for his own Alma Mater, Hereford Cathedral School, I accepted the alternative, the second chance, with alacrity, though none of my particular friends, themselves all bound for Uppingham, Bradfield and Charterhouse, had ever heard of the school. Nor had I. Even when the former Herefordian showed me the framed groups on his study wall of himself as an oarsman on the river, I could neither recognize him, compared with his present image, nor my future. My mind, usually so full of hopeful pictures, remained a blank. Perhaps it was better so, at that moment.

This time, however, the examination papers were closer to my intellectual level. Also it may have been that I was becoming acclimatized. Certainly I was confident in my bones that I had done much better and when the news came the last week-end of term that I had won a sixty-pounds scholarship, I was so overwhelmingly relieved that I had escaped final disgrace that I was ready to believe my destination next term combined all the glories of Eton and Harrow, not forgetting Rugby, packaged into one parcel.

Among the letters that my mother had kept, together with my reports, I came across this one after her death, which indicates the quality of the good Samaritan who came to my rescue at such

Myself at eight months
– the usual pose. *Photo:
The Victoria Studio*

Aged two; with my
mother

Above With my brother at Cherrycroft, Barnt Green. *Below* Summer holidays with mother and my brother, Rodger, at Hunstanton, Norfolk

a crucial point in my development far better than anything I could write myself.

'Dear Mrs Winn:

This has been a specially happy Sunday today. I need hardly say how delighted I am for your sake, for the boy's, and for my own. He thoroughly deserves his success; hard work always does, but doesn't always get it.

'Hereford did so much for me and my six brothers, and I have great expectations for Godfrey. I had a delightfully happy three years there; the beautiful cathedral with its services, and the river, are very great additional attractions.

'The scholarship, of course, relieves the financial situation considerably, but please let me know if you want money for his outfit, or on any other occasion, for any other purpose. I shall be very pleased to be of any financial use while Godfrey is at Hereford, as I have already told you.'

He ended up:

'The cathedral school is small, but is very old, dating before 1381 (older than Winchester) and I have every reason to believe that G. will have a happy and successful career there.

'Yours very sincerely, Lionel R. Browne.'

Moreover, he reiterated his confidence and returned to the theme in the last of my reports, where at the bottom of the page he filled the space allotted to the Headmaster's Latin review with these words:

'I shall watch his career with great interest and confidence. He will always be a welcome visitor to a school where he has done so much in many ways.'

How intensely relieved my mother, too, must have been when she received these two testimonials in swift succession. I have a shrewd idea that she was already reconciled to setting her own sights less high for her second son. If only he would conform to the normal pattern and not come out with these exhibitionist announcements that he was going to be a successful playwright one day, find his proper niche later on, and settle down, and not indulge in idle boasting like his father, all could still be well.

E

For Mr Browne believed in him and Mr Browne was a good man. But then hadn't she believed that about my real father, too?

As for my own reactions, just to see the once-familiar signature of my custodian at that time, on the page, brings back his uncloyed militant goodness with a contraction of my heart that is like a pain, especially when I remind myself how much I took all his generosity for granted. That there will always be an universal provider, turning up from somewhere, in the nick of time. Don't the majority of children feel like that? That period of pre-puberty is probably the most resilient in our whole journey. And certainly I required all the resilience I could conjure up for the major changeover that was coming, though all my thoughts that summer holidays were concentrated on my entry for the Junior South of England Championship.

I had had little practice during August. I was marooned at Richmond, kicking my heels, because my Ludlow cousins did not possess a tennis court, and I knew no one in the neighbourhood who did. In my enforced solitude, I played innumerable matches in my head, turning the narrow strip of garden into an imaginary court, where I swung my racquet like an Indian club. Fifteen-love, thirty-love, down the sideline with my forehand, now a sweeping top-spin drive across court, to my opponent's backhand . . . I won every game.

It was the only way to sustain my morale. Mother was on tour, promoted once again, this time to Henry Baynton's Shakespearean Company where she was chaperoning Mr Courtneidge's younger daughter, Rosalind, and receiving another two pounds a week in salary, Rodger was coaching some small brat whom he found even more of a trial than his younger brother, our American grandmother had left Mary behind in charge of number 16 Queen's Road, the rent of which she was paying, and as a kind of surety that she intended to return one day and buy a property again in Edgbaston where we would all go and live together. She imagined, no doubt, that she would queen it once more as she used to do and patronize my mother as her handmaid, Mary's help. However, she was to die from a sudden heart attack before she could implement any of these projects. In any case, Fate had other plans in store for my mother.

My own plan was very simple if rather stupendous. I hugged it to myself, but I was absolutely determined to win the Junior title, though that event in this famous tournament which closes the grass season was open to boys up to sixteen. All the better, that meant I had the chance of a hat trick! The curious thing is that I never imagined I was going to make any runs in the match against St Andrew's, so I can't think why I was so certain I was going to fare so well in my first open tennis tournament. Nevertheless, it was in an utterly confident mood that I took the train back to Eastbourne on the Saturday before play was due. Perhaps it was partly joy at getting away from the Richmond house, which without my mother's presence was a prison; perhaps it was partly the thrilling expectation of being able to watch the senior players once again in action, but certainly I arrived at the cottage in Meads of Bump's sister, who had most kindly offered to put me up, bubbling over with optimism.

The tournament started on the Monday morning. Punctually at ten o'clock I presented myself in front of Mr Burrows, the doyen of referees, changed and ready to play. He looked at me over the top of his glasses, still studying the lists of entries and deciding about the seedings and the pairings among the champions. He had no idea that he was gazing down at an embryo one. 'Come back later,' he said in a kindly voice.

I was in a fever. Due to present myself, in such a different setting, to report at The School House, Hereford, on Thursday evening, I began to torture myself with the possibility that the boys' event might not reach its climax by Wednesday evening. Supposing I had to scratch in the final? I still can't explain my absolute belief, but for once it was justified. Because on the Wednesday afternoon, at five o'clock, I found myself in the cleaner of my two pairs of white longs, passed down as usual from a cousin, walking on to the centre court as though to the manner born. Only one appendage was lacking to create the sensation of being protected that week by a benevolent spell, inviolable. I possessed only a single racquet, whereas all the senior stars, like Gordon and Arthur Lowe, and Brian Norton from South Africa, whom I had been watching from the players' seats at the side of the court for three blissful days, between my own matches, entered the arena carrying half-a-dozen under their arm, and wearing a white blanket coat into the bargain. Oh well, one day, maybe . . .

My head was ice-calm as I tossed the racquet, inviting my opponent to call. I was going to my destiny, I had no qualms. But later I must have become intoxicated by the trickle of applause from the stands – there had been something of an exodus to the tea tent when the junior finals was announced – for in rushing to the net to perform the *coup de grâce,* I not only bogged the winning smash, but I was appalled to hear an ominous tearing sound at the seat of my trousers. Gingerly I retreated to the baseline, hoping and praying that from this distance no one could guess what had happened. Deuce again. Advantage. Deuce. How thankful I was, for more than one reason, when at last my opponent's return went wide of the baseline.

In the back garden at Richmond, I had practised running gracefully towards the net to shake hands, and had got my little speech pat. 'It was a jolly good fight. Thanks awfully.' Instead, I hobbled nervously forward, then disappeared as fast as I could into the security of the changing rooms. A muffled triumph. Still, on the following Sunday, during yet another of the interminable train journeys which had become so much part of her life, my mother was astonished and delighted to discover on the back page of *The Sunday Dispatch* a small picture of me, leaping at the net, and probably taken at the very second of the tearing asunder, with underneath the caption: G. H. WINN, winner of the South of England Junior Championship, at Devonshire Park, Eastbourne.

I don't imagine she had visualized my sortie in other terms than another children's tennis-party competition, such as we used to have at Barnt Green, until she came upon the picture and the pronouncement in black and white in a newspaper. The very first appearance in print of her younger son, in the paper, the same paper, where exactly thirty years later, G. H. Winn, who had become Godfrey Winn, with the H discarded somewhere along the line, was to have published the serialization of the first authorised biography of Princess Margaret, about to celebrate her twenty-first birthday. The authenticity I entirely owe to the Princess's mother, who as soon as she heard of the project and the commission I had received from the editor of *The Sunday Dispatch,* at that time Mr Charles Eade, commented to a mutual friend, 'If Mr Winn is going to write about Margaret, although she has had no life yet, he had better come to the Palace and meet her.'

The series put on a quarter-of-a-million circulation for the paper that had published my picture all those years before, and after two years voluntary exile, exploring America, brought me back to Fleet Street with something of a bang. In book form, the biography, *The Younger Sister,* sold a hundred thousand copies, and the whole enterprise for the author had a curious affinity with that afternoon on the centre court at Eastbourne, the sensation that one was taking part in a dream sequence.

Princess Margaret received me in her apartments overlooking the Mall. A long room, with high windows, full of light, and furnished, one suspected, more with odds and ends purloined from other suites in the Palace than the expression of her own taste, still in the process of being moulded. For some reason, her absolute punctuality surprised me, though I should have recalled that punctuality has long since been described as the politeness of princes.

One afternoon as I arrived and was taken up in the lift, the lady-in-waiting explained to me that Her Royal Highness had been visiting the Ideal Home Exhibition at Olympia where, surprising act of lèse majesté, the lift had stuck. In consequence, she hadn't been able to return to the Palace till nearly two, and there had been official visitors for lunch. All the same, sharp on the dot of three, the telephone rang in her lady's office. The Princess had found time to change her dress, and now was ready to give me audience.

I sat beside her on the sofa, mesmerized by the unusual colour and brilliance of her violet-blue eyes that I have only seen duplicated in one other face in the whole of my life. The face of Elizabeth Taylor. Although these two human beings are so utterly unalike in most respects, there is an affinity between them. They both were born with that elusive gift, star quality. After Jack Hylton, sitting next to me in the Waterloo Chamber at Windsor, had watched Princess Margaret play the part of Little Red Riding Hood in the wartime pantomime that the two princesses concocted with the help of a local school-master, Mr Tanner, he turned to me and pronounced in the Lancashire accent he never lost, 'I would put her on tomorrow as the soubrette at the Palladium, even if her name was Maggie Jones.'

The inherent shyness of the elder sister, increasing visibly when she had to appear in principal-boy tights, came almost painfully across the footlights. Indeed, she never seemed completely at ease during the performance except when she was singing a duet of *Sur le pont d'Avignon*. Whereas the younger sister, from her very first entrance, was in complete command both of herself and her audience. I can see her now, advancing down-stage to the microphone, tapping with her foot and giving a signal to the colonel who was conducting the army band, as she broke into her first number, *Sing a Song of Tomorrow Today* . . .

Tomorrow was to bring all the stresses into her life that her mother rightfully felt were still lacking at the age of twenty. At that moment when she was on the brink of her coming-of-age, she remarked plaintively to the first of her biographers, 'The papers *have* to make Lilibet the serious one, so as a contrast they will turn me into the frivolous one. You don't know what it is like always to be the younger sister.'

'But I do understand,' I answered promptly, making a mental note at the same time that here was the perfect title for the book. 'You see, all my life I have suffered, too, from being very much the younger brother.'

The ice was broken, and unexpected concord established that was only disturbed by the ringing of the telephone somewhere in the room. As my hostess rose to answer it, I walked to the other end of the room. Standing by one of the long windows, I looked down and away across the Mall. So often I had seen this scene, in reverse. The beds of scarlet geraniums, the Changing of the Guard, the flag flying from the roof to show that the monarch was in residence. Now I was gazing the other way at the stream of Whitehall workers, on their way to catch their buses or trains at Victoria. It was a beautiful early summer's evening, the kind of evening that exiles in the arid heat of Freetown dream of as they change their soaking shirt yet again.

On a sudden impulse, as the princess put down the receiver, I started to walk towards her, pointing out the stream of commuters passing the Palace gates.

'Don't you feel that you would like to be one of those girls, hatless, anonymous, spending your evening as you choose . . .'

'No, never,' she interrupted me vehemently. Her eyes blazed, not with anger but with an inner fire, as though with an inner vision too. 'I can't imagine anything more wonderful than being who I am,' she exclaimed, and then crossed to the sofa, where our interrupted conversation returned to conventional subjects, such as her favourite records, books, colours.

Not surprisingly, that demonstration of her belief in her own destiny made a greater impression on me than anything else we discussed.

* * *

As for my own destiny, my tennis racquet left behind, I felt very much cut down to size, and the victim of anticlimax, when, after a long day spent in the train, from Eastbourne to London, and then on to Hereford, I found myself entering, not a palace apartment, but the school yard.

New boys had to report a day early, and on my arrival I found no one in sight except a West African, considerably larger than myself, standing at one side of the asphalt space on a raised mound, which in due course I learnt to refer to as The Acropolis. The first demonstration of glories long since faded. Another was to follow swiftly.

'Hi, fellow, do you want to know where the bogs are?' It was his effort at a friendly greeting, as he nodded his head behind him. Walking past him, I found round the corner that he was referring to the latrines. Not a single one, as in the Lynfield days, but half-a-dozen in a row. To my astonishment, and growing horror, as my eyes went from one to another, it dawned on me they had no doors. On the floor of the first one opposite which I was standing, there was a dirty piece of newspaper discarded by the last user. It was a page torn from last Sunday's *Dispatch*. Could any welcome have contained more unconscious irony?

I spent two years at Hereford. The School House was Bleak House. What still impinges most of all upon my mind was the sense of dismay, heavier and more constant than a stomach ache, unshiftable as a load of undeserved guilt, because I could never again be completely honest with Bump, the devoted old boy of the school, about my own reactions.

He himself continued to take a warm interest in my welfare. Every week a parcel of tuck arrived from a grocer's shop in Eastbourne. It was extremely welcome, for the food was literally almost uneatable. I recall a diet of squashed swedes for every meal, and pieces of gristle floating in a sea of congealed fat. Even Oliver Twist would not have gone back for more.

Across the road from the main buildings was the Headmaster's

House, with an unkempt garden. There the boarders ate. Dr Crees, the then unmarried headmaster, sat at the head table at dinner time, with the plump, homely matron and one or two others. I am sure it is all utterly different today, the depressing air of run-down seediness long since dispersed. But I used to stare down in loathing at my plate, and in between cast surreptitious glances at that bird-like figure, with the long talons, the ivory skin, the ageless and ignoring face, holding no conversation with his neighbours, gazing fastidiously into space.

I never surprised the Head with a fork actually lifted to his lips. The legend grew that he just sat there at meals as a token symbol; to suppress by his cold presence any rumbles of rebellion, and then as soon as we had shuffled, unreplete and unappeased from the room, scurried to his study to the tray awaiting him there and on it the juicy chop. But I have a feeling, in retrospect, that we did him an injustice. He did not relish food any more than he seemed to relish human beings, in a personal way. He was one of those people who would have preferred to exist on a capsule taken once a day, had it been scientifically possible, so as not to have to waste any time, or any effort in going through the motions of polite intercourse.

Our own paths crossed principally at English classes. I see that his report on my first term acknowledged that his new pupil had taken 'great pains with his essays but his style is laboured and faulty in expression. His writing is difficult to read and he should try to improve in this and in his spelling.'

I am still trying, but now there is no one to stop me from having a dictionary permanently on my desk, and a typewriter, which I have never mastered but approach haphazardly with two fingers. It is the kind of compromise, the rueful acceptance of one's limitations which comes with the erosion of the years. Although disappointed with my essays, I did not get the impression that my new headmaster was *in toto* a disappointed man so much as someone, instead, who was utterly aloof and impregnable. The only time he showed us a glimmer of personal pleasure was when he was batting on the school ground down by the river. He lacked a spectacular off-drive, but with his long wrists he had a crisp way of cutting the ball through the slips, sometimes right to the boundary. A polite trickle of applause would then come from the ramshackle pavilion, whose paint was beyond peeling, but the batsman entirely lacked the personality to set the Wye on fire. After the robust friendliness of my previous headmaster, I was at first dismayed by Dr Crees' desiccated appearance and manner, and then gradually came to accept it as part of my new monochrome environment, together with the nasal voice and anonymous grey clothes of my house-master, Mr Mayne. The boarding side of the school was so small at this time, we were all at close quarters, though an ill-assorted lot. Most of the other boarders were Welsh boys from the New-port and Cardiff areas, and they seemed less surprised by the con-ditions under which we existed than I was. The majority were older than myself – the average age of the class in which I was placed my first term was almost sixteen years – and they kept their spirits up by endless speculation of an anatomical nature about the town girls we passed to and from the playing fields. It was a completely strange language for me, so that I felt, uneasily, blaming myself, out of step.

In the holidays, Bump very generously took me off my mother's hands, at any rate for part of the time. She was still on tour. So St Christopher's was a godsend, even though I felt like a boy whose parents are in India, painfully thankful for small mercies, to be allowed to sleep, instead of in a dormitory, in one of the masters' rooms. Anything would have seemed luxurious after Hereford. I was going through an unattractive phase, my face covered with the spots of puberty and I was shooting up too fast, so that I was very thin and awkward, partly from malnutrition, partly from the poison of isolation. I found it difficult to talk easily any longer to my old headmaster. He was neither one thing nor the other, my mentor or my confidant. This wasn't his fault, but entirely mine. I had betrayed our former relationship by not surrendering in fealty to his Alma Mater of which he himself had such romantic memories framed upon his study walls.

I tried to pretend as best I could. Yes, the boarders still attended the Sunday evening services in the cathedral, and the singing of the choir, especially in the anthems, more than matched the evocative splendour of the massed candles. I did not add that I felt loneliest of all there. After the intimate atmosphere of the chapel at St Christopher's, with Bump himself pounding away at the toy organ, in comparison the vast, shadowy spaces of the cathedral seemed like one of those very grand hotels where you wonder uneasily whether you will be able to pay your bill in the morning.

Yes, I was holding my own in class, and on the football field, and I was learning to play fives, in the court behind the Head's house, which I greatly enjoyed. (Here my voice had a genuine note of enthusiasm.) And the first summer term I took the Senior Oxford Locals, which I passed more than adequately, so that my second year I was promoted to having one of the few studies, which I shared with the son of a clergyman called Hoyle, who had a brick-red face and large hands to match. We had nothing in common, but we devoured my weekly parcel of tuck, so that at least was a bond between us, because momentarily we ceased to be hungry. I never saw Hoyle again, or any other Herefordian of my time. Except once in the Second World War, when I was on a whistle-stop propaganda tour for the Ministry of Information. I was describing life on convoy duties in the North Sea, when at Loughborough – at least I have an idea it was at Loughborough – someone came up to me at the end of my talk in the Town Hall and introduced himself to me as the Town Clerk. 'I am Davies. Do you remember me at Hereford?' Which I did at once. In his smart black jacket and striped trousers, he was still the boy who had always pipped me for first place in class. Davies took me into the Mayoral Parlour and gave me a glass of sherry, which was extremely civil of him, but I could not think of anything to say. All I could think of instead were the dreaded Sunday afternoons, when at two o'clock sharp, whatever the weather, like landladies and holiday lodgings, you were turned out of the gate and had to stay out till four.

After a time, I discovered a small newsagent's shop that was open and would buy myself a copy of *The Observer*. I would order one from week to week, in order to fortify myself with the theatre reviews of St John Ervine who dazzled me by the power of his invective, the sweep of his vocabulary, and above all the width and extent of his theatrical knowledge. Some latent longing from my barnstorming ancestors welled up in me and I would forget the cold and the rain oozing down my neck as I huddled under a hedge along the river bank. In the summer, of course, the Wye meandered very pleasantly through the blind, lush meadows. Then in addition there was the company of my other newspaper hero, someone called Wallis Myers, who wrote in *The Daily Telegraph* about Wimbledon and the international tennis matches. The school house provided a copy of *The Telegraph* every day and I had no compunction in stealing the week's supply, hoarding them for a re-reading session on Sundays. The other pages not in use made a substitute for a rug against the long grass. Although I hated the Sunday afternoons most of all, and even now still dread the sound of summoning church bells (so impregnated for ever with the echoes of my loneliness at the period) the confident, effortless prose of my two literary heroes on the subjects which meant most to me in the world, did help considerably. They blotted out and banished the nagging picture in mind of the more dashing among the other boarders, bolstering up each other's courage, going off in gangs, having first stuffed their betraying school cap in their pockets, to meet 'birds' in secret rendezvous. Perhaps nothing really happened. Much talk, little action. Nevertheless, my own imagination was first stirred, then tortured. Though part of me longed to participate, to go with the crowd, something held me back. And for ever.

I had also come upon another discovery, the novels of Compton Mackenzie. He became the third of my literary gods at that time. *Sinister Street* parts I and II exactly matched my own mood, while, in contrast, *Guy and Pauline* seemed the most satisfying love story in the world. So much passion and yet so much purity. I have made countless pilgrimages to Burford, in later years, to stand beside the stream close to where the vicarage stood – or where the author made it stand, in the days when he was an undergraduate at Oxford; perhaps he also carved his name, as Guy did, under the poem he had written on the glass, in the long summer vacation – which is a little life in itself, a burgeoning and sometimes a withering, too. And Pauline? Is the original of her portrait still alive and flourishing as the author is himself? I would like to imagine so. I must have read their story a dozen times; it has for me the kind of distilled ecstasy that each new generation finds in Keats' *Ode on a Grecian Urn* – '*For ever wilt thou love, and she be fair.*' The expectation and the longing.

I am puzzled as to how I secured the succession of copies of Compton Mackenzie's novels from Boots' library, in the town which was at all times strictly out of bounds except for the direct route to the playing fields and when the streets were deserted on Sundays. Perhaps I invoked the aid of one of the day-boys as a messenger – Greenland perhaps, the gangling, good-tempered son of the owner of the city's largest drapery stores who in the August holidays of my second year teamed up to partner me in the Public Schools tennis tournament at Queen's Club, where, alas, we were defeated in the first round. How I envied the day-boys going home each evening. Going home. I have no recollection of being invited into any of their homes for Sunday tea. I was too proud to hint, though what an oasis that would have been. I cannot imagine I would have forgotten it, even after forty years.

My mother only managed to come to see me once in term-time. She had made a cross-country journey, partly by bus, from the town where she was appearing that week, and over a hurried lunch together she abruptly started to question me about my practical awareness, if any, of The Facts of Life. She actually used the expression, as though it were in italics, adding apologetically, 'You haven't a father to talk to you about these things.' Somehow this reference only made the whole conversation more jarringly out of tune. I had imagined that she had wanted to be shown over the school, which she had not seen, and I was prepared to bluff that out, with my downy upper lip in full control, but now I began to suspect that it was this bogey which had prompted the awkward visit. Had she, I wondered, gone through a similar catechism with my brother? And how had he extricated himself? He and I were not on the terms where we could even hint at the intricacies of sex.

The Kardomah café food that I had looked forward to with dribbling desire, congealed, wasted upon my plate as I hung my head, unable, for once, to utter a single word. I was appalled that my mother should seek to cross such a masculine frontier. How could I tell her about the sporadic gropings in the dark shadow of the Acropolis any more than I could describe the pitiless lack of privacy by day of the latrines themselves? Or comment on the instinctive pairing-off of the protective with the unprotected, the clumsy experiments to find an outlet for one's dawning, puzzled, adolescent longings? As yet I had taken little part in the skirmishings, was still uncommitted, but not ignorant. Had I broken my communion vows so soon? Was I contaminated and unclean? Until that moment I had not envisaged myself as being so, but it was something I could not bring myself to discuss with my own mother. Someone else's, perhaps, but not my own. Even when the problem of sexual and emotional outlets became finally crystallized in my personal philosophy. Then as a kind of compromise for both of us, I returned to share the running of a house, trying to diminish the barrenness of her widowhood, reconciled myself, or largely so, to the pointed label of perpetual bachelor.

That afternoon in Hereford we walked in a mutually frustrated and resentful silence to the bus depot. Only at the last moment did we suddenly become close to each other again when she started to confide in me how an old school friend from Edgbaston called Violet Martino had come back into her life. At first I did not appreciate why Mother made such a point of describing this unknown character to me, in some detail.

'Dear Violet likes to think of herself as a blue stocking. She has a French friend called Andrée, who is a famous journalist in Paris and Violet herself always carries a copy of *The Spectator* under her arm, wherever she goes. It is her Bible. She doesn't care in the least about her appearance or whether her petticoat is showing. She has henna'd her hair into a bright scarlet thatch. Some people might find her a little eccentric or even peculiar, but she has been very good to me. So very good,' Mother repeated, with a transformed look on her face of surprised happiness that I had not seen for a long time. 'And Violet makes a splendid chaperone.'

Here Mother stopped abruptly as though she had been on the point of some further revelation. However, the description had created a visual diversion, I was instinctively intrigued as I always was by anything in the least different and I had the sensation, too, that the conversation was somehow more important than it appeared to be on the surface. In any case, the next moment a clue appeared that I was able to accept at its face value.

'Violet is a wanderer. She has no liking for domestic ties, but she is comfortably off, like most of the Martinos, and very independent. She prefers to stay a lot at her club in Dover Street in London.'

'I didn't know women belonged to clubs. I thought only men did.' My interest quickened.

'Violet also stays quite often in rooms in Winchcombe, in

Gloucestershire,' Mother continued, ignoring my interruption. She was coming to the point at last. The introduction, the alliance. 'Winchcombe isn't very far from Hereford, is it? Violet says she will invite you for the week-end, at half term.'

'Is she a confirmed spinster like Aunt Edith?' I asked. After all, she must be old, I thought, if she was at school with Mother.

'I don't think she would like to be described in that way. Of course, she is very emancipated and advanced in her views. But she can be quite coquettish sometimes.' Mother smiled at the vision, and everything was all right again.

'Then I had better introduce her to Doctor Crees.'

I didn't really mean it, such match-making was the kind of absurdity to save the day and we were both laughing now. All the same, in due course, it came to pass and I still relish every detail of the afternoon that Auntie Violet, as I soon slipped into calling her, insisted on coming to a cricket match, dressed in a buttercup-yellow linen dress of uncertain vintage, with insets of *broderie anglaise* here and there, a huge hat perched on top of the haystack, and long kid gloves, as though she had been invited to a Garden Party at Buckingham Palace. She was determined to do me proud, and insisted, too, on talking to our Headmaster about the leading article that week in her beloved *Spectator,* while he put his pads on to bat. And when subsequently the worst occurred, and he was out l.b.w. before he had scored, she persisted in continuing her harangue, sublimely oblivious – or pretending to be – of his martyred expression of mounting fury. Who will rid me of this woman?

I suppose some schoolboys, saddled with such an odd sort of visitor, might have been overcome with embarrassed shame. But I was for ever egging her on, having established at first sight the kind of mutual aid society which sometimes happens between a stripling, starved of personal drama and a suppressed exhibitionist of either sex and uncertain age, eager for any kind of audience – even her landlady at Winchcombe, with whom she seemed to be on excellent terms. Violet did however confide to me that she suspected her landlady, without a shred of evidence of course, of having tried to poison her with some home-brewed wine. 'I think we had better stick to the cider, as it is bottled by other hands, this week-end.' The sagas were endless and confused, but full of colour. I enjoyed them all hugely.

Even more I enjoyed being treated and confided in as a fellow grown-up, a contemporary almost; such a gesture is always irresistible, especially when, as in this case, my new-found ally was prepared to listen to my reading my compositions aloud, and each time I reached a passage starting, '. . . as the famous historian . . . or as the famous philosopher says . . .' never stopped me to enquire *which* historian, *which* philosopher. Until one day I confessed of my own accord that I had just made up all the quotations to fit whatever theory I was trying to advocate and that Dr Crees, though he had his revenge in never marking my essays higher than a Beta, had not dared to challenge me just in case his own ignorance of some eighteenth-century writer was laid bare. Violet, thinking this was a tremendous joke, dissolved in helpless giggles, having to wipe her glasses several times before she recovered sufficiently to exclaim, 'Oh dear, Oh dear, I must write and tell Andrée that at once. Who knows, you might become a journalist yourself one day, a Foreign Correspondent, and cover conferences at Geneva for your paper, as she does.'

It was the first time that bell rang for me. While on the first occasion I met my new benefactor, my fellow conspirator as she was soon to become, she produced a ten-shilling note from her shabby purse – so often a sign of hidden riches – and tried to press it into my hand as I was leaving to catch the train back to school. She had already sent me more than sufficient for my return ticket and Bump besides had enclosed a half-term tip in his weekly letter. So I was in funds and on a sudden impulse, remembering the bus-stop departure, the abortive, frozen lunch, I said urgently, 'Please, you are seeing Mother before I shall. Won't you buy her something? Some stockings or a small bottle of lily-of-the-valley scent. Or would that cost too much? But something she wants, something nice.' I meant anything frivolous, not a necessity. 'She never buys herself anything these days,' I explained.

There was no need. 'Don't worry about your mother, but you are a good boy.'

'I'm not. I'm not,' I burst out furiously, as a wet mouth was pressed against my cheek. I had not meant the conversation to take this kind of turn at all. My newly-acquired relation had a musty smell at close range, totally unlike my mother. I was unaccustomed to any other female embraces. Nevertheless, I was mollified when she added in a mysterious whisper, 'You see, I am planning something for your mother. A splendid idea all round.' She put up one hand to her mouth, like a ritual mime in a morality play. I waited hopefully. But that was all, for the moment. All the same, I returned to school from my half-term break far less depressed than I had expected to be and, instead of a sense of anticlimax, a promise that my benefactress would take lodgings shortly in Hereford. I had the premonition of a turn for the better in the family fortunes. She was not unlike a pantomime witch, dressed in modern middle-class clothing, and she was about to wave her magic wand. Something was brewing, and my instinct was right. Nor did I have long to wait for the next development. Dr Crees was simply a side-plot.

That August I went as usual to stay at Eastbourne, but this time not to take up residence at St Christopher's but instead as the guest of Aunt Violet, in a small hotel facing the side of The Grand where the ballroom was. Mother was there, too, her tour over, and another Martino, Violet's half-brother, who had black hair parted down the middle, a dashing cavalry moustache, and a friendly twinkle in his dark eyes that softened his image of a big-business man in lofty control of a successful steel company.

He possessed courtly good manners, too, making me wonder if far back there was some Italian blood to mitigate the Brummagem stock. I watched him treat Mother as though she were a girl of eighteen. It was touching and endearing. I had the feeling that I had missed the first act of the play but it did not matter because the plot would be explained to me in due course. At least, I understood now my mother's reference to her former school friend as filling the rôle of the perfect chaperone. Wherever the other two grown-ups went, she went, too. While I practised my tennis shots at Devonshire Park they set off for drives along the coast, with Violet tactfully snoozing in the back of the car, with its long silver bonnet, the only outward sign of wealth, or buried herself once again in *The Spectator,* this time on a deck chair on the lawns, to allow the other two to catch up with all that had happened to them since they had briefly met at Edgbaston coming-out parties, in their uncluttered youth. Then in the evenings to The Grand ballroom, from whence the sounds of Jenkie's band tuning-up invitingly would reach us as dinner was finishing in our own hostelry across the road.

Neither my mother nor her middle-aged but still dashing beau had danced for years. My mother, because that side of her life, which she had once upon a time so spontaneously enjoyed, had disappeared with the disintegration of her marriage; he, because of the vicious, recurring attacks of asthma that prevented him from ever sleeping the whole night through in peace. Yet his gallantry and his guts were undefeatable. If you courted a lady, you took her dancing. While in tow, behind them, trotted the chaperone in a variety of extraordinary *ensembles* run up in some haste by a Winchcombe dressmaker. Reluctantly at half-past ten I went upstairs to my room, not to sleep but to crouch by the window in my pyjamas, watching the shadowy couples caught for a moment in the light of an open window.

How seductively enticing is the rhythm of any band, when the music reaches you with the muffled overtones of distant enchantment. I can never pass a house in a London square, with the striped awnings out across the pavement – because a dance is being held indoors – without remembering those other summer evenings when I longed with all my heart to be inside, instead of outside able to gaze in with only snatched glances at the paradise that was forbidden me. So many times the pattern was to repeat itself in the years ahead.

At that first confrontation, with myself as the eternal observer instead of as the participator, which most of us seek to be, my reactions did not include antagonism towards the newcomer. On the contrary. He had so clearly, by every gesture, every glance in each other's direction, brought my mother back to life and taken the defeated look from her face that had begun to seem as though it was carved in stone. I can truthfully say that I never became jealous of him, in the way that stepsons often are, especially when they reach that ticklish transition to their own potential manhood. He was too disarmingly generous-minded in his attitude regarding people unlike himself. I could only marvel at his genuine tolerance, his patient efforts later to understand why I could possibly prefer the insecurity of an actor's existence, compared with a safe seat in his office or the opening that would surely have been found for me in my grandfather's flourishing works. Edward Martino ordered his clothes from a London tailor and took some pride in his appearance. But he never forgot that his suits and his cars were paid for by good Midland money. Therefore, the belching factory chimneys in a brilliant frieze across the night sky gave him all the aesthetic satisfaction he needed – so utterly different from the emotions conjured up for me by the lighted windows and the music of the ballroom, still out of bounds.

I tried to hide my bitterness that I was not considered old enough to make the trio into a quartet. After devouring Compton Mackenzie's *Sylvia,* I felt so sophisticated and worldly-wise. I would willingly have had a shot at whirling Auntie Violet round the floor; I should not have cared even if her petticoat had fallen to her feet, just for the emancipated joy of finding myself part of that glittering, adult setting. It seemed so unfair, because, after all, hadn't I been the first of them to learn to dance to Jenkie's jazz rhythm, her indefatigable fingers tapping out the tunes on the school piano – *And her Mother came too, Kitten on the Keys, Limehouse Blues,* – with the encouraging french chalk sprinkled on the gymnasium floor at St Christopher's, once a week during the winter terms? We had had to make do without girls for partners in our prep-school days, all in preparation for the real thing, the glamorous nights at The Grand.

I felt cheated in the evenings and increasingly puzzled during the days as to what the climax was to be. Until I could suppress my curiosity no longer and asked the chaperone point-blank whether her services were to be indefinitely prolonged.

'Is Mr Martino married? I mean, he talks about his son, Ted, who was at Dartmouth, where Rodger would have gone, and who is now at sea, Ted I mean, as a snottie in the *Queen Elizabeth.* And about an older grown-up daughter, Peggy. And about Horrie – was it? – the other son who died. But he never mentions Mrs Martino. Is she dead, too?'

'No, she is not dead. She has run away to Australia.'

'But why?' I persisted, thinking that my confidante made it sound like a death.

'It all started in a convalescent hospital which she used to visit near her home, during the war. It was a case of cheering up the poor wounded Tommies too much.' Her hand went up over her mouth in the now familiar gesture, followed by her usual sex-starved giggle. The next moment, however, her expression and her manner had changed. 'Poor Edward. It was a complete surprise for everyone concerned. I told my brother he had to have a divorce, it was the best way out of a messy business. Of course, he himself was utterly blameless. Except that he was too good and kind. Like your mother. I gather she was too good to your father. Too meek and self-effacing. It doesn't pay in the long run.'

'Do you mean over being married, or always?'

'I mean always. You can get so dreadfully hurt. Like your mother was, and my brother. When I first heard what had happened to her, how she was playing small parts in a fit-up tour, and living in lodgings without a proper lavatory, I couldn't believe it, she was the prettiest girl in my form, everyone taking it for granted that she would find Prince Charming. I went to see her, and thought immediately of my brother. So on my next visit, I took him with me, as a surprise. You can imagine what it was like for your mother, coming out of the stage door and finding the car there. Waiting for her. And instead of going back to a kipper in her digs, supper laid on at the local hotel, where Edward and I stayed the night.'

'And from then on you started playing your own part as chaperone. I see it all now,' I exclaimed. At least, I imagined I did.

'Don't you think it was a brainwave on my part? They need each other. They will restore each other's confidence.'

I nodded, sagely. This was like the resumption of one of the conversations we used to have, opening the windows of the stuffy, over-crowded rooms at Winchcombe, and at Hereford. Only my essay book open on my knee, to start the conversation off, was missing. No longer needed. Dear Violet. All my original affection for her, my recognition, as children have, for what can lie behind a façade of eccentricity, came flooding back. I bent gratefully to kiss her own starved cheek.

All the same, it did not occur to me at that moment, or for long afterwards, that the conjured picture of the stage-door johnny was in reality an impatient passionate lover only prevented by the shadowy presence of the King's Proctor from leaping into bed with my mother. I was not yet fifteen, my mother was over forty, though she had the figure and the skin of a girl. Automatically I assumed, as so many other sons have done, that that side of her life was over. But companionship and kindness, to be made to feel wanted and attractive again, that was a different matter, and as I watched the transformation proceeding, the reburgeoning day by day, my own heart was full of relief and gratitude towards her saviour.

My mother herself was too shy to speak yet of what was happening, except where it concerned me directly. She had taken such a battering that it was not surprising that she should be wary of challenging Fate, in a big way, openly. Though it seemed big enough to me when on our last day of the holiday together she came into my room at the hotel to pack and announced that she wasn't going back on tour, but had taken a small furnished house off the Hagley Road, in Edgbaston. Before I could ask her why on earth she should want to go back and live in a suburb of Birmingham again, she added:

'You won't be going back to Hereford next term.'

'I won't be going back?' I was dumbfounded. I could not believe what I had heard. 'You don't mean I've been expelled?'

'No, it is I who have written to Doctor Crees. Edward helped me with the letter.' Soon she was to refer to him as 'Dad', but not yet. Already, though, she was enjoying the pleasure of bringing him into the conversation. It gave her a sense of reassurance like sewing on buttons for her children's clothes. And picking up my tennis shorts and folding them into the case. 'I knew from the day I came to visit you that you weren't . . . happy.'

It was not the word that she had wanted to use but she could not think of the right one, the all-comprehending one.

'I am sorry. I would have stuck it out. It might have got better. I did try.' It was so much easier explaining to Auntie Violet, I thought.

'As long as I was on tour, there seemed no solution. Till Violet appeared on the scene. It was her suggestion. She offered to take rooms in Edgbaston, so that you could live with her and go as a day boy to King Edward's. The Headmaster has accepted you as a scholar, because you did so well in your Oxford Local Examinations.'

'So I shan't cost you anything?'

'The school is in New Street. It's one of the oldest grammar schools in the country and Edward says he knows many old boys from there and that it has turned out some splendid men. It has a great reputation for rugger, too. I know you will do your best to settle down this time and finish your education. There is a very fine Headmaster, Dr Carey Gilson, a very different type of man from Dr Crees. Violet and I went to see him together. It was all her idea.'

I longed to ask what the chaperone wore on this historic occasion. But the moment was too serious, an epic moment in my life; nor was it over yet. My mother had finished the packing and was at the door. She had kept something back to the last. 'You'll be going to stay the first few weeks of next term with your Aunt Edith in Newhall Street, till the house I've taken is free. Your father is not paying the rent, but there is some money coming at last from Granny's American estate.'

'It will be nice to see Auntie Edith again. I'm very fond of her,' I said quickly, not wanting to talk about my father, seeing too clearly my mother's face the day that she had had to plead for my dentist's bill to be paid.

'Yes, I know you are, but you may find her changed.'

'How? Older, do you mean?'

'Aunt Edith is very upset because I have started divorce proceedings against your father. She keeps on writing to say that there has never been a divorce in the Winn family. She is horrified at what she calls "the scandal to the family name". She won't believe that your father behaved as he did behave. It would be no use my going to see her, but you are her godson and you are a Winn. To her that is very important. You and Rodger are the only two grandsons. Your Aunt Edith has the right to see you, and you mustn't blame her for supporting your father. Families are like that. Besides, she has had a very shut-away life.'

I felt she was trying to say: don't blame me for wanting to marry again, to rid myself of the name of Winn. As if I could. An overwhelming sense of relief flooded my being. I was not going back to Hereford. I was not going back to Hereford. Nothing else mattered. Except my determination to win the Junior South of England championship for the third time running.

But first I had to try my luck in the Public Schools tournament at Queen's Club. My future stepfather had offered to drive me up to London, with my mother, who was taking him to meet her sister Ethel at Mortlake. It was doubly kind, for it meant an extra-early start for them since I had to report to the referee by ten o'clock. Owing to the state of excitement in which I was now enveloped we were ten miles out of the town before I discovered with horror that I had left my only racquet behind. I scarcely dared admit the enormity of my lapse but the driver said nothing, though he had slept badly through an attack of asthma. Because I was my mother's son, he turned the car round and returned to our Eastbourne hotel. My sense of gratitude for this gesture never left me; I was won over for good. All the years he was married to my mother, he only rebuked me once. And mildly, then. 'A car door is not to be slammed like a railway carriage door,' he pointed out.

The South of England championships were being staged as usual at Devonshire Park, at the beginning of September and as usual I stayed with Lionel Browne's sister, at Meads. I was thankful that Bump himself was away, on holiday in Jersey. I could not face the imagined hurt look in his eyes about his old school. But at least, I had not asked to be taken away. Would that have made a difference? As it happened, I never saw him again. Now I have reached the stage when I pause and turn my head to gaze back along the road; then, with the exuberant self-centredness of my youth, I was only interested in what lay round the next corner. However, on the Sunday, the day of strung-up waiting before the challenge began – the hat trick, could I bring it off? – I left my hostess after tea and walked through the village till I came to the red-brick buildings at the top of Carlisle Road that had none of the forbidding air of most schools. Some instinct had brought me to seek absolution, to hold confession, on my knees.

As though to aid my plan, the door of the chapel was not locked. It was the hour when in term time the evening service would have just started. I had never found myself alone in the chapel before but I did not go to my usual place in the choir stalls. I knelt in the front row, where the smallest boys used to be placed, just in front of the lectern in the form of an eagle's head and carved wings.

Shutting my eyes, I prayed as I had never prayed. I prayed that my mother would be allowed to marry her stage-door johnny, and never be disillusioned again, as she had been by my father, or humiliated and defeated. I prayed that I should like my new school and not let the side down, which was one of those phrases that were part of my vocabulary at that time, but most of all I prayed that on the morrow I should start a victorious progress towards the triple crown. 'Oh God, please let me win the championship this week. If I do, I will be good. I promise I will be good.'

How many other pilgrims, in other places, for other reasons, have made similar confession?

Of course, you cannot make bargains with the Almighty. I did not know that yet. In consequence, I walked out into the evening air, wrapped in exaltation. The Hereford cathedral bells had no power again to accuse me. I would never sit in that shadowy transept, close to tears, rejecting the beauty of the pure soprano voices, soon to break as my own was breaking. In contrast, how welcoming the small, modest school chapel had been. And across the grass, the pavilion where with such loving pride I had rubbed down my first bat with linseed oil. It was not too difficult to imagine the familiar smell was still lingering there, to scent victory in the sunset.

Need I confess I did not win? I did not even reach the final. There were bigger guns this year. I lost to a young player with a classical style, called Max Callender. We were five-all in the third set. Then I was pipped at the post. I could not believe that it was going to happen, till the last shot had been played. Because I would not believe that God had let me down. I never spoke of the shock to anyone, though it was a long time before I could pray, with any sense of confidence or meaning, again. Desperately, I tried to do so a year later, when my mother, in a dress of her favourite shade of blue, was married in the Savoy Chapel off the Strand. Surely God would listen this time. Hadn't she been through enough? So I prayed, if not with absolute conviction, at least with the knowledge that I had learnt one of the more important lessons in life. You must never ask for anything for yourself. Solely, selfishly for yourself.

They were still on their honeymoon, a second honeymoon for both of them, in the New Forest, when I came to take up residence – a dull phrase, considering that it means so much more than a casual week-end visit as a guest, instead to have one's own room, to be granted the right to discuss the colour of its curtains – to take up residence in my new home, because it was henceforth to be my mother's home, with the drawing-room thrown out and an extra dressing-room built above it, as a wedding present. Mother had been busy all the spring and early summer, directing operations, like a general, in her element once again as a home-maker, all her former vitality and confidence miraculously restored.

Before that, during the winter, after my visit to Aunt Edith, which had been something of a strained armistice, the gentleman caller arrived punctually every Sunday afternoon at three o'clock and sat in the little back room of the semi-detached box, furnished with the nebulous taste of strangers, while I struggled with the aid of a lexicon and an ubiquitous thesaurus to compose Latin verses on the dining-room table in the front room.

'*Eheu fugaces, Postume, Postume, non reduntur anni . . .*'

It seemed so simple, so inevitable, when you read it from the pen of someone else. Had Horace never had to struggle? Was it the secret of all good writing that, above all, it should appear so effortless? Alas, I was a pedestrian poet, but I went on trying; just as I tried not to be conscious through the paper-thin walls of their increasing proximity to which I had still to adjust myself. Instead, to concentrate with gratitude on my own happiness which was all-embracing. I had found a stepping stone again. I belonged.

Much to my surprise, I had been placed straight away in the Classical Sixth. This meant spending all my working days in a beautiful carved room, like a college library, with a great stone open fireplace, blazing with logs, in front of which the headmaster stood, warming his long legs and the tip of his almost as long flowing white beard. Dr Carey Gilson had a voice with the richness of Paul Robeson, a majestic appearance, and the total air of a prophet of old. He was a figure of awe, but never frightening; only wisdom came from his lips, and when he pronounced that the ultimate salvation of the human race on earth lay in work – of some kind or other – I accepted the dictum so whole-heartedly that it has stayed with me all my life. While instead of those greasy excrescences which had been termed meals at the School House, now I took a packet of home-made sandwiches with me each day and, in the break between morning and afternoon classes, I joined a group of my munching companions, gazing down at the remote traffic of New Street. I was no longer out of step, I was absorbed into the fraternity of those seeking scholarships at one or other of the universities. All the talk was of that. When I let slip what my elder brother had already achieved, it gave me a sort of stature myself, ill-deserved.

Beyond being accepted, what mattered so much was the excess of freedom as a day-boy, and the access, in consequence, of such delights as the performances of the Birmingham Repertory Company. After turning out for rugger on a Saturday afternoon, I would treat myself to a ticket from my pocket money in the evening, to see Gwen Ffrangcon Davies in *The Immortal Hour,* who as she sang 'How beautiful they are, the lordly ones', dressed in Debussy-like, floating green raiment, epitomised for me the merging of Eloise and Pauline and Melissande into a vision that was like an immaculate conception. In contrast, there was the robustious *Farmer's Wife,* later to be taken to the heart of London audiences with such now famous names as Raymond Huntley, Colin Keith Johnston, Melville Cooper and Cedric Hardwicke, who also excelled in interlarded productions of Shaw. A vintage cast, a florescence in that particular repertory theatre which many would suggest has never been since surpassed. I soon became on chatting terms with the lady in the box office, was regaled with backstage titbits, and, having invited her, in exchange, grandly, to 'our family box at the Prince of Wales,' was sometimes, in return, smuggled in for free. The smell of real grease-paint was beginning to tickle my nostrils though I took care to keep my enthusiasm to myself; or at least to camouflage it by announcing that I had been cast for a part in the school play. Antonio in *The Merchant of Venice.* Not much of a part, but it had one good speech which I hammed up for all that it was worth, and more.

'. . . *the weakest kind of fruit*
Drops earliest to the ground, and so let me;'

I wore a long robe with mauve braid trimming the edges. The trimming had been entirely my own idea. The original design, to be made up at home, was surely altogether too drab. For once my mother agreed with my sartorial fancies which was more than the young designer did. He had red hair, his tongue was not as fiery but it was a withering one. There was quite a dispute about the braid. In the end, I got my way, while he got some early practice in dealing with the egocentricity of actors. For that boy was designed to see his name, Alec Shanks, blazoned on the posters outside the Palladium as the designer of the pantomime costumes, the summer shows, and so much besides. And when on a first night I have watched one cavalcade follow another, so many rioting colours, so much exuberance, I have found myself wondering why, even in the beginning, Alec should have minded so much about a few yards of royal purple braid. We were breaking him in, lightly. In the next production, promoted to play Mark Antony in *Julius Caesar* I borrowed a leopard-skin hearthrug from my new friends, the Maschwitzes, and wore it round my loins for the Forum scene, and nothing else, except the enviable self-confidence of the amateur player.

By that time, I was settled in at The Oakalls, just outside Bromsgrove a largish former farm-house, re-painted white. It had gone up in the world, standing now at the end of a long drive, with a lodge at the gates, meandering through a miniature park, with a cluster of out-buildings, a pond imaginatively placed, and a pleasant view across the fields. Here the cows became part of a landscape which was impervious to the fact that there was a new mistress, and a new broom, in a household that had been in disarray since the surprising departure of the previous châtelaine.

I came upon the house only a few weeks ago bathed in the evening light. From the distance of the gates it did not seem to have altered in the slightest external degree. So far from shrinking, as sometimes happens, in the dimensions of one's mind's eye, this half-time refuge, this rallying-place of my youth appeared even more pleasing, exactly right in its relationship to the still untouched surrounding landscape. After my memories of the arid wastes of the Barentz Sea, I approached it with a fresh awareness, an intensity of emotion which surprised me, though I had not been unappreciative, I reminded myself, at the time.

This reappraisal, this chance encounter, happened because I was on my way to Madresfield, after having spoken to a group of teenagers, assembled for a week-end course in a private house at Alvechurch, generously donated to the cause of Midland Youth Clubs by the eternally civic-minded Cadbury family. The title of the week-end course had appealed to me. *A taste for living.* Combined with a taste for honey? One could say a lot about that. In my acceptance to make yet one more speech, I had forgotten how close Alvechurch was to Bromsgrove. Almost within walking distance. As Bardwell, who has looked after me like a watchdog for close on twenty years, sensing my mood, drove slowly through the country lanes, I was worrying, as usual, whether I had left anything out. I put a tick to the headings which I buried in my mind because I have never been able to get used to carrying notes. The importance of independence – to acquire a skill, a training that would make you financially independent, if necessary, of all your fellow human beings, – 'the boys' manners in Nottingham are simply awful,' one of my audience had volunteered – the equal importance of having friends of both sexes, and staying friends, if possible, with your parents who were not necessarily fuddy-duddies; and above all, the importance of believing in something, someone, most of all, if possible in yourself, because if you did not have good cause to believe in yourself, how could anyone else be expected to do so? Whereupon I found myself smiling wryly over the comment of the only girl in the group dressed in a white blouse and skirt instead of the uniform slacks, the solitary one to admit that she did not want to marry or have children, and preferred, besides, mature men to The Beatles.

'Men have all the luck,' she had called out provocatively.

'Why all the luck? Because we don't have the boredom or the pains of giving birth?' I retorted.

'Because a fat, middle-aged, bald man is still attractive to some woman, but it doesn't work the other way round.'

You learn something on every journey, I told myself. Still, was this a cue for the visitor to take his leave? Certainly it wasn't the cue for me to recite the parting piece of maternal advice I had been given when I left home, to fend for myself, in London.

'Take care of your health, its value to you will be beyond that of any money you may earn from now on. Always wear a clean collar and shake hands firmly like a man, and always get up from your chair when a lady comes into the room.'

Considering that no one got up any more in a bus or tube, my audience would have found the final directive particularly hilarious. I had come away wondering if they had found me a rather pompous old 'square', for they looked incredulous when I had begun with the announcement that at their age I had lived only two or three miles down the road. How could I have *ever* been their age or been faced with the male counter-part of their problems, when to be on-coming, when to hold back? I doubt if

I convinced them about anything, although the room did become suddenly still when I related the incident of the girl of sixteen who in desperation knocked at the inconspicuous door of the office of The Council for the Unmarried Mother and Child, tucked away among the shabby shops of the Kentish Town Road, because she was going to have a baby and the moment had arrived when she *had* to tell someone.

'But why not your mother?' the secretary asked, curiously. 'You are living at home, you say.'

'Yes, but there is never any time, we never see each other alone,' came out the answer in a rush. 'You see, we both go out to work, and then in the evenings as soon as the washing-up is done, the telly's on, and then on Sundays *they* go out in the car and I go out on my boy friend's bike. So when could I tell her?'

A simple parable of modern times, proving once again that the art of communication is the most imperative of all, I decided, as the car came up the hill, and there was the house beckoning to me. If I had not already been late for dinner where I was staying for the week-end, I would have told Bardwell to turn in through the gate for a closer view and then asked permission to climb the stairs to the whitewashed room with the bars across the window, presumably a nursery once upon a time, where secretly I had written my first novel, *Dreams Fade,* during 'resting periods', the euphemistic phrase, in the Theatre.

My brother, befittingly, had a more impressive room across the passage, looking out on to the newly-conditioned tennis court which my stepfather had had relaid as a welcoming present. But the best room of all, with its own sitting-room attached, was strictly reserved for Ted Martino, as the real son of the house. I gathered this had been insisted upon by my mother who was anxious to get all the priorities right from the start. However, my newly-acquired step-brother had had to return to his ship as soon as the wedding ceremony was over – as proof that she was the completely guiltless party in the divorce, it had become a vital issue with my mother that somehow, somewhere, she should receive the church's blessing upon her re-marriage, her second exchange of vows – so as a kind of advance guard, Rodger and I found ourselves sent on ahead, to await the honeymooners' return.

He no longer had to spend his vacations tutoring, he was

already something of a swell at Cambridge. Every time his name was mentioned in the family circle, it was to announce that fresh academic laurels had been showered upon his head. Nevertheless, I have an idea that what pleased him almost most of all was that he had been chosen to cox a boat for his college, Trinity, and now possessed at last a link with the world of sport, and the rowing world, with all the uncomplicated lusty comradeship it inspired. Legal tomes make austere reading; indeed, his high forehead already looked as though it needed a barrister's wig to complete his appearance. Without it he was like someone who has dressed in formal clothes but forgotten to put on a tie.

I had regarded with dismay the prospect of being alone with him in a strange house for a whole week but surprisingly it turned into one long picnic, a festive occasion. It was still warm enough to lie upon the lawns, he with his law books, I with a novel by Galsworthy, whom I had recently discovered and who was so soon, in another kind of way, to discover me. I had passed the Higher School Certificate that summer, having satisfied the examiners in Greek, Latin, Greek and Roman History, and English Literature and French, and was to have a first shot at a scholarship at Oxford in the spring. To my relief, my brother made no suggestion that I should be swotting now, and that he would help me on my way as he tried to do once before. But that had only ended in bouts of sarcastic ridicule, and I think he was as eager as I was to preserve our own kind of honeymoon truce. I have the feeling, too, in retrospect that he was just as deeply appreciative as I was that our wrecked family ship had been set afloat again, or at least towed into harbour.

After tea we would go for a walk together, picking the first of the blackberries, with me shinning up the banks and Rodger pulling down the branches with his stick. It was very much in both our minds that if we kept on along that particular road, we would be on the outskirts of Barnt Green within the hour. Only four miles away as the crows flew, if there were crows in those parts, but how much had happened to our fortunes and our personalities in the years between.

'The new maids mother has installed seem to be settling down very well,' he would comment judiciously.

'Yes, we had a jolly good dinner last night, didn't we? I wonder what Cook is giving us tonight.'

It wasn't exactly the fraternal greetings of a Masonic Lodge, but at least there were no tart comments on the width of 'Oxford bags', no warning rumbles of an imminent volcanic eruption. And no more washing-up, no more cockroaches.

My stepfather had three motor cars, the loves of his life, after my mother and his own children, and my mother had three maids under her command, one up on the old days in Barnt Green, for those who were interested or impressed by such one-upmanship symbols. For myself, and I suspect for her, too, what established most strongly the blessed security of the fresh start were the times when we had tea together, alone, in the long drawing-room with the french windows at one end. Dad was not yet back from his office. I would catch, if possible, an earlier train from Birmingham and school, and walk from the station across the fields, swinging my bundle of books tied with a strap; all my inner being was concentrated on the pattern that the flickering flames of the fire would be making on the white walls and the tea-table, set out with the Queen Anne silver. And the lady of the house pouring out, while the parlour-maid, the one who smelt so strongly of perspiration but Mother said we mustn't mind because she did her work so well, pulled the delphinium-blue curtains against the early autumn twilight. Our *l'heure bleue*. The furnishings of the room, the china cabinets, the rosewood and Hepplewhite furniture, the generous sofa, were a larger and more extravagant replica of what had never been achieved at Richmond. This was surely the symbol which really mattered. More than all the welcoming-the-exile-back dinner parties that her old friends at Barnt Green were rallying to give; the bridge evenings; the invitations to serve on the committees of Worcestershire good causes; the no longer counting the money in her purse every day.

'I thought in the Christmas holidays we would give a party ourselves. If we pushed all the furniture back, and took the rugs up, there would be room to dance in here. The morning-room could be used for sitting out, and the dining-room, of course, for a buffet supper. I don't think the parquet floor would get hurt, do you? Of course, we should have to put some french chalk down.'

Like the gymnasium floor. No, more like The Grand.

'What sort of party? A grown-up dance?' I asked cautiously, not daring to become excited too soon.

'A young party for you, and Rodger, and Ted, if only he can wangle some leave. Dad has offered to buy you your first dinner-jacket for Christmas. And you will be able to ask Audrey Charles, and the Ambroses, and Rowena Goodrick Clarke, of course, and the Cohens – I hear Sylvia has grown into such a lovely girl – and John Challen, and Kenneth Sharp.'

And Uncle Tom Cobley and all.

'Who's Kenneth Sharp?' I demanded.

'They're new since we lived in Barnt Green, Auntie Bee says, but very nice. Cousins of the Adies.'

The pleasure that everyone, but everyone, should have this glimpse of her restored image, the gracious hostess, the bountiful party-giver, enveloped her for a moment like a pink cloud. And I was reminded suddenly of Colin Spencer and his mother, whom I had not thought of for a long time. Should I ask him? No, Lynfield was too far away now. On the other hand, there was someone I would like to ask.

I mentioned the name of one of the girls from the female side of King Edward's. We had made friends on the morning tram, the year I was living in the little furnished house off Hagley Road, and her family had invited me sometimes to Sunday supper with a pack of her school friends. We had played games like 'Sardines', that hovered between horseplay and sex exploration. The searchers sometimes did not find one couple for a long time.

Mother had forgotten the name already, but when I reminded her, she said, of course, I was to ask anyone I liked. 'And we mustn't forget the Beeslys, either. We'll have to make out a list.'

'Let's start now. I mean, let's start practising. On the night, you must wear your gold dress to receive.'

I jumped up to put a dance record on the new gramophone on its mahogany pedestal in the corner where today the television set would stand. I pushed back the rugs; immediately our mutual enthusiasm for dancing embraced me. This is how it should have been on my exiled nights in Eastbourne, I thought with a pang, and the memory made me bossy. 'No, you go back with your right foot, and wait for me to turn you round. The man leads, the girl follows, and if there is a muddle it is *always* the girl's fault,' I repeated loudly, several times.

The head of the household, returning, found us in full spate. We finished the record with a flourish. There was no automatic change in those days. 'Now it is your turn, Dad,' I suggested magnanimously. My partner left me at once to welcome back her real lover, to give him her flushed cheek to kiss. 'A young party.' I thought. Including them. But I felt no resentment, only an ever-increasing desire somehow to achieve my own first romance, to put it on display. Leaving them unashamedly holding hands by the sofa, I slipped away to my cold room to struggle with my homework till dinner time.

The table lit by candles, both my parents in evening clothes, that was another interlude which I greatly savoured, including the freshly-established ritual when Tartar was allowed to come out from under the sideboard for his piece of chocolate. Tartar was the first of a long line of Sealyhams, a breed to which I was to develop a life-long attachment, though I freely admit they lack the party manners and show-off tricks of many other dogs. Presently, in the Esher home I was to share with my mother, and still later in my own Sussex home, there was to be Mr Sponge the First, and Mr Sponge the Second, the name lifted from the story of Jorrocks and Mr Sponge's Sporting Tour. To have a dog about the place was another proof of a settled sojourn. I am sure that is why my mother loved Tartar most of all.

Ted was home with his ship in time for the party, which made all the difference because he looked extremely dashing in his dress uniform, and had such an air of gallantry, that all the shyness of the girls vanished and Helen Beesly lost her heart to him, for a while. The party itself went with a swing from the moment that John Ambrose gave his seal of approval to the selection of records we had bought. Only my own specially-invited guest seemed out of things. This was my first experience of how un-consciously snobbish a small clique can be. Did she look different from the other girls? She was far more attractive than some of them, I told myself stoutly, and she followed impeccably as a partner. But every time I left her to do my duty by one of our other guests, I would come back to find her where I had left her, sitting-out on the sofa of the morning-room, until finally, more in desperation than for any other reason, I suggested a tour of the house. When we reached my bedroom, she picked up a sheaf of paper off the desk in the corner.

'What's this?' she asked.

My brother today:
Lord Justice Winn.
*Photo: Universal Pictorial
Press Agency*

With my brother

Aged ten

Aged fourteen

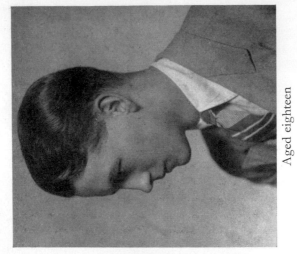

Aged eighteen

'It's a story I am writing,' I said importantly. 'It's called "Primroses." ' With few inhibitions about my literary aspirations, I took it from her and started to read aloud, as though she were Auntie Violet, my best audience to date.

'The trees glistened after the rain. There was a nice fresh smell, Nigel had taken off his hat, and his fair hair was ruffled, seemed alive when Joy put her fingers through it. She loved his plus-fours, with lights of yellow and blue wool worked into the background of brown. She rubbed her cheek against his arm; the stuff was rough, and yet soft at the same time . . .'

I looked up and stopped reading. She had sat down on my bed, and now was lying back against the pillow with her eyes shut. Her skirt was up above her knees. 'I bet you've never put your hand up a bird's skirt,' they used to taunt me. There was a confusion of voices battering at me from those Hereford days, and my heart was thumping against my chest. I must do it, now. Now. As I clumsily half-knelt upon the bed, she helped me by pulling my face down to hers. She put her tongue between my lips. I had never tried kissing like that before. I was not sure if I liked it or not. Liked any of it. One of my hands she drew against her breast encouragingly, but as I pressed down harder I was only conscious of the first stiff shirt I had ever worn with my dinner-jacket, which was having quite a christening. In a panic, I found myself hoping that nothing would show. I don't know how long we stayed like that, but at last I stumbled to my feet, pulling down my jacket, fumbling with my buttons, while she, older and more controlled than I was, powdered her nose in front of the mirror.

I was just about to stammer nervously that we ought to go downstairs before we were missed, when she cut into the silence herself.

'Have you started to shave yet?'

I shook my head, blushing miserably. It was the most dehydrating remark of my life.

However, my male sense of vanity was soon restored, though in a somewhat unexpected manner. I was now turning out regularly as a wing three-quarter for the school Second Fifteen. My greatest asset was my speed and a good eye for picking up a pass. During the first match in the new year I was trying to gain time for my side by kicking into touch when I was collared from behind with the ball still in my hand and went down with a considerable thud. Instantly there was an agonizing pain in the leg that had been taut and tethered. I tried to get up and found myself yelling out in pain. Then I fainted. The next thing I remember was the blurred arrival of the ambulance, and being carted off to the hospital where my family were summoned posthaste. I had torn the cartilage of one leg pretty severely in the pursuit of duty, and in a laudably conventional way, so that I found myself on my return to school a minor hero. Meanwhile, I basked in every moment of my convalescence at The Oakalls, secretly delighted when the doctor pronounced that it was highly unlikely that I would be able to turn out on the rugger field again that term. As long as my tennis prospects for the summer weren't threatened, nothing else mattered. I had been blooded.

The first letter I wrote about what had happened was to a Cambridge undergraduate. Not my brother, because it never occurred to me that he would be interested, but instead to someone who was something of a first-class sportsman. H. A. C. Gaunt was in the running for a tennis as well as a hockey blue, and had won my undying regard by offering without a trace of patronage to knock up with me, during the long summer vacation, on the courts of the Edgbaston Tennis Club; he had even partnered me in the handicap doubles in one or two south coast tournaments.

Tom's home was in Edgbaston where the Gaunts had one of the more opulent houses, filled to overflowing with children of all ages, with a trio of sisters that I would have loved to have possessed. I remember especially the eldest, Nancy Gaunt, and her unmistakable English fairness, with the same affection to this day that I was to have for Ruth Maschwitz, who was in due course to serve unknowingly as the model for Olive, the Junoesque heroine of my first novel. But at this time it was Tom who was my hero, though less so to his father, a similar kind of Midland business autocrat as my grandfather Winn, and therefore bewildered at his elder son's announcement that he intended to eschew the family business and become instead a schoolmaster.

I had been elected a junior member of the Edgbaston Tennis Club, the venue of the Midland championships, the year before and during the summer term when I was still living with my mother in the makeshift quarters she had taken while her divorce was in transit, I used to change into flannels and take the bus to the grounds, every Sunday afternoon. There I would sit in front of the pavilion in a conspicuous position hoping and silently entreating that some other member would invite me to make up a four. No one ever did. So after a couple of hours of miserable frustration I would take the bus back and, too mortified to admit my recurring failure, would concoct elaborate stories about all the coaching and encouragement I had received from the Best Players.

It was left to Tom Gaunt to make, unconsciously, these stories and my dreams come true. He was not too superior to play with a schoolboy, he was the *chevalier sans peur et sans reproche,* and it was almost inevitable that there should develop an emotional tinge to the relationship on my side, the one who had come in from the cold; in the same way as I was exaggeratedly grateful to another Edgbaston family who, starting on the tennis court, had taken me under their wing.

It was true that Ruth Maschwitz did not herself play any game; her time was consumed with writing novels, in a series of exercise books, and she had the tenacity to submit over a dozen before her first was accepted. Nothing disturbed her concentration and she would bring her work to the side of the tennis court, pick up a ball that had fallen at her feet, and continue with the sentence where she had left off. I marvelled at her calm acceptance too, of the disruptive vagaries of life itself. Just as I marvelled at the energy of her father, a portly old gentleman who still bounded about the tennis court, beaming with good humour, and never surrendering until the last point of the match. I delighted to partner him and win, just as I was delighted to take the whole family to our theatre, night after night, when the National Opera Company arrived at the Prince of Wales for a season. Now it was that I had my first introduction to Wagner, with Mr Maschwitz echoing snatches of the recitatives in German, which impressed me greatly, and made me think of Ruth as one of the Rhine maidens. None of my own family could even pretend to enjoy Wagner.

Sometimes at week-ends the Maschwitzes' son appeared from London. He was older than Tom, already down from Cambridge. Indeed, he had had a serial accepted for *The Daily Mirror,* which he had written in six weeks. He never stopped talking, called everyone 'My dear,' and seemed a tremendous man of the world to me, especially when Ruth explained that her parents were very worried about Eric, though for quite a different reason from Tom's father about his son.

'You see, he is in love with a married woman.'

I pricked up my ears. This was like one of Auntie Violet's conversations.

'What will happen? Will she do a bunk? Will there be a divorce?'

'That's what we are afraid of. Mother thinks that Eric can't afford to be married yet, tied down.'

Such was my introduction to Eric Maschwitz, who has set such an enduring example to me, and many others, in that he never allowed himself to become spoilt, despite all his success as the creator of such shows as *Balalaika,* of songs like *These Foolish Things,* or in his august position in the higher echelons of the BBC.

He is exactly the same today, in his bubbling-over, uncarping attitude to life and people as he was when I first met him on his family tennis court. While as for the married woman, that is to say the first wife that he married, and later unmarried, though remaining on the friendliest terms, she was destined to become an unique star in her own right, one of the indestructibles. Only recently, when I was the guest in her latest Television series, just before our light cue, Hermione Gingold hissed with her wickedest smile and her tongue hovering between her teeth : 'Fancy you first hearing about me, leaping over a tennis net. Who was the better player? You or Eric?'

I could claim the victory there, though I was far behind his accomplishments in other arts, just as I was far behind my other tennis partner, in volleying skill. Tom enjoyed going to the opera, too. That was another link between us. When I volunteered that I had become a Wagner enthusiast – mimicking Mr Maschwitz senior – he rather crushed me by explaining that I could never pretend to possess any real musical taste until I found *The Magic Flute* an utter ravishment. Sitting through it together, in the family box, it sounded to my barbaric ears all trills, and no heart, no tunes of the melting rapture of *Depuis le jour* ... from *Louise,* which I had recently purchased, with Madame Edvina as the soloist, on a celebrity label, together with Galli Curci's even more spectacular rendering of *un bel di vedremo.* I was passing through the stage when I scorned the English translations and I played these two records, which I still have today, over and over again, lying on the drawing-room sofa with my leg up during my convalescence, waiting and waiting for a reply to my letters to Tom. A reply which never came.

I must have written half-a-dozen times before it finally dawned on me that there would be no answer. What had I done? How had I offended him? I went through all the torture and the bewilderment of the discarded. Two or three years later, when he was a housemaster at Rugby, on his way to becoming the revered headmaster of Malvern College, he invited me to lunch at the Public Schools Club. He seemed slighter than I remembered him – or perhaps I had expanded in so many ways myself – and had he always had vaguely prominent teeth? He could not have been more charming, more interested in how I was getting on, in the theatre, or more tactful about how he had prevented me from making a fool of myself, dramatising a situation that didn't exist. I suppose the intense tone of my letters had taken him by surprise, embarrassing him, and making it quite clear that this unhealthy devotion must be nipped in the bud. Such crushes were not to be encouraged either for a prospective schoolmaster, or schoolmistress. Silence was the great destroyer, together with time itself. Our lunch was so altogether ordinary, that it would have been absurd to refer to the desolation that I had endured, unable to confess to anyone at the time, even Ruth, though she listened patiently to my outpourings of how I was determined not only to be financially independent as soon as possible, but utterly self-sufficient, too. Here I meant as far as my emotions were concerned. A multitude of other men and women must have endured similar experiences to mine, in their perplexed search for maturity, and wondered afterwards if and why they had cared so much. Yet surely it is better to feel something, anything, rather than nothing. A stone, falling to the bottom of the pool. And I keep in the drawer beside my desk a letter which the last Governor of Holloway, a woman who has had to witness the ultimate degradation of the human spirit, in many forms, and has herself remained uncorroded, wrote to me once:

'I think that the unity of both mankind and the universe is a sort of final aim, and that therefore all friendship, all affection, whether for implements, animals or anything else, is important.

Obviously the highest example of this is marriage, which is why a happy marriage is such a lovely thing. But if that doesn't come one's way, there are lots of other means to use and so increase one's power to love . . .'

*   *   *

In the resilience that one has at sixteen, I swiftly found another outlet for the inherent romanticism in my nature.

I can't be sure how it happened now, but somehow two tickets for the O.U.D.S. production of *Hamlet* came my way. It may have been that Joyce, my ally in the box office at the Birmingham Repertory Company, had been offered them, and unable to make use of them herself; had been touched by my loyalty to the theatre at large. Anyway, there they were in my wallet, next to my season ticket from Bromsgrove to Birmingham. But how was I to get to Oxford and back home again, on the night, so as not to miss school the next morning, since the performances were in term time?

To my undying gratitude, Ted came to my rescue. By good luck, he was on leave again and if he could borrow the small Hillman from his father, he would drive me over. No, he didn't mind in the least sitting through Shakespeare, if it meant so much to me to go. He had that kind of character; I was fortunate indeed in my stepbrother, as in my stepfather. It is always assumed that the relationship is more complicated than dealing with one's own flesh and blood, but I never found it so.

I don't know if today my stepbrother, long since retired from the Navy with the rank of Commander, recalls anything of the evening, and I certainly had no inkling when we set out from The Oakalls to drive the sixty miles to Oxford that I was, in a sense, journeying to my destiny. Some people have confessed to me that the first time they heard a performance of *Tristan and Isolde* was an experience which changed their whole existence, in that it gave them a new standard, a fresh awareness in musical appreciation, linked with a deepening pulse regarding life itself. Something like that happened to me that February evening at Oxford, so that I was too utterly absorbed to want to stir in the intervals, letting Ted go alone to smoke a cigarette.

After our own school attempt at *Julius Caesar,* the efforts of the undergraduates to perform *Hamlet* seemed professional plus; moreover, everyone who saw this particular production would agree that it was an exceptional one in the long annals of the O.U.D.S. It had a kind of alchemy induced by the personality and the performance of the player in the title rôle. The present Lord Kinross, then Patrick Balfour, provided a comic cameo as Osric, the present Lord Chancellor, Gerald Gardiner, was an austere, commanding Horatio, Robert Speaight made his mark as the player King. Others in that memorable cast were John Sutro, as the first grave-digger, and – among the extras – John Counsell who today runs the theatre at Windsor. But it was Hamlet himself, in the person of a tall, well-built, blond young man with a magnetic delivery, who received such acclaim and such spectacular notices from the London papers that it was almost inevitable he should subsequently adopt the stage as his calling, and play other important Shakespearean parts all over the world before settling down to look after his inheritance as a country squire in Northamptonshire.

I cannot myself visualize Sir Gyles Isham as he now is, in that rôle, though I am sure he carries it out extremely well. To me he will always be the unfledged, questing Hamlet, as I saw him, acting for the first time that February evening in 1924, dying as those beloved of the gods do die young, in Horatio's arms. *The rest is silence.* Years later, when in the darkness of a London cinema I watched the film production of *Hamlet,* with Olivier choosing to play the part, for a change, in a Nordic blond wig, suddenly he became Gyles as I knew him in those days, whose hair was exactly that same tow-colour in real life, though he, in reverse, had worn a darker wig for the play. The strange metamorphosis, in my mind, bringing so many memories in its train of that eventful year, when everything seemed to catapult all at once, and my life took a great leap forward, gave me a purging sensation of mingled joy and sadness.

Look thy last on all things lovely,
Every hour . . .

There was a moon riding high, and a brilliantly clear sky, as Ted and I drove home, with the fields canopied with snow. The temperature was well below zero, and the time was well past midnight, but I was still on fire. My impressions poured out of me, I replayed every scene. Ted let me have my fling. He was concentrating on the icy patches of the road, as though he was the officer in the middle watch on the bridge. But I sensed his taciturn friendliness, and he became Horatio at my side.

The sleeping landscape crystallized under the aurora of the untarnished moon was all part of the magical insubstantiality of the evening. We seemed to be floating through the deserted, muffled countryside, the only two inhabitants, not of the earth but of the moon. My ambitions, my waking dreams, were soaring as high as that. Now I knew for certain where my future lay. I must be an actor, too, one day. A strolling player, like my great-grandfather, a strolling player and a playwright as well, like Shakespeare himself. If only I could win a scholarship at Oxford, if not this year, next, and then someone on the casting committee of the O.U.D.S. would somehow hear of my performance as Mark Antony, and of my write-up in the 'Birmingham Gazette' with the result that one evening, when I was swotting, there would be a knock on the door of my rooms in Christ Church . . .

Alas, the knock on the door was a bang from my stepfather, summoning me to the bathroom he had just vacated, adjuring me to hurry or else I would miss my breakfast, before leaving with him, in the car, for the station and another routine day of school. Half-an-hour later, in the stable yard, the sturdy little Hillman no longer seemed like a space rocket to the moon. Its engine was sluggish in the bitter cold, and not surprisingly reluctant to start. Dad cursed softly as he pulled out the choke further but, wrapped in his usual patina of courtesy, still remembered to ask, 'Did you enjoy yourself last night? Your mother and I never heard you come in. You were good fellows to be so quiet.'

At least, he no longer called me a boy, and I was grateful. All the same, what could I reply? 'Yes, I enjoyed myself very much, thank you, Dad, and it was awfully kind of Ted to take me and of you to lend us the car. He drove marvellously.' The words did not sound as though they belonged to me, or anyone. I was still in a dazed trance, not so much from lack of sleep as completely hypnotized.

To Oxford I returned a month later, in a far more sober frame of mind, a candidate for a classical scholarship. As this was regarded simply in the nature of a trial run for me, my headmaster had set my sights high and put down Christ Church as the college that was my first choice. In consequence, I was allotted rooms in the first of those exquisitely-proportioned quadrangles, which I did not know was more familiarly called Peck. But I did know that I was roused in the middle of the night by the sounds of revelry, which seemed more like the hounds of hell baying in the courtyard, for someone's blood. Surely not my own, so soon.

Peering apprehensively out of my window, I was astonished to see converging on the pool, with the child-like statue of Mercury on its rim, poised for flight, but petrified in stone, the dregs of some end-of-term celebration party, who were only too clearly determined to finish off the evening with a drunken display of their own favourite variation of blood sports. Their *bête-noire* in the college had been routed out in his pyjamas and was about to be cast into the pool.

I shivered, and went back to my own warm bed, to toss and turn uneasily. So that when I awoke again, it was with a sense of impending disaster. As though I myself had been the victim the night before. Or at least, it had been intended as a warning to me. By the time I was seated at my desk and had been given my first paper, I was in a nervous panic. Everyone round me appeared to start writing at once, but my mind, like the foolscap sheet in front of me, equally remained a blank.

On one side of me sat a candidate who seemed much more mature than myself, because of his very pale skin and dark, brooding eyes; on the other side was an elegant youth with a pink face and a very pleasant expression, which he still possesses today. In the break, they both took pity on me, cutting short my lamentations, and I discovered that the one with a Calvinist look was called Charles Plumb, was in his last year at Rugby, and his father was the Bishop of St Andrews; while the other was an Irish peer who would be going up to Oxford in the autumn, whatever the results. His name was Michael Rosse, and he seemed to my unsophisticated gaze to be an Oxford man already, with so many friends and fellow Etonians in residence.

When I blurted out that I had been woken at midnight and forced to watch the sacrificial rites, Michael Rosse exclaimed, 'That would amuse Harold. I am lunching with him, is it the day after tomorrow, to celebrate our release. I am sure he would not mind your coming, too.'

Once again I was tagging along, as in my early childhood days at Barnt Green. Everyone always seemed either older, grander or more assured than myself. It was to continue like that all my life. On this occasion, I didn't realize it was to be my first encounter with one of the most legendary characters that Oxford has ever produced, Harold Acton. He received me, among all his other guests, in his rooms, with charming consideration for my gaucherie. Then, fortified with two glasses of hock cup, as I came to the end of my story, which was growing with each re-telling; I added, 'Why do you think they had picked out that particular undergraduate?'

'Because he was an avowed aesthete, my dear, and they were a horde of hearties,' my host hissed in an accent that he deliberately made more exaggerated than it was, on the occasions when he wished to infuriate his listeners. 'Oxford is irrevocably divided into two camps. Hearties and aesthetes. It is one long battle between the brutal majority and the gallant minority.'

'And which camp do you belong to?' I asked.

'I am myself,' he replied, with a smile of self-mockery. Not surprisingly, I was greatly impressed by his reply. By being himself, however unconventional his behaviour, or however punitive his wit, he was accepted by both camps as a leader in his own right, who had the courage of his intellectual convictions and was meticulously aware where he was heading, and what he intended to do with his future. The solid worth, as well as the dazzling incrustations of his subsequent published work, is the irrefutable answer to those who at the time chose to scoff at the flamboyant attitude it amused him to adopt, and at the coterie he collected round him. For my own part, I found him utterly engrossing, a character from a world I did not realize till that moment existed. It was the first of many Oxford lunch parties I was to attend, which have a unique flavour of their own. They provide a debating ground where every kind of subject, from politics to poets, with a garnishing of local personalities, can be discussed without reserve or rancour, loss of face or good manners. I am indeed grateful that in days gone by I was asked to a succession of such parties, considering that I always remained outside, and never became a member of the University.

What my host, at my baptism into Oxford Society, thought in his turn of his stray guest I cannot imagine, and have never dared to enquire. I wore my widest pair of 'Oxford bags', which I had bought in Birmingham, a blue pullover with a mauve border, knitted by my Aunt Edith, as my last Christmas present, and a mauve tie that I had bought to match, that morning, in the High, in the hope that at lunch I would look like an undergraduate-to-be rather than a sixth-form boy who had muffed his exams.

However, I must have had not too debilitating an effect on the other guests, for one of them, hearing of my admiration for everyone and everything to do with the O.U.D.S., offered to take me to the club after lunch, where my recent run of good fortune held. Here, in a group, we came on Hamlet, now dressed in tweeds, in the company of Robert Speaight, who was himself to become equally well-known as professional actor and author. At first sight he lacked the height and authority of Gyles Isham, but he more than compensated for these losses by the intensity of feeling he put into his performances, and his implacable determination to tackle such exacting parts as Richard III. This he was to play for the first time that summer, and I came upon him that day eagerly expounding his plans for the Angmering Shakespeare Festival scheduled for the long vacation.

Certainly the project had a very grand title, though in actual fact it took place in an old Y.M.C.A. hut. What matter? Here was a starting point, diving board, and to its credit the team had secured as its producer Martin Browne, whose wife, Henzie Raeburn, was a professional actress of note, and who himself acquired considerable fame later for his productions of T. S. Eliot's *Murder in the Cathedral,* and other plays by that author. During the Festival, the players would be boarded out in fishermen's cottages, if they were not lucky enough to be invited to be the guests of the Israel Zangwills in their summer home, whose teenage daughter, Peggy, would be playing Ariel in *The Tempest.* At the O.U.D.S. that afternoon, the small group of planners were in the process of discussing the casting of Ferdinand at the exact moment when I arrived on the scene.

'I see the lovers, Miranda and Ferdinand, as a couple of young innocents, don't you, Gyles?' Bobbie was saying. 'As long as they can successfully project this aura, and look right, I don't think the rest matters so much. Don't you agree?' Surely this was the most tactful glossing-over of the gulf between the amateur and the professional that I was ever to hear. And for me, there was better to come. Though I returned home to Bromsgrove with the inner fear that I had made a poor show of my papers, I was buoyed up with a verbal invitation to play Ferdinand at Angmering. I still can't understand why I was chosen, in preference to one of their fellow-members in the cast of *Hamlet*. Perhaps none of those whose physical appearance was suitable was available in August. Perhaps the emanation from the hock cup which had gone to my head enveloped my new friends, too.

Inevitably, as soon as I started to enthuse to my mother about the Angmering Shakespeare Festival, leaving out the Y.M.C.A. hut and rolling the title off my tongue like an incantation, she replied, in her protective way, 'I expect they were just being kind to you, as you were so depressed about your examination papers being above your head this time. If I were you, I'd forget all about it.'

Those examination papers that were never above my brother's head; and into the bargain, I had already had more than my share of waiting for letters that never arrived. Not surprisingly, a mood of anticlimax set in. However, for once, my mother's instinctive defence-mechanism was not required. Not only did I receive a firm confirmation in writing from Bobbie Speaight soon afterwards, giving me an assembly date, when I should be expected to be word perfect, but I also had another letter in an unknown hand. This was from Charles Plumb, telling me that he had been awarded a scholarship at Balliol, and suggesting that we met in London in August, so that we could have a day at the Wembley Exhibition, after I had played once more in the Public Schools Tournament at Queen's; there was an invitation, too, to join him and his family in the cottage that they rented every year at Braemar in the Highlands.

I had been accustomed so long to being the younger brother. It was a considerable boost for my morale to be wanted for myself, and by myself. Notwithstanding, all these future delights paled into insignificance compared with what lay over the immediate horizon. At what had once been the family theatre in Birmingham, during Easter week, Ivor Novello, the Beau Brummel of the day, and constant escort of Gladys Cooper, was billed to appear in a new play, *The Rat,* of which he was the part-author. I was so stage-struck by this time that I had the nerve to ask the front-of-the-house manager if he would conduct me to Mr Novello's dressing-room, so that I could ask him, in person, for his autograph to add to my counterpart of the book that my mother had treasured, at the same age. I already had the signatures of the principal players at the local Repertory Theatre, but this was someone from another constellation.

The star, good-tempered though he was at all times with everyone, must all the same have been rather taken aback to hear his young visitor pouring out all his own aspirations to stride the boards. Perhaps, as a diversion, to stem the flood, he announced that on Good Friday, as there was no performance, he and his Easter guests from London intended spending the day at Stratford-on-Avon. At once, undaunted, I offered my services as guide, since my own home lay close by. Whereupon my fate was decided by another visitor in the dressing-room. A man with an eye-glass and a piping voice that contrasted curiously with his dignified, grey-haired appearance, who, I was to discover, possessed the kindest heart of anyone I have ever met. Which he showed on this occasion by automatically assuming that behind my irritating precociousness there was something worth cultivating and encouraging. Such was my introduction to Eddie Marsh – later Sir Edward Marsh – a lifelong friend of Ivor Novello and his most loyal supporter in that he literally watched his shows hundreds of times, paying always for his seat, though his own literary tastes lay more in the direction of his own delightful translations of the fables of La Fontaine.

Eddie Marsh, who had been at one time Sir Winston Churchill's private secretary, was one of those people of whom it could be genuinely said that he walked with kings and never lost the common touch. Both Lady Diana Cooper and Lady Oxford were close friends of his, and I remember on one occasion discussing with the latter the virtues and faults of a mutual acquaintance. 'But he has no heart,' Margot Oxford said emphatically. 'He is very kind,' I protested in defence. 'Yes,' she agreed, 'but kindness is only the politeness of the heart. Not its beat.'

Eddie himself possessed both the politeness and the beat. And so did Ivor Novello. Because of his triumphantly consistent success with the public, and his striking good looks, his considerable musical and dramatic gifts were inclined to be comtemptuously dismissed by the critics. However, no less an artist than Kirsten Flagstad was a genuine admirer of his, and not long before her own retirement she made a point of visiting the flat in the Aldwych, where memorable parties were given after first nights – though it was surprising the guests ever reached the top floor, so small and creaking was the lift – in order to sing her host's own favourite from her repertoire, with Ivor accompanying his guest at the piano where he had composed so many of his own songs.

'When I've sung my song for you, I'll sing no more.'

As for the small-part players, who are the real testing ground of a star's character and worth, I have often thought since of something one of the members of the chorus in *King's Rhapsody* volunteered to me on a Saturday night when I was standing in the wings, waiting for the show to finish, as I had been invited to drive down to Red Roofs, the Novello country home, for the week-end.

'You know,' he said, 'you can always go and knock on the Guvnor's door and ask him anything. I mean, really anything. You don't have to go through the stage manager, as you do with other managements. He's no different with us than he is with the leads. I've been with him ever since his first show at The Lane – *Glamorous Night* – and I was with him in the war, when we were on tour with *Dancing Years* most of the time. But he'd never go to his hotel when we arrived in the train on a Sunday, in a place like Glasgow or Manchester, until he was certain that everyone in the company was fixed up with decent digs. What's more, once you are in the company, you're there for keeps. You may lose your voice, or your figure, or your looks. It doesn't matter. He'll still find some sort of job for you, even if it's only in the wardrobe room. There are not many like that.'

Six weeks later, there was one less. Neither of us, that unknown voice speaking for them all, from Vanessa Lee, Olive Gilbert and Zena Dare downwards, or I myself, were conscious that what was said that Saturday evening, filling in time before the finale and the descent of the curtain, was an unconscious epitaph. Though the next morning, when I entered the long living-room at Red Roofs, I was startled and shocked by the greyness of my host's face as he sat slumped on the sofa opposite me, in his dressing-gown, having his morning coffee and glancing through the theatre reviews in the Sunday papers. He seemed so wasted, so spent, that I could not believe I was gazing at the same person who only a few months before had given me the secret of his everlasting youth.

'You see, Godfrey, I was never bored when I was young.'

I was never bored when I was young, either. Everything was exciting to me, everything was a treat, and it has remained so to this day. Certainly I was extremely fortunate to enter the orbit of such established figures as Eddie and Ivor at a time when I was still at the most malleable stage of my development. For in their different ways they both had a strongly constructive influence which has stayed with me till this day. Eddie, by his eclectic taste, his awareness of the world and its true values, and his wide knowledge of modern art which inspired me to start my own collection, that has been such an increasing solace to me; Ivor, by his simplicity and modesty, his refusal to be defeated by the critics or mesmerized by his own matinée idol looks, and above all, by the complete lack of malice or small-mindedness in his make-up. I never heard him make a cruel or condemning remark in the long years of our friendship. He was that rare phenomenon, a really good man. Only once did he display signs of bitter anguish, when discussing what it had been like, the month he spent in prison for a trivial war-time petrol offence, which should have been dismissed with a fine, and would have been had it not been so public a figure standing in the dock, he commented: 'I have nightmares still when I am in the exercise yard, walking round and round with murderers on either side of me. I don't think I deserved that.'

He never fully recovered from that ordeal; it left a mark on him that all the make-up in the theatre could not obliterate, and increasingly aware that Sunday morning of Ivor's drained look, I had a sudden awful presentiment that this was the last time that I would see him alive, though I tried to push it aside by reminding myself that he was simply in need of a proper holiday, after a year's run, and would, in fact, be leaving for his Jamaican home in a few days. Surely, that would bring back his voice, as weary as his body, and colour to his cheeks?

At that moment, as if he could read my thoughts, the man whose Keep the Home Fires Burning, Rose of England, and We'll Gather Lilacs, have won for themselves their own kind of immortality, broke the silence to whisper hoarsely:

'Do you ever play the game, Godfrey, where you would want your funeral procession and the hearse to stop on its way to the cemetery? Mine would stop, of course, at number 111, The

Aldwych, because everything started there and I've been so happy there ever since; and at the Prince of Wales Theatre, because I had my first big success there with my own play, *The Rat* – weren't Isabel Jeans and little Dorothy Batley divine – and do you remember how you burst into my dressing-room, at your Prince of Wales Theatre in Birmingham, when we were trying out the play, and started telling me all sorts of ways of improving it, and Eddie was so amused he invited you to Stratford with us, and I wasn't sure he hadn't made an awful mistake, but he hadn't?

'And then there would be Drury Lane, where I played *Henry V,* which was killed by the outbreak of the war, but did the musicals which put the theatre back on the map after all those failures, and The Ivy, of course, because I wouldn't like to add up how many times I've lunched there, with Lilian or darling Maria Tempest at the next table, and The Palace to end up with, because that's where I'm playing now. I only want to do one more musical, Godfrey. I want to play Monmouth. I am writing the score now, and hope to get it nearly finished in Jamaica. There's never sufficient time left. You'll find that, too, one day.'

I gazed at the crumbling head, slipping sideways as though he wanted to sleep and sleep, the flesh disappearing from the bones, the death mask in its place. Where was the indestructible profile now? I was appalled by the transformation. I wanted to cry out, Ivor, don't, don't go on, but I could not not speak. I was so afraid.

'And Eddie's flat in Gray's Inn, of course,' he was ending up. 'Dear Eddie.'

Eddie's flat, filled to overflowing with pictures, so that there wasn't an inch of space even on the lavatory walls, was presided over by the most superb Mrs Mopp of all time called Mrs Algy. If Mrs Algy approved of you, then you were in, but I am afraid that she did not approve of some of the odd-looking young artists who turned up at all hours, with canvases under their arms, seeking a patron. Eddie wasn't rich except in goodwill, but he never sent anyone away without a meal, or a few pounds in their pocket for an example of their work. Moreover, he had an unerring eye for real promise. It was at Gray's Inn that I saw my first Duncan Grants and Paul Nashes, and it was to this twentieth-century patron of the arts that I owed my introduction, too, to the Georgian poets which he had edited in a series that is still on the bookshelf of my writing-room. It was a source of wonder to me that he should actually have met in the flesh such war poets as Julian Grenfell and Wilfred Owen, and should have been Rupert Brooke's most intimate friend and biographer. It was not surprising that I was eager to sit at his feet. In the Easter holidays I went to London for special tennis coaching at Queen's; I was overjoyed – since I had no money left over for such pleasures – when generously he offered to take me to the theatre, his almost nightly ritual.

I put on my new dinner jacket, for in those days almost everyone in the stalls wore evening dress, and the play we saw was *Our Betters*. Just before the lights went down, the play's author came into the stage box. I would not have known had not my host explained to me who the man with the head of a Chinese mandarin was – the man who although he was then only in his early fifties, already looked to someone of my age older than any eastern god.

Yes, but how wonderful, I thought, to have the right to take your seat in the stage box and watch the characters you have created perform, and listen to a packed house laughing at the scintillating lines you have written, and applauding with such warmth at the end of each act. Surely that must be the ultimate satisfaction in life, and I was more than ever determined that it should be mine. 'With a great sum obtained I this freedom,' St Paul remarked, and it did not occur to me that night at what a great price, in laboured concentration and long hours shut away from the sun, such really creative work is produced. It all seemed so effortless, so inevitable, as though Margaret Bannerman, whose biggest glittering success this was, was talking and behaving exactly as she would talk and behave in real life. That is the ultimate test of the playwright's art, though I did not give the author sufficient credit that evening, as I would today. Any more than it did not occur to me to imagine that our own paths would ever cross, or that I was in due course to have the good fortune to become his literary protégé, to be disciplined by him as far as my professional life was concerned, and would in consequence owe him a debt to my own dying day.

All the same, it was not surprising that I returned to King Edward's for the summer term in a restless mood. I had been vouchsafed too many glimpses of other worlds, other ways of life.

I did my best to concentrate on sitting for the Higher School Certificate again, though having passed once, there seemed little point. Automatically, I entered myself for the English prize, stimulated to discover that the Shakespearean choice this year for study was *Antony and Cleopatra*. A far cry from Ferdinand and *The Tempest*, which I was studying secretly at the same time, but, inevitably, I was intoxicated with the passionate verse, reciting reams of it aloud to myself in my bedroom at night, determined to try and persuade Mr Hammond, who decided these things, to do the play next Christmas. But where would we find a Cleopatra?

> *Let Rome in Tiber melt! and the wide arch*
> *Of the rang'd empire fall! Here is my space;*
> *Kingdoms are clay . . .*

Yes, but this was no longer my space. My fellow sixth-formers argued unceasingly about the Idylls of Theocritus, the value of the Professor Jebb translations of Sophocles, and the erotic subtleties of Catullus, while all my thoughts, as I munched my sandwiches at lunch time, kept turning to the night I had visited the Globe Theatre, to see *Our Betters,* and had been startled by the silhouette of the author in his box. From the windows of our classroom, we gazed down upon the scene below, at the same isolated elevation as from a box at the theatre. Yet here the drama was lacking. I had been blooded in a different way from the sacrificial victim in the quadrangle pool.

When in due course I won the English prize, and Dr Carey Gilson, at the presentation ceremony, warned me that if I was able to achieve any success as a writer myself, I must read and read the work of established authors, in the hope that something would re-emerge with the stamp of my own personality upon it, I spent the two-guineas voucher at Cornishes across the road, which still stands there today despite the wholesale annihilation of most of the other landmarks of my youth, in a city that must be having the most expensive facelift of all time. One of my purchases, a slim, morocco-bound volume, remains on the table beside my bed. Housman's *A Shropshire Lad.* The other choices, after much pondering, became finally the collected edition of the plays of Eugene O'Neill and *The Forsyte Saga.*

I was to meet the author of *Anna Christie,* which would scarcely cause a ripple for the outspokenness of its language today, at lunch on the Riviera. He had come to pay his respects to the owner of the Villa Mauresque the first summer that I was to stay there, five years later. It should have been a great occasion for me, the meeting of the two literary giants. But having noted that my fellow guest had the deep-blue eyes that so often those who have a feeling for the sea seem to possess, I was unfortunately mesmerized for the rest of the meal by his false teeth which wobbled alarmingly at every mouthful he took. Somehow, I hadn't associated such a virile writer with what seemed to my irreverent gaze to be a symbol of dotage.

I was equally disillusioned on the only occasion that I met Bernard Shaw, also in the South of France. This time I was staying with another celebrated author, Mary Borden, who had taken for the summer the Villa La Leopolda, high up on the hill above Villefranche, so that she could work in comparative peace on a new novel to follow up the deservedly world-wide success of *Jane Our Stranger.* The Shaws came to lunch, and you would have thought that Mrs Shaw, muffled up against the heat, was the young master's nanny from the way that she fussed over her illustrious husband. After he had had his rest in the garden shade, we all trooped down to the pool to bathe. Mr Shaw had apparently brought nothing to change into, and all the younger members of the house party were much intrigued as to what the great man would do. Whereupon, with no trace of embarrassment, he discarded his top layers of clothing and entered the water in his short Aertex pants. Emerging again, he now seemed to be wearing a dripping loin-cloth lashed against his loins, and with his impressive beard, and the halo of the setting sun behind his head, he had the look of an Elijah, so that those of us who had not been placed within earshot at lunch now waited hopefully, impatiently, for some noble and historic utterance that might, who knows, have influenced our whole future. The skin of his body, as he sat cross-legged in his loin-cloth beneath a pomegranate tree, shone like that of an untouched youth. I was just deciding what a splendid advertisement he was for a life-long vegetarian diet, when the Delphic Oracle began to utter. One subject seemed to obsess him. Over and over again he returned to it. Nothing to do with the state of the world's moral decay. Nor even the reform of the alphabet. Neither of those themes was mentioned. Instead, he was solely concerned . . with the limitations of boxing. Why, for instance, were lady protagonists never encouraged to enter the ring? What splendid sport that would make.

Increasingly today, public figures, not only politicians, who have always been considered fair game, are expected to provide sport for the television-fed masses, and it is not surprising that many of them shrink from being exposed with such greedy cruelty to the public gaze. After all, it is impossible for anyone's halo not to slip sometimes, though in a recent letter to me, Gladys Cooper, expressing her disgust at 'all that stuff that is being written about Willie' (Maugham) 'and such inferior muck, too,' adds : 'I had a long and happy and very successful time with Willie. In the theatre he was the most unconceited and generous of authors. I was very fond of him, and I loved Syrie, too, who was one of my best friends.' I cannot imagine a more searching and naked confrontation than that between an author and his leading player, during the wracking strain of rehearsals, and in similar circumstances, though of course in a very minor capacity, I was unexpectedly given the opportunity of studying John Galsworthy at close hand. In my case, too, my already abounding admiration of the author of *The Forsyte Saga* was only enhanced by each new revelation of the man himself.

I can see him now, with his high, domed forehead, wearing the bow tie and the very clean linen and the dark-grey suit, that were like a uniform, bending gravely towards me to shake hands when I was presented to him that morning in the green room at The Haymarket. I might have been Norman McKinnel, his massive leading man in this his last play, instead of an unknown applicant for a two-line part, the office boy in *Old English*.

Out of the blue there had arrived for me a telegram, which my mother had opened as I was, of course, at school. On my return that afternoon, rushing into the drawing-room for the ritual of tea, it was to find her standing in front of the fireplace, as though to give her height and authority, with the expression on her face that she had worn the day she had tried to discuss with me the facts of life.

She did not kiss me, or ask what sort of day I had had. She simply handed me the telegram, which I took in dread. Telegrams usually meant bad news. I looked down, and in bewilderment read:

'Harrison of The Haymarket wants to see you at eleven o'clock tomorrow morning. Casting the new Galsworthy play for the autumn.

Eddie.'

Harrison of The Haymarket, the doyen of managers, the friend of my grandmother, whom my mother had visited herself in vain. From her subconsciousness she recalled all the humiliations, the heartbreak. I didn't. All I felt was an overpowering sense of excitement mingled with gratitude to Eddie who had listened to my yearnings to get a start on the stage, and succeeded in putting a word into the right ear at the right moment.

My mother was speaking now. 'It will mean your missing a day from school, and just before your exams. I refuse to pretend that you are ill.' Her voice was vehement, almost accusing. With every fibre of her being, she instinctively protested against the idea of a son of hers becoming an actor. She had too many memories of the juveniles, on her own fit-up tours. A profession where half its followers were out of work all the time. A profession where you went to work at a time when other people were breaking off, going home, and painted your face, in an unreal light. Her own aspirations and what had come of them had made her more than ever convinced that it was no life for a man, no life at all.

However, in the end she did not stop me going. It was Dad, arriving half-an-hour later, who took charge, telephoned the school, explaining the position so reasonably that leave was granted, and a telegram of acknowledgment sent to my sponsor. But dinner that evening was a difficult meal, and Tartar's antics with his chocolate created a welcome diversion.

'Perhaps I won't get the part,' I said, as a peace-offering at bedtime.

As it happened, I looked right for it, which was all that mattered, in this instance. Mr Harrison had a florid complexion, and a benevolent manner. He was as courteous to me as the play's author. They combined to put me at my ease, but I had no inhibitions or shyness. I imagine it is often like that, the first time.

Hardly had I been ushered into the room by the stage-door keeper than I was blurting out about having played Mark Antony, and taking the precious cutting out of my pocket I handed it to Mr Harrison, and pointed out the appropriate paragraph. With reluctance, that he scarcely showed, surfeited by thousands of such yellowing cuttings from obscure provincial papers, he made himself read:

'High praise must be handed to G. H. Winn, who as Mark Antony dominated the stage whenever he was on it. To say that he was far ahead of his fellows is not to disparage them, but to elevate him to conspicuous heights. In the Forum scene, with its many pitfalls, he was convincing and certain, and throughout his stage presence was excellent. Altogether, his was a very creditable performance.'

'Capital . . . Capital,' said Mr Harrison, but spared Mr Galsworthy, to whom I now turned my attention. 'Would you like me to do the funeral oration over Caesar? You know, it starts, "He was the noblest Roman of them all." '

'No, I don't think there is any need for that,' broke in Mr Harrison hurriedly, for I had the impression that Mr Galsworthy, in keeping with his views in *Justice,* was prepared to submit himself to anything. 'I think he had better just walk across the stage, so that Teddie Swete can see him, don't you?' Mr Harrison added.

So I walked across the stage in my school flannel suit, and a rich, ruby port, melodious voice from the darkness of the stalls called out: 'Pretend that there is a window over there, and you are looking down on a crowded street, and a tram is just pulling into the kerb. You are watching it, and some of the people who are getting on it. "There they go," you call out. "Ting-a-ling . . ." '

I did as I was told. I pretended to myself that I was back in the sixth-form room at King Edward's, staring down into New Street. Except that there weren't any trams. It did not matter. Was I not an actor now? 'Ting-a-ling, there they go,' I shouted out with conviction, using the same voice as I had done for Mark Antony, in the leopard-skin scene, and the crowd were roaring ominously back at me.

'That will do, thank you,' said the producer, Lyall Swete, who remained a shadowy figure with the blurred outline of his flowing, silver locks, and his beaky nose. 'That will do nicely,' he repeated, and my heart missed a beat. Did that mean that he was satisfied, or simply that he was ready and anxious to pass on to his next audition? He himself belonged to a school of acting that scarcely exists today, but his performance as the Earl of Warwick in the original production of *St Joan* has never been equalled, let alone bettered.

I did not quite know how to make my exit – should I back as though in the presence of royalty? – but somehow I got myself to the green room again where Mr Harrison assured me that I had passed my test, and was engaged. My salary would be four pounds a week, and a contract would be sent me.

'I hope you will be happy with us. This theatre has a great tradition.' They both shook hands with me again. It was like being blessed in turn by a bishop and an archbishop.

As a gesture of conciliation, Eddie came to stay for a week-end that July. The plan was that he should mollify Mother, who had invited both Aunt Ethel and Aunt Violet to meet him. They were the nearest that she could get to what she considered was his intellectual level, unaware that very clever people, on the whole, enjoy most very simple pleasures and tasks. I remember the delight that Eddie showed once at being asked to act as ball boy for a tennis match in which I was taking part. Mother should have put him on to a session of weeding, standing over him while she harangued him for having shown her son these first steps along the slippery path. Instead, she punished him by allowing Violet to have a field day. The old girl never drew breath, so that Ethel had little chance to discuss her admirable work and the interesting cases she had to deal with as a woman magistrate. In his turn, Eddie was an excellent listener, pleasant to everyone, and like a child eager to please and show off his latest toy, recited for them his most recent translation from La Fontaine. This provided Violet with a splendid lead-in yet again to her friend Andrée, and her views about the whole French Cabinet, together with the tottering state of France.

I had keyed myself up for a drama which never happened, at least not in the shape or form that I had expected. A scene in which Eddie won my mother over by explaining that he had recognized my potential talents at sight, and that only in the metropolis would I have the chance to give full play to their development. Instead, his voice was heard raised in shrill protestations of quite a different nature. Very early on the Monday morning, dressing for his departure, our poor guest could not find the trousers of the suit in which he had arrived.

I was summoned. Dad was in the bathroom, Mother did not feel that it would be dignified for her in her dressing-gown to make a personal search, and kept up a running commentary of suggestions from off-stage. It was like a scene from a French farce. Eventually the mystery was solved. The housemaid, who was unfortunate in one respect, had excelled herself in zeal, having been instructed by Mother to add to her duties that of valet to the distinguished visitor from Whitehall. In the course of which, she had conceived the bright idea of putting his city trousers under the mattress to press.

One thing was certain. During all the week-ends that Eddie had spent in other people's houses, like Chatsworth and Blenheim, not forgetting Red Roofs, in the course of a wide and indefatigable social life, that was something which had never happened to him before, or would ever occur again. Somehow he managed to keep smiling to the end, but I do not doubt that it was a relief to escape back to the more familiar ministrations of Mrs Algy. Equally for myself, it was an escape to lose myself in the bohemian atmosphere of the Angmering Festival, where the bagginess or grubbiness of anyone's trousers passed unnoticed, and where there was no hope of a bath, unless either the Zangwills or the Konstams took pity on you.

Nancy Konstam, a tender, submissive girl with beautiful dark eyes and hair to match, cascading down her shoulders, was playing Miranda opposite me, while her cousin Phyllis was supporting Bobbie Speaight in *Richard III,* as Lady Anne. The cousins were a complete contrast. Phyllis remained a Londoner by the sea. She might have been on her way to the hairdressers, rather than to a rehearsal. Or to a date for lunch at The Ivy. Her largish mouth was outlined strongly with lipstick, and she held forth in a far more worldly manner than the rest of us. She made me, despite the contract for The Haymarket that I proudly displayed, feel a poor relation. In consequence I found myself much more in sympathy with Nancy, which was just as well considering the affinity between us that we were seeking to achieve in our parts.

Yet how often in life one's snap judgments of those we

encounter for a short time turn out to be contradicted by events. The odd man out at the Festival was a plump, colourless student who was a lecturer in a Welsh College at Aberystwyth. It was only too obvious that he would never make an actor in a thousand years. Whatever instructions the producer gave him, he muffed. One did not feel sorry for his clumsy efforts so much as complete indifference. In between rehearsals, he wandered off on his own, possessing none of the easy affability of other members of the company, like Robert Holmes, over whose crinkly hair the girls swooned, or Bobbie Speaight himself, who was ready to sit up all night discussing every aspect of every character in Shakespeare. So my surprise can be imagined when four years later I opened the papers one morning to discover that there had been a tremendous success the previous evening for a new playwright. *Young Woodley* by John Van Druten. Who knows, if perhaps I had taken more trouble to be pleasant, and had been less concerned with my own performance, and the approval of the more showy members of the company, I might have been playing one of the schoolboy parts in that memorable production, or been offered the understudy for Frank Lawton, who in the name part became a star overnight. Who knows.

It is cynical advice to suggest that one should always make a special effort with the shy girl, hidden away in the corner at a party, since one never knows whom she may marry, but it certainly never occurred to me for one instant to imagine that Phyllis Konstam would in the end marry Bunny Austin, and become utterly absorbed in the Moral Rearmament Movement. Today she is as absolutely dedicated to a life of unselfishness and unselfseeking as is her husband. Watching him in the days when he was struggling to reach the final at Wimbledon, a frail figure in his schoolboy shorts, beside the more confident, extrovert Perry, I always sensed that something was lacking, some final spur to victory. He possessed all the strokes but not the staying power. He has found that now, supported and sustained by his wife, for whom it could not have been easy to sacrifice all the adornments which mean so much more to a woman than to a man. To wear no make-up, to spend no money on pretty clothes, to have no luxurious, social life, such as she had enjoyed as the daughter of well-to-do parents. No, it cannot have been easy for her, not easy at all. It happens that I myself am inclined to steer away from such mass demonstrations of faith as this movement encourages, instinctively feeling instead that one's religion is a more private affair. And yet I sometimes wonder whether of all of us in that small Sussex village, as fortuitously drawn together as the characters in *The Bridge of San Luis Rey,* it was not the one person who was inclined to alienate me at the time who has in absolute terms made the most success of her life.

The three weeks that I spent that August at Angmering were so utterly satisfying that although I live only a few miles away along the coast today, I have never gone back, lest I should look in vain for something that I could no longer find in this now sophisticated week-end resort. I was the only member of the company of players actually fixed for a London production in the autumn. It gave me a status far beyond my technical accomplishments. Four pounds a week seemed a fortune to any teenager in those days, and I was careful to remain extremely vague as to the actual scope of my part. After all, an office boy might have a whole series of cheeky interpolations. Was I going to play it cockney? I was asked, and always had my answer ready. 'That would depend on the wishes of the Producer.' Ting a ling. The irrefutable point was that it was a Galsworthy play, and I hugged the comforting knowledge to myself as I joined in the theatrical discussions in the evenings, or walked across the cornfields behind the village, too engrossed to want to play tennis, although there was a club with some excellent courts.

'*Our revels now are ended. These our actors,*
As I foretold you, were all spirits, and
Are melted into air, into thin air:'

When the Festival was over, and Prospero had spoken his immemorial lines for the last time, I did not go home because I dreaded the spell being broken. Instead, I went to stay a few days with Gyles Isham and his parents, at Hastings, and then to Scotland. I could not face my mother's reproachful, anxious gaze. All her life she was to remain apprehensive lest I should be too easily satisfied with the gloss, instead of seeking more solid goals. She was conscious, too, that charm can be a curse, bringing instant gains but little permanent security. All this I only came to understand much later. At the time, I resented being kept so short of travelling money, which was the only way left in which parental control could be exercised. My stepfather had heard of a residential club called The Connaught, near Marble Arch, where many public schoolboys and ex-undergraduates billeted themselves when they came to London to take up appointments of some kind. It was reasonable enough. Thirty shillings a week, for bed and breakfast, and I would have my own small room. 'And you can send your washing home each week.' When Mother announced that, I accepted the gesture with relief as a kind of reconciliation. A guarded truce.

Auntie Violet and Auntie Bee, Audrey's mother, had also played their parts. Mother had an admiring opinion of Bee Charles's almost masculine sense in the management of her own affairs. Of course, it is always far easier to support the cause of someone outside your immediate family circle. You not only appraise the situation more objectively, but also without the burden of full responsibility. I am sure Auntie Bee, whose own husband owned a factory at Redditch, would have been horrified had a son of hers announced that he wished to become a barn-stormer, but having no son of her own, she had always taken an affectionate interest in my welfare. Indeed, during my two starved years at Hereford, she had invited me for half-term week-ends, stuffing me like a turkey. While in the immediate future, when often I was to go hungry in my passionate determination not to break my vow of independence, each time she came to London to shop she would always invite me to a meal at the Berkeley, where she stayed. Gazing back, acknowledging one's debts, how much one owes for the sum total of such meals, provided tact-fully, without any strings attached. Today when I am asked to lunch, except by close friends, I am afraid that my instinctive reaction is: now I wonder what *they* want.

I wanted my return fare to Scotland, and it was irksome to have to write home for it. Yet how important the awareness of this kind of discipline was for me in the long run, though I was not conscious of that truth in the train travelling north, sitting up all night, because there wasn't sufficient left over for a sleeper. One day I will be able to afford to travel first-class all over the world, I repeated, each time I shifted my position to ease the crick in my neck. Such grandiose prophecies did not help much, though my peevish tiredness and my stiffness vanished together the moment that I was in the friendly local train to Ballater the next morning, and the scent of the heather, and the fresh, unfakeable Highland air was in my nostrils for the first time.

Charles was on the platform to meet me, looking far less formidable in his plus-fours than in the examination room, and after a huge breakfast and my introduction to the rest of the family, and to a surfeit of Banff cakes, he carried me off for a walk over the hills. Each day, whatever the weather, we took sandwiches, and spent the whole day out of doors. He, too, was going through a crisis in his own family fortunes, though of a very different intensity from mine.

In the sitting-room of the cottage, which seemed unnaturally dark after the light on the hills, Charles' father sat, with a rug over his knees and a faint, sick emanation of decay surrounding him. Nothing was said in so many words, the dread sentence was never spoken, but it was poignantly clear that this man of God was fighting a losing battle against the coming of the angel of Death. On our long walks, we lay to rest in the heather, and Charles, whose inherent shyness had prevented him from confessing till this moment that he was something of a poet as well as a classical scholar, recited his latest sonnet: – *and that ambrosial act which lovers do* – whilst I, in my turn, not to be outdone, quoted from *The Waste Land* and *Ash Wednesday*, which had come to haunt me in the last few months, with the fresh impact of their discovery, as strongly as the insistent motif of youth's swiftly passing joys that is the recurring message of *A Shropshire Lad*.

Because I do not hope to know again
The infirm glory of the positive hour.

Charles was to have the satisfaction of being loved by many women, while his ambition to blossom into a major poet escaped him, and he settled in due course into the ranks of the Civil Service. Would he have been happier the other way round? Which of the many fleeting glories have the power to sustain us till the end? My own major ambitions at that time, to write a play and see it performed on the West End stage, and to have my entry accepted for Wimbledon, were never realized, either, though I came very close to the latter positive hour. No matter, I am content, even if no longer armoured by my youth, which, in contrast, seemed all the more invincible when returning in the evening to the quiet cottage, our chatter died away, confronted with this implacable manifestation of yet another appointment in Samarra. No matter how holy you were, or how much you prayed. It was the first time in my life that I had been close to the coming of death, and I marvelled at the manner in which Charles's mother went about her duties with such stoical calm. Until I found myself filled with the guilty longing that, in return for all their kindness to me, their acceptance of my presence in their midst, at such a moment, I could substitute my own father for the figure with the yellowing skin and the gaunt head staring past us into eternity. At the same time it struck me, too, with a sense of even greater guilt, that I had scarcely thought of my own father for a long time and that he no longer meant anything to me. Alive or dead.

So much so, so irrevocably deep had the chasm become between my childhood at Barnt Green and my place now as a member of the Bromsgrove household – four miles away – that on my first evening in the metropolis, when after unpacking my trunk at the club I wandered into the park, overwhelmed suddenly by a spasm of homesickness, and desperate for the reassurance that at least I knew one family in London, just one person I could ring up and say, 'Hello, I'll be seeing you,' it never occurred to me for an instant to go in search of my father, now living in Twickenham, having married the nurse who had brought him through a particularly brutal attack of his recurring 'sickness'.

Instead, I drifted from group to group, listening idly to the Sunday speakers, braying out their panacea for paradise on earth, who had been there the Sunday before and would be there again the Sunday after. In the end, my feet grew tired, so I went and rested on a seat by myself, innocently eager that someone would sit down beside me and exchange a few friendly words. It was then that I was reminded of those other Sunday afternoons, when I had changed hopefully into clean flannels and taken my tennis racquet and sat outside the pavilion at the Edgbaston Club, but no one had given me a word of encouragement, either. And because, from quite early in my development as a human being, I found that it helps to surmount the personal crisis of the moment by comparing it with other incidents of the past that seemed so utterly catastrophic at the time, but somehow one survived, I made myself now relive every detail of my arrival as a new boy at

Lynfield; I remembered how, like a whimpering puppy, I had crept for warmth into the bed of the dormitory captain.

Things were better than that. Much better, I told myself reassuringly. At least, I had learnt not to whine. All the same, I was back at the beginning again.

Part Two
The Growing Years

Above House where I was born – Rosemary, Woodbourne Road, Edgbaston, Birmingham. *Photo: The Birmingham Planet.* *Left* Tudor House, Broadway, Worcestershire, the country home of my American grandmother. *Below* King Edward School, when it was in New Street, Birmingham

My mother's rose garden at Barnt Green

Below
The Oakalls, Bromsgrove, Worcestershire

THE CURTAIN at The Haymarket was due to rise at eight-thirty. All the cast had been in their dressing-rooms for hours before. There was the lovely girl of seventeen, nearest to me in age, with the Titian hair parted in the middle and the look of a Rossetti heroine, Joan Maude, the bearer of a proud name in the theatre. Then the older woman, buffeted by many years of character parts, usually cross-patches, Louise Hampton, who would stand in the darkest corner of the wings, during rehearsals, whispering her lines over and over again to herself. And Norman McKinnel, the leading player, whose massive monolithic appearance was not so different at a first glance from the phalanx of extras, with whom for the next few months I was to share each evening a glorified garret at the very top of the back-stage labyrinth.

For many of these extras had been featured players themselves in the past, though others – it was true – had never reached further than being part of the crowd. The three pounds a week now offered them would just about keep the bread-line at bay. As we waited, I for the first time, for the familiar echoing cry of the call boy up the stairs, 'Half-an-hour and beginners please,' I sat squeezed in next to the only other youthful person in the room, who was playing the junior office clerk in the play. Together we watched the rest, old enough to be our fathers and grandfathers, open flat cigarette boxes containing precious stubs of hoarded sticks of greasepaint, which they carefully started to dab on their chalky, parchment cheeks. Our comrades were there because a group of shareholders were needed for the company meeting that was to be addressed by 'Old English'. No one in the audience would see their blurred features, only their bulk, filling out for that scene one side of the stage. No matter. The tradition rites, almost like dressing for dinner in the jungle, must be preserved. Some of them had brought in a bottle of Bass to fortify themselves and drink success to the run of the piece, which they fervently hoped would see them over Christmas. Others kept up their spirits by boasting of former first nights in which they had more largely participated – the glories of yesteryear. None of them would have dreamt of whistling, to prove how much at ease they were, since that would have meant instantaneous bad luck for all concerned with the evening's performance.

Cecil Trouncer, the clerk, with not many more lines to speak than myself, though in due course he was to return to The Haymarket, for an all-star revival of *The Doctor's Dilemma,* and be allowed a very different dressing-room, had helped me at the final rehearsal to put on a straightforward number five and number nine make-up. Of course I pretended I knew, but I had only the sketchiest idea of how to do this. At Angmering, our lighting had been on the primitive side, while for our theatricals at school a professional of sorts had taken charge of the principals. Now I was a professional myself. Almost. Later, as we stood in the wings, the clerk and the office boy, waiting, long in advance, for our cue at the end of the first act, we were grateful for the appreciative chuckles from the audience we could not see. I thought of my mother and my stepfather in their seats in the dress circle, which I had managed to secure for them, and of Eddie Marsh, my benefactor, in his usual place in the fifth row of the stalls, who had promised to join us for a celebration family supper party afterwards.

Now. 'Good Luck,' whispered Cecil, pushing me ahead of him, and we were through the door, on to the stage, and as I started to cross to the far window, the sudden flash of the footlights almost blinded me, making me feel dizzy, though not with nerves – for you do not feel nerves at the beginning, only later. Nevertheless, I was trembling as I counted ten, which I had been told to do by the producer, before shouting out the curtain line: 'There they go. Ting-a-ling.'

I was blooded. On the West End stage I had spoken my first lines. I was different from the grizzled warriors, with whom I had shared that attic dressing-room. Little did I realize how short-lived the difference would be, and that the next evening I would arrive at the theatre to learn, with rebellious consternation, that my only line had been cut out, considered at the morning-after-post-mortem to have held up the first-act curtain too long. So my only reason for appearing at all was to help on 'Old English' with his overcoat. Scarcely an opportunity for a dramatic portrayal.

I should have had a premonition at supper, for that turned into an incongruous anticlimax, too. For some reason, perhaps because as usual he wanted to make a generous gesture, Dad had chosen the Piccadilly Hotel instead of some quiet grill room. I am sure Eddie had never found himself in such a setting before, and the cacophonous din from the band completely drowned his protesting, piping voice. Mother had doubts about the pulling power of the play, which she made no effort to disguise, while Dad, hemmed in by the stiff shirt for his dinner jacket, by the tables crowding in on him, and the conglomerous heat, was overcome by a series of asthmatic spasms. Desperately I sought to keep the evening, my evening, afloat. When midnight came, I pleaded that we should stay up for the first editions of the morning papers, and the play's notices, for I had read in one of Stephen McKenna's novels that that was what the actors did after a first night. However, my exuberant suggestion filled the senior members of the party with such mutual dismay, that they vied with each other as to who could drop me off quickest, by taxi, at my hostel.

The next day my family, having done their duty, returned to Worcestershire, and it was back to The Prompt Corner for me. This was a little snuggery in Rupert Street, much patronized by theatrical folk because you could get a capacious meal there for one and sixpence. In my perpetual search for ways to eke out my four pounds salary to last the week, I also discovered an excellent eating place off Leicester Square. There were windfalls, too. Mrs Byam Shaw, the widow of the artist, who had been such a figure of the Broadway scene in my grandmother's heyday, and who had a son, Glen, of the same age as myself, also just beginning to serve his apprenticeship in the Theatre, was extremely kind and fed us both with scrumptious high teas at her home in Addison Road. This meant I could cut out supper altogether on those nights. An enormous help to my budget.

I didn't aspire yet to the *Criterion,* in the heart of Theatreland, where the cheapest set meal, starting with a grapefruit, and a cherry on top, was three and sixpence, till some time later, when I used to sup there with a fellow player, who was understudying at Wyndham's, next door to the New, where I was playing the juvenile lead, such as it was, in *Prince Fazil,* with Henry Ainley and Madge Titheradge in the main parts. Eric and I had to be very careful not to stay too late, talking of our ambitions, or we would miss the last bus home. And neither of us could afford a taxi.

For several years, my companion with the ruddy cheeks and very blue eyes, had been playing leads, heavy, light, character, straight, in summer stock in Halifax, where the mill-girls acclaimed him, and he was a local hero for the season. But in between, no matter how hard he tried, he could not get a break of any kind in the West End. Yet in his heart he was convinced that he was a better actor than many of those whose names were in large letters on the hoardings, and I often find myself scribbling the name of 'Eric Portman' on the pad beside me when I open yet another letter from some young man or woman pleading for a chance to prove what they can do. How does one explain that it is all a question of hanging on, of timing, of being absolutely prepared when the opportunity arrives? For if you possess the talent, that opportunity always does come in the end. I am completely convinced of it.

At the unpretentious eating house off Leicester Square, where so many hungry aspirants foregathered at lunch time, hoping to hear news of a production that was being cast, there was one frequent visitor with the air of an eagle, despite the fact that his grey flannel trousers were poorly pressed and his hair was already receding, making him appear older than his years. Already John Gielgud was inclined to wear rather a serious air, though he had a gentle smile and possessed the Terry charm, but I recall him on one occasion being very angry and bitter because of the mauling he had received from the critics after some special performances of *Romeo and Juliet* in which he had played opposite Gwen Ffrangcon Davies. It was his first showy chance and it looked as though it had passed him by, for he was even accused of not being able to walk across the stage, and the outstanding beauty of his voice, for speaking verse, was but grudgingly acknowledged.

It all came back to me, the picking of the cheapest and most filling dish upon the menu, the endless chatter of theatrical shop, which I so eagerly devoured, when I read Ivor Newton's* absorbing account of his life as an accompanist in the world of music, and his description of the day that he invited Sir John

* *At the Piano* (Hamish Hamilton).

Gielgud to meet Lotte Lehmann at lunch in his London home.

Naturally, there was a great deal of talk of the opera and the theatre, and at the end of the meal, the man who has long since been acknowledged as being without a peer in his own particular brand of costume rôle said quietly, 'If only I were young enough to play Romeo again, I know now how it should be done.'

'How well I know the feeling,' replied the singer, whose Marschallin in *Rosenkavalier* has never been surpassed. 'I feel now how to act the Marschallin – if only I were young enough to do it.'

The whirligig of time brings many such regretful longings, and many such demonstrations, too, of the innate modesty of the truly big artist; equally it brings many unconscious revenges. Not long ago I was talking to Sophia Loren concerning her early struggles for recognition, when she described to me how as a girl in her teens she managed to secure an interview with the producer casting a new film, who looked her up and down before dismissing her contemptuously with the barbaric comment, 'You have the neck of a Neapolitan giraffe.'

I was fortunate myself – too fortunate, perhaps, for it all seemed too easy in the beginning – that I did not yet have to endure such humiliations : to be herded like cattle into an outer office or left to hang about in a passage outside an agent's room, waiting for the summons to the inner sanctum that so seldom came. The very week that *Old English* closed early in the New Year (as usual, my mother's instinct had been right) I was invited to become a member of the company of Lewis Casson and Sybil Thorndike, who were transferring *St Joan* to the Regent Theatre, opposite King's Cross, and needed someone of my age and height to take over the brief part of the court page. This time, instead of calling out, or rather not calling out, 'Ting-a-ling,' I stamped my beribboned stick of office upon the ground, crying for silence. I wore tights, and a royal blue velvet jerkin, with a diadem across my forehead, from which was suspended a strutting plume. Altogether, as I pranced about like a circus pony, I secretly thought the effect was rather fetching. Notwithstanding, the far better part of the other page, who had the chance of showing real acting ability, in the kingfisher, wind-changing scene, was played by an ex-Italia Conti pupil whom I envied passionately, except that he was so pleasant and friendly I could not hate him for long. His name was Jack Hawkins.

Once again I received four pounds a week, and once again I shared a huge barn of a dressing-room right under the eaves of the theatre with a strange conglomeration of extras, who played noblemen in the court scene, and monks in the trial scene, while placating their frustrated hopes of fame by understudying the principals. These principals included Robert Horton as glowering Dunois, Raymond Massey who doubled the parts of La Hire and d'Estivet, O.B. Clarence who had the final terrible judgment to deliver, and spoke it with such delicate, gentle clarity that I have been conscious ever since that it is the quiet ones of the earth who are those to fear, not the blusterers, not the bullies. Then there were Lyall Swete, who had produced *Old English* in between playing the Earl of Warwick, and Bruce Winston with a minor rôle but a major influence backstage, because it was his personal task to superintend the weekly bleaching of Joan's locks, herself with no patience for such frippery, necessary though it might be to enhance the Maid's ethereal air. And finally there was Ernest Thesiger, an unforgettable Dauphin, who filled in the waits between his scenes doing the most exquisite *petit-point*. Where all the other actors were content to employ conventional sticks of make-up for their disguises, he chose to paint his face with liquid washes, like a water colour, now dipping his brush into this mysterious bottle, now into that. Sometimes he allowed me to watch the transformation, a real work of art, while he kept up a running commentary about the other members of the cast. He repeated, for example, the *mot* of Mrs Patrick Campbell concerning our leading lady, when she first appeared as a bright new comet bang in the centre of the other's fading sky.

'Dear Sybil, she is so clever. She is the only woman I know who has teeth and looks as though she hasn't.'

Ernest Thesiger, too, had a formidable wit, and woe betide anyone who tried to cross verbal swords with him. He also enjoyed what can be a dangerous pleasure, putting people right. On one occasion he was playing opposite Dame Marie Tempest, and at rehearsals, when she stumbled over a line, he instinctively corrected her, presenting her with the right reading and the right pronunciation of a certain word. All she did in return was to glare at him for his solicitude, and for the next few days there was an extremely frosty atmosphere in their scenes together. Then suddenly, one afternoon, the delicious artist, with a flair for high comedy that has never been surpassed, broke away from a stage embrace to dissolve into laughter, her whole face crinkling up in the way that her audiences adored.

Testily, her husband, Graham Browne, rebuked her from the stalls, where as producer he was ensconced in the nebulous darkness. 'Mary, Mary, we have less than a week before we open, and you do not even know your lines. Please let us rehearse seriously.'

'I am sorry, Willie dear,' came back Dame Marie's answer, floating across the footlights, 'but you have no idea how funny his face is close to.'

Honours easy. From that moment, they became firm friends, both respecting each other's talents. After I had come off stage, in the court scene, I would linger in the wings night after night, never tiring of watching the subtle touches the Dauphin would bring to his emergence before our eyes, from a petulant, effeminate creature into a royal prince, with a renewed sense of his own destiny, under the blazoning zeal of the Maid of Orleans; so uncouth a figure herself, in that setting, surrounded by all the foppish courtiers, and yet inspired by such compelling sincerity that from the side of the stage, however many times I watched, I longed to cheer her on, to shout out 'Good for you'. I have seen many other Joans since, but none of them could hold a candle to that original conception by the actress whom Shaw had in mind when he wrote the part.

With the curtain coming down on the court scene, I was not finished for the night. I was made to earn my four pounds a week this time, and certainly there was no harm in that. On the contrary, the more that was demanded of me, the better I responded. It is still so. Out of my finery I changed into the rough habit of a monk, and mingled with the louring crowd in the background of the Trial scene, the play's climax. I suppose it was something like forty minutes that I stood there, unmoving, my head covered by my cowl. I have often thought of all those forty minutes strung together, and what use I could make of them now. Especially did they come back into my mind when, not long before he died, I lunched with Bernhard Berenson in his treasure house of pictures in Florence; of all the exchanges in conversation that day with B.B. what stays most vividly in my mind was when this most distinguished of art critics and connoisseurs remarked sadly to me, 'When I go for my drive in the afternoon, I long to stop the car beside the Ponte Vecchio, and put out my hand to each of the passers-by, and say, "Please could you not spare me just an hour of your life?" '

At sixteen, you do not count the passing minutes, but all the same, that forty often seemed more like four hours. Though, on the other hand, sometimes much less, when the moving simplicity of Brother Martin's last plea, so superbly delivered by Laurence Anderson, and the agony of the victim's final cry of self-justification beating against the weary, inexorable logic of the Grand Inquisitor, took possession of my senses. All the same, I was invariably thankful when the flames surrounding the stake began ominously once again to flicker across the backcloth, and I knew that my own release was imminent. One night, dashing out of the stage door to cross the road to catch the Underground from King's Cross, I stopped dead in my tracks, astonished to find the whole sky was mirroring the stage-lighting effect on the painted scene that so short a while ago I had left behind me. As though by some ingenious arrangement of reflecting mirrors, and on a much more stupendous Valkyrian scale. It was an eerie sensation. Was I back on the stage? Was this real life? Where was I?

Swiftly I was to realize exactly where I was. In the company of the hundreds of other spectators, drawn by the portents in the sky from far and near, I was gazing at the gutting of Madame Tussauds by fire. And what excitement, what pleasure this bonfire to eclipse all bonfires provided, since everyone's conscience was aware that no human sacrifices, such as Joan of Arc's, were pinned to a stake within those crumbling walls which, silhouetted against a molten sky, had exchanged their prosaic shape to assume the crenellated outline of some vast, medieval fortress.

My own overriding reaction was that it was a pity this unexpected example of *panem et circenses* was not taking place on a Sunday, for it was the empty week-ends in London that I had begun increasingly to dread. To be in the centre of the metropolis entirely on one's own, on the sabbath, with few contacts and no money to spare, is the most dismal of prospects. This was before the era of transistor sets and free television in the public rooms of all large establishments. I would come down late from my cubicle to have my minimum set-breakfast of tea and toast, hungrily missing the eggs and bacon at home, in the heated silver dishes on the sideboard; then looking round the almost empty dining-room of the Connaught Club, I would wonder wistfully where all the week-day occupants were spending the day. During the whole time that I was billeted in the Club, I cannot recall a single helpful overture from anyone. It was the most impersonal lodging-house in which I have ever found myself, and whenever today I drive past its doors, I cannot help wondering whether, now that it has changed its name to the grandiloquent one of the Victory Club, the servicemen who are transient guests there suffer from a similar sense of isolation. I sincerely hope it is not so.

To go home to Worcestershire for twenty-four hours was too extravagant a pleasure, but sometimes if I could manage the lesser fare I would catch the last train down to Oxford on a Saturday night, and stay with Gyles Isham. He was now sharing digs with Paddy Monkhouse, son of Allan Monkhouse, whose play The *Conquering Hero*, about the First World War, with its underlying pacifist message, had created the kind of intellectual stir which is today provided in a more exaggerated, violent way by John Osborne's work. Paddy himself, prosaic in appearance and manner, had little interest in the Theatre, but he received me into his circle with genuine north country tolerance, and today he has followed in his father's footsteps to become an outstanding figure on the editorial side of *The Manchester Guardian*.

At the time, I certainly had no inkling that he was to attain such a coveted position in our future mutual calling. He seemed so pragmatic in his approach to all the things that set my own imagination on fire. It was different when one week-end, at an Oxford party, across the room I caught a glimpse of a stocky young man, with pursed lips, staring with the eyes of a gremlin at the uninhibited, noisy scene. All the other faces were so vulnerable, so untouched, his alone seemed already to be cast in a different mould, his body, in some strange way, to be isolated, in space. My curiosity aroused, I asked his name. Evelyn Waugh, I was told. It meant nothing to me. We did not speak. I never met him, but in the years ahead, when I read with immense admiration his novels, such as *Brideshead Revisited*, I was confronted, as though it were a physical emanation, with his presence again in the observation corner of that crowded room.

Some time about then, during another of my many Oxford week-ends, this time to see the OUDS summer play, or rather two plays by Rostand, performed in the gardens of Merton College, there was a plump pigeon of an undergraduate playing the part of a waiter in one of the productions, with a napkin over his arm. I am sure it was no larger a part than my own in *St Joan,* and yet there was something about him that made me stir in my seat. So that I was eager to meet him at the party for the cast afterwards. He spoke with a lilting Welsh accent, and he told me that night that his first play had been accepted for production by J. B. Fagan, who at that time was running the Oxford Playhouse.

So my hunch had been right, Entirely right. For this was Emlyn Williams, who apart altogether from his overflowing gifts as a writer, and an actor, and equally as a *raconteur,* has something even more important in his make-up, an immense capacity both for living and feeling. When his fellow-countryman, Richard Burton, fell consumingly in love off the film set, still uxoriously under the spell of his Cleopatra, Emlyn made a special journey to Rome to plead with him, and to try, for Sybil Burton's sake, to save the marriage. In vain. After that for a time Elizabeth Taylor must have regarded this Welshman more as a foe than as a family friend, yet when the moment arrived for Burton to essay Hamlet on Broadway, it was to Williams that she instinctively turned, pleading that he should come and sit with her husband on the long, nerve-ridden afternoon of waiting, before the curtain rose on the first night. Tactfully, she left them together, in yet another of those over-luxurious hotel suites. The boy from the Welsh hills, who had started with nothing but a passionate desire for learning, calmed and set at peace the spirit of the youth who had journeyed an equally long way from the Welsh valleys. Thus fortified, Richard Burton went on to the stage that evening to score a considerable success. There are certain bonds that are far stronger than those of consanguinity, or any kind of emotional tie. These remain eternal.

I once asked Emlyn Williams, Noël Coward, Terence Rattigan and Somerset Maugham the same question. Where, if they had to live in America, would they consider the climate most conducive to the production of first-class work. Unhesitatingly, they all gave me the same answer, San Francisco. I understood at once their choice. For you can lose your identity more easily in San Francisco than in any other American city comparable in size, and that is what an artist needs to do. However, if I was ever forced to live out of England, which I try never to contemplate, I would myself choose either Marrakesh, that oasis of such enchantment in the desert, or Rome. I have had a love affair with Rome, built like San Francisco on seven hills, ever since I was privileged in my youth to be one of the vast concourse who watched Pope Pius XI carried towards the Basilica of St Peter, on a vociferous wave of acclamation, at the ceremony of the Beatification of the English Martyrs. Returning again last spring, summoned this time to a private audience with Pope Paul VI, the sense of belonging – although I am not a Roman Catholic – and of having climbed the Spanish Steps in another century, in a previous incarnation, was stronger than ever. Has not almost everyone experienced the reassurance of such a waking dream, somewhere?

On my return from Rome and impressed most of all by the overriding simplicity of the human being with such temporal power in his hands, I was asked the same question by many friends. Supposing His Holiness had been stripped of his gold and scarlet vestments, supposing the setting had been far removed from the impressive apartments of the Vatican, supposing, for instance, we had met, two casual travellers in a railway carriage, would I have still been so overwhelmingly aware that I was in the presence of someone whose goodness and nobility were in excelsis? It is difficult to be absolutely sure, but I would aver that in more cases than not, those who have been chosen for a special destiny, even if their pilgrimage has scarcely begun, do seem to wear upon their brow a kind of invisible stigmata that you nevertheless sense is there.

When Eleanora Duse was still a child, she travelled with her parents, who like my mother were members of a third-rate stock company. One winter day in a hill town, the leading lady was taken ill, and at a few hours notice this child of fourteen was called upon to play Juliet. She was quite calm, quite unmoved by her fortune, till an hour before the performance she came to her mother and said, 'I cannot play Juliet tonight unless I have white roses in my hair.' Her mother was only too aware that there was snow in the streets and she had not a lira to spare in her purse. Her only possession, for a bargaining exchange at the pawnbroker's, was a treasured piece of lace. Silently she went on her search. And thus it was that her daughter, who was to become the most internationally famous actress that Italy has ever possessed, made her début as Juliet with real instead of artificial roses binding her hair.

This was the beginning of the road. As Anna Pavlova's body lay waiting for her soul's release, suddenly – moved by an invisible power, and in delicate, precise movements – the arms of this now legendary dancer lifted themselves from the coverlet to make the last fluttering movements of The Dying Swan. That was the end of the journey.

I first met Sybil Thorndike, and came under the benevolent influence of the Cassons, when she herself had reached the middle stretch of her own journey. I was not so much in awe of her, for she was on christian-name terms with the whole company, extras included, as a bashful acolyte. Automatically, I would press myself against the wall of the passage-way each time we passed on the stairs leading to the dressing-rooms. On Saturday nights, however, instead of a smile and a wave of her hand, the leading lady in her mail armour would stop and speak to me. It became a ritual.

'Godfrey, are you all right for your Sunday dinner?' she would ask. 'If not, come and have it with us.'

I could have embraced the Dauphin's saviour in gratitude. But my pride only allowed me to accept one invitation in three. Then we would bowl down the High Wycombe road in their old Morris Cowley, with Lewis at the wheel, to visit their daughters at school and take them out to lunch, too. I was not in a position to return the Cassons' hospitality until many years later, or to discharge my debt completely, ever. Still, not long ago, we had a most happy reunion in my London home, with the other pageboy from St Joan at the lunch party, too. 'You were two, dear, well-behaved boys,' Sybil gave us her blessing. Whereupon Jack and I glowed, more pleased by this accolade than with anything that had happened to us in the years between. 'And what a lot of fair hair you had in those days, Godfrey,' she added.

Her own hair is now silver white, rising from her forehead

like a tiara. Seated in one of the tall chairs in my living room, she made its covering seem like cloth of gold – herself a queen, magnificent, indestructible. So that it came to me that, were I asked to compile a list of the ten most striking-looking women I have ever encountered, I would certainly include Sybil Thorndike as she looks today, since the beauty of her character and the beauty of her mind shine in her face. On an impulse I asked her how it was that, in her eighties, she still succeeded in projecting such an image of youthful vigour and vitality. Whereupon she replied briskly, 'I think it is because I am still determined to learn something fresh every day of my life.'

And she does. Equally, she was always eager, and indeed insistent, that those around her should do likewise. Rightly she believed that we all required an absolute knowledge of our particular craft, and as the end of the run of *St Joan* approached, she took the trouble to use her personal influence for me to go up to Liverpool to join the company at The Playhouse. Here a Scotsman, William Armstrong, once upon a time himself an actor with Mrs Patrick Campbell, had found his real *métier* in running a repertory company. Robert Donat, Michael Redgrave, Diana Wynyard all passed in turn through his hands; at that moment the juvenile lead, Hugh Williams, was leaving and a replacement was needed. When the theatre's producer met this Casson protégé, he took one look at me on the station platform and exclaimed: 'Good God. Do you think you could wear a hat at rehearsals?'

I was naturally rather taken aback by this greeting, till it was explained to me that my predecessor, several years my senior, and, in fact, about to be married, was far more groomed and sophisticated in his appearance than I was. Would a trilby hat perhaps provide a semblance of maturity? Fortunately, in the first part I had to play, I did wear a headgear of sorts, the cap of a newly-commissioned second lieutenant in the army. This was J. M. Barrie's *The New Word,* and the only line I now recall from it was spoken not by me or by my father, that splendid character actor, Herbert Lomas, but by my sister, Primrose Morgan: 'Maréchal of France, now that's the best of all.'

Best of all. What I remember about those apprentice months in Liverpool was the generosity of the two elderly sisters who took me into their house off Rodney Street, and cared for me and washed my shirts and socks and gave me a hot supper when I got back from the theatre, as well as a substantial breakfast before I left for reheasals, and all for thirty shillings a week. How many men and women of my age must look gratefully back to some unknown landlady, long since dead, who in their student days, far from home, in some strange town, took them in, asked no questions, but made them feel not just another paying lodger, but wanted and secure. I have been back to Liverpool more times than I can count. After Edinburgh, it is my favourite among our larger cities. Strangely, I have more of a welcoming sense of coming home there than in my native Birmingham. However tight my programme for any visit may be, I always find a moment to stand in front of *The Playhouse*; I gaze at the frames of pictures of the current company, wonder if the younger members still walk back to their digs at night, to save the bus fares, staring down at the dark outline of the Roman Catholic cathedral; I remember how consumed I was by recurring moods of panic that life was rushing past and I must hurry or I would get nowhere. Nowhere at all.

Not that Merseyside in any way gives you an impression of existing in a vacuum. On the contrary. It is the most rumbustious and gregarious city in Britain. I love the feeling of the sea just over the horizon, the ever-changing bustling activity of the river down by the Liver Building, while higher up, in the equally lively shopping streets, there is the sharp reminder – of which any visitor cannot help being aware – that here, far more than in the run of inland towns, you have a mixture of many races, many creeds, such as you will find in other international ports like San Francisco. For me the refreshing atmosphere of tolerant acceptance was summed up in an encounter I had, on one of my return visits, with a coloured woman teacher from North Carolina, who was spending a year on the exchange system, coping with eight-year-olds in a multi-racial school down by the docks. She had an illuminating story to tell me of her birthday, just past. In the afternoon, after her work for the day was finished, feeling rather homesick she made her way back to her lodgings. To her astonishment and delight, she discovered that a party had been surreptitiously organized in her honour by her landlady. It seemed that the whole street had come to tea, and there on the centre of the table in her landlady's own sitting-room was an impressive iced birthday cake, home-baked. Whereupon the alien from another shore was invited to light the candles while her temporary neighbours stood round, chanting 'Happy Birthday to you.'

In London, I doubt if in similar circumstances so imaginative a gesture would have been made; but it was typical of the goodwill that was shown to me, too, in a multitude of ways during the months that I spent as the most junior member of The Playhouse company, where most of the plum parts that year fell into the hands of an actor whose talent for light comedy was already manifesting itself. More than a quarter of a century later, I found myself, much to my astonishment, pinioned upon the stage of the Television Centre at Shepherd's Bush, being told by Eamonn Andrews, whose professional skill is concealed beneath the charm of his Irish accent, that This was about to be my Life; the first person from the parade of my past to greet me, and put me at my ease, was Cecil Parker, who had led the Company that year at Liverpool – and whose picture I am looking at at this moment, on my desk, in a composite group of us taken on an outing to Port Sunlight. Cecil, I see, is wearing a hat and I am not. It should have been the other way round.

Months of secret research and tapping of possible sources of information laboriously went to the planning of each of the 'This Is Your Life' programmes. Many of the suggested names had to be discarded *en route,* because, despite all precautions, the victim became suspicious as to what was in the wind. Like other members of the public, I had occasionally wondered whether the whole structure wasn't a fake. Till it happened to me. Although elaborate plans had been laid weeks in advance to persuade me to accept an invitation for an editorial dinner in London that evening (for like all thorough detectives, the BBC had discovered that it is my habit to spend Mondays working peacefully in the country), they were taking no chances of a last-minute hiatus. Indeed, they took double care to ensure my presence in the metropolis by casually ringing me up on the Friday before, to invite me to record at Broadcasting House itself, at six o'clock that same Monday evening, a television plug for a very popular radio programme which I annually compère for a week. The fact that I had been chosen out of all those whose names are equally connected with the programme, was too much for the natural vanity of a performer. I swallowed the bait in one gulp. If there had been any mention of Shepherd's Bush on a Monday night, I might have been suspicious. As it was, I blithely turned up in Portland Place to do my piece, and hardly had I been briefed by my director in the BBC's own TV Studios, and was going through, as I thought, my first rehearsal, when Eamonn Andrews walked through the curtains like a cat burglar – except that physically he would be rather too big for such a rôle. Whereupon the open-mouthed bewilderment on my face was instantly captured by the cameras.

After that I was the fish on the hook, and there was an anti-climatic hour of waiting before we were due to continue the pro-gramme, whose prologue was now in the can, at Shepherd's Bush. Eamonn suggested that we should go into hiding in the flat where he lived at that time in Lancaster Gate. Here his delightful and attractive wife, Grainne, fed me with sandwiches to soothe my nerves, which centred chiefly round the knowledge that my brother, because of his austere legal position, viewed with in-stinctive horror the idea of any personal publicity. As soon as Eamonn was able to assure me that Rodger, at his own request, had been entirely left out of the programme, and for that evening I was the only Winn in our family, I felt I could face anything else.

Afterwards, I discovered that as soon as Rodger had been warned by the BBC what was in store for his younger brother (but he had the perfect alibi against appearing himself, as one of Her Majesty's judges) he decided he could go so far as to hire a Television set, until that time an entirely unknown quantity in his life, to allow himself and my sister-in-law Joyce to look in, having steeled themselves for the worst. As soon as the pro-gramme was finished he said to Joyce – no doubt greatly relieved to know that the BBC had kept their promise, and that no skeletons in the family cupboard had been rattled and produced upon the screen, 'I suggest we switch over now to the other channel. Before the set goes back. I may as well have a look at those Commercials that I've heard so much about.'

The switch-over took place. Now my brother was really interested. Leaning forward in his armchair beside the fire, with his beloved budgerigar tweeting away in its cage beside him, he became utterly absorbed in the enticements offered. 'Joyce, do we use that cleaner for the kitchen sink? What about that toothpaste? Quick, get a pad.' The next morning, my sister-in-law was dispatched to Harrods for an extra spate of household shopping. The next evening my learned brother, returning from a trying day in his own world, and finding the Television set was still there, most reasonably decided that another swift glance at whatever was on either channel might release his tensions before he sat down to dinner. Once again the alchemy worked, and my sister-in-law was on her way with yet another shopping list the next morning.

Today, that Television set has taken up permanent residence, and though the commercials have long since lost their magic, there is no doubt that the set's owner has become a far more enthusiastic viewer than his younger brother; perhaps because, unlike myself, he does not have to try to cope with the medium, and die a thousand deaths each time before the camera. Anyway, I have heard him explaining to other visitors to his home that as my sister-in-law has sometimes to rest a troublesome leg, a Television set has proved – for her, of course – a solace; indeed, a godsend.

I wish that William Armstrong had lived long enough to have been able to watch two of his company meet, so many years later, on the screen, in a programme that incidentally would have provided the perfect setting for his own warm personality. William was that rarest of creatures, someone without an ounce of malice or vanity in his own make-up, and without an enemy in the world. One evening he came to my dressing-room to show me a telegram he had received from Lewis Casson. It asked if he would be willing to release the newcomer to his company to play Marchbanks in Shaw's *Candida*. The play that the management had put on after *St Joan* was doing poor business, and they were considering a revival with Sybil as Candida, a tailor-made part for her. But to take such a chance on me! I was filled with wonder and gratitude. 'You are a very lucky boy,' William announced in his mournful, Scottish voice but without a hint of irritation on account of having to recast his next production. His only thought at the moment was for my unexpected break. When eventually the project was dropped, and another telegram came, William – seeing my utter dejection, since for a whole enchanted week I had become the poet reciting his dreams as I walked back to my lodgings each evening – characteristically invited me out to supper at The Adelphi after the show, as he sensed that such a treat would restore the balance of my usual optimism.

From my seemingly static salary of four pounds, I could not contemplate entering the swing doors of that most imposing among grand hotels in the provinces, except occasionally for a cup of tea in the outer lounge. On one occasion I enjoyed a cup with the most faithful supporter of The Playhouse Company – a young man in his twenties, who reminded me a little of Charles Laughton in his physical appearance. He was the most all-embracing stage-door johnny that I have ever encountered. Not content with coming to every production on its first night, and often paying several repeat visits, he would on other evenings hang about the company's dressing-rooms, blissfully content just to sniff the scent of grease paint. I have met many actors *manqués* in the course of my career, but few with the good sense of this one, David Webster, who realizing at once on leaving Liverpool University that there was no future for himself on the boards, settled for commerce straight away and gave himself over to the guidance of the business chief who, in the war, was to achieve a small footnote to History for the way in which he fed the nation with Woolton's Pie. Frederick Marquis, later Lord Woolton, had an extremely shrewd eye for picking and assessing executive talent. When I first met his latest protégé, who was also The Playhouse's most devoted follower, David Webster was spending his days being put through the hoop, and performing such menial tasks as directing the customers to the right departments; later he was to rise to become the much respected general manager of the Bon Marché store. And today, when I watch Sir David Webster, the general administrator for Covent Garden Opera House, settling the Queen and the Queen Mother into their seats, under the canopy of the royal box at some special gala, I gaze from afar at this portly, now middle-aged figure with the sparse grey hair, in his immaculate tail-coat and white tie, and wonder if he ever looks back to those early days in Liverpool, and is as surprised at all the bounty that life has brought him as I am at all the astonishing good fortune that has been mine.

Most people are more interesting on their way up than after their arrival. But which road to take for the safest ascent to the summit? At the end of the current Playhouse season, its director assured me there was a place for me in the company in the autumn, at the same salary. However, before that could happen, I was offered another minuscule part in London, this time in a revival of Pirandello's *Henry IV* at The Everyman Theatre in Hampstead, with Ernest Milton in the title rôle.

Once more, as in *St Joan*, I stood about on the stage, but in this instance I was consolingly dressed in a most striking costume designed by McKnight Kauffer. My big moment came when the mad king of Bavaria, after a long soliloquy, and much dramatic manoeuvring, paused in front of me and demanded my name. 'I am Momo, Sire.' Seeking to put a wealth of subtle meaning into my answer, I must have succeeded because much to my gratification I was picked out for favourable mention by the critic of *The Times*, Charles Morgan. He was, of course, simply an anonymous figure to me in those days, but towards the end of the Second World War – then not so much as a shadow across the far horizon – this much-admired novelist and playwright chose for me the title of my book describing my life as an ordinary seaman. 'Why don't you call it *Home from Sea*?' he suggested. I had dined as his guest at The Garrick, and now we were on our way home in the blackout. 'And don't forget,' he admonished, 'that the quotation is "Home is the hunter, home from the hill, and the sailor, home from sea." *Not* from *the* sea. Everyone will get it wrong,' he added, with the satisfaction of a scholar. And he was right. They did.

I was to wonder apprehensively whether I did wrong not to go back to Liverpool, to continue my apprenticeship in a monthly variety of parts. Or to another Repertory Company, since during the brief run of *Henry IV* a different director from William Armstrong, after seeing a performance, came backstage to offer me the princely salary of six pounds a week to go to Hull.

Stupidly, I consider now, I finally refused both these opportunities to gain more experience in the profession which I imagined at that time to be my permanent one. It is only by acting that one acquires authority and ease upon the stage, just as it is only by writing, by sitting anchored day after day at one's desk, that one learns to write with fluency and a lack of self-consciousness. Unfortunately, there was too much optimistic talk of *Henry IV* being transferred to another theatre in the West End, with its complete cast including Robert Newton, who showed no signs yet of the disintegration which was to bring about his tragic early death; and Nancy Price, that undefeatable trouper, gallantly making a new reputation for herself today as the champion of a bird sanctuary near the Sussex coast. I came upon her one evening standing in front of the communal long mirror, backstage at The Everyman, pulling at her draperies, and exclaiming with a devastating self-honesty not often found in the Theatre, 'My husband always said I looked like a horse.' Be that as it may, they had produced between them an enchanting filly in Joan Maude, who had been with me in *Old English*.

I was influenced in my decision, too, to stay in London, because I had the tempting offer of moving into a flat in Talbot Square, near Paddington, which several ex-undergraduates were sharing. But the play didn't transfer, in the end, and from having been continuously in work for a year, beginner's luck, I now discovered what it was like to be 'resting'. Trying to find my share of the rent each week, without begging for funds from home, became something of a nightmare. By standing all day in a queue outside the Sydney Jay agency, I managed to get a few days filming as an extra at a guinea a day in a Betty Balfour film; soon after, I had my hopes raised by being cast as a chauffeur with a couple of lines and some bag-carrying to do in a Leon M. Lion production of a play by Monckton Hoffe at The Garrick, called *Christilinda*. Alas, despite the appeal of Isobel Elsom, then at the height of her fame, the play was so ill-fated that it only lasted ten days, and now there was nothing for it but to burn my boats temporarily, borrow my fare and retreat to Worcestershire. It was early November, not the most prepossessing of months to be idle in the country, and I tried to keep up my morale by regaling my old Barnt Green friends, like Rowena and Audrey, and John Ambrose, the doctor's son, whom I was particularly anxious to impress (because he always had the latest records, such as *I've danced with a man who's danced with a girl who's danced with the Prince of Wales*) with titillating accounts of high life in the metropolis in which I had personally participated.

Actually, there was only one story with authentic glamour attached to it, and I made as much as possible of the incident. This concerned an evening when I had been invited to a supper party at the 50-50 Club in Wardour Street, given by Ivor Novello, one of the club's sponsors and founders. I had been loth to drop into his dressing-room between performances, at The Prince of Wales Theatre, because now that I had become a very minor member of the same fraternity, I was acutely conscious of the professional gulf between us. He, on the other hand, with the enveloping generosity that was so much part of his nature, had made a point of inviting me on an evening when among his party were Constance Collier and Tallulah Bankhead, as much the toast of the town then as Gertrude Lawrence was to be in the 'thirties.

The excellent idea behind the club was a supper *rendezvous* when the day's work was done, where actors and actresses could each pay for themselves, without embarrassment, or, for that matter, women for the men, if one was working and the other wasn't. In this admirable atmosphere of freemasonry, and equality of the sexes, I became emboldened to ask the star of 'The Green Hat' if she would care to dance. 'I shall be delighted, my dear,' she replied in that husky, vibrant voice which made of the least utterance a historic pronouncement. In a way, this was one. For scarcely had I projected my partner once round the crowded floor, holding her reverently and gingerly at arm's length, when the most unexpected climax occurred; one of the other dancers caught his foot round hers. Thrown off balance, because I was not clutching her tightly enough, she slipped and fell, sprawling on her back with her beaded skirt above her knees. I was stunned, and as I stood there, a lump of stone, there flashed through my mind an absurd scrap of country lore I had somehow acquired to the effect that if a sheep fell upon its back, it could never right itself and tragedy might follow. On this occasion, it was more a case of tribulation than tragedy. As soon as other eager helping hands had hoisted my partner once again to her feet, she cut short my appalled apologies, removing the huskiness out of her throat to boom like Clara Butt on the stage of the Albert Hall. 'After him, my dear.' After whom? I hadn't the least idea which of the other dancers was to blame, all I did appreciate was that Miss Bankhead was in the mood to hack at everyone's shins. My relief can be imagined when the music ended, and I had the excuse to conduct my handle-with-care partner back to her seat.

That was the point where I ended the story each time I repeated it with embellishments, in the home circle; not with my

ensuing sense of mortification that what should have been an evening of delight, with myself seated among the gods and goddesses,
in full view of the nymphs and shepherds at the other tables, had
turned into a near-disaster, as far as I was concerned. For had
I not been given by my host the opening for a *rapprochement*
with the darling of the 'twenties? Instead, how badly I had
muffed it. Better, I realized ruefully, that I should stick to partnerships on the tennis courts. In my schoolboy days, I had been made
a junior member of Queen's, the doyen of tennis clubs, and now
my stepfather had offered to keep my subscription up for me,
as a senior. Thus, whenever I was asked, I was able to make
up a mixed-doubles four with the wife of one of England's key
industrialists; she, rather surprisingly, possessed a passion for
the game and, much to my relief, always insisted on paying for
my share of the new balls and the extra cost of the indoor wood
court.

Mrs Samuel Courtauld was the mother of a dark, gauche girl
with a strong jaw-line, who had often come to stay at Barnt Green
at the Pump House, as she had been at Roedean with Helen
Beesly. Sydney, an only child, was more my brother's age than
my own, for they were fellow undergraduates at Cambridge.
However, as soon as she heard that I was now living in London,
barnstorming, she insisted on inviting me to the family mansion
in Portman Square, though ironically she was increasingly unhappy there herself. Once my tennis skill had been tested out by
her mother, there followed a plethora of free meals, and of a
quality I had not yet encountered. It is galling to have to admit
how much of my adolescent thoughts centred round that recurring
problem as to from where my next meal was coming. I was still
growing, and in consequence always hungry. Actually, I am far
more aware now, looking back, of a different kind of pang which
was assuaged for me each time I was invited to lunch, or to one
of Lil Courtauld's supper parties after the opera. On the walls
of the dining-room glowed masterpieces by members of the
Impressionist school, like Gauguin and Van Gogh, such as had
never swum into my ken before. While my body was fed with
rich dishes, I enjoyed a revelation of the spirit that was
to return to me on the day that the Rijksmuseum was reopened
and restored to the Dutch people at the end of the German occupation of their land. On that September Sunday afternoon in

Amsterdam, along the road leading to the museum there was a silent procession stretching for miles; all were dressed in their church best, waiting their turn to incline their heads in gratitude before the Rembrandts that are so much a part of their country's heritage. I doubt if any of the burghers and their wives had eaten that day, since in exchange for the food coupons provided us, a chosen group of writers invited from England by the Government, we were given – in the leading restaurant in Amsterdam – a bowl of almost tasteless soup, nothing more. It did not matter. It was over. This was a day of triumphant rejoicing, in which we could share, when the national treasures, more precious than any jewels, had been brought out of their hiding places in the sand-dunes, symbols of something at once more permanent and more powerful than any machinery of war.

In a similar way was I hypnotized by the glory of the Courtauld collection, and I imagine my silences at table were put down to the same debilitating shyness which, like the cancer which was one day to kill her, consumed the daughter of the house. I would watch her stalking ahead of me down the corridors, an exile in her own country. Sydney was utterly guiltless, and yet she had committed the crime of not being a male member of the species. Her mother found that she had nothing in common with her awkward, coltish daughter, who was making a reputation for herself as a blue-stocking at college; her father found it difficult to conceal his disappointed longings for an heir to his great empire. Between them, I could sense the smouldering volcano of mutual accusations. To have so much and yet so little. Sydney hated the social life at Portman Square, the large parties, the endless entertaining that was so exciting for me, who came from outside. It was all such a prison to her that she insisted on taking a small flat in Notting Hill Gate, and refused to wear the kind of clothes her mother wore, ignoring and despising all the trappings of a rich heiress, which her contemporary, Edwina Ashley, later Mountbatten, so frankly enjoyed. The second married a sailor, the first an embryo politician. In both cases, I suspect, it was the unshakeable strength of their characters, rather than their considerable dowries, which did most to further the careers of their respective husbands.

Even with those for whom she had a certain childhood affection, like myself, Sydney Butler lacked an easy manner, and her marriage, though an overwhelmingly happy one, did nothing to help her relax in public, since her husband, Rab Butler, brought into his personal encounters the same equivocal air that he has always displayed as a politician. I only stayed with them once in their home in Essex, soon after they were married. I still have a wry note in my memory of the man who was to take a just pride in being the architect of the Education Act, showing me – in the course of a Sunday afternoon walk round the estate – the hatches in which the baby pheasants were being reared and fattened up for future slaughter. I found it difficult to hide my dismay. The contrast of what seemed to me such pointless inhumanity, with the stoical courage that Sydney herself showed during her last illness, when her husband's own suffering, because of his shy devotion, was much commented on in the Westminster community surrounding their house in Smith Square, has often recurred to me as one more example of the different levels of feeling at which even the most civilized of human beings live out their lives. Today, whenever I hear Rab Butler described, politically, as 'a cold fish', I remember the pheasants, but I also remember other things.

In Worcestershire, that November, as I walked every afternoon, to kill time, through the sodden fields, a solitary pheasant sometimes rose protestingly on the wing, but its passage across the mournful, autumnal sky had no message for me. Except in times of war I have never held a gun in my hand. What was exercising my mind at that moment was not the need for launching a crusade against cruelty to animals so much as the unpleasant fact that Christmas was looming on the horizon, and I hadn't a penny with which to buy presents for my family. My parents were refraining tactfully from any 'I-told-you-so' comments about my choice of a profession, but I was only saved at the post by the arrival one morning of a letter from the Daniel Mayer Organization, with whom I had enrolled as my agents in the Business. This was to tell me that a revival of the play *The Rising Generation* was to be put on for a Christmas season at Wyndham's, and there were good prospects for me, since the action was provided by a tearaway group of teenagers who decide to run the family residence in their own way, during the grown-ups' absence.

Right up one moment, right down the next. It is the one characteristic which all theatrical folk share in common. With my confidence restored overnight, I pleaded for my fare back to London and the next afternoon was reading the part of the ringleader among the juvenile revolt in front of Tom Walls, the show's producer, who gave the impression that he would much rather have been spending the day in the grand stand at Epsom. He had a mottled complexion and a bellowing voice. I was to discover, however, that his bark was far worse than his bite, and this master of farce and fancier of horse-flesh taught me more about timing, during rehearsals, than I learnt during all the rest of the four years I was on the stage.

Another first night in London, and this time even Rodger had agreed to be present, as I had such a good part. Much to my relief, in the clean white flannels that I had bought for the occasion, I found that I was able to stand up to the veteran skills of Ena Grossmith and C. V. France. As soon as the opening tensions were resolved, there was a holiday atmosphere in the theatre too, and the weeks went all too swiftly. At matinées, the house was full of children who roared their approval of our larking antics, and after the climax of our parents' unexpected return in the last act, and the clearing up of all the mess that we had so joyfully made, I admit I enjoyed to the full the moment when the cast took their curtain calls, and I found myself for the first time bowing from the centre of the stage. Applause is heady wine, and once you have tasted it, the liking grows. I was soon to be relegated to my right place once more, in the line-up for *Prince Fazil,* but as another spring approached, and my inborn restless longing for having always more to do began to assert itself again, I was unexpectedly summoned to the presence of that theatre rajah, Tony Prinsep, a very rich entrepreneur, presiding over the fortunes of the Globe Theatre. Here he dutifully put on a succession of plays for the actress who was now his wife, Margaret Bannerman, at that time a very beautiful woman.

Behind the desk of Mr Prinsep, as he received me courteously in his office, was a full-size portrait of his permanent leading lady as she appeared in *Our Betters,* in a white evening dress which set off to perfection her dazzling fairness. There was a time later when I would gladly have thrown vitriol at that portrait, had

I had the opportunity. But on this occasion, how flattered I was to be told that the reports on my performance in *The Rising Generation* were so universally excellent that I had been chosen to play the son of eighteen, in an adaptation from the French to be called *There's No Fool*. It was explained to me that the plot revolved, in typically Gallic fashion, round the triangle of a father and son in love with the same woman.

'She has been his father's mistress, and now the son, returning from college, suddenly grown-up, meeting her for the first time, is so bowled over by her that he proposes marriage. There is a big scene for you at the end of the second act, when your father finds out the truth.'

'Will the part of the woman be played by Miss Bannerman?' I asked with rising excitement.

'At a later stage, perhaps,' it was cautiously explained. 'We are going to try the play out first for a six-weeks run in the provinces. We can offer you a salary of fifteen pounds a week.'

'Fifteen pounds a week,' I echoed. That was what really mattered, I thought, as I hurried back to The New, where *Prince Fazil* was playing, to ask Mrs Henry Ainley if I might be released. There cannot have been much reluctance to let me go, for that same evening, so swiftly does the grapevine work in the theatre, another member of the cast knocked on my door to ask if the rumour was true, because if so, she was anxious to put in for my part, for her son-in-law. 'By all means,' I agreed loftily, 'I will speak to the stage manager myself, if you will tell me the name.' This turned out to be Val Gielgud, unknown to me then, though we were in due course to have another link. For like myself, he changed careers in mid-stream, and wisely so, since he was to end up as head of the Drama Department of the BBC. I wonder if today he remembers anything about our jointly-shared part in *Prince Fazil*. I don't, except that we were certainly not playing the Prince.

What I cannot forget even now, with the cold shiver of recurring insecurity down my back, was the gruelling time I had during the rehearsals for *There's No Fool*. I arrived at the stage door of The Globe for the first reading, over-confident though I was soon to be utterly deflated. My father, I found, was to be played by Bertram Wallis, who for years had been almost a fixture at Daly's, in a series of Ruritanian musicals, so that he looked strange and lost, out of thigh boots and without a riding whip or sword in his hand. He was inevitably stiff and mannered at rehearsals, but he had a commanding presence, and got off lightly compared with myself, who was held up to ridicule day after day by the producer, Stanley Bell, in front of the whole cast. It reached the point when, in an agony of nervous anxiety, I could do nothing right, and I would arrive each morning feeling so physically sick that I am sure I would have thrown my hand in, had it not been for the sympathy and understanding shown me by someone who was herself at that time fighting for recognition in the Theatre. She only had one small but telling scene in the play: the dialogue of a discarded mistress calling on her former lover. This she spoke and underplayed with such finesse, that she made it sound as though it was the first time such a scene had been played or written, and the same delicacy of perception that she brought to her performance she displayed even more abundantly in real life. Martita – for it was Martita Hunt – to try and cheer me up, suggested that we should share digs during the tour. I appreciate now that she unselfishly sacrificed her own reserves of the confidence that she so badly needed herself, for without conventional looks, managers refused to consider her for leading parts. It was considerably later that through sheer perseverance, which is as necessary as a blazing talent, Martita was to come into her own, and today whenever we meet at a party or in a restaurant, I long to throw my arms round her and thank her all over again for the way that she gave me something to hold on to, something strong and unsentimental, in those far-off days when I was so lacking in technical resources.

Yet I did possess something that was to manifest itself equally in my early published writings. A kind of directness of appeal which owed nothing to art or professional skill, everything to my instinctive eagerness to communicate. As soon as there was an audience in front of the footlights, the gulf was bridged. No longer did it seem to matter that I was clumsy in making my entrances and exits, in all the bits of 'business' I had to get through, even in sitting down in a chair. The public, who in the end are the ultimate arbiters, broke into spontaneous applause at the end of what Mr Prinsep had described at our meeting as my 'big scene'; applause which was only lacking in Glasgow, because of the rows of empty seats. It was the middle of the

General Strike, the April of 1926. On the night that the future Queen of England was being born in Bruton Street, far away in London, I could hear the chanting of 'The Red Flag' in the streets outside, and my dresser rushed into my room for my quick change into my brand-new tail coat, which had cost a whole week's salary and which was supposed in the play to establish the proof of my transition from adolescence into manhood: 'Och mon,' he cried out excitedly, 'they're burrrning the buses noo.' How could we compete with such a free show?

We struggled on to Birmingham where I was able to hoard my salary by living at home for the week, and be driven back to Bromsgrove each evening by Tom, my stepfather's chauffeur, in some style. I had secretly hoped that all Edgbaston would turn up to see the local boy on his way to making good, but in actual fact, we were still playing to very moderate houses, because of the country's state of emergency. Indeed, it was not till we reached Brighton, on the last lap of the tour, and settled down at the Theatre Royal, that most charming of all small seaside theatres, that I began to feel that I was really getting the most out of my part. Brighton gives you that sensation always, that everything you do, even walking along the front, has some kind of significance – is an event larger than life. The air really is like champagne, and I still find it intoxicating now that my working retreat is only a few miles away under the protective crest of the South Downs.

The truth is that it is impossible to be unconfident in Brighton for long, though there were ominous backstage whisperings that Miss Bannerman and Mr Prinsep had slipped down to take a private look at the mid-week matinée, without coming round, graciously, like Royalty, to congratulate any of the cast or speak of future plans. I pushed away the sinister implications, and on my return to London, since there was no call for my immediate presence, I left a forwarding address with the Daniel Mayer Company, and decided to spend the money I had saved during the tour on my first visit to the Continent. All thirty pounds of it. A fellow actor, Robert Harris, whom I greatly admired for the superb quality of his speaking voice, in the way that one admires those players who appear on the centre court when one is still struggling to have one's own entry for Wimbledon accepted, offered to be my guide in Paris, where he himself was bound after making a considerable impact in the title part in *The Marvellous History of St Bernard*.

The first evening of our arrival after our long train journey, I was content just to wander through the twilight streets, before going in search of the Arc de Triomphe. It was the end of May, and in the Bois the chestnuts, with their white and scarlet flowers, like myriad candles, illuminating the dusk, were not yet snuffed out. The week passed in a dream. On our last afternoon, we climbed the cobble-stoned road to Montparnasse, lingering for a time in front of the canvases painted by the students of the day, on display in the street, in a search for a new Cézanne or Seurat, until we came to that unsurpassed view, the plateau in front of the Cathedral of the Sacré Coeur, where all Paris, like the panorama of the world with which the Devil tempted Christ, is spread beneath you. Inside the cool, shadowy church, I lit another kind of candle, different from those on the chestnuts in the Bois, praying silently that whatever life had in store for me in the years ahead, I would never allow myself to be corroded or disillusioned, but keep my faith, my faith in my God, but equally my faith in my country and in myself. For if one did not believe in oneself, how could one expect the rest of the world to do so? Every time I return to Paris, I light another candle.

We were taking the evening train to the south. By pooling our resources, we had sufficient funds for another ten days, if we were prepared to sit up all night, packed like sardines, in a fourth-class carriage. Bobbie had been enticed by an account of an undiscovered village on the coast near Perpignan and the Spanish border called Bagnolees-sur-Mer. My companion was eager for some real Mediterranean heat. Like Italian tenors whose voices feed rapaciously on a diet of the sun mixed with spaghetti, Bobbie was a worshipper in the days before sunbathing had become an almost universal cult. I gladly acquiesced. It was all experience to me so that it was, on my part, in a mood of bubbling expectancy that we made our way back to the Place de la Madeleine, to visit Cooks at the corner of the square, to see if any post had been forwarded from England.

Afterwards, I wished we had not gone, though I suppose it would only have been a postponement of the bitter tidings. There were two letters for me. One was from my mother, full of cautionary advice about the pitfalls of 'going abroad', though she was somewhat relieved to know that I was in Bobbie's care, since he had stayed with us in Worcestershire, and had greatly impressed my step-father by the factual account of his career since the days when he had been a Gold Medallist at the RADA and won an enviable contract with Basil Dean.

The other letter was from Angus McLeod, the head of the Daniel Mayer office, informing me that Mr Prinsep had decided to bring *There's No Fool* into The Globe straight away, with his wife in the star part, but otherwise the cast unchanged – except for the son. 'They consider you are too young,' was the gist of the explanation.

On my return I heard that an actor already in his thirties, Leonard Upton, had been chosen, which made the plot of the play palpably absurd. On the other hand, it would save the leading lady's face from an accusation of baby-snatching. I can appreciate the logic of that now; at the time I was too overwhelmed by dumb misery to argue coherently. Had I not been cheated out of my inheritance? What was the use of all the applause I had received during the tour, the extremely favourable notices in every town? Bobbie tried to comfort me by admitting that he had thought very little of the play when he had seen it in Birmingham, and had only refrained from telling me so until this moment because he hadn't wanted to dash my hopes. There was poor consolation in that. The point was that everyone would know that I alone had been dropped from the cast. There's no fool ... like a young fool, I kept on repeating over and over again to myself, as we sat, squeezed upright on the unforgivingly hard seats, enveloped in a cloud of garlic from the other passengers, seeking to quench our thirst with a bag of small, unripe apricots we had bought at the station. This was my punishment for being too trusting, too innocently expectant.

I found myself comparing this night with the one when I had sat up in the train to Scotland, to stay with the Plumbs, and how I had kept up my spirits then by envisaging the time when I would be able to afford first-class facilities wherever I travelled. Almost two years had gone by (and at eighteen that seems like a lifetime) but I was no nearer my goal. Would I ever be? I will. I will. I must. That night, as the train sped south, I swore a more binding oath to myself, more solemn even than my prayer in front of the high altar of Sacré Coeur blazing with votive candles, that somehow, whatever the cost, whatever the self-sacrifices or the self-discipline demanded, I would make myself invulnerable to all the caprices and the prejudices of those in power. I would become my own master, as far as anyone can be. All the shame that I had endured at rehearsals, all the agony of heart for what seemed, from my side, like a brutal betrayal, welled up and suffocated me, until utterly spent, sweating and aching, I fell into an uneasy doze, my head on a stranger's shoulder.

I wonder how much Bagnolles-sur-Mer has changed in the forty years since that moment and this. Are there now a row of smart hotels, striped umbrellas, apéritif bars? In those days there was one small, unpretentious inn, with lobster pots close by, so that you could choose your own sacrificial victim for lunch, and wash it down with the second brew of *Château Yquem,* which to my unpractised palate tasted just the same, the sweet nectar of the gods, and cost an absurdly few francs. Indeed, nothing seemed to cost anything and the free sun shone all day from a pure, cerulean sky. Bobbie lay upon the rocks, roasting himself like an ox upon a spit, turning copper brown, while I, consumed by some inner force I could not explain, shut myself away in my bedroom, writing, writing. The only paper I could purchase at the village's general store had thin, criss-cross lines on it, quite unlike anything I had ever seen in England, and this in its turn became part of the strange, unreal mood that now possessed me. These pages of foreign foolscap I covered with the first draft of a novel called *Tangled Roots,* a self-conscious title which I subsequently changed.

The combination of my unexpected, savage disappointment, together with the impact upon my senses of the romantic florescence of Paris, and now of the burning coastline with its sienna-red boulders and cobalt sea, had acted as a powerful medicine upon my being. Galvanized into a creative fury, I only saw Bobbie at mealtimes. All the rest of the day, until in the cool of the evening we sat at the one open-air café, watching the locals dance in their berets to the accompaniment of an accordion, I stayed behind the shutters of my room, closed against the sun, surrendering to my subconsciousness. Instead of the sea, a spate of words poured over me. It has never been quite the same since, and not surprisingly my companion could not understand what was happening. In his eyes, it was the ultimate folly, existing as we did in a grudging northern climate, to refuse the bounty of the sun. I could not explain. During the vigil I had kept that long night in the train, I had been first stripped naked, and then re-clad, with a new armour, a fresh incentive. It was no use pinning your hopes, your beliefs, on other people. In the end you must be self-contained, self-sufficient. And how better to achieve this philosophy than through being a writer, when all you needed as your props were a pen and a pad of paper?

If only it really was as easy as that. At the same time I am strongly convinced that nothing in our progress through life happens by chance. That exorcism had been needed, its repercussions were entirely salutary, although, ironically, by the time we returned to England the play was already off. Savaged by the London critics, shunned by the public, it scarcely survived a week, and proved Miss Bannerman's worst failure to date. I had been well out of it, and stayed well out of it for the rest of the summer, content now to settle down at home, no longer on the defensive for my idleness, for not earning my keep, for was I not writing a Book? Only Auntie Violet was permitted to read the opening chapters. This position of trusted, literary confidante so pleased and flattered her that she praised what I had written extravagantly to my mother, who remained, however, still unconvinced as to which of my now two proposed professions was the more chancy. I wasn't sure myself. Returning to London in the autumn, I celebrated my nineteenth birthday by dividing the morning between visiting the Daniel Mayer office in Golden Square, to prove that I was now truly equipped for grown-up parts, and sitting on a chair in the outer offices of the Sydney Jay film agency. Despite such conscientious overtures, the only work I could secure that October had nothing to do with the Theatre, or for that matter with writing, except indirectly, as future copy. Once again, practical assistance came to me through one of my tennis partners.

Anthony Bradley, the tall, blond son of the owner of Pope & Bradley, the Bond Street tailors, had won the junior West of England Doubles with me in his last year at Downside, and still occasionally invited me to the family home on Kingston Hill at week-ends. His father, who at sight looked a bluff, forthright businessman, was an ardent spiritualist, and séances attended by

Above View from my mother's drawing-room, at Esher. *Below* My mother in the garden at Esher. *Photo: Topical Press Agency*

My studio at 115 Ebury Street. 1930. *Photo:*
E. J. M....

My writing room at Esher

Hannen Swaffer on occasion would be in progress behind the closed curtains of the drawing-room, while we were enjoying ourselves on the hard court. Anton Dolin, who imagined that he was as proficient at other pastimes as he was as a dancer in the Diaghileff Company, had been unwise enough to challenge me to a match, with five pounds as the prize. I had accepted with alacrity, not seeing myself as a confidence trickster, and the bet had kept me for a week. Anthony knew the form too well, but he did ask me bluntly one Saturday how I existed between jobs. Had I an allowance from my family? I shook my head, explaining my almost superstitious aversion to dependence of any kind. Had I anything in prospect? Again, I had to shake my head. 'Then you had better come and work for us. We need a new junior assistant in the shop. See if you can sell yourself to the customers. I'll give you a week's trial.' He was trying to imitate his father's manner; and he added as a salvo to practical considerations: 'And you can choose any material you like for a new suit, or an overcoat.'

I promptly settled for a winter overcoat, which I badly needed, in dark-blue cloth, and as promptly presented myself the next Monday morning at nine, much to the surprise of the senior assistant in charge, who had not been warned. I enjoyed myself as a salesman, especially the challenge of flattering the ego of any potential customers who came my way – 'You would look very slim in this material,' to the old ones; 'This is the kind of cut and cloth that we find is popular with the ladies,' to the younger ones – and I sometimes pretend to myself I might still be there, since after a fortnight I was doing so well I had been put on a percentage, had I not received an urgent call one day to present myself at the Jay office.

All the occasions that I had sunk my pride to haunt the outer passages had at last paid off. A film to be made about the First World War, with the nostalgic title of *Blighty*, was shortly to go into production, and there had been, apparently, some difficulty over the casting of the young lead. Not surprisingly, since the sponsors were searching for someone who looked sufficiently like Ellaline Terriss, already cast as his mother, Lady Villiers, and Lilian Hall Davis as his sister; again young and fresh enough, on the one hand, to cause sadness in the hearts of the audiences at his untimely death upon the fields of Flanders, yet sufficiently

H

experienced to carry off a torrid love scene with the refugee with wild hair and enormous, expressive eyes, who before the last reel was over, was to bear him a son. Altogether, Robin was quite a lad. Mr Jay had given them my photograph, and on the strength of that, the film-makers had offered an interview.

The film was being directed by Adrian Brunel, an artist who achieved his best effects by never raising his voice, and produced by a new name in the celluloid world, a fellow-Brummie of mine called Michael Balcon, whose very first full-length feature this was. The British side of the industry had been passing through a very depressed period, and, in consequence, the film was to be made on an extremely tight budget. I was given a test and told that the part would carry a salary of four pounds a day. A day! This, I am afraid, made me over-register in front of the camera, while I prattled on about the coincidence that I had already played one newly-commissioned second-lieutenant at Liverpool. Then I went home to Worcestershire once again to wait for confirmation. I could not concentrate on the customers in Bond Street, now my original choice of vocation had so tantalizingly loomed again. Equally in vain, I tried to concentrate on my book, sitting at the small oak bureau in my bedroom at The Oakalls, which still goes wherever I go, as a mascot.

Each time the telephone rang, and I heard the sound dimly from upstairs, my heart seemed to stop beating. And then after a month, when I had almost given up hope, it did ring for me, and of all times, on a Sunday night. It was the film director himself at the other end, who apparently had voted for me from the start. Fortunately, no better possibility had turned up, despite an extensive search, and I was in. Definitely in. Would I please report for further tests, as regards my clothes and make-up, at Islington Studios, on the Tuesday morning. Would I? Would I . . . ?

The story line was a rather simple one, and by current standards a corny one too. Yet the picture was so sensitively directed by Adrian Brunel, that it has withstood to a remarkable degree the erosion of Time and changing tastes. The proof of this is that a couple of years ago, *Blighty* was unearthed for a war film series at the Festival Hall, and I was asked by the promoters, together with Sir Michael and Ivor Montagu, who had been responsible for the script, to appear on the stage at the end of the showing, and make speeches. I was torn between dread and curiosity. Supposing what we were now going to see resurrected should arouse laughter in all the wrong places, with the cast's movements and gestures as jerky as an early slap-stick comedy? On the contrary, what is now a period piece stood up remarkably well, and was most cordially received. I could not applaud, in the darkness, I could not move till an usher came for me. I was Robin again. Seeing my image on the screen, after all these years between, still strongly recognizable in some ways as a person, so utterly remote in others, had brought back such an odd jumble of recollections.

The trench-warm that I had worn in one scene had been lent me by the young floor manager who had been 'out there' himself. Bill O'Bryen, who was to become an important film executive in due course, and marry a glamorous young star, Elizabeth Allen, and be among my Brighton neighbours today. Jack Cox, the camera-man with the moustache, cropped hair and flow of language of a company sergeant-major, had taken an unreasoning dislike to Nadia Sibirskaia, a Russian actress who looked a little like Nazimova, and could not speak a word of English. This did not matter, as ours was a silent film, but what did was her adamantine determination to play all her scenes with the rest of the cast, including myself, with her own head never full-face to the camera, never profile, always in a three-quarters position. This naturally caused considerable complications all round. 'The bloody bitch,' muttered Jack from behind the stockade of his camera. Those within earshot smiled broadly, and so did the star brought from a foreign land, mistaking his muttered imprecations for compliments for her powerful emoting.

Nadia needed no artificial aids to encourage the tears to run down her cheeks, but my film mother, in the scene where she said farewell to her boy bound for the front, asked for a record of 'Evensong' to be played at the side of the set. That helped us both immensely, though I suspect the technicians must have been satiated with the treacly melody by the time the scene had finally been shot to the director's satisfaction. Throughout the weeks we spent at Islington, Lilian Hall Davis behaved with a hectic, brittle gaiety, off the set, as though she was secretly conscious that time was running out for her. The other leading male part, that of the family chauffeur who, joining up on the same day as the young master, ended – thanks to the democracy of the war – by his asking for the hand of the daughter of the house, was played by Jameson Thomas. In contrast to Lilian, he gave off such a strong scent of melancholy that one could not help being aware of it, and inevitably one was puzzled, since Jimmy was obviously turning in a first-class performance. I suspect the explanation was that the industry itself had been in such a parlous condition, and that Jameson Thomas himself had been out of work too long for him to be able to hope with any confidence that the tide had really turned for him. Out of the proceeds of the success he made in *Blighty*, he bought a ticket to Hollywood, seeking to make a name for himself, in that more flourishing and sunnier climate, as a second Ronald Colman, but alas, it was too late. The long period of malnutrition had undermined his health to the extent that he became an easy prey to tuberculosis, at about the same time as his bride in the film was to end her own life in a moment of mental instability. Only Ellaline Terriss indestructibly lives on, as much an Edwardian beauty as ever, now that she has entered the nineties; indeed, so little changed from the days that she embraced me over and over again to the sound of 'Evensong' on the organ, that I found myself asking her not so long ago her recipe for eternal youth.

Ella was engagingly direct in her answer. 'I go to bed every afternoon,' she said, 'and sleep for at least an hour, like a child, with the curtains drawn, and you know, I managed to do this even in the early days when I was partnering Seymour.* Don't you remember, Godfrey, that I even did it when we were filming together? I had my rest put in my contract. They either had to agree to that, or I wouldn't have been your film mother.'

Of course I remembered, and how I had rejoiced. For my film mother's absence from the set, after the lunch break, could mean an extra day's work for her son. Another whole four pounds. I would look at Jack Cox, hopefully, pleadingly, as our producer with an extremely authoritative air arrived on the set from his Wardour Street office, complaining that we were behind schedule. This has been the stereotyped lament in the making of all pictures, whatever their budget, since the beginning of the film world. The artists versus the moneybags. In the end, I made almost a hundred pounds in the course of the film's shooting, and went on my way rejoicing, though completely unaware that

* Sir Seymour Hicks, Ellaline Terriss's husband.

within a few weeks I would find myself rehearsing the part (this time without music) of the son of another leading lady (elevated to the status of an eighteenth-century French marquise) who equally put her trust in the health recipe of a sleeping amnesia every afternoon. (Except on matinée days.)

'But you must get right into bed, and take off all your clothes, and when you get up, bathe your face in cold water, and start afresh. Sitting in an armchair, as Willie does, is a waste of time.'

Marie Tempest only gave me that piece of advice long after I had ceased to be a member of her Company. She was explaining to me her antidote for blitz-menaced nights in the war. Though she made it equally clear that this routine of cutting the day in half, and refilling her reservoir by sleep, had been a rigid part of her régime – even in those early days when she had been more of a singer than a comedy actress, and revisiting the convent where she had been educated, had been surrounded by the novitiates and nuns in their black habits, entreating 'just one more song for us before you go back into the world, just one more song.' Now the time for such enchantments, for sitting down to play her own accompaniment on the spinet, or insisting on eating an apple while her husband and her lover fought a duel, as they did in *The Marquise,* was over and gone for ever. Instead, we sat at lunch in her flat in Regent's Park, she as impeccably up-right and composed as ever, pretending that I had not reached her building over a devastation of rubble and broken glass. At any other time I would have been astonished to find my hostess dressed in slacks, a kind of feminine edition of the familiar and comforting Churchill siren-suit. As it was, her dignity and her charm – a rogue in porcelain, as she had been christened by the critics, after Meredith, – remained utterly unassailed. I marvelled, since I have often felt that few women would wear trousers, except for household chores, or for sporting occasions, if they ever took any serious trouble to examine their contours from behind. Madame the Marquise, however, succeeded on this, the last time that we were destined to meet, in appearing as undefeatably elegant as she had been in the dresses of silk and brocade and the *poudré* wigs copied from Fragonard, when she had set such an example in poise to all the male members of the cast of Noël Coward's play. Especially to such a gangling youth as myself.

I was fortunate to have been engaged for the production at all, since, except for playing Sebastian opposite Fabia Drake's Viola, in a Sunday night production of *Twelfth Night,* I had no experience of costume parts. Luckily, Bobbie Harris was playing the other juvenile in the play, the suitor for the hand of the Marquise's daughter, and hearing that the part of the son had not yet been cast, put in a recommendation for me. Whereupon I was summoned to the presence of the Graham Brownes, and appreciated at once that I was for the first time in my life in the presence of Royalty. Instinctively I stood to attention throughout the interview, and did not dare to stand at ease even after rehearsals had begun and I had been engaged by the Criterion management at ten pounds a week.

Not without just cause, Dame Marie, as she deservedly later became, had the reputation of being something of a martinet in the theatre, and I waited apprehensively for explosions. One morning, after I had finished going through the opening scene of the play, the leading lady beckoned to me to join her on the other side of the stage. I advanced nervously, wondering what was in store for me. Correction over the way I had spoken a certain line? Her opening comment took me completely by surprise.

'Boy, strike me here,' she commanded, pointing to her waistline.

'Strike you *there*?' I echoed, bewildered and appalled.

'Yes, *here,*' she repeated, pulling my hand towards her and beating it against what seemed to my bruised fingers to be a belt of steel, beneath her dress.

'That,' she explained in matter-of-fact tones, but with a twinkle in her eyes at my discomfiture, 'comes from correct breathing, the system that my singing teacher, Garcia, taught me when I was your age. Until you learn to breathe properly you cannot hope to control an audience, let alone yourself. All control in life,' she continued with mounting emphasis, 'comes from the control of the diaphragm, which is only achieved through correct breathing.

'Now let me see you do it, boy. Push your stomach *out,* as you breathe in deeply, hold it, then breathe out, pulling *in* your stomach tightly as you let your breath go. Yes, continue to do that half-a-dozen times.' Now it was her turn to place her hand on my diaphragm. 'You can do the exercises at home, you can do them in the wings, when you are waiting at rehearsals, until it becomes second nature to you. You will find that it casts out fear.'

Her prophetic promise was to come back to me often in the war. Standing on the bridge of a ship in the Barentz Sea, and assailed by successive waves of Focke Wulfs, like flies upon the ceiling of the world, pinpointing the convoy, dropping their bombs all around us, terror possessed my bowels. I was a reporter with a pen in my hand, I dared not shut my eyes. I could not pretend to myself that it wasn't happening. Then, as a direct hit was scored on a tanker close to us on the starboard side, which proceeded to disintegrate into a blaze of flames and cauldron-black smoke pyramiding in protest to the heavens, I found myself, almost subconsciously, repeating that lesson of long ago. I started to breathe in, hold it, breathe out, and after a few minutes I had regained control, not only of my stomach muscles but of myself, as my tutor had promised me all those years before. All fear had truly left me, even as it had done for herself with myself as spectator, at the première of *The Marquise*.

It is always an ordeal to have the opening scene to play on a first night. But on this occasion, Miguel, as I was called, was greatly assisted by the gay, bubbling *insouciance* of his sister Eileen Sharp, recently promoted from soubrette parts with the D'Oyly Carte Company. In consequence, as I made my exit, there was a trickle of applause which the star of the piece, waiting in the wings for her own first entrance, heard, and she put up one hand to touch my cheek.

'Good boy,' she whispered approvingly. 'First blood to you.' It was one of those moments that you remember always. I stood there, warm with happiness, though very conscious that the hand which had touched my face had been ice-cold and trembling. It was then that I watched the transformation take place. As her maid removed the white dust wrap from her shoulders, to reveal the Watteau blue of her dress beneath, she seemed to me, with the cruel chasm of the years between us, a frightened, shrivelled, old woman. Until she started to breathe, in the manner that her famous singing teacher had instructed her. Whereupon before my eyes, I saw the transformation happen. The consuming attack of first-night nerves which, oddly, only increase and feed upon success, was halted and contained to such a degree that now, to my astonishment, I was gazing at an alluring actress in her prime, dressed as an elegant · eighteenth-century French aristocrat, glowing, utterly assured. The next moment, she had walked through the door on to the stage, to receive an ovation and to give one of the most effective performances of her long career.

The author was not present on that first night to take a curtain call in his own right. Instead, on his return from the States, he called the cast together for a run-through, and I was struck at once by his sense of authority and of all-embracing stagecraft. Here was a born leader in the theatre; someone who knew exactly what he wanted from his players, and equally what was within their compass. Someone who knew, too, not only how to sell himself to the public, but to his troops. It was my first view of Noël Coward at close quarters, in action, and he wasn't at all what I had expected or imagined from having watched his remarkable performance in *The Vortex*. Here was as strict a disciplinarian as Miss Tempest herself. In consequence, I have never quite got over the feeling of awe of that first encounter, even though, on hearing that my own ambition was to become a playwright myself, he found time to invite me to tea one afternoon, in the apartment he kept for his own use in his mother's home at number 111, Ebury Street.

Typically, I found him at his grand piano, improvising a number. I imagine he was in the throes of creating another Cochran revue; songs like 'Dance, dance little lady,' which were to outlive their era and create their own kind of immortality. As I sat there, listening gratefully, watching, hypnotized by one of his fingers raised in mid-air before it wagged at his audience – his habit when he is giving advice – it was impossible to imagine that he had ever been in my own supplicant position. Yet it had been so. Only ten years divided us, in age, but already a lifetime, in experience.

There was one experience he never brushed aside. It had happened when he was as immature and unrecognized as I was that afternoon I walked Ebury Street for the first time, from the bus stop at Victoria. He had made the same kind of anxious entrance as I had done, but his was into the sitting-room of a Manchester hotel, and instead of the manuscript of an unfinished novel, he had held in his hands a bundle of unpublished songs, which he was desperately anxious to sell to an actress already established both as a *chanteuse* and a *diseuse*.

She invited him to sit down at the piano and play his own compositions in his own way. They were charming, she decided, when he had finished, but they were not for her. Equally, she recognized that here was a budding talent of real promise. So instead of sending the unknown composer on his way with a few phrases of polite regret, she rang for tea and talked to him without condescension, and as encouragingly as she could.

'You need to show yourself off with more bravura,' she counselled him. 'The only way to sell yourself in life is to present yourself in a big way. Look, like this.' To demonstrate what she meant, she took her guest's place at the piano, where she struck a series of triumphant chords with a flourish. 'Next time you play your songs to someone, start off like this. It will pay you in the end. I promise you.'

The very raw, very young composer thanked her for her advice, and disappeared into the Manchester fog. As the tide of fortune flowed for Noël Coward, the actress who had helped him on his way, noting the unchallenged progress, must have wondered sometimes whether he had long since obliterated their conversation from his mind. But he hadn't. For one morning Ivy St Helier's telephone rang in her London flat, and at the other end of the line was the voice of the man who by that time had been given the accolade of The Master by his fellow performers. 'Will you please come down to His Majesty's Theatre, to try over your music in the show?' he asked in the voice that so many have in vain tried to imitate.

The show was *Bitter Sweet*, in which Miss St Helier was to make an outstanding success in a showy part which contained exactly the right amount of bravura. After all, it had been created for her, with that phrase from the past in mind, a cellophane package done up in ribbons and presented with the gratitude one reserves for those who are kind and helpful in the beginning.

That afternoon when we talked of the foundations for a writing technique, either as novelist or playwright, neither *Bitter Sweet* nor *Cavalcade* had yet been conceived. These works were still as embryonic as the notion that not only would I one day live next door, in Ebury Street, and go on living there for the next forty years, but far more binding a link, our two mothers would find their own final resting place round the corner in the same house in Eaton Square, one of the first to be converted into post-war flats. Neither son was aware of this unexpected juxtaposition. Then one day my mother remarked to me, after enthusing over the view from the wide windows of her second-floor apartment, and how at night the ever-flowing lights of the traffic reminded her of the Champs Elysées, 'Did you know that Noël Coward's mother lives in the flat on the ground-floor?' When I shook my head in surprise, my mother added, 'Poor dear, she is very deaf, I understand. She is always seated at the window every time I go in and out.'

Very deaf and very old, finding the last of her pleasures, and her company, in watching the passers-by, while her world-famous son still took his place in the centre of the stage, crossing and re-crossing the Atlantic, but always returning to that corner house in the square, whose Edwardian façade had been so appropriately restored. Until the moment came for us both to take our respective farewells. Inevitably I was to find this second coincidence a haunting one, joined as it was with the undoubted fact that, through my first meeting with the author of *The Marquise*, I later discovered a room for myself in a neighbouring house in Ebury Street, where I have been so content and which has brought me such good fortune, and where I intend to go on living whenever I am in London, for the rest of my own days on earth.

After I had left number 111 in good time to get to the theatre, I stood outside the house a few doors away where I had been told that George Moore lived, whose own *Conversations in Ebury Street* had recently come into my hands, a street with such double literary connotations, a street where there was also a plaque, near the other end, establishing and commemorating the house in which Mozart, as a boy, had composed his first symphony. What luck might it not bring me, could I also have lodgings there?

At the corner of the street nearest Victoria, there was a stationery shop, still in occupation today, with cards in the window offering this and that for sale, a kind of unofficial mart and domestic agency, with studios and lodgings in the vicinity, thrown in for good measure. As soon as my book is finished, I'll come back and have another look, I told myself. Or rather, if my book is finished and accepted – that was what I really meant. A sort of carrot, an incentive to myself, as though I would not merit to live among such neighbours, unpublished. At that moment, I had a room in Charles Street, the one off Trevor Street, in Knightsbridge. In those days that vicinity possessed a different charm from Ebury Street, less raffish, more conventional. All the same, I used to wander out in my pyjamas on to my balcony in the mornings, when I woke up for a late breakfast. It never occurred to me that my dressing-gown appearance was an object of speculation to the neighbours. A few years later I was to meet a young woman with brilliant scarlet hair who had lived in the house opposite. 'We used to have bets about how many times we would see you in your pyjamas each week,' she told me. 'We wondered what you did to be dressed like that at eleven o'clock in the morning. I guessed you were an actor.'

'I was working on my first novel,' I answered loftily. 'I had just come out on to the balcony for a moment's breather.'

Mollie Panter Downes had written her own first novel at the age of sixteen, and it had caused something of a sensation. *The Shoreless Sea* was clearly the work of a naïve schoolgirl, and yet it showed in parts such a surprising awareness of adult emotions that it is not surprising that its author has won a rather special reputation for her London Letters in *The New Yorker,* a literary market where many other English authors have drawn a blank, in contrast with her own lasting success.

I had no idea that there was a fellow author of the same age as myself in our street; I was entirely preoccupied with scribbling away to my heart's content on non-matinée days. *The Marquise* had settled down to a run, which meant that I could afford to have my sheets of foolscap, covered with my schoolboy handwriting, typed (and the spelling corrected) by a first-class agency. A refreshing discovery at that time was how much better any kind of literary work looks when it comes back to its creator cleanly and clearly typed, with all one's corrections and crossings-out eradicated from each page.

'The gift of spontaneous laughter is beyond value. Young men possess it in excess, but as they grow older it generally fades away into just a smile. That is terrifying, especially to the next generation.'

A year in the life of a boy of sixteen, inevitably autobiographical as the majority of first novels are, and when the year was over, and like myself the hero, Michael, was leaving his family home in the shires to try for fame and fortune in London, I took the last pages to the Margaret Watson agency, beside Westminster Bridge, handing them over to the principal as though I were entrusting her with the Koh-i-noor diamond. In a way, I was. I have never felt quite the same about any book which I have written since, except perhaps *P.Q.17*,* since that, too, was composed with my life's blood.

One Sunday morning, with the precious typed manuscript on my knees, I drove home for the rest of the week-end in the car of a friend, whose family had been another of my kind meal-providers, and who himself had taken the trouble to read the chapters as they were written, urging me on to the completion of my task. Robert Blundell had been at Cambridge with my brother, and in due course had also been called to the Bar. There their ambitions had divided. Robert did not aspire as high as Rodger, though he, too, had a strong, secret determination – to take his place one day on the London Bench, an ambition which he more than fulfilled, since he was to become the Senior Metropolitan Magistrate presiding over the Bow Street court. Thus when in the evening papers I came across the reports of the justice he had meted out that day, I sometimes found myself remembering that spring Sunday when we drove through Oxford and on to the Stratford road, until we reached the home stretch, with all the fruit blossom once again in full flower. Somehow the fields of blossom cascading with such abandon on either side of the hedge-rows matched my mood of overflowing relief that my book was finished and typed, for better or for worse, my first literary effort complete. Besides, hadn't Miss Watson herself assured me that she was lucky for first novelists?

I started to talk about it the moment that we sat down to lunch. Robert and my stepfather were discussing the performance of the former's Austin. One hundred and twenty miles in five minutes under the four hours. That was quite something. I brushed aside their mutual congratulations, their car 'shop', to announce:

'Miss Watson says that her agency typed the first novel of Pamela Frankau, also of Anthony Gibbs.'

Sharp as a dagger through my heart came my mother's instant retort. 'What a pity, dear, that you will break her record.'

It was to become an affectionate family joke. Years later, for instance, when I was sharing her home at Esher in her widowhood, she was heard on her way to bed one Saturday evening to give this good night exhortation to a visitor staying with us for

* A story of a ship on the Russian Run, published by Hutchinson.

the first time: 'I do hope you'll find the bed comfortable and that you'll sleep well. If you don't, there's one of Godfrey's books on the table beside your lamp.'

That, too, was something which could have been phrased differently, though my mother always defended herself by pointing out that in the first instance she had only been anxious to prepare her son for the worst which could happen. 'I did not want you to be disappointed.' As I myself have been so often disappointed in my own life, she meant. Little by little her personal philosophy had grown into a state of eternal wariness, of being prepared always for the sun clouding over on a summer's day, a cold wind tugging at one's back, from nowhere – soughing suddenly through the trees.

Fortunately this time the worst did not happen. On the contrary. I had been given an introduction to Duckworth's, the publishers, whose offices are still in Henrietta Street, Covent Garden, and there on my return to London I delivered my manuscript in person to a dark, clever-looking young man in the outer office. I was to come to know him much better during the ensuing months, since it fell to him to correct my grammar and tidy up some loose ends, but he never looked down his nose at my artless outpourings, as well he might, since he himself was destined to become one of the major novelists of this age. For his name was Anthony Powell.

All the same it was not Anthony Powell, but Mr Balston, a senior partner in the firm, who actually decided my fate. Within a week I had been recalled to Henrietta Street, and almost before I had entered Mr Balston's sanctum, he announced, 'We are going to do your book, but we would like the Epilogue cut. It is superfluous.'

'Yes, of course ... anything you want,' I stammered, unable to believe my ears.

'I will have a contract drawn up this week, the usual contract allowing an option on your next two books, and as soon as it is signed we will give you an advance of fifty pounds. It's a little late for the autumn list now, but we should be able to publish you early in the New Year, when there's not such a spate of books coming out, so that you'll stand more chance of reviews.'

The New Year seemed a century away, for this was only May, but what matter? I was a fully-fledged author and soon I should have a cheque for fifty pounds to prove it. Actually, it had never seriously occurred to me that you were paid for writing, in the same way as you were for acting or serving behind a counter. Writing was a labour of love. At least, it had been so far.

'Oh, there's one more thing. We don't like the title.' For the first time since I had entered the room, the face of the friendly figure opposite me, with the old-fashioned manner, puckered in distaste. '*Tangled Roots*. It's the only indigestible thing about your book,' he added. 'We think it might put people off. Will you try and think of something else, and so will we, this end.'

A moment later I was out in Henrietta Street again, in the dusk of an early summer evening. I started to run as though I was taking part in the school sports. In actual fact, I was searching for a post office, before closing time. I had a telegram to send, the most important telegram yet of my life. '*Book accepted straight off by Duckworths. Fifty pounds advance. Love Godfrey.*'

Surely the mention of the money, such a concrete, not-to-be-sneezed-at sum, would convince them at home at last? I myself was in such a state of excitement that evening that I did something unheard of, dead against every backstage rule in a theatre where Miss Tempest was reigning. As soon as I was dressed in the thigh-length hunting boots that I wore for the first act, I thumped along the passage and greatly daring, I knocked on the door of the star's dressing-room.

As usual, the leading lady had been driven to the theatre an hour before she was needed. To compose herself. To empty her mind of everything except the challenge of her nightly rendezvous with her audience. Not like some of the flibberty-gibberty young-sters of today, she would often complain. The girls were the worst offenders, rushing through the stage door long after the 'half hour and beginners' had been called. In consequence, few ingénues had an easy ride in her Company. Eileen Sharp was so pretty and so unspoilt that I would have imagined that no one could have found fault with her, but unfortunately she was an incorrigible giggler, and we were both reported for this heinous crime in one of our scenes together. It was really entirely my fault. For it happened on the night when there was a gap in the middle of my front teeth, so that I hissed every time that I opened my mouth. I had gone to Brighton for the day and suc-

cumbed to a stick of rock on the pier. At one point, Eileen became too convulsed to go on with the play. However, the smile
swiftly faded from both our faces when we were summoned after
the performance to The Presence — just as all my exuberant self-
confidences swiftly evaporated when I actually found myself inside Number 1 dressing-room, standing awkwardly beside the
star, who was setting out her patience cards. A nightly ritual, after
her make-up was done, her wig dressed and put on to her critical
satisfaction, the dust coat wrapped round her shoulders.

'And what is the reason for this intrusion, may I ask?' she
demanded.

I blurted out the news that to me was so overwhelmingly
important. 'I am awfully sorry, Miss Tempest, I didn't mean to
disturb you, I know I should have waited till the end of the performance, but . . . but . . .'

'Yes, boy?' Her voice had lost its edge of anger. There was
a whimsical look of almost tenderness in her eyes, which encouraged me to finish what I had come to say.

'You see, I wanted to ask your advice. You are so wise. Do
you think I should continue with acting as my profession, or
should I give up the stage, and devote myself entirely to being
a writer?'

That I should have spoken like this, imagining that anyone
in her position would be as absorbed in my future destiny as I
was, seems extraordinary to me now. Indeed I am filled with dismay for my effrontery, yet in a way, I am thankful, too. For had
I not burst in upon her that evening, floating on the first tide
of my rapture, not stopping to pause and think how I was breaking all the rules and the conventions in regard to Royalty,
I might never have received the blunt, realistic answer that
I did. Or, at some other time, it might have had less of
an impact.

Of course, I longed, I half-expected her to reply, 'Why, there
is no question, you must stay on the stage. Willie and I will want
you in our next production, or if there is no part for you, we
will recommend you to our many friends in the profession. We
are both agreed that you show real promise. Especially now
that you have learnt to breathe properly, and taken fencing
lessons, to improve your deportment, as we suggested.'

I must be honest and admit that she said none of these things.

All signs of temper had completely vanished now, and she was smiling in the way that she had smiled at Ernest Thesiger. It wasn't my face that was funny, close to, it was this revelation of my taking myself so seriously, with so little to show for it, yet. But, at least, I wasn't one of those silly girls. So she took the trouble, and I shall be eternally grateful, to weigh her words with some care before she passed judgment.

'If your first novel has been accepted by the first publisher to whom you submitted it, and within a week, clearly you must show promise as a writer. To me it is quite clear where your future lies.' There was a pause, and then with all the knowledge of the heartbreak in her own career at the back of her mind, she added words that have often returned to me now that I am a member of the audience, safely on the other side of the footlights.

'Juveniles in the Theatre are two a penny.'

It was not the answer that I had hoped for, but it left such a deep and lasting impression on me that when the run of 'The Marquise' came to an end I did not spend the rest of the summer and autumn haunting agents' offices, nervously seeking work as I had always done before, but with the promise of another fifty pounds on publication day, was quite content to sit back to see what happened to *Dreams Fade,* the title with my mother's unmistakable touch about it.

So I was at home in Worcestershire on the day of publication, January 19th, 1928. I had started another novel with a background of stage life that autumn, having been promoted from the cramped desk in my bedroom to the sitting-room in Ted's suite, now that I was a paid writer. Christmas was, in a way, the best I could remember, because as a kind of present to myself I was able to display the book's dust-cover as a conversational gambit, to make everyone in the neighbourhood promise that they would ask for it – 'The title is from a quotation of Walter de la Mare,' – at their local library, to create demand. At all the Christmas and New Year parties, I felt I was regarded with a new respect. But alas for the mounting triumph, when the week of publication itself arrived I suddenly came out in a rash of spots. Mother's first instinct was to put it down to a spate of overeating, too many parties. Moreover, being so stoical herself about any form of sickness, she viewed with disapproval my increasing complaints that I was beginning to feel really ill.

However, the moment arrived when my stepfather, returning from his Birmingham office, insisted that the doctor was sent for, and that night, full of contrition, she sat up with me, giving me sips of water, for my temperature had soared alarmingly. Delirious, and my face burning, I demanded that the first copy of my book, which had arrived by the afternoon post, should be placed in my hands.

Later it had to be consigned to the flames before anyone else inside or outside the sick-room, had touched it, or had been contaminated. For the next morning the doctor pronounced that, undignified though it might seem for a budding novelist, I had measles, and an extremely severe attack.

But how enormously pleasant that luxurious period of convalescence, the aftermath, turned out to be. As I sipped the midday glass of Wincarnis prescribed for me, I was not for once depressed by the bitter cold of another Midland winter, by the roses reduced to black frozen sticks in my mother's beloved borders, for was I not basking in the sun of being a real live author? As the reviews started to appear and were sent on to me by my publishers, I stuck them into my first scrapbook with a pot of home-made paste, a pastime which I have never enjoyed so much since; while, out of the second instalment of my royalty advance, I bought myself a typewriter, surely the unchallengeable insignia of a writer's professional status.

However, I did not start using my portable Royal, which is still in commission, and has gallantly stood up to many batterings in my world travels, for the draft of my second novel. That, I decided, would have a diminishing, almost a coarsening effect. After all, one day my manuscripts, written in my own handwriting, might be bid for in auction rooms, or acquired by museums. In fairness, there was some excuse for such outrageous flights of fancy. My first published effort received almost universal praise from the critics.

Auntie Violet was the member of my family to be most outwardly impressed. It was almost as though she had written the book herself, and she was particularly delighted with the outbursts that it contained concerning the conventions of family life. On yet another of her sporadic visits, she crouched over the morning oom fire reading and re-reading *The Spectator*, or with a pad on her lap writing endless, long screeds to Andrée, in Paris. Here was her one link with the kind of Bohemian existence that she had longed for but never attained, and whenever a particularly flattering mention of my book appeared, she would with a proprietorial gesture enclose a copy with her letter to Paris. Already she was convinced in her own mind that she had prophesied it would all turn out exactly like this, in the days when I had read out passages from my essays to her in her Hereford lodgings, to take her mind off her suspicious preoccupation with the landlady's meals. Though they had seemed like a series of Lucullan feasts to me, after the barrenness of school fare.

Violet relished particularly the impressive list of quotes that the publishers inserted in the Sunday papers, to announce that a second edition was already on its way. The first two thousand copies, in those days considered a more than average sale for a first novel, had been exhausted in a month.

'*"Dreams Fade" is a sensitive, courageous attempt to do an almost impossible thing – to render, in the intelligible terms of art, those strange, shy hungers and dreams and discontents that haunt and drive and irradiate adolescence*.'

This was from Gerald Gould, in *The Observer*. He had first been my Sunday companion in the solitary walks beside the Wye, and was now considered one of the most important literary pundits of the day. It was an unexpectedly encouraging pat on the back.

The Sunday Times told its readers that I had 'begun very well'; *The Evening Standard* called the book 'a remarkably good first novel'. Using the same words, *The Daily Mail* added as a rider, 'Full of sympathy and understanding,' while *Punch* went so far as to suggest that 'Mr Godfrey Winn, in the play between the puzzled mother and her son, has performed a feat that is nearly related to genius.'

True, I had been ignored by *The Spectator,* but *Punch* was *Punch,* and in my parents' eyes the kind of magazine that you liked to see come into your house. That notice was the real accolade in their eyes, and it was not surprising that for a few weeks I existed in a fantasy world, where the only jarring note was struck in *The New Statesman,* where Cyril Connolly, then at the beginning of his extremely distinguished career as a critic, lambasted me without mercy.

He started his notice with the words: ' "*Dreams Fade*" *belongs to the worst class of autobiographical novel*'; he ended with the ominous foreboding: '*Perhaps when Michael grows up, for he is only sixteen, he will be able to stand alone, without the infinite promptings of the author's tenderness. For the author, as well, will one day be a man.*'

It was a body blow, indeed, and not surprisingly I hid the copy of the magazine both from my family and Auntie Violet, consoling myself with the thought that at least this cutting-down to size had not taken place in her own literary Bible. Writing today, when the fires have long since died down, and a defensive immunity against such devastating criticism has imperceptibly been developed, *faute de mieux,* across the years, I am bound to admit that I fully appreciate the reviewer's reactions.

Although in defence of Michael's creator it could be said that I was most eager to grow up, to fend for myself, to achieve a living space of my own, at this moment when I was about to receive the keys of the door.

Restlessly that spring, I returned to London, en route for Cambridge, where I had been invited to a May Week party, which included Oliver Messel, just commencing his career as a designer, and Nina Seafield,* who with her reddish-gold hair, parted severely in the middle, bore a striking resemblance to some of the early portraits of Queen Victoria. There was also in the party a most beautiful girl of eighteen, with the kind of completely natural ash-blonde looks that only America seems able to achieve. Charlotte Brown had come over to be presented at court, and she and our host, Sir Basil Bartlett, seemed an admirably matched couple. The rest of the party took bets as to whether the engagement would be announced before the week was over. I am still surprised that it wasn't, since the atmosphere was so extremely conducive to romance. We danced all night, we lazed on the river in the afternoons, we went to see if Rupert Brooke's clock at Grantchester still stood at ten to three. I remember whirling Charlotte round and round the panelled room at the King's College Ball, at four o'clock in the morning, praying that the music would never stop. I had achieved my elixir of

* The Countess of Seafield.

delight. All thoughts of earning my living, or serving a fresh apprenticeship, were far away that week.

Basil, with impressively spacious rooms looking out on to King's Parade, lived a very different kind of life from my brother, at the University. At the time it was only natural that I should relish the contrast, but on reflection, and in the light of all that has happened to us both since, I have a suspicion that Basil had been given too many gifts at his birth by his Fairy Godmother. He was too rich, from the start, too good-looking, too attractive a personality to be allowed by his ever-widening circle of friends and acquaintances to slog away at his books. With a potential first-class brain, his talents were too diverse, his own enthusiasms too demanding. He appeared as Coriolanus, and had created almost as much a furore as Gyles Isham had done with his Hamlet at Oxford, he was already translating plays from the French, he was invited to all the débutante dances in London, he drove about in a lush-looking Packard. In fact, he possessed everything that I lacked, and his air of assumption that it all belonged to him by right I found awe-inspiring. Unconsciously, however, he set me a treacherous example. For he made everything seem too easy; and I was to discover in due course that nothing in the matter of lasting achievement or the establishment of permanent values is easy; nothing at all. I should have learnt the lesson sooner.

A rising young barrister would sometimes invite me to the theatre. Afterwards, I would suggest that we went on to supper somewhere. Cyril always refused. Not because he was unsociable, but because he must burn the midnight oil. It would be two o'clock before he was satisfied that tomorrow's briefs were properly studied. But it was all worth while in the end, because today he is Viscount Radcliffe, Lord of Appeal in Ordinary. And now I come to think of it, I can't remember a single evening dining with my brother in the days when he was an advocate, that he did not have to leave my sister-in-law and myself directly the meal was finished, for the solitary companionship of the law tomes in his study.

Unfortunately it is so very pleasant to be idle, if you can get away with it – and ignore the consequences. Suddenly, I was finding myself in social demand, and it was an extremely agreeable if distracting sensation. As an author with a successful first novel on display in the bookshops, I started to receive many more invitations than in my days as an actor. The only 'prop' I needed was the tail-coat I had acquired during the run of *There's No Fool*. Moreover, my evenings now were free, and one invitation that I accepted with alacrity came from a sanatorium in Scotland.

Here, incarcerated all that winter, with one lung useless and the other in poor shape, lay a still-youngish man who had almost dissipated a huge fortune in the pursuit of enjoyment and in giving pleasure often to worthless hangers-on, because his own sincere motivation, his one abiding ambition, eluded him. Ned Lathom longed to be acclaimed as a playwright; not to be known, instead, in the gossip columns as the peer who was one of the biggest theatrical 'angels' in the West End, even to the extent of financing his own plays from time to time, so that they could be given a production by some Sunday-night Society. Classed as 'that inveterate first-nighter, the Earl of Lathom,' he had under the mask of flippancy that he wore in self-protection a passionate craving to achieve – just once before he died – a commercial success in the Theatre on his own merits, like his friends Eddie Knoblock, who had hit the jackpot with *Kismet* and *Milestones,* and Willie Maugham, to whom he had with characteristic enthusiasm sent on my book after he had read it himself in the sanatorium.

Ironically, the latter had also had his first play produced by a Sunday-night Society. However, in Maugham's case, *A Man of Honour* had been such an instantaneous success with the audience that immediately it was transferred to another theatre and put on for a run. Immediately, too, the other managers, who had until that time studiously ignored this newcomer's talent, while he languished in exile abroad, existing on a small legacy left him by his mother, searched in their drawers and brought out other plays that had been lying there, unread. They were, not surprisingly, anxious to muscle-in on the drawing powers of this new theatrical discovery. But it was too late to bring the author of *Mrs Dot* and, later, *The Circle*, the kind of uncorroded joy that I had experienced in the reception of my first novel, when even *The Daily Herald* suggested that if I could spare the time from my studio preoccupations – a reference to *Blighty* – my succeeding novels should be worth reading 'more than once'.

I have never been able to erase from my mind the picture

that Somerset Maugham drew for me once of the Sunday evening when the first of his plays was performed, at last, and how he had been torn in half with mingled relief and rage as the audience began to explode with laughter at his witty comedy lines. He wasn't a young man of twenty-two any more, as he had been when his first novel, *Liza of Lambeth,* had appeared. He was thirty-five when recognition finally came, and he had been in the literary wilderness ever since his second novel had failed dismally to repeat the impact of the first one. In consequence, as is the way of the world, he had been dropped by the society hostesses, who liked to sprinkle their parties with the latest lions of the moment.

In the end, he had to wait, to endure, for thirteen years before he was taken back into the fold. He hated 'them' for fawning on him once more; he hated himself for accepting their adulation. As he sat in the author's box on each subsequent first-night – soon he had four plays running at once in the West End, a record that has never been surpassed since – with the spontaneous applause assaulting his ears, the persistent shouts for 'Author' at the fall of the final curtain, he could only see before his eyes the succession of sleazy *pensions* in which he had had to exist in Spain, at that time the cheapest country in Europe. It was a memory that was part of him for ever after. It not only took away the sweetness of the final triumph, but it also clouded his whole future attitude to life, and to the world. Of course, it can be argued that he was being unreasonable, perverse; but having been orphaned almost from birth, and with the cruel burden of a stammer to bear in public, that added considerably to his sense of apartness, he has created in Philip, the hero of *Of Human Bondage,* also published that year – an *annus mirabilis* for him – a self-portrait which explains exactly the strange, conflicting ingredients in his character, a character longing to be loved, even by a worthless creature, and yet was for ever searching for the worm in the bud. This long novel is today considered to be his masterpiece, but he confessed to me that he wrote it first when he was twenty-five and had to rewrite it half-a-dozen times before his publishers would finally, grudgingly, accept it, ten years later. Meanwhile, the iron had entered into his soul, and once that has happened there is seldom, if ever, any effective means of exorcism.

Richard King, in what was an established column of the day, called *With Silent Friends* in *The Tatler*, had most generously given up a whole page to discussing the merits of *Dreams Fade,* ending his review with words that did not strike me at the time as having any particular personal application, though now, as I turn back the yellow pages of that first scrapbook, I am forced to realize, in the light of so much subsequent experience, that they do exactly describe the situation with which Somerset Maugham himself was faced throughout his life.

'The *"different"* people always make trouble for themselves and others, but principally for themselves. Their doom lies in their "difference".'

Ned Lathom, on the other hand, despite the consistent failure of any of his plays to be put on in the West End, had none of the same bitterness or sense of martyrdom in his own make-up. Like so many other tubercular sufferers he was overflowing with optimism. In between the increasingly long periods that he had to surrender himself to the closed order of a whitewashed cell, he would feverishly embark upon bouts of entertaining in London, as though, despite his front of frivolity he was secretly aware how rapidly the candle was burning down for him.

One of his less spectacular and more conventional forms of enjoyment was to spend an evening playing bridge, and when his own leave from the sanatorium coincided with a visit of his old friend, now living in the South of France and recently divorced from his wife, Syrie, he always arranged a game for him, since, throughout his life, bridge remained Maugham's chief source of relaxation. And it was to one of these sessions that I was summoned, little realizing that the evening was to prove so portentous a one for me, or that my whole writing future was to be involved.

Graham Greene in his latest novel, *The Comedians*, puts forward the theory that the first twenty years contain the whole of experience for a writer – the rest is observation. Well, I had just concluded my own first twenty years, which, if they had in no sense been as unhappy or frugal as those of the orphan brought up by a spartan clerical uncle, starved of affection in that Broadstairs vicarage, had nevertheless left me with a deep-rooted sense of insecurity concerning the lack of lasting stability in most relationships; this was, I appreciate now, to colour all my own creative efforts for a long time. I had no inkling, however, at that moment, that I was to assume the rôle of observer that I have deliberately schooled myself to do, as in due course the journalistic side to my career developed. All the same, I was abundantly aware, and naturally very excited by the prospect, that I was on my way that spring evening to meet for the first time the man who in his short stories, if not in his plays, is acknowledged to be the supreme observer of the foibles, the idiosyncrasies and the motivations of the human heart.

Once, a long time ahead, I was to ask him at the end of quite a different kind of evening, when we had been to a party which in an extrovert mood I had found extremely entertaining, why he himself had worn such a glum look all evening. Was it the food, the heat, the noise? The people?

'I will tell you why, Godfrey,' my host at the Villa Mauresque replied bleakly. 'You see,' and he began to stutter, which he only did, in his own house, when he was very tired or very bored. 'You see, when people chatter and chatter to me, saying all the flattering things that they imagine I want them to say, I know what they are really thinking underneath – what a disagreeable old party, and how dull he is in real life! How can he ever write all those clever books and amusing plays?'

'You mean, you can really see into people's hearts and minds? What they are thinking, when they are saying something quite different?' I queried.

'Yes, it is a gift from the Devil,' he replied grimly, and proceeded ahead of me up the wide staircase, to bed.

On the landing he turned back, and looking down the stairs, asked:

'Did you know Alfred Mond?'

'I knew his son, Henry Melchett, and Gwen, of course.'

'Well, you see that Chinese statue on its plinth?'

I did, indeed – carved wood, as old as Time, an exquisite thing.

'Well, Mond came to lunch and asked if he could see all over the house. When the tour, an exhausting affair, was over at last, he paused on the staircase and said, "I will have that." I could not help being struck by his choice, because it is the only really museum piece in the whole house.'

At his doorway, turning to say good night, he added: 'The

very rich are like that, you know. They have a special kind of nose.'

All the flushed warmth lingering from the party left me. I felt suddenly shrivelled and forlorn, and looking into my bathroom mirror, as I cleaned my teeth, I was faced by the dark, sombre, fathomless eyes of the man who so often chose to play the part of skeleton at the feast.

I could sympathise with the guests at any party, struggling to make conversation with this shy, inhibited figure, who had the reputation of being so hard on his female characters, though in real life he liked to surround himself with elegant, vivacious women, such as Daisy Fellowes,* Annie Fleming,† Juliet Duff‡ and Pamela Berry.§ Throughout his life, he had many more close friends from their sex than from his own. As our own friendship gradually matured, though he remained to the end in my eyes my literary mentor, and I myself remained the pupil, I found it, much to my chagrin and puzzlement, increasingly difficult to talk naturally to him. He made me feel as my brother had done one morning at breakfast in my youth, when looking up from his paper, to still my flow of conversation in full spate, he had said, 'Consider that statement in the light of reason.' It was unreasoning that I should be often ill at ease in Maugham's presence, when I was so full of admiration for his achievements, and of gratitude for his help, and I can only put it down to a sense of my own inadequacy. For he had the most courteous manners, and went out of his way to be kind and welcoming whenever I visited him. And right up till the time when a curtain came down over his mind, he would always give me frank answers to my questions.

For instance, when I asked him why he had stopped writing plays so much earlier than he had given up writing fiction, for he produced *The Razor's Edge,* one of his major works, when he was seventy, he replied:

'No author should continue to write plays after he is fifty. He is inviting derision if he does. Fashions change in the Theatre much more radically and more swiftly than they do in other forms of art. You try to adapt yourself to the new mood, and

* The Hon. Mrs Reginald Fellowes.
† Mrs Ian Fleming.
‡ Lady Juliet Duff.
§ Lady Pamela Berry.

only succeed in seeming old-fashioned. I had two failures running, and so packed up.'

Exceptions come at once to mind, such as Bernard Shaw, who
started writing for the theatre late in his life, and again, Noël
Coward, who has recently had a remarkable renaissance with a
trilogy of new plays, although himself not far off the seventy
mark. There was, one felt, a certain irony when surely to the
author's own surprise, some of the critics insisted on recognizing
a likeness between Noël Coward's own portrayal of the aged
English writer, living out his last years in a Swiss hotel, in *A
Song at Twilight,* and Somerset Maugham, who had been a life-
long friend of Coward and given him such generous encouragement in his own early days as a playwright.

What struck me at once was that the leading character in
Coward's play was made of much more brittle material than
Maugham. He showed himself to be very vain too. Whereas
Maugham, throughout his career was extremely modest about
his achievements, referring to himself as a story teller, nothing
more. Again, for long periods in the play the dialogue is of so
feline a character that at one moment the ex-mistress of the
Master cries out, 'What a bitch you are!'

Whatever Maugham's detractors may now suggest – since the
law of libel conveniently has no powers to reach beyond the grave
– he was not that. It is true he had a sharp tongue – in the same
way as he had a sharp pen – and could be devastating on
occasions, when his stammer allowed, but he never failed to give
the impression of what was truly the core of his being. First and
last, he was a man of letters, a most disciplined craftsman
who never deviated from his belief that the art and skill of the
writer, or for that matter any other creative artist, must be put
before all worldly considerations of any kind.

On almost the last occasion that I saw him alive, when I had
been invited by Alan Searle, who looked after him with such
devotion for the last thirty years of his life, to spend his ninetieth
birthday, as I had his eightieth, at the Villa Mauresque, I took
with me the only trifle that I thought might still give him
pleasure. Forgetting that he was almost as blind now as he was
deaf. A programme of the National Theatre, with many striking
pictures of the players between the covers.

My host was seated in his favourite leather armchair, wearing a faded velvet dinner jacket. As though he was an old player waiting in the wings, he was waiting for his dinner; he had just finished the dry Martini, which like his food he still relished.

'Good evening,' he said politely, though on my arrival from the airport he had greeted me by name, and embraced me. 'Are you one of Alan's friends?'

I put the programme into his hands and he stared at the cover for a long time. I only realized fully later with what difficulty he traced the wording. 'OTHELLO by WILLIAM SHAKE-SPEARE.' The silence lengthened between us until he finally broke it, saying sadly, 'I can't remember, you know, when I wrote that.' Although there was a fire blazing, a shiver touched me and it was as though my own grave yawned.

Alan had not prepared me for this. 'Where is Alan?' he kept on asking petulantly. I looked towards the door of the long salon with the great Florentine golden eagle over the Provençal stone fireplace that I had seen put into place the first summer I had visited the villa, but there was no sign of any rescue. So desperately, feeling the sweat gathering on the palms of my hands, I tried again, almost shouting this time:

'Noël had also had a big success with the National Theatre, with a revival of *Hay Fever.*'

'Noël? Noël who?' he echoed coldly.

'Noël Coward.' Now it was I who was doing the stammering.

Again there was a pause, in which there was time for me to have a vision like unto the procession of the headless figures in the scene of Banquo's ghost in *Macbeth,* before he spoke again. These were his words:

'I seem to recollect the name, but I cannot recall the face.'

It was like an epitaph delivered in perplexity, rather than tinged with malice.

Alan at last appeared, and taking both our arms the old party, as he liked to refer to himself, made a slow procession into the dining-room where we ate our meal in silence. If Alan and I spoke to each other at mealtime during the week I stayed on, he would be suspicious that we were talking about him; if we bellowed to reach him through the cold corridors of his deafness, it seemed discourteous, and I found myself thinking with regret how different it had been on his eightieth birthday. On that occasion it had been a brilliantly sunny day, with the bulbs already flowering in the garden though it was only the end of January, and we had driven up the hill over Villefranche in a brand-new Rolls-Royce, for a celebration lunch party at what is perhaps the most extravagant restaurant on the *Côte d'Azur*.

'Why have you changed cars?' I asked him. 'In the past you've always used French makes of cars. You said it was more convenient for these roads, and also because you lived in France.'

'I know I did, Godfrey, but they promise me that a Rolls is good for ten years.' That would make him ninety, I told myself. A bold gamble, but in the reckoning he was almost exactly right and, as though he could sense what was in my mind, he went on: 'You know, people seem to regard death as an indictable crime. They are shocked if you mention it. I wait for it now without rancour or surprise. Every morning my valet tiptoes into my room as though he expects to find me dead in my bed – but death, like constipation, is one of the commonplaces of human existence. Why shy away from it?'

Changing direction I was delighted with the relish which he put into his next remarks. 'And do you know what we shall have for lunch at the Château de Madrid, Godfrey? We shall have fresh asparagus, baby lamb, and strawberries out of season. I am told there will be eight in the party, and do you know what it will cost our hostess, including the view? Well over fifty pounds.' He said those last words with childish wonder. Like myself, he never forgot what it had been like to be very poor, and we sat back, enjoying the luxurious feel of the car, savouring the prospect ahead, relaxed, and for a moment very close.

And yet, though I knew him for thirty-five years, and received so many confidences from him, as well as so much constructive advice, after a time I began to find it more compatible, to my own surprise, to spend an evening in the company of his ex-wife, Syrie. A woman of genuine warmth, great taste, and enthusiasm. Some people give, some people take. She was a giver and again a giver. It was true that there was nothing she relished more than a shrewd bargain in antiques, a *coup*, and equally she enjoyed charging an extravagant price for her services as a decorator, but then everything went back into the melting pot. Rightly she took up the attitude that the rich without taste should pay for the support of struggling young artists, in whose work she glimpsed a reflection, however faint, of the promised land.

Cecil Beaton was one of her protégés, whose merits she was never tired of extolling, not as a photographer but as the painter and designer for the Theatre that he has become. While for my own part, it gave me great pleasure that towards the end of her own life, when the fires of her enthusiasm had begun to burn themselves out, and she was increasingly frail, I was able to invite her to rest sometimes for a quiet week-end in my Sussex home. This was a small return for all the hospitality she had given me, and the many kindnesses she had shown me, both before the war and after her return from the States. At the end she lived in a flat in Park Lane, just opposite the Dorchester where her former husband always stayed in the closing years of his literary apotheosis.

To Syrie he was still the man in his prime, with whom she had had a tempestuous love affair in Positano, with its patchwork-quilt roofs, just before the outbreak of the First World War. The daughter of Doctor Barnardo, she remained an extremely handsome woman, with delicate features, an ivory skin, and striking eyes, until the end of her life. She had had many admirers, but the one a woman loves most, the one who gets beneath her skin, is the one who finally escapes. Notwithstanding her defeat, she never spoke in a deprecating way about her lost lover, as so many women do after a divorce – railing unceasingly to anyone who will listen. Instead, she went on seeing what she had originally seen in him until the end. She would sit in her flat and without venom, without reproach, think of him, a stone's-throw away, in his suite at the Dorchester, and the first thing that she would ask me when I arrived to dine, to play a game of canasta for two afterwards, in a version that she had taught me – as a refuge against middle-age – would be: 'Have you been to play bridge with Willie? How is he?'

Nor had her enquiries about his health anything to do with her knowledge that at his death their daughter Liza, named after the heroine of his first book, would inherit the bulk of her father's fortune. Instead, the simple truth, astonishing as it may seem to some, was that she went on loving him until she died. He was in her blood stream. Even despite what happened on the last occasion when they came face to face by chance, just after the retreat from Dunkirk. It was zero hour, a moment of desperate decisions and heart-searchings. Syrie had decided to take Liza, who was expecting another child, to safety in the States, while Willie himself had just reached these shores in a tramp steamer, usually more accustomed to carrying a cargo of coal but now pressed into the services of the English refugees from the South of France.

In a way, it was entirely suitable that they should meet in the anonymous atmosphere of the lounge of the Dorchester, like two ships passing each other in the English Channel.

Surely the exigencies of war, the breaking down of so many barriers, would make a difference? Acting on a spontaneous impulse, she stopped her ex-husband and told him her news about their daughter. Wearing his mask of a Chinese mandarin, he looked at her and his upper lip curled back. It was a dangerous sign. He started to stammer. At last he succeeded in getting out his answer.

'Well, S-S-Syrie, I am assured that when you find yourself in the water, if you open your m-m-mouth wide, it's all over much more quickly.'

She forgave him even that. Though many of her friends could never forgive the last of his published work, scraps and dregs of poorly-composed autobiography, when he mercilessly denigrated her name in a dozen disgraceful ways. He was so very old, and so very sick, already wandering in his mind over the battlefields of the past. The poison welled up in him, an excess of the bile that had cursed him all his days, and he foolishly was allowed to give it expression in a manuscript that should have remained locked away until all the protagonists were long since dead, and all the old scores erased. For what happened there could be no excuse, a degrading episode for the accuser, not the accused; but for the rest, I find myself writing in the margin of my own pad the biblical warning, 'Judge not, that ye be not judged.' Moreover I find it extremely ironical that those who hardly allowed time for Somerset Maugham's ashes to be buried close to the precincts of Canterbury Cathedral, and in the shadow of his old school, before they published, for doubtless very fat fees, their holier-than-thou condemnations, their scurrilous revelations, were hardly those whom one would have imagined would have been anxious to cast the first stone.

The first stone, the last stone; I have no wish, no right to cast either; just as I had no consciousness of any portents that first evening when I met the man who was to have such a profound influence over my working life. Everything seemed to go with a swing. It is only when you are twenty that you harbour no doubts about prattling away, blithely unaware that you are not necessarily God's conversational gift to the party. Fortunately my luck was in that night. Having cut my future literary mentor for three out of four rubbers, I held consistently good cards. It does not matter how well you play your cards at bridge, in the end it is a plethora of aces and kings which win the rubbers. My partner was delighted with me. He got up winning a fiver, and pocketed it with transparent pleasure. To me, accustomed to playing for threepence a hundred, it represented a month's rent, and thrilled with my windfall, as we sat back enjoying a nightcap, I was bold enough to embark upon a personal anecdote that illustrated another aspect of beginner's luck, which I hoped would amuse the story-teller of the party.

Soon after the appearance of *Dreams Fade,* I had received an invitation to a Hunt Ball to be held in a neighbouring county, where my hostess for the night, herself possessed of literary aspirations, was married to a hunting squire. Perhaps she felt that a kindred spirit would help her survive the rigours of the evening. Little did I appreciate, when I answered her letter, what lay ahead of me.

All the male guests except myself, at the large dinner party before the Ball, wore the insignia of a pink coat. Gazing round the table, I felt like one of the black-beetles that had swarmed across the basement floor of our Richmond house. Vermin. As the women left the table, I cast a despairing glance in the direction of my hostess, who was sensibly – or perhaps symbolically – dressed in black. My feeling of being completely out of my *milieu* only increased when my host, in a hospitable gesture, beckoned to me to come and sit beside him. As he pushed the decanter of port towards me his face shone like the midnight sun. I filled my glass automatically before moving the decanter on to my neighbour, deep in conversation as to what had happened that day at the last covert they had drawn.

For once I was nonplussed. I had absolutely nothing to say. My host tried valiantly. 'My wife says you've written a capital first book. Anything in it about horses?' I had to admit that there wasn't; there was something about sheep, but nothing about horses. Rather foolishly, I proceeded to announce that I could neither ride, handle a gun or a fishing rod. At that his scarlet countenance assumed a glazed look. 'Good God,' he muttered, and relapsed into silence himself. A few moments later, with in-bred politeness, he tried again. 'What do you think of the port, my boy?'

The heat of the room, the alien atmosphere, enveloped and confused me. I felt myself trembling, unable to produce any of the stock phrases about wine, such as 'bouquet'. This was not surprising, since my knowledge of any kind of alcohol was so limited, my own palate non-existent.

'Well?' my host demanded. His tone of interrogation sounded extremely menacing. I took a sip and then a gulp, draining my glass so that I was on fire. There was a sudden silence down the table, as I held the empty glass up towards the candlelight. All the other guests seemed now to be leaning towards me, wait-ing for my answer, their sporting pink merged into a phalanx of advancing troops. I must, I must say something. For no reason at all I blurted out 'I think it's corked, sir.' 'CORKED,' echoed my host. 'Good God. He raised his own glass, while the silence became agonizing. Surely I would be frogmarched out of the room, ignominiously ordered to pack my bag, banished before I could have a single dance. I half rose from my seat in expecta-tion of what was to come.

However, the sequel turned out quite differently from my phantom fears.

The squire, who had not missed a day's hunting for the last twenty years, gargled the port round his gums, then put down his glass with a look of surprised admiration now on his face. 'Good God,' he exclaimed again, 'the boy's right. Ring the bell, some-one.' In came the butler, and a bottle of the best port in the cellar was commanded forthwith to be decanted. Indeed we all had to remain in the dining-room till it was. Then a second and third glass was forced upon the expert wine-taster, whose status had been so unexpectedly transformed.

When we finally joined the ladies I could hardly stand and had to consume several cups of black coffee. It did not matter, because my host's arm was around my shoulder, and this was the judgment he subsequently pronounced to his wife: 'That young protégé of yours ought to do well with his writing. He's a first-class judge of port.'

Winner of the South of England Junior
Championship, aged 13. *Photo: Illustrated
London News*

Tennis partnerships – Billie Yorke and Jack Lysaght,
Godfrey Winn and Susan Noel

Above Winning South of England championship 1921. *Below* Suzanne Lenglen. *Photo: Radio Times Hulton Picture Library*

'Of course the port was no more corked than yours tonight, Ned,' I explained, unnecessarily, in parenthesis. For Somerset Maugham, of all people, was only too aware how easily the world is deceived by a sufficiently bold assumption of absolute knowledge. However, I could see that my narrative had not bored him; moreover, it gave him the opportunity to lead in to an experience of his own.

'I had such an excellent valet when I lived in London,' he started. 'I shall never find such a good one again. Alas, he left me.'

Ned took up his cue. 'Why was that, Willie? Did he dislike the idea of going to live out of England?'

'No, the reason was quite different. As you know yourself, Ned, in the days before the war, when you stayed at week-ends in grand houses your valet or the lady's maid brought by another of the guests always had to sit at mealtime in the servants' hall, in strict social precedence according to the rank of their master or mistress. As I was invariably the only guest without a title, let alone with relations in Debrett, my poor fellow found himself always placed at the bottom of the table. Out in the cold. In the end, he couldn't stand it any longer.'

'You should have kept him by accepting a knighthood. I understand you have been offered one on several occasions.'

The affectionate mockery beneath Ned's tone apparently escaped the narrator of this side-light on the social façade of the Edwardian era. But then snobbery is not a failing that anyone ever recognizes in their own character.

'They knight jockeys these days,' the author of *Our Betters* retorted contemptuously, and the evening was over. No, not quite. As we left our host's house, my fellow guest offered me a lift in his car. He had chambers himself in Half Moon Street, where he always stayed now during his periodic visits to London at this time of the year to attend the cycle of *The Ring* at Covent Garden, for music, like bridge, was one of his few lasting pleasures. While I had recently acquired rooms of my own in Ebury Street.

As we approached across Eaton Square, I explained how I had come to settle in the neighbourhood, just on the edge of Pimlico. 'I have Noël Coward two doors away from me on one side, George Moore three doors away on the other. I am hoping

I

desperately that some of their literary lustre will penetrate the walls between, and rub off on me.'

'Hmn,' was the non-committal reply I received. 'The last time that I ran into old George Moore was on Paddington Station, and when I enquired politely whether he was engaged upon some fresh piece of literary creation, do you know what he said? "Maugham, the only thing that I am interested in at the moment is whether I shall ever again be able to pee through my penis."'

This depressingly caustic comment concerning a fellow author who scarcely seemed any older in my eyes than my companion, then in his middle fifties, decided me to try again in lightening the atmosphere, as I had apparently done with success earlier in the evening.

My scrap of repeated dialogue was also about a famous author, and with a medical flavour, too, though of a rather different kind.

'A nurse told a friend of mine that when Rudyard Kipling was having an operation, and they were giving him the anaesthetic in the operating theatre, his subconsciousness floated to the surface and he went under crying out, 'I am the greatest writer in the world, I am the greatest . . . I am . . . I . . .'''

The car had reached number 115, where I still live today. I could sense that good humour had been restored. So on the spur of the moment, after offering my thanks for the lift, I added, 'Would you care to play bridge here one evening, Mr Maugham? I would ask Ned, and I have a friend at Cambridge who plays an excellent game.'

'Certainly. That would be very pleasant.' A night was fixed for a fortnight ahead. I had not yet come to appreciate that no invitation is unpleasing to someone who is rich, from someone who is not. The rich grow so weary of being sponged upon, always expected to do the asking and the paying. They are touched and disarmed when those with few resources set out to make an effort on their behalf.

'I used to write all day in my house in Chesterfield Street, and come down to dinner dead tired and not knowing one of the guests in my own house, eating my expensive food. They had all been invited by my wife,' he was to tell me, not that evening, of course, but in due course when he came to speak, though with a certain ingrained reticence, of the events which had resulted in his taking up his final abode in the large white box on a hillside at Cap Ferrat, built in Moorish style, round an open court-yard. The previous owner of the property had been a retired bishop from Morocco, and it changed hands originally for seven thousand pounds. Untroubled believer though he must have been, that cleric still felt it was necessary to carve a symbol against the evil eye on the gate posts, and over the front door. The symbol that Somerset Maugham was to adopt himself, and have inscribed on his writing paper, the covers of all his books, and even on his patience cards.

As regards my own front door, I still felt a thrill every time I saw the brass plate with my name on the panel of fellow lodgers in that lofty, eighteenth-century mansion which had fallen on to shabby days. All the same, that night as I climbed the stairs, which invariably seemed to smell of cats, I had a sudden attack of the kind of panic I had experienced on the evening of the port gargling episode. How would I entertain my first real literary celebrity? How would he accept the approach to what must seem like a garret? And what would I give the bridge players to eat?

I need not have worried. Rich guests are delighted with a sample of *la vie de bohème* when their own memories of such an existence are far behind them. They enter with relish into the spirit of the preparations on their behalf, they drink the sherry from the grocers as though it contained the formula for the high spirits of their own far-off youth. Besides, in this case I had a new-found ally in Mrs Hubbard, who bustled up from her base-ment, spreading bonhomie like thick butter on the fare of the evening.

Deborah Hubbard had only come into my life a few weeks before. I had kept my promise to myself from the afternoon that I had gone to tea with Noël Coward. As soon as I returned to London, after the publication of my book, I had made a special pilgrimage to the stationers at the corner of Ebury Street opposite the grocers, and amongst the cards in the window I had found, with a leaping heart, as though it were an act of Fate, one that stated there was a studio, with sleeping accommodation thrown in, to let at number 115.

I hurried on down the street. Destiny was beckoning to me. A small, jolly woman wearing a pinafore, and with apple cheeks, led me up the stairs to the second floor, and unlocked the door facing the landing. A tiny, airless lobby led into a big room, that seemed even larger in comparison. Stripped of furniture, the floor completely bare, it awaited a transforming wand. Hideous strips of decaying brown paper hung forlornly from the walls, and there were equally forbidding stains on the ceiling. Even so, I refused to be discouraged, though it was difficult at that moment to visualize how the same room looks today; or for that matter, how it was to look a month later, after my mother had taken over the decoration and the furnishings, as a twenty-first birthday present in advance. My own only addition was a second-hand oak kitchen table, to be used as a writing desk, which I acquired in a sale for a couple of pounds. I have refused to part with it ever since. Indeed, I use it every day in my office on the floor below, when I am at Ebury Street. For I am very superstitious about the feelings of objects that have helped me on my way. They are never inanimate to me.

Having inspected the slit of a bedroom next door, just space for a narrow bed and a wash-hand stand – we painted the ceiling a Mediterranean blue, in compensation – I returned to the barren studio, where the early spring sunshine was streaming in encouragingly through the wide windows that ran almost the whole length of the wall facing the street. My mind was made up and the moment had arrived to enquire the name of the guardian with the bunch of keys at her waist. When she told me, adding that her own habitat was in the basement, which she shared with her husband, Fred – 'my darling was wounded at Zeebrugge,' she told me proudly – I suggested with a smile of alliance, 'I am sure, Mrs Hubbard, *your* cupboard will never be bare for me.'

And it never was. Nothing was too much trouble for her. Deborah Hubbard. She certainly lived up to her name. She never scolded, she never complained, even when I forgot my keys and brought a sleepy-eyed Fred to the surface by ringing their bell, long after midnight. However, like the good, Norfolk-born countrywoman that she was, she started briskly.

'The rent's twenty-five shillings a week, but that goes a quarter in advance to Miss Fuller, the landlady, who lives in Bath,' she explained. 'If you would like me to do for you, being a young bachelor, that will be another five shillings a week that you will pay, to me. And I will give you a nice breakfast for one-and-sixpence.'

'And what do I do about washing?' I asked. 'I mean, hot water?'

'Well, there's a ring, look, at the side of your gas fire, where you can boil a kettle to make a cup of tea, and use for your shaving water. And the lavatory's on the floor below, and if you want a bath, there's one for all the tenants to share, with a geyser and a slot machine. You can get a lovely hot bath for three pennies.'

You could, and I did, but on one occasion, something went wrong, there was an almighty explosion, and the next thing that happened I was shot across the room, and discovered naked by Deborah, in a dazed condition on the floor. She promptly forced me to swallow a glass of milk – 'to kill the fumes' – and with the resilience of youth I soon recovered my nerve, and my singed eyebrows their lustre.

The geography of the house – of which I am now the landlord myself – having been fully explained, I moved in and gave my first dinner party. We ate off the bridge table. Deborah provided an excellent roast chicken, carrying it up all those stairs without demur, and the guest of honour asked for a second helping. Afterwards, as though he possessed *le droit de seigneur*, he announced, 'Godfrey and I will challenge you, Ned.' Fortunately, my luck held a second time. I had even better cards, and the evening ended up with a lay-down grand slam.

Two days later, I received a note from Half Moon Street inviting me to stay the whole of August in the South of France. 'I hear your tennis is even better than your bridge, and you'll find that we are all eager to improve our game, and ready for some expert coaching. I write every morning, and no doubt you'll want to do the same. In the evenings there's usually a game of bridge. If the stakes are too high for you, I will insure any losses.'

With typical thoughtfulness – and there are many others who could give evidence of far more expensive gestures behind the scenes, though never discussed – a cheque was enclosed to cover my first-class fare, in the Blue Train. I accepted the offer at its face value, and how sensible of me to do so, for it is still paying dividends. My brother, in his summer holidays from Oundle, had taken coaching jobs, and I now placed myself in the same category. Though to the world at large I boasted of my invitation, without implying that there were any strings attached. I felt that it gave me an added aura when I played Puck in the Warwick Pageant opposite the Titania of Lady Cynthia Asquith, who had been Sir James Barrie's amanuensis, while Lady Bird – of Bird's Custard fame – was a much-bedecked Queen Elizabeth, in a motley and bizarre collection of figures from history, on which the rains descended indiscriminately, as always seems to happen when pageants are planned in England. There are few things more disagreeable than having to spend the day wearing damp tights, and I began to long with an aching eagerness for the southern sun. Certainly, I told myself, I would not waste my days indoors this time, as I had done at Bagnolles.

Fortunately, the weather improved for the week of the Stratford-on-Avon tennis tournament, where my partner, George Pinney and I somehow bundled our way through to the final of the men's doubles. The Pinneys in their Coleshill home had staying with them a young cousin from Australia, a languid youth with a plangent voice. We considered it good for his moral fibre to be roped in as a ball boy. Little did I imagine that I was handing out prefect's orders to someone who was to become one of the most celebrated art critics in the world. Douglas Cooper lives nowadays in a castle at Avignon, and who knows, had I been less scornful about his antipathy for the game I loved, I might have long since received an invitation to view his own collection of masterpieces.

It is not only on the race-course that it is difficult to pick winners. My host that August was taking a considerable chance. So, in a way, was I. I had no idea how much was to be added to my previously constricted knowledge of human emotions. In any case, a month is a long time to be a guest in anyone's house. I found that Barbara Back, the handsome wife of a well-known surgeon, Ivor Back, was presiding as hostess at the Villa Mauresque. Gerald Kelly, the leading R.A. who had painted a succession of memorable portraits of our host whose close friend he had been since their early days in Spain, was staying, too; a Maugham niece and her husband completed the party.

When I presented myself in the salon, before lunch, on the day of my arrival straight from the train, in my orthodox English grey flannel suit, my host took one look at me and gave me my first marching orders.

'No tie, no jacket, no socks. This is the South of France in August, not Finals Day at Wimbledon.' When I returned from my room for his reappraisal, he added, 'Gerald, take Godfrey into Nice this afternoon, and get him some linen slacks, shirts and espadrilles at the *Bon Marché,* like yours.'

I glanced across at the man dressed in candy-pink beach-clothes, who was handing round drinks, and instinctively something in me revolted. *I don't want to look like you. To resemble you in any way, ever.* I had been given no briefing about the undercurrents that on occasion were to blow at gale force through the cool splendour of the villa. This other Gerald, in permanent residence at the Villa Mauresque, Gerald Haxton, the man who had been Maugham's companion on his extremely fruitful world travels, was, I suppose, at that time in his late thirties. Already the signs of the dissipation that was ultimately to destroy him were beginning to show on his face, and in his increasingly bloodshot eyes. He smoked as well as drank far too much, and puffed away ominously. The inborn American vitality, the party spirit which in the early days he must have had, and the completely contrasting power to unlock a door inside Maugham's shut-away secret wall, were now clearly on the wane. Only when he dived gracefully from the plank at one end of the pool, set high on the hillside and surrounded by oleander bushes, did he capture and echo the charm of his surroundings – although for myself, that was cancelled out by his insistence on always bathing naked, even when there were women sunbathing on the yellow cushions along the marble verge. I clung to my brief shorts throughout my visit. It was not so much that I was prim, as that I was still unfledged. Inevitably, however, I began to notice signs and curious moments of tension. There were days when Haxton was grey beneath his tan, and his hand shook holding the cards at the bridge table, when he would speak to my host in a voice that was hardly that of an employee, let alone a privileged companion. Whereupon the man who was my literary god, instead of silencing the rebellion from his throne, where he sat wearing for the evening the black silk mandarin trousers that he had bought back from China, was himself silent and seemed – or was it my own literary imagination taking over? – to gaze back in fear.

Then this mood would be blotted out by a period of intensive, violent gaiety – 'Come on, Willie, you don't want to go to bed yet' – when Haxton, becoming more and more blurred in his speech, would insist on staying up all night, lingering behind the rest of the party at the casino in Cannes or Monte Carlo, visiting later a succession of squalid bars or bordels, about which he would drop lurid hints subsequently in a bout of alcoholic confidences, only creeping into his own bed in the room next to his guarantor when the sun had long since risen on another burnished day. The playboy's losses at the various casinos he patronized were paid up grimly by the partner over whom, as the weeks passed, I began to suspect he had the kind of hold which a blackmailer exerts. Was this what was really meant by the expression 'your evil genius'? I baulked from recognizing the full implications of a situation that I realize now had its roots in the past rather than the present. Instead, I buried myself gratefully in the company of the other guests, determined that my antipathy to Haxton should not spoil any of my enjoyment of the sort of luxury that I had not visualized until that moment as really existing.

I wrote home enthusiastically, describing the moonlight *bouillabaisse* picnic that we had joined on the island across the bay from Cannes, and how I had actually bathed in the pool with Mary Garden, then in the full glory of her powers as an opera star, and met Eugene O'Neill at lunch, reiterating with some emphasis how my tennis coaching was greatly in demand.

That note had been struck right from the start by my host, who, on the day of my arrival, had announced firmly as we went in to lunch, in the dining-room leading on to the portico, where the walls were covered with pictures by Marie Laurencin in silver frames, 'Godfrey is going to improve all our forehands. Especially yours, Gerald. We'll make a start this evening. I have asked the house-party from Maryland to join us.'

To my delight I found that there was an excellent newly-laid hard court with exactly the right kind of background. It was too hot to make a start before six o'clock but then the conditions were perfect. Automatically it was assumed that I would partner my sponsor, who played very much better than I had anticipated. He really did possess a forehand drive, though with it, little knowledge of court craft, or how to deal with a smash at the net. Haxton, in contrast, ran at the ball as though he had a butterfly net in his hand. He was clearly irritated by his lack

of prowess, compared with his skill as a swimmer, and the few
suggestions that I offered across the net were received with an
ill grace. The general effect was of vicarage party tennis, though
in a rather more exotic setting. I could not help showing off,
and I admit I basked in the approbation of the spectators on the
bank. When Haxton, at the first opportunity, led an exodus towards the swimming pool, I suggested to my host that he should
stay behind for a few minutes so that I could knock up balls to
him from the other side of the net.

'The pace of the ball does not come from the actual force with
which you hit it, but is much more a matter of footwork and
general co-ordination. Come forward on your left foot, as you
swing at it; take it opposite your right hip. Try not to get too
close to it, or too far away. Yes, that's *much* better. But keep
your head down, and never look where you mean to hit it. You
know that, already in your mind. At least, you should have a
picture of the whole court marked out in your mind. Try again,
and lock your wrist this time, and try to keep your arm in one
long, firm line. Look at that! It was a winner all the way.'

The enthusiasm that I have given to any project all my life,
now flowed across the net. This was my host in a new rôle that I
could sense was giving him intense pleasure; equally, I found
myself taking to the rôle of sporting coach with alacrity, passing
on the tips that Gordon Lowe had given me, between his matches
in the South of England championships at Eastbourne, where he
had been year after year, the leading player. In consequence, because of that early coaching at a most malleable period, my own
forehand has remained my most effective scoring weapon. I was
on safe ground here, and I was determined to earn my keep.

Unfortunately and unwittingly I was to earn instead my literary
mentor's grave displeasure.

One morning, when I had been at the Mauresque for about a
week, my host's valet came to my room at a very early hour and
explained that 'Monsieur Morgan' wished to see me on the
terrace. Still in my pyjamas, I obeyed the call with a faint sense
of unease, as though I had been unexpectedly summoned to the
headmaster's study.

My host had had his breakfast already and was smoking his
pipe. He looked up from the French work that he was reading.

'Oh, I sent for you to enquire what progress you were making with your new novel.'

I felt, rightly, that there was more behind this polite remark, as I shifted nervously from one foot to the other.

'I am afraid I am stuck,' I said.

'Stuck,' He repeated the word with disdain.

'Yes, my inspiration seems temporarily to give out.'

'Is that why you have been spending your mornings up at the pool, while I have been in my study?' he demanded.

I don't think he expected an answer. He understood exactly what had happened, how I had been seduced by all the abounding beauty, the richness and the novelty. I had felt like Antinous, lying on the orange cushions, with the sun caressing my body, and in the shimmering distance the sea and the wide curve of the Bay of Nice. I had excused myself for my idleness by promising to try again tomorrow, and surely one or two days off from work didn't matter.

But it did matter. It mattered violently, compulsively to the man whose whole output and reputation as a craftsman had been built on a most austere and rigid self-discipline.

'I did not pay your fare to come down here in order that you should spend your days lazing beside the pool. You are too young to need a holiday, what you need is discipline. I wanted you to learn from my example. I hoped that it would not be necessary to have to speak to you so plainly. Your first novel was fresh and showed such promise that I was anxious to meet its author. I was not disappointed. But I am now.'

When I made no reply, overcome with shame and dismay, he continued on a quieter note, but with tremendous vehemence underlining every word.

'There is no such thing as inspiration. At least, if there is, I have not discovered it. There is, instead, dedication and complete absorption in your craft. I am a self-made writer. I started with a poor prose style, and had to fine it down as best I could. I have been moderately successful in my profession, and you must appreciate right from the start that writing *is* a profession like Medicine or the Law.

'Don't be misled by the so-called glamour of authorship. There is none. You will have to endure recurring moods of depression, as we all have to do, and the only way you will conquer these black patches is by the comfort of habit; going to your desk and staying there. At least, when you shut the door, you shut out all your other worries and worldly anxieties. You are alone with your pad and your pen and you must grow accustomed, again through habit, to that loneliness which will stay with you throughout your writing life.

'As you know I started my career as a medical student, and later transferred what talents I may possess to becoming a story-teller. It is the oldest art in the world but that does not mean that you do not have to work as hard as any navvy. I keep the same regular hours today as I did when I was a medical student. I suppose you could say that today the public are my examiners, and life itself provides the substance for my next books. I am self-taught as a writer, as you will be. Therefore it is all the more important that you should never take time off. You cannot afford to do so.'

He got up and put away his pipe. 'Every morning at this hour I go to my desk in my writing-room on the roof, and there I write in my own hand not less than a thousand words. Some-times it is a good day, sometimes a bad. Then I start the next morning by revising my output of the day before. But the final total is usually the same before I join my guests for lunch. You will have noticed that I don't talk about my work, I simply get on with it. And you will do the same, during the rest of your stay.'

'But . . .' I began.

'There is no but.' And suddenly, though he was small in stature, he seemed to tower over me. 'You will go to your room where I took care to provide a desk for you, and you will start again where you left off. You will pick up the threads of your novel and you will write not less than four pages of foolscap, and bring them to me at ten-to-one. If I don't think you have made a real effort, you will have no lunch. You know the way up to my writing-room?'

I nodded. At least I would now see the Holy of Holies. But that was no consolation, and still in my pyjama trousers I crouched over the table in my bedroom, feeling as I had done the first time I had sat for a scholarship at St Christopher's, in despair because so many of the questions seemed beyond me. But I was grown up now. Or had believed I was, until this moment. The author of a published work, not a child to be punished and sent hungry to bed. But where, oh where, had the fluency with which I had written *Dreams Fade* vanished? Sneeringly the flies buzzed round my head, until I reached for the Flit and sprayed everything in sight, watching a greasy mark spread over the accusing, empty page.

'*In the years to come, Tonie would in a moment of unhappiness bring out her store of memories . . . as people do when the present seems hell and the past paradise . . . and blow them high up in the air like toy balloons, and for one lovely, bitter moment, watch them drop nearer and nearer the edge of a chair – then prick, bang, they vanish and the room is empty again.*'

The balloons were pricked all right. It was a very subdued and contrite pupil who later climbed the stairs to the white box, placed on the flat roof of the house. Here, during that summer, though he never gave an inkling of what he was engaged upon, even when Hugh Walpole's name cropped up in conversation, he was in actual fact half-way through the novel that at a later date the author confessed to me was his own favourite, *Cakes and Ale,* in which Walpole is cruelly mocked in a thinly-disguised caricature.

I knocked, and the headmaster's voice said 'Come in.' I held out the sheets that I had written, and he put them down beside the San Remo pad, on replicas of which he wrote every word that he ever published. He bought them from The Times Bookshop, and they suited him because each page took exactly two hundred and fifty words of his handwriting.

I looked round the room nervously, while he read what I had written. One part of the window was taken up by the glass panel on which Gauguin had painted his last picture, and which the traveller to far-off places had brought back from his visit to the island in the South Seas, and to the hut itself where the painter had died. Maugham was overjoyed by his discovery of the painting, but the hut's owner was very reluctant to part with the panel, until the visitor had the inspiration to offer the erecting of a fresh door. This had much more value in the owner's eyes than the painting itself.

I noticed with surprise, that first morning, that my taskmaster was seated with his back to the view. Later he explained to me that he found it too distracting to look towards the freedom of the horizons; better for his contemplation and concentration to gaze always inwards, in this case towards the bookshelves opposite; it is a habit I follow myself today.

'You see the third row from the bottom, Godfrey? It is exactly on the level of my eyes. When I look up because I am momentarily at a loss for the right word, I remind myself, however weary I am, that the whole of that shelf is filled with copies of my own books. And I remind myself, too, how often I struck a blank patch during the months I was writing them, and yet somehow they were all duly finished on time, and appeared in print not without success. One day, no doubt,' he added, 'you will have a full bookshelf, too.'

He only made one constructive comment about the lines I had brought him.

'Cut out those dots. That is an untidy and messy kind of writing. It is simply a cover-up for poor construction. On the other hand, do not worry too much about the present paucity of your vocabulary. Use the same, the most ordinary word, if it is the right one in the context. When I was your age, I used to make out lists of beautiful-sounding words wherever I came upon them, and tried to work them into my writing, but the only effect was that all action was suspended, and I became a poor imitator of Pater.'

He was in a mellower mood now – perhaps because his own morning stint was over – and he could be very mellow, and even benign. His fund of compassion he hid from the world – when my mother died, his was the most tender letter of condolence I received – his forbidding mien stemming partly from shyness, partly from disillusionment, was more often on show.

We went down to lunch, and never had food tasted more delicious. As I wolfed my helpings, I caught my host's eye upon me, but the look he gave me was almost a conspiratorial one. I had the notion that, having passed a test, if not with flying colours, at least adequately and with a good grace, there was from this time on a bond between us, shared by no one else in the party, strengthened, too, each day upon the tennis court, until the climax came on the evening before I was due to leave.

Michael Arlen had been staying that summer on the Coast. Having conquered London with his novel *The Green Hat*, he was now possessed of a very different ambition. To excel at sport and the sort of outdoor pursuits that westerners enjoy. To look like a bronzed statue on an aqua-planing board; to play such an aggressive game of tennis that the mystery surrounding his origins would be suspended. Each morning he was to be found having a lesson from the professional at the Carlton Club at Cannes. Stripped to the waist, he sweated and ran. Now the moment for the triumphant proof was surely close at hand. Meeting us all at one of the many parties that summer, and hearing about the sessions on the Villa Mauresque court, he promptly challenged my own pupil to a duel.

They would play a single on the Mauresque court, in the cool of one evening. From all the excited swirl of talk, one would have imagined that their places in the literary race were equally at stake. It was only too clear that they both minded enormously about the result. I kept silent myself, though I was very keyed-up underneath, sensing, in some strange way, that my own future was involved. Of course, I had no proof as to whether we should accept Michael's self-assessment of his prowess, but I rather doubted it. True, he was considerably younger than Maugham, but I reminded myself that a tennis professional is inclined to flatter his pupil and make things as easy as possible for him on court. We, in contrast, must make it as difficult, and I set to work taking exactly the opposite approach, sending my host harder and harder shots across the net, daring to bully him as he had bullied me in such a different context. When the evening of the pay-off arrived, I was reasonably hopeful. He was an admirable listener, in real life, it was part of his stock-in-trade as a writer, and on the tennis court he had responded equally admirably to every suggestion I had made.

The news had spread. All Cap Ferrat seemed to have turned up for the match. It started in a blaze of badinage and applause, but it soon settled down into an awesome spectacle, a life and death marathon. I began to feel that the first set, let alone the match, would never end. Not because the two opponents were so closely matched, as that they both seemed to suffer suddenly from the most extraordinary lapses of eyesight.

In their understandable desire to be proclaimed victor, any ball within a foot of the baseline was called 'out'; any fast service was automatically proclaimed a 'fault'. Five-all, six-all, seven-all. The game was turning into a negative rather than a positive contest; moreover, the spectators were beginning to be bored, their own eyes longingly on the vision of the Mint Juleps that were awaiting them on the terrace, brewed from the recipe which their host's secretary had brought back from their joint travels in the Far East. All round me on the bank, faces were being turned in my direction, reproachfully, demandingly. Dusk would soon be falling. The older player was beginning to show obvious signs of distress. Could nothing be done?

Certainly it could. At ten-all, I announced, tactfully, that owing to the diminishing light, I would take over the umpiring. There will be no surprise at the sequel. My prized pupil finally ran out the winner at thirteen-eleven, though he had to be helped off the court. One set had proved more than enough. After all, it had lasted well over an hour, and honour was satisfied all round. For my own part, I had been only too conscious in what a delicate position I would have found myself had not the challenged one finally carried off the bay leaves and the crown.

As it was, champagne was produced in my honour for dinner, and I was assured when I said my grateful goodbyes the next morning that I would be invited again to The Mauresque. I was. The next spring. But before the first of many return visits, under such varying circumstances, in the years to come, my literary mentor and I were to meet in London early in the New Year. He was there for the production of his latest play, *The Sacred Flame*, in which Gladys Cooper once again was starring and financing the production, while my second novel, *Squirrel's Cage,* was about to appear.

I am not suggesting there could be any comparison in importance about these two events, but there was, nevertheless, a personal connection. For in the evening, after the author had spent many hours in the anonymous darkness of the empty theatre, enduring the dress-rehearsal of his new work, he had invited me to join him for supper on the balcony of Ciro's.

I arrived, relishing the treat ahead of me. The reunion, the richness, the splendour of such company. I was in any case in bubbling good spirits, because earlier that same evening the literary critic of the BBC, Mrs Agnes Hamilton, a woman with a considerable reputation as a blue stocking, had given my new book a most encouraging launching. As I thought.

'His own mind is interesting, and the minds of the people he describes are interesting, too, and real.'

I had sent the very first copy of the book which I had received from the publishers, by hand to Half Moon Street. On the flyleaf I had written, 'In sincere gratitude for all your good advice.' I was about to receive another discourse, though I had no pre-warning of what form it would take, as I seated myself opposite him, looking down over the balcony at the dancers gyrating below us to the languorous strains of a Tango. Turning back to my host, I noticed now with a shock how weary he looked, his eyelids drooping, as they did when he was wearing what I had secretly christened his baleful look, boding no joy. I put down his tiredness to his long incarceration inside The Play-house.

'How did the dress-rehearsal go?' I asked solicitously.

He shrugged his shoulders, as he lit a cigarette.

'Like all dress-rehearsals. One is quite certain one has a disaster on one's hands. Besides, this is in a different key from my earlier plays. Once you get a reputation for writing one kind of play, or one kind of book, the public will never allow you to write any other. They will pretend not to understand this play. But it can't be helped. I had to write it.'

He was being unusually communicative, I thought, as the waiter came and took our order for food, with the small red-shaded lamp between our heads bent over the menus, casting a night-club glow. It was all incongruously escapist. As soon as the interruption was over, my companion started again, but I was completely unprepared for his change of direction.

He had cut short my soothing noises – actually, his pessimism was unfounded, the play ran for nine months – and broke in icily:

'Whatever happens tomorrow night, nothing could be so appalling as what I feel about your new book.'

'Oh, you have read it?' I echoed stupidly. I suddenly began to feel sick, staring down at my plate. *'The other night when I was having supper with Willie Maugham at Ciro's.'* I had looked forward all day to our reunion. And now this.

'Indeed, I have read it. Every word, though I am not a masochist by nature.'

'You never told me you didn't like what I was writing when

I brought you each fresh instalment at lunch time,' I replied defensively.

'I wasn't concerned with the subject matter. I was simply seeking to ingrain self-discipline into you.'

'Well, I've already had a good review in The *Times Lit,* and a rave notice over the radio this evening.' I was still trying to make a fight of it, though instinctively I knew already it was no use.

Again he cut my counter-attack short.

'I am not interested in anyone else's opinion, though I hope you will read and digest what Cyril Connolly has had to say this week in the *New Statesman.* He honours your *feuilleton* with a whole page review.' He made the word *feuilleton* sound like another name for an illegitimate baby. 'He is a reviewer,' he added meaningly, 'for whose judgment I have an increasing respect.'

That week's issue had come out that morning. Usually, bad news travels even faster than this.

'In "Dreams Fade", Mr Winn's first novel, there was at least a hope for better things, a vestige of emotional reality at the core of his gelatinous egotism, but if anything is heading straight for the cheap editions on a railway bookstall it is "Squirrel's Cage." If it lacks the conspicuous faults of the earlier novel, it lacks almost everything else as well. An anthologist would not know where to begin were he to select a paragraph for an Oxford book of English slop.'

It is said that Bloody Mary exclaimed when she died that they would find the word 'Calais' written on her heart. That paragraph has been written on my heart and in my mind ever since; as well as every word of the conversation on the balcony that night at Ciro's.

'I am sorry, Willie,' I said at last. I meant, sorry that I had been so foolish as to argue, not to accept his judgment at once as an absolute one. After all I had surrendered myself to his literary care. 'What ought I to do now?' I added hopelessly.

'I will tell you what I think you ought to do. You should make a switch.'

'You mean, go back to the stage?'

'If you like, but combine it with journalism.' His anger had subsided – his anger directed not at me, but stoked by his disappointment in me – so that his voice was gentle as he continued :

'I have come to the conclusion that you are too subjective a writer ever to become a really first-class novelist. But I believe if you will work you could become one of the most successful journalists in the country. You have an ear for dialogue, for repeating conversations correctly and catching their echoes, and you make your characters come alive, but you lack a real sense of a story line. If you are not writing about yourself, thinly disguised, or expressing your own views, at once your lack of invention shows itself dismally. Now you must learn how to become an accurate reporter, and try your hand at writing profiles.'

I had already tried my hand as a freelance for a year now. Almost as soon as *Dreams Fade* appeared, I started receiving commissions from editors seeking provocative articles about the views of the new generation. My very first piece had been published in *Everybody's Weekly*, for four guineas. I was very grateful for the fee and still am; especially as it was followed by an offer to write a series on Wimbledon during the summer. The paper is long since deceased, but its editor at that time, R. J. Minney, whose encouragement I shall never forget, was to become well-known in due course as the author of *Clive of India,* to edit *The Sunday Referee* and to become an important film producer. Recently, 'R.J.' has come to live near to me in Sussex, and we have been able to renew an old friendship. He writes his books and I write mine, and we meet at week-ends in each other's houses. The clock has come full cycle.

'What did you make out of your first novel?' my supper companion was asking me bluntly.

'I don't know exactly. About a hundred and fifty pounds, I should say.'

'I should say so, too. That is far above the average for a first novel. Supposing you make the same amount out of this one. Or even two hundred and fifty pounds, for I do not deny that in some circles this book may be more popular than the first one. That works out at five pounds a week, for the best part of a year's work. The same sum as I existed on myself for years. It isn't a very pleasant way of living, you know.

'Oh, I am fully aware that you receive a multitude of invitations of all kinds. For the next few years there will be plenty of people ready to provide you with meals and invite you here and

there. And then what? Your kind of looks and the sort of charm
that goes with them are not likely to last for ever. Believe me,
you will find journalism a far less degrading mode of existence
than what virtually means being kept.'

I was startled by the comparison. It made me conscious of the
titles of some of the recent commissions I had fulfilled. *'Do we
understand our parents?'* *'Are women worse snobs than men?'*
'Have we failed the Dead?' A special Armistice Day tie-up for a
Sunday newspaper. *'The girl I hope to marry . . .'*

Was this literary prostitution? But then it was being suggested
that I had no real talent to prostitute, and I was certainly finding
it more pleasant sitting in editors' outside offices, than in the
corridors outside film agencies. Someone who had been particularly kind to me, and was providing me with an increasing
amount of magazine work, was a tall, striking dark girl
who was very much a rising power at Fleetway House. Peggy
Sutherland in her twenties already edited two magazines and was
to create the extremely successful *Woman's Journal* before becoming a member of The Amalgamated Press Board. She
believed in my potentialities for the magazine market right from
the start, and did not with obvious condescension dangle titbits
before my hungry eyes, but instead treated me on terms of
friendly equality, as though I was already as established as other
well-known names on her list, such as Clemence Dane, Philip
Gibbs and Rebecca West. One never forgets such debts. At least
one should not.

Now that I had received this unexpected reassurance that my
efforts to break in to the freelance market were not frowned upon
– but the very opposite – I was eager to announce that as it happened I had made as much in the last three months out of my
journalistic efforts as I had received through the sales of *Dreams
Fade.* I had sold pieces to the *Sunday Graphic* and *The Star,*
I had broken into the columns of the august *Morning Post,* I
had even been invited to join a symposium on youth's point of
view in Auntie Violet's weekly.

My companion listened, not with impatience, to the catalogue
I now produced. I had the feeling that he was relieved that a
responsibility was being shifted from his shoulders.

'I have never written anything for a newspaper myself,' he told
me. 'Though I am often asked and offered a hundred pounds to

express my views on this or that. Alas, I haven't your knack.
I am completely unable to put an article together. But that doesn't
mean that I despise such mediums for self-expression, or earning
a living. That would be absurd.

'Remember it is all grist to the mill,' he added. 'It did not
hurt Trollope to have to go to the city and work in an office all
day and do his writing in the evenings. Some people have
foolishly dismissed Dickens as a literary hack. He certainly wrote
to order, and untidily sometimes, but his works make vivid
reading, perhaps because there is so much of the journalist and
the thinly-disguised reporter in him.

'Believe me, no one writes better through starving in a garret.
Comfort yourself with that knowledge when you find yourself
writing to order. It will not hurt you to have to turn out a
thousand words on a variety of subjects. Everything that you write,
whether you sell it or not, will teach you something; above all, it
will increase your sense of ease on paper. I am not sure that that
is not the most important asset of all for a writer. And it is certainly better that your name should appear in *Comic Cuts* occasionally, or *Home Chat,* if it ensures your maintaining financial
independence.'

Thus the evening ended on a far happier note than it
had begun, and his words came back often to spur me in the
months ahead during which I worked in what had once been the
white cell of a monastery, perched high up on the hillside overlooking the sea which on a good day was the colour of crushed
butterfly wings, at Amalfi in Southern Italy, just round the corner
of the bay from Naples.

In the spring on my way home, I was to visit the Villa
Mauresque, and again in the summer. But the rest of that
winter I was to spend at the Hotel Cappuccini, and the following
winter too, tackling, undaunted, another novel, a long family saga
this time of three generations, set against the hunting shires,
which took me three equally long years to complete. Because most
weeks I had to break off to dispatch short pieces home, to keep
up with the surprising number of journalistic offers I was now
receiving, and equally, to keep the pot boiling.

Fortunately the hotel at Amalfi, which was turned into a leave
centre for our troops after Italy packed up in the war, was

absurdly cheap in those days. Moreover, the sunshine itself was free, and the long terrace, where the lizards basked, and the orange blossom and the fruit hanging side by side in the abundant grove stretching up the hill. It was an idyllic setting for a honeymoon. All the same I did not feel lonely on my own. In the mornings I stayed in my cell, working at the table that was set for me in the bay-window, but I could not make myself turn my back on the theatrical backcloth of vivid blues and sienna shades, as if for any Italian opera, set below me. Usually I returned for an afternoon session too, when the light had at last faded, out of doors. After lunch, when the hotel would be invaded by scores of Americans with their ciné kodaks, perching like shrill cockatoos to take their pictures of each other against the orange trees, I would walk along the coast road, or make the stiff climb up to Ravello. Here in the local hostelry Wagner wrote one of his last operas, and here, too, there is a most romantic villa perched on the top of the cliff, belonging to the Grimthorpe family; I have coveted it more than any other resting place on my travels.

On those still, warm afternoons, with the promise of spring all round me, I would lie full length on the grass, with the scent of mingled herbs in my nostrils, a carpet of freesias at my feet, looking down at the sea far below, and the sense of isolation, set in the framework of such natural beauty, was intoxicating. This was the distillation, the crystallization of so many vague longings and desires. Surely if I could stay here, or return here often enough, I would never grow old, like so many of the faded visitors in the hotel, fleeing from the February fogs at home.

What I could not escape from – or indeed wanted to escape from – was the increasing flow of commissions in my mail, all obtained for me by a bustling, new agent on the literary scene Rupert Crew, who for the next twenty years was to take me under his wing. Sometimes I would sigh and curse inwardly at having to return to my typewriter, and leave the manuscript which I was writing, in longhand, a symbolic switch-over; until I reminded myself again how extremely fortunate I was to be spending the winter in such a setting. Whereupon I would concentrate once again with a good grace to produce as competently as possible a diatribe on youth's more pressing problems of the day (as viewed through editorial eyes) which in due course would appear under some such title as *'It's not much fun being young,'* (in the *Sunday Dispatch*) or *'Why the young are bad-tempered'* (in the *Daily Mail*).

There was a small group staying in the hotel, who had been coming there for years, and were in consequence in a rather privileged position. They might easily have been upset and bad-tempered at the arrival of another English artist on the scene, however minor, and that he should have discovered their hide-out, for they kept themselves very much to themselves. The group consisted of Osbert Sitwell, his brother Sacheverell on occasions, a family friend, David Horner, with all the airs and graces of a dilettante, and a young musician from Oldham, with palely-fair, long hair, a pale face and eyes to match, who always looked half-starved though he had an excellent appetite, and whom the Sitwell family had virtually adopted, recognizing his genius before the rest of the world. This last was William Walton. In some ways, he seemed an incongruous figure beside the others, because he had clung to his Lancashire accent, and possessed none of the courteous manners of Osbert, whom at first I was rather nervous to meet on account of his reputation at that time for engaging in implacable literary feuds. To my surprise, I found Osbert instead a most urbane guide to the neighbourhood, nor did he ever patronize me because of the obvious gap in our intellectual stature. Often he would invite me to join his party for their after-noon walk, when he would eagerly ask me for any titbits of gossip I had gleaned about the latest arrivals, in whom he took an enormous interest, from a distance. So much so, that on our return he always insisted that we had our tea in the crowded communal sitting-room, and would suddenly remark, as though I was one of the characters in *Before the Bombardment,* 'Do you find your listening apparatus is working well today, Godfrey?'

Later in the evening we would compare notes, our day's dis-coveries, in the only private sitting-room that the hotel possessed. In one corner there was a very dilapidated upright piano with several notes missing, at which, while the others stayed in their rooms, Willie composed during most of the day. By the time the evening came, he would often look so white and exhausted that one felt rather concerned. The first year we met at Amalfi, he was putting the finishing touches to his great choral work *Belshazzar's Feast;* the second, he started composing his first symphony.

At one moment he was utterly convinced that he would never finish it, and in fact the last movement he did add at a much later date. Osbert sometimes would join in the gloomy chorus. He had not, he assured us, written a word that passed muster that day. While often I had struck another bad patch with my book. Anyone looking down from Mars would have imagined that we were in a prison camp. Only David Horner would appear unruffled by the cares of creation; he was the onlooker who always seemed so secure on the sidelines. Willie Walton had brought with him a portable gramophone, and a selection of his own favourite records. On evenings when our morale was at its lowest ebb, he would cheer us up with a concert. Each of us would be allowed to choose a record in turn. And I never hear the haunting music of *The Walk to the Paradise Garden,* of the lovers in Delius's score, without being momentarily back again in that plush-coloured room, furnished with an odd mixture of Italian and Victorian furniture, seeing in the lamplight the patrician features of Osbert, whose autobiography was to be hailed in due course as a small masterpiece, and the sad pierrot face and drooping figure of Willie Walton, whom I can scarcely recognize today in his white tie and tail-coat, so filled out, so confident, when he takes up the baton to conduct one of his own acclaimed compositions in front of a crowded audience at the Festival Hall.

Osbert Sitwell and Somerset Maugham, although their styles differed so diametrically, had a high regard for each other, and when I arrived at the Mauresque again that spring I brought fraternal greetings. My host's own publisher I found was another guest, a jovial, kindly man, clearly with an enormous regard for an author who was such a perpetual gold-mine. I cannot help thinking that the bones of Charlie Evans must be rattling in their coffin at the idea of a subsidiary of the firm over whose fortunes he presided so admirably, publishing, the moment that Maugham himself was dead, such a waspish little book, in such odd taste.

Old soldiers are inclined to boast of past victories; artists, whatever their quality, have a reputation for being self-absorbed and garrulous about their triumphs. But I never heard Willie Maugham ever expatiate, for instance, on a triumph such as when a million copies of his books of collected stories had been sold in their Penguin edition, in one year alone. Indeed, the solitary occasion when he made any mention of the astronomical sums he earned was when his secretary brought him an offer, in a letter, one day before lunch. The three of us were alone, and they discussed it freely in front of me. A cable must be sent off straightaway to New York. Did he want to accept? The offer was for six new short stories. They were to appear in the *Cosmopolitan Magazine* in the States, in *Nash's* in England, and in the equivalent kind of German magazine. One thousand pounds for a single short story, and only the first rights at that. My eyes boggled, as Haxton produced the letter which had arrived while my host was in his writing-room.

I watched them standing side by side, as Willie read it through and considered the proposition and how it would fit in with his current programme of work. The two men seemed to have nothing in common except the one thing which surely is long since dead, I thought. 'It's an awful bore, Gerald,' Willie decided wearily, 'but I suppose I had better say "Yes". We need every penny at the moment.' Was there some special emphasis in the way that he said that? It had never occurred to me that he could be short of money, for a moment. Then why? Was it that Haxton's excesses were costing more and more? Not only his gambling excesses, but his emotional ones, too. Their relationship, whatever the nature of the original bond, or what dark secrets held them together, was becoming an increasingly strained one. Things were easier in the summer, when the house was full of a succession of guests, but when I was there at other times, and perhaps the only other person staying in the house, I could not help being increasingly conscious of the mounting tensions, the sudden glimpses of a waking nightmare. Such as happened on the day that some rather special guests were coming to lunch.

The old Duke of Connaught was a neighbour at Cap Ferrat and often brought his sister, Princess Louise, to a meal when she was staying with him, or again his granddaughter, Princess Ingrid. The Mauresque's owner had broken his morning's pattern by coming downstairs at half-past twelve. He was clearly uneasy, and not surprisingly. There was no sign of Haxton, who had been out on the town the night before. 'Where's Gerald? Has no one seen Monsieur Haxton? Is he in his room?' Willie asked the butler, the footman, myself, anyone in sight. Everyone shook their head, there was an increasingly nervous silence. Then suddenly the reveller appeared through the doorway, dishevelled, unshaven, a tramp.

He staggered as he came towards us, as though he was walking in his sleep.

'Gerald . . . don't talk now. Don't say anything. Just make the cocktails. Do you hear? MIX THE COCKTAILS. That's all you're fit to do, and then go and clean yourself up.'

A quarter of an hour later, he was not on the front door step as he should have been. Willie stood there himself. The ADC arrived eventually, just in time to slink into the dining-room behind us, and I noticed that all his usual *bonhomie*, his American unself-consciousness, had deserted him. He sat glassy-eyed, while Willie stammered his way through the meal. As soon as the guests had left, Willie went to his room for his afternoon rest, without speaking, and for the rest of the day the house was filled with an ominous silence. Haxton did not appear that night at dinner, nor at lunch the next day. This time I found myself seated opposite my host, alone. He looked as though he had not slept at all. I was desperately sorry for him, for the horror he must be feeling, at the ruins and the death's head spread out in front of him, no longer to be able to pretend that it was not so. But what could I say? It would be impertinence to offer advice to someone more than old enough to be my father, whom I had been encouraged to regard as a father-figure concerning my work. All the same, I longed to plead with him, to urge him to make this *débâcle* the excuse for a final showdown.

'Get rid of him now,' I kept on repeating to myself, as I ate my avocado pear with the special sauce that was a *spécialité de la maison*. 'Get rid of him now, before he does you further harm. You can't go on like this indefinitely.'

Of course, I said nothing. Though when people talk to me about this situation today, and ask me how could it have been allowed ever to happen, or to deteriorate to such a degree, I ask them in turn if they have never had one single bad influence in their own life, no relationship which seemed so carefree, and amusing to begin with, and ended up so disastrously. Not one single one? And then I tell them what this victim who punished himself deliberately, for his own imprisonment, finally admitted to me, that day at lunch, when something welled up in him bursting the dam of his usual ingrained reserve.

'You do not know what it is like, Godfrey, and I hope you never will, to be married to someone who is married to drink.'

I had no answer. Yet did I not know? I was suddenly back in the house at Richmond, and we would be waiting for my father's return. What condition would he be in? I saw my mother's face as she bent over her mending, her ear pitched for the sound of the front door being opened. There had been horror then, but a different kind of horror. Nothing like the final *dénouement,* the final breaking asunder of the unholy bond, when the truly evil one in the partnership lay half-conscious in a New York hospital, his liver, destroyed by alcohol, crumbling to dust.

Although the partnership had long since broken up, and Haxton's place at the Mauresque had been taken by someone whose influence was as good as the other's had been bad, Maugham insisted on visiting the dying man during the final period of disintegration. Not just for an hour of duty; instead he sat there all day and night, quietly, at the side of the bed in that aseptic room, making no sound himself, accepting his punishment. The patient, who bore no longer any physical resemblance to the young companion with whom Maugham had journeyed round the world, in search of copy, was wandering now hopelessly in his mind, as his own last journey was about to commence, possessed by hallucinations of a terrible order. Hour after hour he screamed and railed against the only real friend he had ever had, the friend who had been so incredibly generous to him. Appalling, venomous obscenities poured forth from his subconsciousness. No sedation, no drugs seemed to make any difference. Instead, terrifyingly, they only heightened the stream of molten lava. The doctors and the nurses tried to lead the solitary visitor away. He would not move. His vigil lasted right until the end, until the last accusing mumblings were stilled, the soul had fled. And the devil had been exorcized.

This was the only kind of catharsis that Maugham understood and believed in, hell on earth. Towards the end of his life I did however sense in him a slight turning away from the atheism that had been his avowed philosophy, a half-expressed longing for something to hold on to, as the diminishing years dragged on for him, something that would convince him, against his eclectic reasoning, that we do not inevitably, wastefully, go out like snuffed candles.

There was, for instance, the only time that I saw him weep. It was when he was describing to me a journey that he made to Strasbourg, to search for the grave of Goethe's sweetheart, since he was engaged in writing a long essay on this German writer whom he greatly admired. Instead of the grave that he was looking for, he came upon, in that same churchyard, a row of simple wooden crosses to mark the bodies of a British bomber crew, shot down in the second of the wars to end all wars.

Each of the crosses bore the name and rank of the buried remains, except one that was inscribed simply: 'HERE LIES A YOUNG ENGLISHMAN KNOWN TO GOD.'

It was then that the tears unashamedly coursed down his parchment cheeks.

I found myself wishing, each time I visited Cap Ferrat, that I could turn back the clock so that he might have a second chance. Time was running out very fast for him now – he was to be ninety-one in a few days time – and it was increasingly clear that he was ready, almost eager, to be rid of his mortal bondage. And did he long, too, in the depths of his being, this man who will go on being known to millions through his published work, to be known himself to God?

That evening the telephone rang, and Alan who for weeks had scarcely left his side, went to answer it, in the hall. It was London calling with the grievous news that Sir Winston Churchill had had another stroke, and was slipping into a deeper sleep. Had Mr Maugham any message to give the world, about his old friend?

There had been three of them at the end, I thought, the three elder statesmen of their respective worlds. They had met every week, during their last winters in the south, either at Monte Carlo, where Sir Winston had a suite at the Hôtel de Paris, or at the Mauresque, or at the villa at Cap d'Ail which Lord Beaverbrook had bought from the most celebrated *couturier* of his times, Edward Molyneux.

Churchill and Maugham were both inexorably enclosed in their deafness. This, in a curious way, was an added bond between them, as they soliloquized about the past, and Lord Beaverbrook fed the fires, while Alan, who seemed almost a young man in comparison, acted as interpreter and referee.

Now the second of the trio was on his way, and only this gnarled figure, for whom his favourite armchair with the leather back seemed too large, was left. We had dined as usual off the Georgian silver; the food, cooked by the female *chef* who had been with him over thirty years, was up to its usual high standard; servants hovered attentively. But the trappings could not soften his growing terror as to what lay ahead, the absolute negation of death.

Alan came back and whispered to me the news. But how to make it clear to him? The one old friend who had seemed immortal. And how to reach the one left behind, at the end of the long corridor of his deafness, baulking at being confronted with any form of reality? But later, as though he had sensed what we were talking about, I heard him stammer, almost to himself, 'Winston . . . none of us would be here without you . . .'

Then for a short time he became almost his old self, demanding:

'Tell Godfrey what happened the last time Winston was here. What? Yes, that's it . . . the story of the boy.'

Originally, Willie and Alan had heard the story from another source, and were anxious to confirm it.

A small boy, as a great treat, was taken down to Chartwell to lunch by his mother. He had been promised that he would see the greatest man in the world. Unfortunately, Sir Winston had one of his not-so-well days and didn't appear. So on the drive back to London, the mother expected her son to be disappointed; yet instead he was jubilant. 'But I *did* see him, Mother, I *did*. There was a man taking a tray along the corridor so I followed him and went in behind him into the room. There was an old gentleman in bed, and I went up beside him and asked him out-right: "Are you *really* the greatest man in the world?" And he looked at me very straight, and said, "Yes, I am, and now you buzz off." '

Sir Winston has assured them, yes, it was true, and after lunch that day he had made an unexpected request; he had asked if he could visit his host's writing-room, the smaller box set on the top of the parent one.

When I made the same request on my own farewell visit, my

host replied with his typical liking for understatement: 'You will find some bits and pieces missing,' adding, 'I don't go up there any more.'

I could understand why. The empty bookshelves facing the desk gaped and yawned like the grave. The other changes – such as the Gauguin panel, gone to be auctioned in the sale-rooms – one hardly noticed, but the books, generously despatched to form a new library for his old school at Canterbury, which today bears his name – that was so different, because here had been his armour, the most precious part of his birthright.

As instinctively I touched for luck the plain flat walnut desk on which he had written so many manuscripts, I saw myself standing there beside him, on that first morning of my tuition, and I relived all that he had said to me about the books, his own books, on the third shelf at eye-level to the desk. Would my own contributions, all twenty-five of them, be sufficient to fill the shelf now? Certainly, though not comparable in quality. Still he understood I had done my best. That was why I was here, the last house guest of all. I had worked as I had promised him I would.

The desk itself was so unnaturally tidy, compared with my own, I thought. There was a fresh, unused San Remo pad, and beside it a surgical glove. It seemed to have a strange life of its own, it was the ultimate landmark. When writer's cramp began to threaten him increasingly, and his right thumb became virtually useless from having written so many words in that unpretentious calligraphy that was an integral part of his personality, he tried the support of the glove, in vain. It was the beginning of the long, bitter, losing battle, which lasted too long for humanity's sake.

'Can't we go into Nice tomorrow and change my glasses?' he kept on saying, like a petulant child, that evening. Even though it would be a hopeless expedition, it was at once soothingly agreed. That afternoon he had driven into Beaulieu to have his hair cut, which was noticeably more luxuriant since his visits to Doctor Niehan's rejuvenation clinic in Montreux.

On his return from the barber, my host had greeted me, almost gaily, like his old self. 'I haven't had my hair cut for fifty years, not since we used to play tennis together, Godfrey.'

But the call from London about his old friend had somehow,

contrarily, seemed to steady his mind again for a little while. He was even able to babble about the most beautiful women he had ever known, stretching from Lily Langtry to Vivien Leigh. After saying that *The Letter* and *Rod* were his own favourite stories, he proceeded to tell me with a surprising exactitude the only plot he had never used.

Called simply *The Mother,* with a Spanish setting from the years that he had spent in that country, in hungry exile, it would have told the story of a woman who loved her son with such a primitive, possessive passion, that though he went to prison for a stretch, she cosseted him all the more on his return home. Until she discovered, in a fury of rage, that he was deeply involved with a girl whom she did not consider in any way worthy of her precious son.

The mother was an excellent cook. Thus her son always ate every morsel, every titbit, set on his plate. 'Did you enjoy your meal?' she asked one day. 'Very much, thank you dear mother.' 'Then let me tell you, you have just eaten the liver of the girl who tried to steal you away.'

With something of an effort, he reached the climax, and then, spent, lay back against the chair in which he had sat for so many rubbers of bridge, the happier evenings of his life. 'Time for bed,' Alan announced, with a dumb-show gesture at his watch. It was half-past eight.

But though he obediently rose, the story-teller had not quite finished.

'It was founded on fact. You must understand that. Like all my stories. I could only write if I knew there was a foundation of truth. That gave me confidence.'

Surely in all our lives there is one true story, too terrible to relate in public, and his own life was no exception, I decided, as once again a little procession formed. Slowly we went up the marble stairs, to the first floor, where the wide corridor runs round the inner courtyard, with its giant bronze statue of Buddha which, on some days, I had the odd fancy had become its owner's blood brother, demanding his share, too, of the richest estate that any author has ever left. After all, it could be argued that they had so much more in common, in their philosophy, than Maugham had had with his own brother, the formidable Lord Chancellor of his day, or for that matter with his nephew, Robin, who was now left with the unenviable task of trying, in literary circles, to perpetuate the family reputation.

Through the open doorway of the bedroom of the only Maugham whose name will live, I could glimpse on the mantelpiece the framed picture of his mother, who had died when this son was eight.

'Not long ago,' whispered Alan, who by his own innate goodness of character had held life together on a more even keel at the Mauresque, 'not long ago, I found him, his head on his arms, weeping silently in front of the picture. Although her death happened over eighty years ago, he has never got over it. He is haunted by it as though it happened yesterday.'

'What are you saying, Alan? What are you saying? Speak up.'

I would have to speak up, too, one day for everyone's sake I reminded myself the next morning, as I wandered down in curiosity to discover how the tennis court had survived. Of course, it was not, as had been suggested the previous evening, from some clouded picture forming in his muddled mind, fifty years since the days when I had coached him for the historic match with Michael Arlen, though it seemed almost as long ago. Certainly it was many years since the court had been used, and I was not surprised to find that a crop of weeds had sprouted through the terra-cotta surface. So that I did not have a feeling of guilt, as I walked about the court in ordinary shoes, suddenly remembering the answer that I had given to the interviewer in the TV programme who had demanded what I considered were the two most important assets for a young man starting out on life. 'If possible, he should be an above-average tennis player and possess a mastery of the rudiments of Contract Bridge.' The questioner had looked very surprised; he had almost accused me of quibbling, not considering his question with due gravity. But on the contrary, I had been very serious. Most serious indeed.

In my own case, surely it was the right answer, I told myself again, as Jean came out of his garage, breaking off from polishing the Rolls. Did he believe that the more he polished the longer his master might live? They had been friends, as a good employer and his staff can be friends, for forty years. He was plump and heavy now, and his own hair was grey; in the brilliant light, it surprised me to be made aware of how much Jean himself had changed from the days when he would be dispatched sulkily in search of Haxton on the mornings after one of his 'benders'; or would meet me, with a beaming smile, on my own arrival at the station, or later at Nice Airport.

'How is "Monsieur Morgan" this morning?' he asked.

I shrugged my shoulders. All my emotion was used up, but he himself had something else to add, with a note of touching pride. 'Il n'y aura jamais un autre comme lui.' Upon which, he resumed his polishing, while I found myself thinking now of the tennis court at that other villa, along the coast at Cap d'Ail, where I had also stayed with such carefree enjoyment, in the springs before the war, and again, before it had been bought from its owner who had furnished it with such taste, by Lord Beaverbrook. Then I went back again to the Villa Cappucina, where the tennis court is suspended beside the sea, and across the tiny bay you can glimpse the lights of Monte Carlo beckoning at night, to dine with my boss whenever I was in the vicinity and he himself was in residence. It was at once a privilege and a command. How exhilarating were those evenings at Lord Beaverbrook's table, how fraught with pitfalls, and how instructive in a different manner from the days when I had been blissfully unconscious of my gaffes, sublimely armoured by my youth. In a pause in the conversation, while I was wondering if I should suggest a new topic, or wait for my host, I could hear, far off in another life, the voice of Helen Morgan on the gramophone, singing *'Why am I here, why was I born?'* I would imagine I was smelling the drifting scent of the great pots of madonna lilies along the terrace as I recalled in my mind, as though it were yesterday, how the exquisite drawing-room had looked, with its white walls and pale upholstery – 'people and flowers should provide all the colour in a room' – wasn't that what Edward had always said? And certainly the people were colourful enough.

People like the Grand Duke Dimitri and his unspoilt American wife, Audrey, and Doris Chapman, who was as English as a teashop in Eastbourne, and yet you could not think of Monte Carlo without her, and a posse of tennis players, such as Mrs Lambert Chambers and Phyllis Satterthwaite, and Esmond Harmsworth, towering over the company, who could have been absolutely first-class at the game had he not had other preoccupations. I would gaze across the terrace, before lunch, at Dimitri with his sad, spaniel eyes, and lose the thread of the chatter round

Ferdinand and Miranda,
at the Angmering
Shakespeare Festival,
1924

At the Angmering
Shakespeare Festival,
with John van Druten,
walking on in *Richard
the Third*

With Eileen Sharp in *The Marquise* by Noël Coward, at The Criterion. *Photo: Sasha*

Marie Tempest in *The Marquise. Photo: Radio Times Hulton Picture Library*

me about who had won or lost most at the casino the night before, and what length skirts would be that season, and would Suzanne resist the challenge of this new girl from America. Instead I would think with wonder, but was he really present at the murder of Rasputin, the monk, together with his cousin, Prince Yussupoff? There is nothing to show it. He looks like any other White Russian of his world. Did nothing show ever, on the surface?

The villa's owner in those days, Captain Edward Molyneux, who had won an MC in the First World War, and been wounded no less than eight times, had had to surrender his ambition to be a painter, because of damaged eyesight, and had become a dress-designer instead, serving his own apprenticeship under Lucille. He had an absolute fetish about keeping fit. In Paris he rode every morning at seven in the Bois; here he hired a tennis professional each morning from Monte Carlo, whom I was allowed to share. Unconsciously, too, he continued my education in self-discipline where my other host had left off. Although the atmosphere of the villa was invitingly sybaritic, after a fortnight he firmly turned his back again on the delights of the South, refusing to be seduced. Back to the job, and an iron routine.

One spring, early in the 'thirties, he drove me up to Paris in his Rolls, which was the badge of ultimate success in the 'thirties, and invited me to stay on for a few days, in his château at Neuilly, so that I could see something of the city by day, while he was closeted himself at number 5, Rue Royale. This magnificent building, furnished entirely in dove-grey, with glittering crystal chandeliers, he always referred to laconically as 'the shop'. He hated all frills, all fancy talk. 'I make clothes, I am a shopkeeper,' he insisted. His attitude was a revelation to me.

All the same, I had vaguely imagined that in the evenings we would be going out to parties, to First Nights, to such functions as were à la mode. On the contrary. He would come back, deadbeat, from his studio on the top floor of Numéro Cinq, have a bath, get into pyjamas, eat very little, drink nothing, and go to bed.

Naturally it was a disappointment to me. 'Don't you enjoy going out and seeing smart women wearing your clothes?' I asked wistfully.

K

'I have had to live with my clothes since they were a gleam in my eye, I have had to make drawings of them, and put them together, first as a sketch, then holding the materials against a model, revisualizing them over again. I have slept with the clothes for weeks before they are finally shown. Then, after the Collection, I have the special ones among the clients insisting on consulting me themselves, asking my advice about this dress and that, while I am trying to concentrate on the trends for the next Collection. The last thing I want to do is to go to parties, simply to see the clothes all over again on someone's back. And probably worn with the wrong accessories.'

Abashed, I tried again.

'What do you think are the three most important things for a woman to consider when she is buying clothes?' I was learning fast to play the part of a reporter wherever I went. As my mentor had said, it was all grist to the mill.

He considered the question carefully before he answered.

'She should realize that white is a colour that every woman wears once too often. That you should always exclaim, "What a pretty woman,' not 'What a lovely dress,' meaning that the dress should always be complementary to the personality of the wearer, never the other way round.'

'And the third dictum?'

'Dark blue, with touches of white at the neck – a bow, a collar, or again cuffs – will always – and I repeat, always – be the safest bet, the most becoming outfit for the daytime.'

'Is that why you yourself always wear a dark-blue serge suit, and a white silk shirt?' I asked, smiling.

'No, I wear the same suit all the time because I never have time to shop for anything else. In fact, no time to shop at all. So my secretary just rings up my tailor and says, "The Captain wants another couple of suits," or the shirtmaker for another half-a-dozen shirts. It simplifies life. Maybe you will find the same thing one day.'

I have, and wear a similar uniform myself today. Indeed, I was wearing it when I went to call on him in his suite at The Crillon, almost thirty years after our original conversation. At seventy, the Captain – as everyone knows him – was about to stage a come-back, not because he was in need of any sustenance, for on the contrary, he is deservedly rich through the commonsense he brought to his business right from the beginning. No, it was quite simple why he was coming back, to face the fashion jungle once more; he was bored.

'The mornings are all right,' he told me, on the eve of his first Collection, starting all over again once more in the Rue Royale. 'I paint in the mornings at my house at Biot, above Antibes, but it was the afternoons, when the light began to fade, which dragged in the South. I don't play bridge, and I am not interested in gossip. What else was there to do?'

He stood up restlessly, in the blue uniform that matched my own, and I noticed how lean he was still, how carved his profile, as he gazed out on the lights of the *Place de la Concorde* that somehow epitomize Paris.

'What fresh advice have you to give women about their clothes?' I asked.

'Exactly the same as I gave before,' he answered promptly. 'But there is a warning that I ought to add. I have a horrible feeling that skirts are going to jump, not just above the knees but incredibly almost to the waist. The "mini-skirt".' He pulled a face. 'I am appalled at the idea. For, *sans doute*, my friend, the ugliest part of any woman's anatomy is the back of her knees, leading up to her thighs.'

'Few women would wear trousers,' I suggested, 'if they looked at themselves from behind.'

'That is also true.' The waiter had brought our dinner, and when he had drawn the curtains and gone, my companion added a postscript, coloured by a burst of emotion that is rare to his nature.

'Whatever happens tomorrow, they can't take one thing away from me. When it was announced that I was coming back into business, all the silk manufacturers from Lyons, with their samples, called in an unceasing procession at the Rue Royale. Some were the sons of the men with whom I used to deal in the old days, but all had come with the same message. "If there is anything here that you like, it is yours, to use exclusively." Such loyalty can't be bought. It is worth all the rest.'

Of course, his success was assured again. Because, like his one-time apprentice, John Cavanagh, he creates clothes that are kind to women; soft and feminine clothes such as he used to design for Gladys Cooper for all her plays, and for Gertrude

Lawrence, and for the beautiful, young Greek princess, then living modestly on the left side of the river, for whom, in admiration for her looks, he would occasionally make a dress, to be rewarded in a most unexpected fashion, as so often happens in the end. For when Princess Marina became engaged to Prince George, he was the only designer in Paris who was commanded to create not only her wedding dress but equally the dress that she wore when she drove through London in an open carriage beside Queen Mary, to be introduced to her future country, and to win all hearts. Like the other princess from across the sea, this time from Denmark; Alexandra, whose family was equally in modest circumstances, and who on the eve of setting sail to become the wife of the future King Edward the VIIth, wondered so much what the future held for her and what destiny awaited her. In her commonplace book – so popular in those days, and where you expressed yourself under such headlines as 'My favourite author,' 'My favourite colour,' 'My favourite flower,' 'My favourite ambition . . .' – she wrote, 'I want to be loved.'

I suppose everyone wants that. Certainly I was no exception. If I look back now a little ruefully to that period of self-realization in my life, I do so without rancour. One is as one is created, and must accept whatever crosses come one's way. My brother was now married to exactly the right life-partner for him, and his utterly different weight of loneliness from mine, stemming from the restrictions caused by his childhood illness, was lifted for ever. While my stepbrother, Ted, looking very handsome and dashing in his naval uniform, led, as his bride down the aisle of St George's, Hanover Square, the sister of the man who in the same way as my brother turned an initial physical handicap into an eventual asset, was to crown his life, too, with complete victory in his own sphere of action.

Through meeting as fellow ushers at Ted's wedding, I was to come to know Dick de Quincey well. He and his fair, graceful, wife spontaneously invited me to spend the rest of that winter with them, instead of going to Amalfi for the third time, at their Queen Anne house on the river at Bodenham just outside Hereford. With such unhappy memories of my schooldays in that vicinity, I was apprehensive at first about accepting. But how thankful I was afterwards that I did.

Ann de Quincey spoilt me, insisting that a comforting coal fire should be lit every morning in the room where I worked at the last chapters of *The Unequal Conflict,* while Dick, in all weathers, was out and about the farm. By nature, and upbringing, he had been in his youth completely urban in his outlook. However, after being battered in the First World War, the doctors warned him that his only hope of survival was to lead an outdoor life from then on. So reluctantly he bought a farm in Herefordshire and decided, a complete novice, that he would create a herd of Herefordshire cattle, little guessing that in due course he was to become the greatest producer of champion bulls in the world, carrying off all the top prizes with monotonous regularity, and becoming, in addition, a huge exporter-earner for his country.

He was so utterly unassuming that, if you encountered him walking down St James's Street you would have imagined that he spent his life in some club such as White's. But these sorties to the West End became rarer as the years went on. Right from the start, he made a rule that he must be awakened at any hour of the night, summoned for every birth, present at every mating. In five years, he understood more about cattle breeding than any of his staff, who worshipped 'The Captain', and were delighted with his sallies, as when on one occasion, taking round an important buyer from South America he remarked that the only drawback Herefords had were their pale eyelashes.

It wasn't only with cattle that Dick was to discover that he possessed, immensely to his own surprise, the equivalent of 'green fingers' in a garden. Towards the end of his life, he was to amuse himself by experimenting with trotting ponies, and within a couple of years was carrying off all the trophies there, too. Humming birds and orchid-growing he took in his stride, as sidelines, while early on, he was accepted without contradiction as the finest breeder of Sealyhams in the country. An astonishing record for someone who had expected to live out his days as a confirmed townsman.

One morning at breakfast, during my initial visit to The Vern, there came to our ears a muffled wailing that might have presaged the fall of the walls of Jericho. 'What on earth's that?' I asked my host in astonishment. But he was already at the door and I followed him, full of curiosity.

In a barn off the yard, knee-deep in muck, I found the most unexpected sight. A dozen Sealyham puppies were holding a protest meeting round an empty trough. The cry of the banshee, the followers of The Beatles could not have exceeded their keening. And what on earth was the matter? Was it because the trough was empty of water? 'No,' explained their breeder, unexpectedly. 'Not water, but orange juice.' He went on to explain that they had a ration of orange juice each morning, full of vitamins and good for their back legs, arresting any tendency to rickets. 'Look at that little beggar, he'll never be any use for showing, as it is.'

Dick pointed at the smallest of the group, who, instantly aware that we were discussing him, subsided on his hindquarters, to hide his imperfections. When a few minutes later one of the farm hands arrived with a fresh supply of nectar, having opened another crate of tins, all the other recipients stood on their hind legs and buried their noses in the trough, to lap up their ration for the day, except the one that Dick had pointed out. Alas, each time, poor fellow, he tried to reach up, his back legs let him down. It was only natural that I should lift him over the heads of his brothers, so that he would receive his fair share. Absolutely delighted at this bounty, he wagged his tail joyfully, and when we made a move to return to our own breakfast, he followed after me, into the yard, and had to be shooed back to join the rest of his family.

I could not get this waif out of my mind all day. Somehow, I suppose he had aroused in me my protective instinct. At breakfast next morning, I cocked my ears. No sound from the stables. All must be well. Except what about the one I had rescued? As soon as I had drunk down my own glass of orange juice, without saying where I was going, I slipped out of the room and waded across the yard. It was exactly as I had suspected. The others were all gobbling down their quota, my new pal was the odd boy out. At my arrival, he came nuzzling hopefully against my legs. 'Here we go,' I told him, and up over the heads of the others, once again, he went. It was the same the next morning. After all, he would be expecting me now. I could not let him down. Whereupon my host, amused by my Good Samaritan act, suggested that I should have the rescued one for my own. 'He's got the most magnificent head and shoulders,' Dick explained, 'but quite frankly, as I told you, the weakness in his back legs will prevent his ever taking prizes at Cruft's.'

So we compromised. I adopted my chum for the rest of my stay, and christened him Mr Sponge, after *Mr Sponge's Sporting Tour*. But how could I keep him for ever? I only had my rooms in Ebury Street, and was dead against keeping a sporting dog cooped up in London, especially when there was no one to look after him, if I was out or away.

Yet my heart was irrevocably won over now, so that when the spring came I could not bear to leave The Vern without Mr Sponge. Instead of going back to London, I moved on into Wales, where on the Tremadoc Bay estuary I had heard that in the grounds of a hotel, newly designed and opened by the distinguished architect, Clough Williams Ellis, there was a campanele, and scattered small cottages, overlooking the water, ideal for painters or writers seeking a working sanctuary. I could come to an arrangement by which I had my meals in the hotel, an old house that had been neglected, now refurbished, and be left in absolute seclusion for the rest of the day, if I wanted it so. It proved the perfect retreat, for a time, and I could not have arrived at a better moment, since the long walk to the end of the Point, through the woods where the azaleas and the rhododendrons grew in wild profusion, their scent strong and very sweet in the May sunshine, is one of the most evocative vistas that I have encountered in the whole of my journeyings. Indeed, when more spacious travellers start describing the delights of Tibet and Kashmir. I am rather inclined to interrupt their flow with my own loyalty for Portmeirion, which I used as part of the background for the last of my novels, *Communion on Earth*.

I really did find communion there, though I was still struggling to finish *The Unequal Conflict*. Nevertheless, all the concentrated effort, the re-writing and the re-polishing that I gave this book paid off in the end, because its publication produced an even better press than *Dreams Fade* had done; so much solid acclaim, in fact, that Cassells, a rather more important publisher than the House with which I had started, offered me a fresh contract with a guaranteed advance of three-hundred pounds for each of my next three books. I was overjoyed at the offer, though I can't think now why I should have been. It was still a slave wage. However, the contract was something to show my stepfather, as the businessman of the family, the proof that I was making concrete progress, if at a slow financial rate, as a serious author, and it gave me in addition an excuse to give my first literary party. A christening party, for the new book.

Rather cheekily, I decided to consult one of the Quaglino brothers, who gave their name to the restaurant which is still flourishing in Bury Street, St James's. It was very much the smart eating place of the 'thirties. I had twenty-five pounds, at the most, to spend on the party. Did Signor Quaglino think that such a sum would provide a bar waiter, to create a special cocktail named after my book, a lot of ice and a certain amount of drink? I explained that *The Tatler* had offered to send one of their photographers to take pictures, and all sorts of well-known figures in the literary world, such as Louis Golding, Ethel Mannin, Eddie Marsh, Theodora Benson and Betty Askwith, who wrote novels in partnership, had already accepted my invitation.

'Certainly we will do it for you, it will be a pleasure,' the Italian restaurateur replied promptly. No quibbling, no looking down his nose, when I explained that the bathroom for storing the ice was on the floor below, and that there would only be one room for the party. What's more, 'Quag' sent three waiters, a lorry-load of cocktail stools to transform the scene, and even came himself to perform the actual christening, pouring his own concoction over the book. My studio was absolutely jammed; the stairs resembled a tube station in the rush hour. Far more guests arrived than I had ever expected, let alone asked. In the middle of it all, Ernest Thesiger almost caused a riot by opening his shirt to display the rope of pearls he swore that he always wore round his neck. Someone said he ought to have been the book's fairy godfather. I am sure he would have obliged. But there was no doubt about it, the evening was a huge success and gave me my first taste for being a host, and my first lesson in party giving. It is far better to have too many guests than too few, and after the initial half-hour, there is no need to provide an excess of alcohol; people are lit up on their own eloquence, mingled with the sensation of being at the right place, at the right moment, for once, in the swim.

The next morning I paid another visit, before luncheon, to the restaurant in Bury Street. I hoped this was the most tactful moment for a quiet word. I was not suffering so much from a hangover as from a sense of remorse allied to acute anxiety. 'I am awfully sorry there were so many people last night,' I blurted out. 'I don't know where they all came from, and I am afraid they must have drunk much more than twenty-five pounds worth of your liquor.'

The book's christener, who was as much a figure of the London scene at that time as Ferraro was at The Berkeley, up the road, cut short my apologies with a bland wave of his plump hand. 'Do not worry. Do not give it another thought, please. You will more than repay me one day.' He turned on me the penetrating gaze of assessment that he used if he was deciding where to seat a party of customers. 'You see,' he continued, 'it is part of my business to know such things, you are on the way up.'

I had no such inner conviction myself. I never seemed to have more than a few pounds in the bank, perhaps because I had rashly acquired my first 'bus', on the never-never system. Naturally, it was the joy of my existence, a small blue Wolsey Hornet, conspicious with much aluminium in the way of external fittings, and a wicked-looking exhaust pipe. In this I used to hurtle down the Kingston by-pass, oblivious to the only memorable remark that the Lord Baldwin of the day ever made. Opening the first of the motor-ways, he commented sombrely that the cemetery already in place at the Putney end was not enough. 'There should be one at each end,' he declared with a prophetic prescience which he scarcely showed regarding the need for rearmament on a giant scale.

At the far end of the by-pass lay Esher where my mother had recently persuaded my stepfather to buy a home for his retirement from his steel business in Birmingham. He had aged considerably, looking much older and greyer than his years, and she hoped that the Surrey climate would be kinder to his asthma. Each summer, during the twenty years that she was herself to live at Esher, she would remark with the same note of relief and wonder in her voice, after the passing of another winter, 'The first blooming of the roses here is a month earlier than it used to be in Barnt Green and Bromsgrove.'

Broom Cottage had white frame woodwork, like a Virginian house, on the garden side, and a seasoned wistaria growing along it. Standing in a close of houses, a few hundred yards from the Portsmouth Road, there was nothing much to distinguish it otherwise from the others until Mother, with her usual flair, set about altering the garden, making terraces of roses where there had been a tennis court, and painting every room white to give a country rather than a suburban atmosphere. Thus in the end, the garden and the house became entirely complementary to each other, and the final effect was wholly charming. The house itself was not so large as The Oakalls, a deliberate choice, but apart from the maids' quarters I noticed on my first tour of inspection that it had two spare rooms. So I automatically presumed that the one at the top of the house would be mine. But I presumed both wrongly and rashly. For it was explained to me at once that this was no longer to be considered a family home, though of course I would be welcome for visits, from time to time.

Mr Sponge settled down more easily, under the terms of sufferance, than I did. There had always been a Sealyham in our house, and now there was one again. He was absolutely sure of his welcome, always. Not that my stepfather was not his usual courtly, kindly self, but though nothing was actually said I sensed that they both were in complete agreement that what I needed was not a dog as a companion, however endearing his ways, however faithful his moist eyes, but a wife who would make a real home for me. Of the three brothers of the two families, I was the only one left, untied, the odd man out. Of course, I was considerably younger than the other two, but both the longing, on the one hand, and the desire to conform, on the other, were equally strong in my own veins at that moment. Indeed it touched me to hear the note of delighted expectancy in my mother's voice when, soon after my probationary visit to Broom Cottage, I rang up to invite her and Dad to a night out in Town, as an independent return for their hospitality. A theatre, always her favourite treat, and supper afterwards at Quaglino's. 'And will you both dress up, please, because there is someone I want you to meet.'

The evening cost far more than I could really afford, but then Leonora was special. Very special. Not because her mother was married to P. G. Wodehouse, and therefore she had lived a very sophisticated, amusing life, meeting everyone, going everywhere, treated as though she were Plummy's own daughter. Not even because she was lovely, in a spun glass kind of way, with delicate bone structure, soft fair colouring, and the sort of figure that would have been worth a fortune to any model. The best point of all about Leonora was not her appearance but her character.

She was fundamentally so nice. A much berated word, but here intended in its original, comprehensive sense. Without being fulsome, or insipid, Leonora managed to be nice to everyone. Yet without, too, surrendering her critical judgment. At the same time she succeeded in making anyone with whom she came in contact, even to exchange a few words, feel that they were the only person in the world of any importance at that moment.

I met her first, I think, at the Cazalets' house Fairlawne in Kent, where today Peter, the younger son of the family, trains his winning stud of racehorses. In those days, his elder brother, Victor, was alive, who, a squash champion, as well as an MP, was equally energetic on the tennis court. Like his sister Thelma, who was herself to become an MP. And we were all roped in, the tennis brigade, like Catherine Willoughby* and Charles Hope†, to canvass for her in Islington. Two players of Wimbledon standard in the family, two Members of Parliament. Not surprisingly, the week-ends at Fairlawne, both mentally and physically, were extremely lively, and it was a high-water mark for me when I was invited to stay for a whole week to join the house party for a local tennis tournament. It was here that I met Jack Lysaght for the first time too, and was paired up with him by my hostess in the tournament. But although he was an Oxford Blue as well as the Somerset champion, and was soon to be tried for his England cap, we went out in the first round. I could not play well in the right court, being a left-hander; he could only play his best in the left. Strangely, this ignominious defeat was the beginning of a lifelong friendship.

Although the sun always seemed to be shining in those days, I don't remember Leonora ever watching the tennis, let alone playing. You could not really think of her as an out-of-doors girl at all. As a change from her life in New York, she had taken a mews flat for herself, off Bruton Street, where she enjoyed giving bridge evenings, or sitting about playing the latest American hits on the gramophone, just talking and laughing. She had a wide mouth, perhaps through laughing so much at the absurdities of life, and there was a slight lisp to her voice which made everything she said seem more original or more amusing

* Lady Catherine Willoughby.
† Lord Charles Hope.

than it was. It did not matter, I was in thrall. I remember one June day I had been lunching with Johnny Farrow, an Australian with the very blue eyes of someone who loves the sea, who was destined to become a big Hollywood director and marry Maureen O'Sullivan, and sire seven children, including one called Mia. After we had finished our meal, we both exclaimed simultaneously, 'Let's go and see if Leonora is at home.' Johnny was a little in love with her, too, at that time. Every man was. At the corner of Berkeley Square, there was an old woman with a basket of madonna lilies. Between us we bought all that was left of her stock, and carried the bunches triumphantly through the summer streets. The scent of the lilies, the warmth of the sun on our faces, the positive knowledge that we were both young and ardent, all surged to a climax when Leonora opened the door. At sight of the bouquet she embraced us both, as though she had never been bunched before. 'Johnny . . . Godfrey, how divine.' I hoped she meant us, not just the flowers. Anyway, we stayed with her all afternoon. Only when I was with her did I never have any sense of guilt that I should be at my desk. I knew already in my heart, that my suit was hopeless, there were so many much grander suitors than I, but I went on hoping, pretending to myself that I had a chance, and it was typical of her all-embracing warmth that when I described my mother to her she insisted on being allowed to meet her.

By then the summer had vanished over the horizon. I should have realized at the time that the fog which descended so disobligingly that November day we had chosen for our party, was an omen. A bad, bad omen. Early in the afternoon, Mother telephoned that Dad was not prepared to take the car out of the garage. 'Couldn't you come by train,' I suggested, 'and get a taxi to the station, and stay the night in Town?' In the end they did that, a sluggish, cold, insufferable journey, so as not to disappoint me, and themselves too; so as not to let down the side. The fog penetrated into the theatre, affecting the singers' voices. Manfully Dad tried not to cough or wheeze – falling back on his pills for special emergencies. He was most gallant with Leonora, and she adored him. The show was the musical hit of the moment, with Mary Ellis in the star part, and Leonora was too nice – that word again – to admit till long afterwards that she had seen it before in New York. All through supper she took the most enormous trouble, without showing it, to make them both believe that she was having the gayest evening of her life, though because of the fog, the restaurant was almost empty. By the time we dropped my parents at their hotel, my mother was equally under Leonora's spell, and kissed her good-bye, a most unusual gesture for her. How she hoped, I could tell from her face, that she was kissing her future daughter-in-law for the first time, and later, when she knelt down to say her prayers, as she never failed to do, I am sure she mentioned it, too, to the Almighty.

But it was not to be. When I finally plucked up courage to ask directly if there was any hope for me, Leonora managed to turn me down with her usual grace. 'Oh Godfrey, I'm much too extravagant and spoilt for you. I should ruin you in six months. Besides I think you're too young even to think of marriage yet. It would interfere with your writing, and Plummy says you've got a big future. He does, really.'

She was determined that I should not feel diminished, even at that moment. Deliberately she gave me the line to take, the self-protective armour to adopt, hereafter. She herself in the end chose Peter Cazalet of all her *beaux*, and went back to stay at Fairlawne, this time as its châtelaine. Soon after they were married, I drove over from Esher for the night, and after dinner Peter took off his shirt and Leonora rubbed his back, which was sore from a fall, with embrocation, as though she had been look-ing after a horse-trainer all her life. She still treated everything, even domesticity, with the lightest touch, and I found myself hoping jealously that Peter appreciated his good fortune. Later, the war came and I lost touch with them both. Peter was in the army, like his elder brother. I was most of the time at sea. There were no more tennis week-ends for anyone, no more theatre parties all dressed up, since the black-out proved more stultifying than the worst pea-souper. And then one afternoon, one bitterly cold March afternoon of '44, I was battling my way against the wind, round the corner of Berkeley Square, with my head down and my feet dragging, when, just at the spot where I had bought the lilies, a century ago, I ran full tilt into a woman in a mink coat with a scarf round her head, and it was my first love, my only real love.

'Leonora . . .'

'Godfrey . . .'

We stared at each other, like two ghosts, in the bleak twilight. I could guess what she was thinking. How thin he looks, how changed. My skin was the colour of putty, hers was delicately made up, and as usual she wore a million-dollar look. The scarf made no difference, no difference at all. After months in a naval hospital in the north, and an unsatisfactory convalescence at Esher, I had gone in fear to see my old, peace-time doctor, and just left him after a second, gloomy consultation. He was usually so optimistic but on this occasion he had looked grave, hinting that he feared there was some kind of obstruction in the lower bowel. In consequence, he had decided that in the circumstances, the best thing for me was to become an inmate in a clinic in North Wales, at Ruthin, where more elaborate tests and a complete set of X-rays could be carried out without fear of enemy interference.

I started to blurt all this out to Leonora, as she took my arm affectionately, and her coat made a tent for us against the wind. The scent she used was the same as the old days. I felt a nostalgic tide of emotion rising within me. 'Come and have a cup of tea,' she suggested. 'I'm picnicking in Anthony Mildmay's house, over there.'

We went into the house of Peter's greatest friend. She lit a fire in the library, which was partly under dust sheets, and made some toast. As she bent gracefully over the grate, I decided that she was more desirable, if more unobtainable, then ever.

Then when I had finished my story, she told me hers.

'It's the most extraordinary coincidence, but I had just come from seeing my doctor too. Like you, I've got to go into a nursing home. Just for a few days. Mine is nothing, just one of those small tiresome tidying-up things that women have to have done to themselves, sometimes. And I am sure your tests will all turn out negative, too. The truth is, you're just worn out, after all those Russian convoys. And no wonder. What you need is some sun, and feeding up.

'So Godfrey, promise me as soon as you get back to London,' she continued, handing me a piece of toast on a fork, 'that you will let us know and come and spend as much of the summer as you like at Fairlawne. We get chickens off the farm, and things like that, so you won't be gobbling up the children's rations. I shall be alone with the children, because Peter will be with his regiment and I have a feeling that he will be going over-seas, that they are preparing for something big. Of course, I don't know, but I just feel it, and it will be such fun having you to keep me company and stop me worrying. It will be like the old days. I love Fairlawne, don't you?'

Yes, I loved Fairlawne, and all the fun we used to have, once upon a time. I accepted gratefully, eagerly, trying to pretend that nothing had changed. But of course, it always has. I never saw her again, there was no second flowering on the tree. For a week later, on the very morning that the matron at Ruthin Castle came into my room, accompanied by the head doctor of the clinic, to announce that I could cast away all my fears about cancer, (be-cause all I was suffering from was a nervous spasm of the colon, induced by the Arctic cold), with a great rush of thankfulness, after they had gone, and I was alone again, I picked up the copy of *The Times* lying on my bed, and there on the front page my eyes turned idly to the lists of births . . . and deaths.

It was no one's fault. The million-to-one chance. I could not believe the cruel, bare announcement, except there was never any mistake in *The Times*. It was as omnipotent as God. Later, when the shock had begun to diminish a little, I felt another wave of thankfulness, a different kind, that we should have had a last, gentle meeting, a bonus for me to carry always. Just as it makes me very glad today to have the link of playing tennis with Leonora's son, Edward, who has married the daughter of a Sussex neighbour, and who took the decision which his mother would have approved, of surrendering his fame at its height as a superb point-to-point rider, to tackle the more mundane fences of the Bar, as his profession. While again, it is always a pleasure for me to see Sheran, Leonora's daughter, who possesses the same quality of being at ease in any company, and perhaps more precious, a gift for making one feel, even at my age, much taller and more vital than one really is.

Equally, my mother was able to do that for my stepfather, to make him forget his accursed asthma, to fill him with the confi-dence of a man still in his virile prime. They had ten idyllic years together, and then suddenly in a week, it was over. And ironically nothing to do with his asthma, which so long had been his mortal enemy. So that when Mother rang me up to say that Dad had been taken ill in the middle of the night, and rushed to a local nursing home, I was not at first unduly alarmed. After all, I had recovered from a burst appendix myself.

Still, I drove down to Esher at once, where I found my mother was as calm and composed as she remained almost till the end. It was the days when the use of the antibiotic drugs, to combat peritonitis, was in its infancy, and they – the mysterious 'they' who take absolute charge on these occasions – were apparently apprehensive as to the effect on Dad's heart, because of his painfully-laboured breathing. Mother went into no explanations at the time, and it was only when she suggested that she would like me to stay at Broom Cottage that I began to feel suddenly afraid. More so when Auntie Violet, uninvited, arrived with the expression of a female undertaker. She had recently discarded the henna bottle, and given up the futile struggle over her hair. Unfortunately, from the years of rough dying, her mop had coarsened so much that it now refused to be disciplined by an army of combs. The general effect was oddly disturbing. I had never worried about her eccentricities before; in fact, I had rather encouraged and revelled in them. But now I surprised her giving Mother a malevolent look, the kind that witches assume as they utter their curses, and I could not understand why, until it came to me that she felt cheated – she was boiling inside because she was being kept from her brother's sickroom. But so was everyone else except his lawful wedded wife. His son had been sent for, but he was the other side of the world in his ship. Meanwhile, Mother was determined that her beloved one should not be subjected to the indignity of being stared at as he fought and gasped for life. Thus Violet felt thwarted; thwarted of her pent-up longing for drama, and the breaking down of human barriers, in a wallowing exchange of gruesome, sick-bay details. My mother came and went, and said nothing. And Violet, who in her ghoulish haste had forgotten to bring her current copy of *The Spectator,* now found herself to her disappointment a spectator of nothing. In the end, rather to my surprise, I found myself taking charge, bundling her, protestingly, out of the house and back to her Ladies Club in Dover Street. 'We'll keep in daily touch,' I said firmly. 'There is nothing you can do here to help.'

There was nothing really that I could do, either. Mr Sponge pattered round the house behind me with his tail at half-mast. I thought of the evenings at Eastbourne, when I had knelt on the side of my bed, in the darkness of my room in the hotel, watching the silhouettes passing to and fro, in the ballroom across the street, the frieze of dancers that I longed so passionately to join; I had been too young to understand fully then what those evenings had meant to my mother, the reburgeoning, the mating of their steps upon the ballroom floor. And, too, the morning when I had forgotten my tennis racquet and my stepfather had turned his beautiful, purring, limousine on the way to London, without a word of reproach from either of them. I thought of so many things, as in my suddenly too-bright sports car I drove my mother to and from the nursing home, where she would disappear and I would impotently wait in the untidy, shabby garden, so very different from her own.

One afternoon, when she re-emerged, she said that Dad was sleeping and that she would like to go for a drive to get some air. It was a calm, early October afternoon. She did not automatically admonish me, as she usually did, to drive carefully. I took her along the Portsmouth Road, to the Hog's Back, above Guildford, where she always made the same comment that Londoners could say what they like but the view was not as really inspiring as the one from the top of the hill at Broadway; and then on to the Punch Bowl. This was the spin that my stepfather and she often took, stopping for a cup of tea half-way. They enjoyed enormously their little car outings. I did not think she would want to face the alien eyes of a hotel lounge today, so I stopped the car on the verge, beside the great hollow where you feel a giant once trod, and she got out and started to crouch among the bracken, as though she was a fugitive from life. I took her hand and it was so cold, that I put my tweed jacket round her shoulders. She started to shiver violently, though the afternoon was surprisingly warm, but when I suggested getting into the car she shook her head. It would mean turning back, it would bring nearer the return, facing what had to be faced.

'He was such a wonderful man,' she said at last, in a whisper almost to herself. 'He never said one single unkind thing to me. I never knew what it meant to be loved till he came into my life. If only it could have been earlier. If only we could have had more time together. He was always so good about you and Rodger.'

I realized with a shock that she was talking in the past tense, though she was not aware that she was doing so. I stopped myself from uttering some ghastly bromide like 'while there's life there's hope', and led her back to the car. Even after we reached home, she was still shivering in violent spasms, and I persuaded her to have a hot bath. She must have just climbed into the water, when the telephone rang, because when I knocked on the door she opened it, with a towel round her, and her face very pink and wet like a child's, which made it even worse having to tell her it was the nursing home and would she come at once.

She stayed at his bedside all that night. The next day he was gone. It was then that I marvelled at her composure. She only said one thing ever, about that week. 'With the beard that he had grown, Dad looked like a crusader.' That clearly comforted her. She had always hated herself in black, and had never worn mourning for her own mother, but from somewhere she raked up a black dress, to placate Violet and all the others. Ted was back by now, and he and I went down to Worcestershire together, to see about his father's ashes being placed in the Martino family tomb. He drove my car, and on the way, on the other side of Oxford, we had a head-on collision with a lorry coming towards us up a hill. In the split second before the crash, I remember thinking: 'Mother has just lost her husband, and now one of her sons. What a week.' But the front of my tiny car staved in without protest or a struggle, and miraculously neither of us was hurt.

When I rang up Mother from Birmingham later that evening, she even accepted this piece of news as though I was telling her about the weather in the Midlands. It was only when the public parade was finally over that the reaction began to set in. I stayed on at Broom Cottage, not knowing whether she wanted it that way or not, until the evening that she finally broached the subject herself.

'Dad has left you and Rodger each five hundred pounds. That was very generous of him. I have been left this house for my life, some free capital, and the interest on a certain sum. The rest has gone to Ted and his daughter Peggy. That is right, of course. Dad has put the administration of the estate into the Public Trustee's hands, and I am sure he believed that I would have enough to manage on my own, but with rising prices I can't help worrying about the future. Besides, I could not bear being here alone, always.'

There was a pause, and she added: 'I was wondering if you

would care to come and share the house now, and pay something towards the weekly bills? You could have Dad's study as your writing-room. I know that you have your Ebury Street studio, but you are always saying that you work better on your books in the country.'

I could only guess at what this long speech for her had cost. I was too moved to answer, and she continued again, because there was something else that she must first get straight in her mind. Once and for always.

'I had hoped, and Dad too, that you and Leonora . . .'

I shook my head.

'And there is no one else?' she persisted, but it was the only time in the whole of our relationship that she ever referred to this side of my life, in direct terms.

When I shook my head again, not meeting her eyes, she went on with a note of pity in her voice that she never used for herself: 'I am so sorry, my dear.' She bent her head over her sewing, and there was silence in the room. Methodically, she had chosen to darn a pair of my socks, as there was no point any longer in mending anything belonging to the man who would never again sit in the chair opposite her, reading his evening paper.

'I know you always think I take a pessimistic view of things,' she said at last, breaking off to glance up again. 'But look what happened to Dad. He was such a good man. Not like your father, who you and Rodger will end up having to keep. If it had to happen to one of them, why could it not have been your father?'

I had no answer to that, either. All over the world at that moment, I reminded myself, someone was asking the same kind of hopeless question, railing against an inscrutable Fate. On the tallboy beside her, there was a fresh vase of late michaelmas daisies, of different shades, arranged with her usual instinctive taste, and close by a silver bowl of scarlet *Red Letter Day* roses, which always did particularly well in the autumn.

I looked from one to the other of the vases appreciatively, and thought; this was a sort of red letter day. At least, a day of decision.

'All right,' I said, 'let's have a shot at it, and see how it works out.' I wanted to say all sorts of other things, too, about how much I had admired her gallantry this last month, but I knew she would not like that. So, on a sudden impulse, I got up and went across to the corner, where on a pedestal stood the gramophone which we had used for our teenage dances in the drawing-room at The Oakalls. All the records were stacked underneath, and deliberately I chose a gay fox-trot from *No, No, Nanette*.

'Come on, darling, let's dance.'

She looked up in surprise, but without demur left her mending as though she sensed, too, that this was somehow a symbolic gesture. When I took my partner in my arms, she was very stiff and gauche at first. 'Now remember your right foot goes back, as my left foot goes forward. That's better.' Slowly she began to release herself, surrendering to the rhythm as the music itself began to drug her mind.

'Tea for two, and two for tea,
Just me for you, and you for me.'

*   *   *

It became a ritual, after my afternoon work, before settling down at my desk again, to come into my mother's blue-and-white sitting-room, with the long expanse of windows looking out on to the borders of 'Ophelia' and 'Madame Butterfly' and 'Betty UpRichard' roses, and find her pouring out China tea from the familiar Queen Anne teapot. Mr Sponge, pleasantly weary after his run over the heath, or exploring the scents of Oxshott woods, would go to her to be petted, and then back to his master, to lie between us happily, on the rug. I took care not to sit in the chair in which I knew my stepfather had always sat but I no longer felt that I was simply a guest in my parent's house. I belonged here.

All the same, it was not easy at first, especially for Mother to enter the room on the other side of the house, that she had planned, and so recently, as a den for Dad, and find me installed there at my typewriter. I resented the interruption, she the intrusion, though we were both scrupulously careful to guard our inner feelings. And then I had an idea. A good idea. Why didn't we spend the rest of the winter abroad together? I was, as usual, embarking on a new novel, but after all, I had worked well enough in my bedroom at Amalfi. That was the obvious choice, until I remembered that on my advice they had spent a few days there, when they embarked on their own version of the Grand Tour, in the interim between shutting down his Birmingham office and settling in the Esher house. For them it had been a kind of second honeymoon.

So Amalfi was out. Then where? Someone suggested Majorca, which was at that time almost as unknown territory to travellers as was Peru. However, we were assured that we should find it warm and inexpensive, and with plenty of accommodation in Palma, the capital. 'I have no idea about the rest of the island,' our informant explained; as though the interior might be inhabited by head-hunters.

The journey, too, was a very different proposition from today. No morning flight, with lunch on the beach that same day. We went by train to Paris, then spent a night in the train to Barcelona. And then another night *en passage,* before we could take a boat to the island. Actually, we were rather disappointed by our first sight of the capital, perhaps because there was no sun. But the second day we were there, the skies cleared, and I suggested we should hire a car and explore. So we took the coast road past Vallomosa, which George Sands and Chopin had found such a romantic setting for their love; and no wonder, with the clouds of almond blossom in full flower against a brilliant sky. Our spirits rose, especially when by midday we had reached a tiny bay, called Port Soller.

We both were enchanted by it at sight. There was a hotel by the water's edge where we lunched, and over our coffee we looked at each other with the same suggestion on our lips. 'Let's see if they have suitable rooms, then we will come back tomorrow and move in.' They had and we did. Now, at last, mother began really to thaw, not towards me so much as towards the world at large that had dealt her yet another brutal blow. Her cotton frocks came out, and her French was aired, together with a few words of Spanish, and after we had been there for a week she looked excited and pleased, like a child bursting with news, when we met for the first time that day at lunch.

'On my walk this morning, on the other side of the bay, I tumbled on such a charming little villa, with a wide terrace, and it was to let most reasonably. It's furnished perfectly adequately, and an old maid goes with it, called Marie, who is French, so there will be no language difficulty there. Shall we take it for a month?'

That afternoon I stood on the terrace, looking down at the Homeric-coloured sea and the orange trees stretching to the road which led away to Soller itself, at the end of a short tram ride. The villa was simply a bungalow, but it had three bedrooms, one of which could be turned into a writing-room for me, built round a central living space where we could eat and sit in the evenings. It seemed exactly what we wanted. An omen of better luck, I thought, as I exclaimed enthusiastically:

'Let's take it for three months. Six months.'

Elizabeth wrote *The Enchanted April* about Portofino, but this equally proved an enchanted spring. In a way, it was the happiest interlude of my life, while this breathing space for my mother unconsciously settled our relationship into the right mould for ever. We shared a sense of mutual freedom such as we had not experienced before, and felt like millionaires, because everything was so inexpensive. In any case, nothing seemed to matter, everything was a joke. There were endless *histoires* about Marie, who arrived each morning dressed as though for a funeral, with a voluminous bag to contain the household shopping that she had done on our behalf. However, it had a two-way purpose. Into it went the left-overs, to take home to '*la petite*'. Until the day came when '*la petite*' put in an appearance, and she turned out to be a strapping wench who towered above her provider. So now we appreciated why Marie's bag had to be so capacious.

Then there were the fluctuating, colourful members of the port colony. Like the retired civil servant from India, with the dusty skin, who wasn't at all dried up underneath, and went with us for expeditions at week-ends, to places like Pollenza, to see the coral beach, and to Formentor, where the hotel that is now such a landmark on the island was in the process of being built, and all the sites for the surrounding villas were going at five hundred pounds apiece. I immediately had an enthusiastic plan that I would use my stepfather's legacy to buy myself one of the plots of land, close to the shade of the pine trees, but Mother's instant anxious reaction was to be apprehensive at the thought of my putting all my eggs into one basket. 'You may need the money. Keep it in the bank,' she implored me, and she received strong support, though for other reasons, from my literary adviser, who wrote back from Cap Ferrat by return of post, reminding me of how little of the world I had seen, and how essential it was for any writer to roam a great deal more in search of experience and material before tying himself to the same retreat in the sun, however pleasant. They were both right, of course, from their respective points of view, though I can't help being a little wistful sometimes when I hear of these same plots changing hands now for twenty thousand pounds.

Such boggling sums did not enter into our life in the port. The rent of the villa was four pounds a week, and altogether our expenditure was seldom more than a tenner. It suited us all very well, including Tony the plump Italian who insisted on Mother giving him free English lessons and in return kissing her hand with extravagant suction noises. In the colony were several other English couples of assorted partnerships, besides ourselves. Two very correct, middle-aged ladies from Cheltenham, who were exploring the venue as a possible site for the inevitable English teashop, and two younger girls, whom I never saw except in grey flannel trousers, which astonished all the men working on the port, though I imagine they would not glance twice at their attire today. After our initial month was up and we had renewed the lease for another three, and yet another option after that, we decided to give an evening party to which everyone was invited, including the regulars at the solitary port café where I would sometimes venture in the evenings to listen to the juke box. My café companions, with whom I chiefly conversed in sign language, immediately offered to put on an entertainment consisting of flamenco music. Mother was enchanted with the idea, and equally with the star turn, who gargled and gurgled in his throat, and finally disappeared into the outer rim of the darkness, escaping from the lights of the terrace where everyone had been applauding so enthusiastically, and was violently sick for a long time.

During the inevitable post-mortem about the party's highlights the next day, when I explained that the singer had had to drink an extra ration of wine, in order to lubricate his throat for his special kind of chanting, and this was a usual Spanish custom, my mother nodded sympathetically. 'Of course, I understand, my dear. What a polite man to leave the party as soon as he felt he had to.'

When one is far away from the restrictions and the routine

of one's ordinary home life, how one's values change in the drugging sunshine. She never spoke of her loss, nor of the cost of widowhood. Only of her pleasure in picking oranges for breakfast from one's own garden, and on the day that reluctantly she left for England at the beginning of May, we stopped on the way back to Palma at a property belonging to a Spanish family from Madrid, where all the fig trees looked as though their foliage had been freshly sprayed with shiny green paint, and there were huge, intoxicating banks of freesias. Mother, like myself, had been used to small bunches in a florist's window, buying one bunch with twelve blooms at a time, because of the cost. But her hostess urged her to pick as many blossoms as she could carry, and when we said good-bye, Mother exclaimed, with a break in her voice she could not control, 'I shall never forget this sight. Never.' It represented, I told myself, all that the escape, these halcyon months, had meant to her, and I was full of joy that I had contributed something towards creating this bridge from the past into the future.

I myself was staying on for another month, as friends were joining me from England now that it was warm enough to bathe. I had no fears about allowing her to return to Broom Cottage alone. She seemed a whole person again, healed, but alas I was sadly wrong. When I finally got back at the end of June, it was to find her in bed, looking very changed from her Port Soller self. It was a considerable shock, for she had never taken to her bed as long as I could remember, and she complained, alarmingly, of giddy fits and recurring bouts of nausea. So I sent for my own doctor from London, Isaac Jones, one of the wisest and most understanding of all the fellow pilgrims I have encountered in my own Odyssey, and he promptly diagnosed that she was suffering from trouble with her middle ear. 'I can prescribe the right things for that, and she will get up and about again and the attacks should grow more infrequent. But what she is really suffering from is delayed shock. That is something which only time can heal.'

I was silent, and he sensed at once the reason. 'That is only a platitude, my dear boy, because it is so true. You'll see if I am not right.'

I did see. I went into her bedroom to find her standing with her cheek against one of the mahogany supports of the four-poster, with its shiny chintz hangings of pink and white roses.

Her voice was quiet and controlled when she spoke, though I was startled by her words.

'I've just made up my mind about something, my dear. I'm going to have this bed cut in half.'

'Cut in half?' I echoed. 'But it's such a fine example of a four-poster, and you were so delighted when you and Dad found it together in that antique shop in Worcester, and . . .'

'I know. I know.' After a pause, she went on, in the same toneless voice, 'Dad and I never slept apart for a night during the whole ten years of our marriage. And he never was able to sleep himself for more than two or three hours at a time, because of his asthma. But it did not matter. We had each other. He knew that I was always there at his side, and I knew that he was at mine. It was very comforting for us both. Now I lie awake, and the bed seems so big, so empty, I can't bear to part with it alto-gether, so I shall do this. And perhaps now I shall sleep better.'

As well as she had slept in Port Soller? But I did not remind her of that. It would have been too cruel, and what was the use? I watched the carpenters come, and start making the necessary alterations. A new mattress was ordered, the room itself expanded, and visitors going into it, like our American relations and their friends who would descend on us in the summer, would exclaim : 'My, Joan. What a cute four-poster. I never knew they made them that size. Now what period does that belong to?'

It belonged to the present; the same period as the built-in white-wood desk which, that autumn, I installed in my new writing-room. Dad's old-fashioned mahogany roll-top affair went to my brother's chambers; the bookshelves already there were added to, so that they now stretched over the whole of one wall to the ceiling; a long lounging chair covered in tweed on which to read, and rest my back between working sessions; finally, a telephone extension was installed and the transformation was complete. It was *my* room now, and it was in this room that I was later to write *Home From Sea* and *P.Q.17,* as I looked out thankfully—instead of at the wastes of the Barentz Sea – at the yew hedges, the green of the lawns, and the immemorial beech in the field beyond that was also ours. No, not strictly ours, but at least the property of the Martino estate. In any case, Broom Cottage had taken on a new lease of life, and for the next twenty years I shared the running of the house with my mother, with Mr Sponge, for much of that time, as a sort of mediator between us. If ever there was an atmosphere of temporary strain in the house, as during the time I was refurnishing Dad's study, he kept on gazing up at his mistress with pleading eyes, until he won the day and peace was restored.

What I shall always recall with gratitude, what was so remarkable about my mother's attitude during this period, was her rigid refusal to interfere in my affairs. She was determined that I should consider myself absolutely free to lead my own life, in my own way. She played fair. She used no blackmail and no sighing technique. If I looked bleary-eyed at breakfast, and she was obviously aware that I had driven back from London in the small hours of the morning, she never questioned me as to where I had been, or laid traps. If I was to be away for the week-end, I just gave the dates in good time but no details, unless I wanted to; if I wished to invite anyone to stay, she welcomed without criticism the friends of my own age, but equally without expecting to be included in our plans. However, she showed disarming pleasure if anyone offered to help her in the garden, her garden, which was a sure way to her affections. With amusement, waiting for the sequel, I noticed that it was always the obliging amateur who retired first and needed a strong drink. I still receive letters today from those who, meeting her at this time, speak of her charm and her vitality, and above all, the gaiety of her spirit. Yet despite the brave front that she put up, nagging doubts kept on recurring in my mind, though I tried to brush them aside.

I was away for frequent periods altogether, either in Ebury Street, or at Portmeirion, or staying with tennis friends, like the Lysaghts at their place in Somerset, close to Minehead, where Jack's parents had singled me out of his many friends, to regard me almost as another son, insisting on taking me with them to Madeira each Christmas. I hoped and prayed that Mother was not too unhappy, too lonely underneath her brisk façade as treasurer of the local Nursing Association and running the amateur theatricals side of the Women's Institute. The kind of good-cause activities that widows, with gapingly too much time on their hands, are encouraged to take up. Basically, a son must be a poor substitute, as a companion, for a husband. Moreover,

I began to have secret fears that I was a poor substitute as a breadwinner too.

On the surface everything seemed smooth enough. With judicious coaxing, and the efforts of my agent, I still received a stream of commissions, chiefly for the women's magazines, but I began to suspect that I was getting into a groove. *'The Daughter I would like to have,' 'The Girl I hope to marry,' 'Why I like working with women,' 'Should wives have a career?'* I had aired my views on variations of these themes, and so many more in a similar vein, over and over again. The cheques for my contributions – looking back, I wonder now with awe how I had the nerve to express such positive views, from the sidelines – paid the rent in London and my share of the running expenses of Broom Cottage, but slowly I began to feel that I was getting nowhere fast, that I was working and living in a vacuum.

I was too proud to admit my growing sense of disillusionment with myself. It is true that if I was invited, as I frequently was, to a house party at Sunninghill Park, at Ascot, as the guest of Phyl and Philip Hill, a huge tycoon, I gave myself up to enjoying every moment of the three days of Rothschild-like splendour, revelling in the in-gossip, the friendly tennis matches, on which my host would always have side bets when I was partnering his wife; and finally bridge long past midnight in the library with the green silk hangings that Syrie Maugham had devised. But as I drove home again to my desk at Esher on the Monday morning, reaction would set in. I could not help comparing what I was worth at twenty-five, in hard cash, with all the worldly possessions of the other guests that week-end. Wherever I went to stay, with the Birkenheads at Charlton, with Ursie Filmer Sankey*, Bendor Westminster's daughter, in Nottinghamshire, or at Tredegar Park, outside Newport, where the parties were so large that there was a special plan for you to study, when you came downstairs for dinner, as to where you were sitting, my car always seemed to be the smallest in the drive. And though my prowess on the tennis court, by house-party standards, gave me a certain elevation, I was beginning secretly to see myself as an also-ran there.

It was then that Jack Lysaght, who had such a passion for the

* Lady Ursula Filmer Sankey.

game himself that he would never drink anything stronger than cider at this time, inspired me with a desire all over again to make the grade, his grade, by suggesting that I should have some lessons for my volleying, my weakest point, from a woman who was considered to be one of the best coaches in the country. Mrs Larcombe looked like a Mother Superior in an eye-shade. She had been the first woman to volley on the centre court, to bring women's tennis right up to the net, and she was a superb teacher. Yet although she improved my own volleying sufficiently for me to win the singles at Gleneagles, and to take a set off Vincent McGrath, a member of the Australian Davis Cup Team, in the summer tournament at Bournemouth, and even to lead two-one in the final set, somehow there always seemed to be an anti-climax. The spectators stampeded round our court, scenting a spectacular reversal of form, whereas all that happened was that my Australian opponent, Crawford's doubles partner, decided that now the moment had arrived, that he had been on court long enough, and allowed me only two more points, not two more games. What's more, the next day the wrist of my left hand was so sore and strained from trying to cope with the pace of his two-fisted backhand, which came off the ground at a speed I had never encountered before, that I had to have it strapped up for a week.

Thanks to Mrs Larcombe, I now succeeded two years running in being included in the qualifying rounds for Wimbledon. As I scraped through two rounds, this meant virtually that I could regard myself as being in the first fifty players in England. There were sixty-four coveted – and oh so coveted – entries permitted; cut down to thirty-two after one day's five-set matches; the next day to sixteen; and on the third the lucky, lucky eight names finally emerged, to join the twenty or so British names already in the draw. Despite Jack hovering encouragingly on the side-lines at Roehampton, where this agonizing gladiatoral contest is still annually held, I was always pipped at the post. The brutal truth was, I wasn't quite good enough to make it.

I began to tell myself that this applied to everything. I had set such high hopes on my fifth novel, *Communion on Earth,* which was published by Cassells in the spring of 1936. I knew in my bones that not only was it my best book, but the best that I could do. Yet though, like *The Unequal Conflict* and its immediate predecessor, *Fly Away, Youth,* which I had written mostly in Majorca, the new book received above average reviews, the sales remained stubbornly under five thousand copies. I would never be a best seller, and I could not continue with the label of "the promising young novelist" for ever. From which it can be gathered that my receding store of self-confidence was now extremely low. Especially when Philip Hill, at the urging of his wife, sent me to see the head of an advertising agency which, to some degree at that time, was within his vast financial orbit. I had produced half a dozen advertising slogans, together with some copy for the products which it had been explained to me this firm handled. I stood in front of the big chief while he read them through, my heart beating painfully as I wondered if my whole life was about to change direction. However a few minutes later, the Mr Royds of the day looked up, shaking his head, giving me short shrift. 'I am afraid this isn't the sort of thing that is any use to us at all.'

Perhaps I should be grateful now to the man whose face is only a blank in my memory, for his curt dismissal, because otherwise I might still be occupying an office in some advertising agency, an ageing back-room boy, instead of having been free and waiting, entirely available for the break-through when it finally came. Though it seemed so infinitely far away at that moment that I was even thankful to be employed as a 'ghost'.

I wrote half a dozen pieces for Kay Stammers – to appear under her name in *Home Chat* – who was then about the best of the English players on the Wimbledon scene, and such a pretty, graceful creature on court. I posted them to her home at St Albans to check and approve, thinking that here was another chore done. Instead, two days later a very agitated Kay rang up to say that by some inexplicable mistake, the envelope with the copy had been thrown away into the dustbin when the breakfast table was being cleared. There was a silence over the line, while I considered the exact implication of this. I had stupidly not taken a carbon copy of the articles, so I was equally to blame, I realized. Half of six times twelve-guineas gone. I gulped, and said soothingly, 'Don't worry, Kay. I will do them again.' And did, in two days. I had been counting on the money as much as Somerset Maugham had for the first short story that he wrote for *The Strand* magazine, and for which he was paid twenty pounds.

After that, I won promotion of a kind. I was engaged to

pretend that I was Billie Yorke, covering the women's final at Wimbledon, in a special account for the *Sunday Express.* John Gordon, the canny, robust editor of the paper, had taken a paternal interest in me ever since we had met by chance one Christmas on the terrace at Reid's in Madeira, where he was lunching, off a cruise ship. He told me to come and see him in the office on my own return. He was the first big editor whom I had met. He was genial and full of good stories. Equally he was as good as his word, and when I presented myself in due course, he did not turn me away with a few encouraging but vague phrases, he sent me off to visit the Star and Garter Home at Richmond, not a small boy this time asking the inmates for cigarette cards, but as a reporter, the kind of observer I was one day to become in depth. What I wrote, with more emotion than technical skill at this time, was nevertheless given a whole page in the paper, creating something of a stir. In consequence I should have recognized that this was my *métier*. But strangely, I didn't. I was bemused by the fact that I was writing a weekly page for the *Tatler* that summer on tennis, under the pseudonym of 'Rabbit'. and I used that contract as an introduction to the sports editor of the *Sunday Express,* who gave me *carte blanche* to produce gossip paragraphs about the players – who was pairing with whom for the season, and so on – for which I was paid thirty shillings a par. It at least gave me the right to deliver my paragraphs each week in person, and it was in this way that the Billie Yorke offer came my way.

She had been invited to stay with the Lysaghts at Chapel Cleeve the week-end of the Finals. So had I. One of us had to stay behind and do the job. In the end, it was myself. It meant twenty whole pounds to me and probably more for Billie, since she was then at her height as a doubles partner; indeed, should have been included in the Wightman Cup team that year. In fact, there was a strong case for making her out to be the best mixed partner in the world at that moment, though she seldom got the partners that Elizabeth Ryan did, for the simple reason that Billie preferred to play with a close friend like Jack, and enjoy herself. She was an extremely loyal friend, and on one occasion she even partnered me in the Melbury Tournament. This seemed to be so much straying outside her class that the *Sunday Express* came out with a front page story that Billie and I were about to announce our engagement. In actual fact the closest that our relationship ever became was when I acted as her writing ghost.

Having telephoned my copy, as soon as the match was over, I went later to Fleet Street to check and cut it into the space allotted. This gave me an excuse to stay on, and for once watch the paper put to bed. The editor was no longer a remote being in his office, he was now sitting among all the rest of his team, in his shirt sleeves, sampling and giving directions about each news flash as it came over the wire. When he broke off from reading my proof to congratulate me on the way that I had handled the story by the girl left out of the team, I felt absurdly elated and not in the least jealous that it wasn't my own name at the top of the page. It was only when I came down into the hall, with Lord Beaverbrook's bust upon its plinth, whose eyes seemed to follow me into the street, that I realized with a feeling of chagrin how he would probably never know who had really written the story of the finals match. Whereupon once again reaction set in, as I began to feel as nebulous and insubstantial as a real ghost. I pictured them all at Chapel Cleeve, in the long gallery at that moment, the men in their dinner jackets, very elegant and confident, the women in their evening dresses, smelling of perfume and pleasure, and I was very conscious that in contrast I was sweating and grubby and hungry. Hungry for so many things. I gazed up at the huge expanse of glass of the *Express* building, blazing with light, and said to myself bitterly: 'The street of adventure, indeed.' How little progress I had made. However many people read my story in tomorrow's paper, a lot of good it would do to my reputation. I could hardly go round boasting, 'I am a Fleet Street ghost . . . I am a Fleet Street . . . ghost.'

*　　　*　　　*

Only a month later, I stood on the same spot, and it seemed to me that every bus coming towards me had a large poster portrait of my head on one side of the front, and my name blazoned on the other. 'READ GODFREY WINN'S PERSONALITY PARADE IN THE DAILY MIRROR.'

How could the metamorphosis have occurred, and so swiftly? All this time afterwards, I still find it almost impossible to believe. Yet I know that it all did happen. Just like that. From a working point of view, this was to be the magical time of my life, when every door opened, and nothing was impossible. The ten years that I had been earning my living, standing in corridors and accepting whatever was offered, in my fight to be entirely self-supporting, suddenly, and in the most unexpected fashion, paid off; that part of my apprenticeship was over, for ever.

I had no idea that, behind the scenes, *The Daily Mirror* was in the process of a far-reaching upheaval, having a giant face-lift which was to change its image completely, so that it was to become one of the most powerful and at the same time one of the most responsible media for influencing public opinion, in the world. Compelling new forces were at work to change its editorial approach to the news, as it concerned its readers. How should I have known? True, with an increasing regularity I had had pieces accepted by the woman editor of the day, Ann Bovill, for her pages, but I had never met the paper's over-all editor, let alone the new revolutionary powers behind the throne. In a second, all this was changed. Out of the blue, I was rung up and taken out to lunch in a small Fleet Street restaurant called The Wellington, by a young man, several years my junior, with a head of dark curling hair set above a wide forehead, and the deep set Celtic eyes of a visionary turned fanatic who gave me the impression at sight that if anyone touched him, electric sparks would shoot out in every direction.

This was Hugh Cudlipp, one of four brothers who had come from Cardiff to conquer Fleet Street, and to prove that it was a street for adventure, after all. At twenty-two, Hugh was already the youngest features editor on a national newspaper. But he was only at the beginning of a road that was to lead him to his present omniscient position in the International Publishing Corporation; this has not simply *The Mirror* but dozens of magazines and papers under its benevolent umbrella today. Of all the debts that I am trying to repay in this book – and how foolish to be so ungrateful as to forget one's debts – I shall always feel that I owe this barnstormer from Wales the largest of all. For in every way we were complete opposites; yet he was prepared to take a chance on me. Apparently he had read a guest column that I had written for *The Sunday Referee,* then edited by R. J. Minney who had published my first article of all. Cudlipp had been impressed because it wasn't the usual kind of society

With Elissa Landi, a famous film star of her day. *Photo: Hal Linden*

In *Blighty* with Jameson Thomas

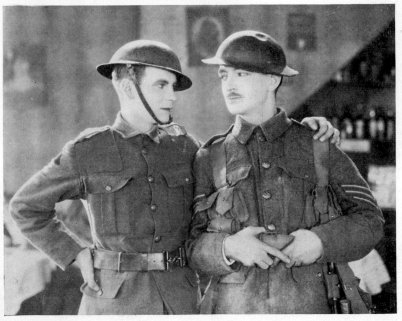

1926. In *The Rising Generation* aged seventeen, at Wyndham's Theatre. *Photo: Camera portrait by Hugh Cecil*

The Company of the Liverpool Playhouse, 1925, including Godfrey Winn and Cecil Parker

chit-chat, which he abhorred, and was determined to banish for ever from the pages of *The Mirror*.

'I understand you are on Christian-name terms with a lot of Dukes,' he started caustically at lunch.

I had to admit that, alas, that wasn't true. I only knew one. This opening gambit made me stare at my companion, defensively, and wonder what was coming.

'I am also told that women read and like what you write. And *The Mirror* has a very large readership among women. But we also mean it to be read by an equal proportion of men, in future. That is why we have hired Cassandra; given him his head, and a daily column of his own. We are now prepared to do the same for you. We are about to kill our already moribund gossip page – we want instead a page about real people.

'They can be famous or unknown,' he continued, warming to his theme. 'It doesn't matter so long as what you write about them and what they say to you really means something in the contemporary world. Duchesses and dustmen, film stars and typists, not forgetting housewives, they will all have their place on the page. Provided they are interesting, as people. This will be a daily column, as I envisage it, in which the writer will also have views of his own, strong views, and isn't frightened to express them. We'll back you up to the hilt, when it comes to a shindy.' His dark compelling eyes glistened at the prospect of an unholy uproar. There was nothing that he enjoyed more because, I was to discover, he always emerged the victor. 'Well, what about it?'

'You mean, you are offering it to me?' I said, unbelievingly, already a little drunk on his eloquence, his passion for words, a spate of words that never faltered, I was to find, but in the end always made sense.

'Yes. A month's trial run in August. A column a day, and your pay will be twenty pounds a week. Well, what about it?' he repeated. And now his eyes were cool and appraising.

'But in August I was going to have a holiday, before starting a new novel.' I protested. 'I am booked to play in two tennis tournaments and stay with great friends in Somerset. It would mean letting down my partners.'

'Tennis tournaments in Somerset? Are you mad, man?' he exploded, more powerfully than any preacher in the pulpit of the village chapel in a Welsh mining valley. The preacher would be

L

offering salvation, at a price, and so was he. 'A daily platform in a national newspaper about to go places. Big places. And you blabber about having a holiday, so as to play tennis.'

I was abashed.

He continued his sermon, with his dark eyes blazing with their unquenchable fire.

'I shall be behind you all the time. I am taking personal charge of the page myself. It is my baby. I cannot allow it to be a failure. Now do you understand what I mean?'

Yes, I did, indeed. I suspect that my initial response which sounds so silly in retrospect was due to an instinctive reaction that after so many snubs, of one kind and another, I couldn't really imagine that I was receiving an offer beyond my wildest day-dream fantasies, that surely there must be a catch, somewhere.

However, there wasn't. A few evenings later, Hugh Cudlipp came down to dine at Broom Cottage, to expatiate further on some of the ideas he had for the page which he was determined should have a strong social conscience, just as much as a fresh and original personality of its own. He did not meet my mother as I would have liked him to have done, for I was always extremely proud to introduce her to my friends; she had unexpectedly chosen to have her own dinner on a tray in bed. 'I should only be in the way of your talk,' she said. The very mention of 'Fleet Street' made her apprehensive.

After we had eaten, my guest stalked up and down the lawn outside my writing-room as though it were his quarter-deck, and I the officer of the watch. Adrenalin poured through his veins. His springy, confident steps, his wiry figure, without an ounce of fat on it, exactly matched his space-age mind. From time to time he would stop abruptly to emphasize some comment, as when he announced, 'A lot of Fleet Street people regard you as a bit of a sissy, but I am going to prove them wrong.' I glanced up nervously towards the open window of my mother's room, and then back to my companion; to the awareness that he was not being critical, sneering, but in his own tough way, protective. It was then that final surrender came, at the price of unquestioning loyalty, and in the same moment, total belief in his journalistic genius was born. The full appreciation of what might be about to happen to my career poured over me in a flood of excitement. It was as though some of his excess flow of adrenalin had been pumped into my own veins. I wanted to leap and jump in the air and only just restrained myself from doing so. Something of my shyness remained, then and always, even though I was absolutely certain henceforth that if I entrusted myself to his care, there was no limit to what the future might bring me. And indeed, my hunch that scented July night, in a garden so far removed from the atmosphere of the editorial floor of a newspaper, was to be proved right. A thousand times over.

I could sense, however, that now my newly-elected partner had had his say, he was impatient to get back to London, and to the scent, not of the tobacco plants, but of tomorrow's papers pouring off the presses. He had come down by train. It would be quicker for him to go back by car; I offered to drive him.

I left him smoking a cigar, the one luxury that was to mean anything to him for a long time, while I went upstairs to change and say good night to my mother. When I returned, I was wearing a white tie and tails.

'What's the get-up in aid of?' he asked.

'I'm going to a Ball at Bourdon House.'

'Who lives there?' he demanded.

'The Duke of Westminster.'

'Then you do know some Dukes,' he reminded me.

'I only know one,' I repeated.

'It doesn't matter.' He flung his arm round my shoulders, in one of his rare gestures of affection. 'In a month's time, they will all know you, man. And I promise you, your picture and the announcement about your column will be on every bus.'

'Our column,' I corrected him, for the first and last time in our working partnership.

An hour later, alone again, walking up the stairs at Bourdon House, to be greeted by Ursie, receiving for her father and looking, as she still does, one of the authentic beauties of the world, I was bursting to tell her my thrilling news. But I kept silent, because I was temporarily back in another world.

Of course, I would not have survived a week in this strange, new, still unexplored territory, as far as I was concerned, without my belligerent and fully-armed supporter. Indeed, it was 'our' column. I soon discovered that Hugh had a fantastic instinct in regard to the make-up of any newspaper page, but especially this one of his own creation, in melding the pictures and the headings and the variations in contrasting type with the text, in such a way that even on an off-day, if the contents were painfully thin, he would still contrive to make the reader imagine he or she was being given something exciting, something special.

Each morning we would have a conference soon after ten as to what I proposed to write about, what names I might be using for an anecdote or to illustrate an argument, and then he would leave me for his own room, to do the lay-out, to brief the day's news conference, and tackle his other work. In my turn, it was agreed that by lunch time my own copy would be polished and ready. Actually, it was imperative that it should be, and now my training at the Villa Mauresque began to pay dividends. Nevertheless, I was so abysmally ignorant of the technical side of newspapers that when my partner took me with him down the stairs to the composing floor to cut and trim the page at the last moment, 'on the stone', I committed a crime which was to become a derisive legend in The Street.

The compositor re-setting the paragraphs, now translated into lead, had an advantage over the author. I had to read what I had written, upside down. In consequence, eager to point out where a cut could be made at the least cost to the continuity of the page's contents, automatically I hurried round to his side of the stone. Instantly, a whistle blew, and all work ceased in that vast cavern. Up to me came bustling the master printer in charge, indignant, accusing. What the hell did I think I was doing? Was I unaware that only compositors, good union men, were permitted on that side of the stone fence? I had nearly caused a strike.

There was scarcely time to apologise, none for the re-telling of the incident, on our own floor of that gaunt building in Fetter Lane. I was too busy learning as I went along, too busy planning and collating tomorrow's material, and for the day after that. Mixed doubles and the Minehead tournament, and drinking Pims at the pub at Porlock on a Sunday morning. How fast it had all receded into a dream belonging to another way of life. Jack Lysaght's mother, Mrs L. as I always called her affectionately, was so upset that I was to miss their annual tennis party, that I made the effort to get down to Washford for a few hours. Alas, I arrived too late on the Saturday to see the finals, and the house party was already beginning to disintegrate, while I in my turn was strung up, with my eyes pricking from tiredness at the end of the week's implacable timetable. Freddie Birkenhead* and his wife Sheila were there that year, both of whom were destined to develop brilliant veins as biographers. I saw with regret that their luggage was already in the hall. We chatted for a few minutes about how the matches had gone, but I had the wry sensation, for once, of being outside the fun and the jokes of the week. Although I had come to regard Chapel Cleeve as a second home, somehow I felt on this occasion an intruder, out of step. Perhaps because unconsciously I was becoming possessed, unable to concentrate on any thing but 'the page'.

At the office, they had given me a small dark room, the size of a prison cell, looking out on to a deep well between the towering buildings, and a secretary, who fortunately brought light and cast a glow upon the scene. Her name was Miss Zelgar, but I rechristened her 'Joan', and turned her into a character on the page, representing all the secretaries who read the paper on their way to work. Like myself, she was unused to newspaper offices, and completely uncorroded. She had a gentle disposition and a beautiful singing voice. Yet however weary she must have grown of listening to mine, re-dictating a passage over and over again, she never hunched her shoulders, she never complained, whatever hours we kept. She was calm and good-tempered and eternally optimistic. The other half of the team could not have made a better choice for me.

Partly to save time, partly because I hoped it would give tomorrow's page an extra urgency, I would pace up and down my cell, dictating to Joan, who took it down direct on her typewriter.

'*Today I filled in one of the missing links in my own chain of experience. I went to visit a pawnshop in Kilburn High Road. I was fortunate in being on the right side of the counter; fortunate to be able to read without personal emotion the neat notice, decorated patriotically in red, white and blue, that said: "Parcels may be put in brown paper and string on payment of twopence." That's another tuppence in addition to the fivepence per pound on credit raised, that has to be paid monthly in interest.*

There was a customer at the counter, herself shabbily dressed, but with her little boy in her arms, smartly turned out in a blue overcoat. With her free hand she pushes a bundle across the counter. I watched Fred, the assistant, unwrap it. Some cheap lace

* The Earl of Birkenhead.

curtains, a pair of woollen pants. All freshly ironed.

"Can I have three shillings?" she asks. Regretfully Fred shakes his head. He offers her half-a-crown instead. "Three shillings," she reiterates more loudly. "Half-a-crown." "Three shillings. Please, mister, make it three shillings."

The young assistant, with his pink cheeks and friendly eyes, so different from the traditional greasy usurer in a skull cap, shrugs his shoulders, and gives way. She watches him take half-a-crown out of the drawer and count out six coppers. These six extra coppers mean so much, I reminded myself, and the pledger is quite jovial now. "Look out, beautiful, how you do 'em up. I don't want to iron them all over again on Friday."

After she had gone, I asked Mr Newnham, the other assistant, what all these references to Friday meant. "I thought they get a month's credit?"

"They get six months if they want it, but most of them never leave their things for more than a few days. They come in on Monday to get a few shillings to last the week out, and then pay it back on Friday when they get their wages. Sometimes they get straight at Christmas through their club funds but it never lasts long."

Afterwards he took me upstairs to look at the warehouses. Rows and rows of bundles were all arranged on shelves according to dates and prices. Downstairs in the strong room there are drawers and drawers of little paper envelopes. Each of these envelopes contains a piece of jewellery, usually a ring.

"What sort of ring?" I asked.

"They've only got one," Fred said. "Their wedding ring." '

In the darkest corner of the room that was now my habitat, there was someone whom I assumed to be a left-over from the page that had been scrapped to create *Personality Parade*. The tide had moved on, leaving him behind. He might have been any age, for he had a timeless look, as though he had already been there for a long time, as part of the fittings. Neatly dressed in a dark suit, I never saw him smile. We had been introduced hurriedly on my arrival, but we had scarcely spoken since. He came in and out of the room at intervals, mysteriously preoccupied with his own affairs, as I was with mine, and in between, he crouched without moving, in his corner. I did notice that it was his habit to write one paragraph on a page, and then place it beside him on the desk, and I surmised, with a pang, that these were 'society pars', which no longer had a place in the paper; still he went on, turning them out from habit, anxious to justify his continuous presence in the office. Later, I began to wonder whether, perhaps, he was the anonymous leader-writer, and his harassed, gloomy air was due to the state of the world. It never occurred to me that far more likely it might be caused by the ill-mannered noise and disturbance I made by my dictating technique.

At the end of my month's trial, it was obvious from the swelling post that the page had got off on the right foot, and I was invited by Mr Bartholomew, whose rise from office boy to *Mirror* chief is one of the Street's happier sagas, to stay on. I am afraid 'Bart' viewed me and my writings with a certain suspicion. We would have stormy meetings in his room, from which I emerged to be confronted by Hugh with the warning that 'Bart' was liable to have a fatal heart attack, if goaded too far. 'Good,' I said, and returned to the fray. Then gradually, as the months went by, an armistice came into being, and we achieved with it a respect for each other's contrasting qualities. Now, in retrospect, I am amazed that he should have put up with my prima-donna tantrums, due mostly to exhausted nerves, and never interfered once with the running of the page, because he had such confidence in Hugh Cudlipp himself, the kind of Fleet Street phenomenon whom he really understood and recognized.

At first I only agreed to stay on till Christmas, still half-hankering after spending the rest of the winter abroad, so that I could start another book in the sun. But that sixth novel was destined never to be written. Here was my growing space, my real place in the sun. As for my stable companion, he disappeared without a word into outer space, and I was given absolute possession of my cell.

'Charm is the plain girl's lifebuoy . . . 'but there aren't any plain girls any more,' retorted my companion, looking round the packed floor of Quaglino's grill.'

I took exemplary care not to plug any restaurants. I did not have to be reminded again that ours was not that kind of column. But I made an exception where Quaglino's was concerned. Had not 'Quag' believed in me from the start, and shown such positive assurance that he had cast his drink and cocktail canapés upon the waters? Now that I had to spend the whole week in London, his restaurant had become my West End 'local'. I could afford it, because I was allowed expenses for entertaining in connection with my column. In consequence there was considerable satisfaction in being able to invite my heroines in the theatre world, like Fay Compton, who, when I asked her why on earth she was playing in the Regent's Park summer season for a pittance, dressing in a leaky tent, when she had just made such a huge success in 'Dear Octopus' and was off on an Australian tour, replied, 'But don't you see, *Hermione* in *A Winter's Tale* is one of the few Shakespearean parts I had never tackled;' and Isabel Jeans, who is still today the best-dressed and most elegant actress on and off stage, and who had treated me, as an understudy of eighteen, with the same grace and consideration as though I had been her leading man; and above all, Marie Tempest, about whom it rejoiced me to be able to write in that same piece which sought to define the indefinable quality of charm :

'The charm of her smile is not its sweetness but its disarming quality. When she starts to crinkle up the corners of her mouth, and there is an imperceptible pause before her smile lifts towards its meeting with the twinkle in her eyes, you know you are lost. You know you would forgive her everything. Indeed, it has made people forgive her everything all her life.'

One day I took Hugh Cudlipp out to a celebration lunch, and it was natural that I should suggest Quaglino's. All through the meal the proprietor hovered round our table, seeing that everything was of the best, and when the moment came that my guest was choosing a *Corona* from the tray of cigars, I remarked casually :

'By the way, there was something I've always meant to ask you but there's never any time in the office. Who was the man who was in my room when we started the page? What does he do on the paper? I think you said his name was "Connor" but I never see anything by "Connor" in the paper. Is he one of your backroom boys? Does he do research? I thought at one moment he might be the leader-writer, but I have met Jennings now.'

My guest looked up from cutting his cigar, a rite that had more meaning to him than to myself, who have never smoked, and gave me one of his louring glances, presaging a message or a command that the hearer did not forget.

'Connor, who incidentally was driven almost insane by your outpourings to Joan, is Cassandra.'

'Good God,' I said.

'Bill Connor is also incidentally just about the best journalist in the world. And will, in due course, be accepted as such.'

I could only nod in agreement, and hurriedly ask for my bill. A few days later I was to have another deflating lunch, on the same spot, though once again, no one was to blame except myself.

My mother was in London for the day, shopping, and I at once suggested that I should give her lunch, moved by the same impulse as always made me so proud to be able these days to take her to a succession of First Nights. The 'perks' for the column were beginning to pour in; a stream of invitations, launching parties, publicity parties, charity parties, tasting parties, welcoming parties to film stars or other kinds of celebrities. But the only invitations that Joan automatically accepted were the premières that brought me in touch again with the Theatre and the Cinema that were part of my birthright.

Being recognized now, from the posters on the buses and the daily pictures in the paper, as I made my way through the crowds outside the theatre, hearing my name screamed out amid the hubbub of near-hysteria was intoxicating for me, a recurring draught of heady wine. One evening, before the curtain went up, I was signing autographs for some of the teenagers of the day who had penetrated into the foyer, when another first-nighter commented to my mother, 'He must get very bored with doing that.' To which my mother retorted sharply, 'He would be a great deal more bored if he wasn't asked.'

She was even more downright and devastating on that day when we lunched together at Quaglino's. I had had a harassing morning, dictating against the clock, while the lead story for the page had broken down at the last moment for some reason outside everyone's control. On top of that, I could not relax now because my mind was full of a difficult interview ahead of me at three o'clock. Suddenly I had a nerve-storm – at least, I suppose that is how a psychiatrist would have described it, though I have never found myself on one of their couches – and spoke loudly and furiously to the waiter who had kept us waiting.

The moment that he had left the table, my mother turned to

me and said in a voice that was all the more telling because it was so quiet.

'Don't let me ever hear you behave like that again, or I shall no longer regard you as a son of mine, and will never wish to be seen with you again in public. To speak to someone like that who is not in a position to answer back, in case he loses his job – what could be more despicable? You tell me that your paper has had to take on a second secretary to cope with all your fan mail. Well, you've certainly lost one fan today.'

Her tone implied that she was referring as much to herself as to the waiter, who on the safe side of the service doors was, doubtless at that moment, letting off steam, and quite rightly so, about me. The overbearing kind of customer who, instinctively, I had always despised. What was happening to me? I was so sick and ashamed, because of her just rebuke, that I could not eat a mouthful of food when our order finally arrived. For the rest of the day, her words kept on repeating themselves in my mind. I tried to put up a defence, to make excuses for myself – Mother did not understand what it was like having to produce a whole page every day, and sometimes out of nothing – but there was no excuse. Hadn't I said over and over again that it was my consuming desire to be the champion of ordinary people, especially the underdog? Then the first thing I must do was to live, as I wrote.

Fortunately an opportunity to redeem myself came soon afterwards. One Friday afternoon, just as I was leaving to drive home to Esher, longing for tomorrow, the one day of the week that I did not have to write, Hugh came into my room with the evening papers in his hands. 'Look at this,' he said. There were banner headlines across the top. 'THE MEN OF JARROW MARCH TO WESTMINSTER.' I took the paper from him. 'Where is Jarrow?' I asked. 'And why are the men marching, with Ellen Wilkinson, their MP, at their head?' 'That's what and where you are going to find out. There's a train leaving for Newcastle in an hour. You can buy a toothbrush and razor on the way to the station. Tell the hotel to send the bill to us. Here's a warrant for your ticket. Get cracking.'

'But I was going to have a quiet week-end at home,' I automatically protested.

He gazed at me with his hypnotic eyes, as he had done the first day we met in the Fleet Street eating house. 'Look, man, this is a great chance for you. To show the south how the north is living at present. The other half. The submerged half. We haven't really felt the slump down here. Not in the way that they have in South Wales, and what they call the Special Areas – a nice euphemistic phrase that – in the north. In Jarrow, fifty per cent of the male population are not working. Can you imagine what that means? No, you can't. You've never been on the dole youself. Go and talk to the wives of the men who are on the march at this moment, because they are sick of standing idle at the street corners with their hands in their pockets. Talk to them in their homes. I am telephoning our "stringer" in Newcastle to meet your train. He'll arrange contacts for you in Jarrow itself. Cheer up and good luck.'

Once again he flung his arm carelessly, reassuringly round my shoulders, and was gone. I turned helplessly to Joan, who was her usual unruffled, sensible self. 'I'll be here at twelve o'clock on Sunday morning, to take your story down over the telephone. You'll want some paper and pencils.' As she started to put them methodically in my brief case, I thought for a moment longingly of the welcoming peace and privacy of my writing-room at home. 'Telephone my mother and explain,' I said, and reached for my coat. I was on my way.

*　　　*　　　*

'It's quite pretty at night,' the stranger opposite me in the Silver Bullet express remarked, as we started to slow down to enter Newcastle. I looked out of the window. You could trace the course of the river by the lights, like myriad Japanese lanterns stretching away into the ultimate darkness that was Jarrow. What should I find there in the morning?

The first thing I noticed was that there seemed to be nothing in the windows of the shops, no special lines of goods, no bargain offers. 'Why are the shop windows so empty?' I naïvely asked Mr Wallace, one of the local clergy, who with his wife had agreed to be my guide throughout the day. My two companions both stopped dead in the street, regarding me with astonishment. 'But don't you see, Mr Winn,' Mrs Wallace exclaimed, 'if there is no money to buy anything except the bare necessities, it would be too cruel, too tempting, to fill the windows with any sort of display.' 'It would simply be a waste of time,' added her husband.

We walked on and at the cross-roads, near the Labour Exchange, it was exactly as Hugh had predicted. Sullen little groups of men with bloodless faces, and all with their hands in their pockets, as though they were loath to show them to the world. For it was not cold. On the contrary, the autumn sun was shining, which gave to the river a sheen of ice. In consequence, everything was too clearly etched in the bright, accusing light.

'My wife and I look after the poorest parish in the place,' Mr Wallace was saying. 'But my parishioners have the pride and dignity of aristocrats in their adversity. Every morning the men come and ask if they can scrub out the church or the chancel steps for me. And I have to remind them that they did that only yesterday. "I know, but we want to use our hands," they remind me in their turn. "We want to use our hands." Some of the younger ones, already in their twenties, have never had a single job of any kind since they left school. Can you imagine anything more soul-destroying – and I mean soul-destroying – than that?'

'They don't expect to be paid, Mr Winn,' his wife continued. 'Not a penny. And they are pathetically grateful when I suggest, as a variation, that they repave the churchyard. They take such care over the work, too.'

The pawnbrokers were shut down, gone out of business, because no one had anything left to pledge. I realized that when I was taken into one of the homes of the marchers who at that moment were displaying their banners in Hyde Park.

The home was one room, sublet for five shillings a week, in Stanley Street. The marcher's wife greeted me wearing a kind of white shift, with a small boy clinging to her skirt. The photographer with me took a picture of us together, as a typical family; typical, especially, in the lack of self-pity this mother showed, as she explained exactly why her man had joined the march. They had thirty-two shillings a week on which to exist, two children to feed, and in the three years since their marriage, her husband had not been able to secure a single day's work. She admitted that she had even sold the dress in which she had been married in order to buy milk for the baby.

Near the station, I was shown the life-size statue of Sir Charles Palmer, who had first brought prosperity to the town in the days when the slogan had been, '*Jarrow is Palmer's, and Palmer's is*

Jarrow.' From Palmer's yards had come such fine ships as *HMS Resolution,* and when the cruiser *York* had been launched, the town had been *en fête* for the smiling young Duchess of York who had been invited to grace the christening.

But that had been ten years before, and now we were in the middle of the depressed 'Thirties. At Palmer's itself I found the man who had once been foreman of the paintwork shop, with a hundred men under him; in contrast, he was the doorkeeper whose only occupation was to greet each morning the demolition squad who were breaking up *The Olympic.*

'We don't want to break up ships, we want to build them,' Mr Black kept on protesting to me.

Throughout the long day, the words echoed in my mind. In the late afternoon, I found myself standing beside a great crane, arched against the sky. All through my indoctrination wherever I had walked, it had dominated the sky line, as the proof of past prosperity. Beside it were the hosts of standards that guard the side of the slipways leading down to the river. Once upon a time these standards, I did not have to be told, would have been swarming with craftsmen painting and fitting out the latest ship on the stocks, and always another to take its place. Suddenly it seemed to me that the figure of Christ that I had been shown in the transept of the Church of St Paul, reputed to be a Van Dyck, the figure of the Christ upon the cross, had pursued me here, and was hanging from one of those gaunt standards. A man with arms outstretched was hanging from each of the standards, and a group of weeping women at his feet.

Of course, when I opened my eyes again, the standards were once again so many poles of inanimate steel, and through their tracery I saw that the evening star was pricking the sky, and that the lights were coming out one by one, like lanterns again, along the river.

'Yes, it *is* quite pretty at night,' I heard myself saying. Then I went back to my bedroom in the Station Hotel at Newcastle, but I did not hear the sound of the trains, or notice the hideous wallpaper; for once I was inspired to write down with passion all that I had been a witness of that day. I realize now that it was a kind of catharsis for me, a turning point in my life. For all the vicissitudes of my youth, I had never understood what it was like to go really hungry, to be deprived of a man's inalienable right to be allowed to work, I had never been face to face with the kind of living conditions which I had found in that room in Stanley Street, where there were only two hard chairs and a kitchen table left, and on the table a small vase with artificial roses in it such as you would buy at Woolworth's. I had always disliked and disapproved of artificial flowers till that moment, but now they represented the undefeatable spirit that I had met throughout the town, even in the lodging houses, which managed to accommodate twenty-five men, paying four-and-sixpence a week, sleeping five in a room, and out of the twenty-five, only one working.

These were the facts; hard news. Like the official figure which the Health Officer had given me of the child mortality, (a hundred and fourteen in every thousand babies born) three times as high as the average in other parts of the country at that time. So I wrote down the facts, desperately anxious to make my readers, especially those who lived in the south, see my tour through my eyes. In consequence it was long after midnight before I had finished, and was satisfied with my account, insofar as there were no exaggerations, nothing that would hurt the pride or damage the self-respect of those who had opened their doors and their hearts to me, all those who had kept on reiterating, 'We don't want charity, we want work.'

I slept badly and woke shivering as though I had the ague. This was the first of many times that I was to have the same sensation of being the victim of some virus, when the real explanation is simply that my nervous system has been disrupted, overtaxed by the strain of some such challenge or revelation as this one. I forced myself to get up and dress, and go through the sheets of foolscap once again, so that I was completely ready when the telephone in my room rang punctually at midday. It was reassuring to be greeted by Joan's cheerful voice at the other end of the line. 'Are you ready?' I asked, and that was all till she had finished. Reading aloud what I had written made my bowels turn to water. At the end, I could not speak any more. I lay down on the unmade bed, and waited for her to ring back with any queries from the 'subs'. However, when the bell did ring again beside me, it was Hugh himself on the line who had come into the office especially that Sunday to do the make-up of the page himself. 'Great stuff,' he said.

I felt the warmth come back to my body, but as the train bore me south again that afternoon, and fitfully I tried to sleep in the corner of my first-class carriage, I could not blot out the imagery of the girders of that dying shipyard from my mind. I was committed, henceforth and for evermore. As a messenger – a crusader was too grandiloquent, too self-important a word – seeking to show one half of the world how the other half lived. It would mean less and less time for my own private life, but that did not matter if I could be of some use, do some good. Like the good which was to come out of my visit to Jarrow. For not only did a Surrey manufacturer start a factory in the town, destined to be the beginning of the turning of the tide, but dozens of my readers offered to adopt one of the families, not simply to send them parcels, but help in a multitude of other practical ways. To make them, above all, feel that they were not forgotten, outcasts. The first manifestation of this was that I was able to go back to Jarrow that Christmas, and with me, in the guard's van, sufficient sacks filled with toys and dolls for every child in every school of that 'special area' town. Not second-hand sets of toy soldiers, or chipped dolls, but every present a shining new one. I did not dress up as Father Christmas, I was simply an envoy, walking round with Mr and Mrs Wallace from schoolroom to schoolroom. The incredulous look on the faces of the children came back to me with a rush, as though it were yesterday it had happened, on the night that I found myself the captive centre of yet another edition of 'This Is Your Life.' Mrs Wallace was by this time in her eighties, with failing eyesight, yet she had been determined to make the long journey from Yorkshire to be there, though Eamonn Andrews had to take her arm to guide her across the stage to greet me. 'Jarrow will never forget you,' she said, and those few words meant more to me than all the other tributes. They were a benediction.

It is strange, but very comforting to me, how the insistent echoes still continue. Only last Christmas I received a contribution to a charity fund I run for a magazine, and the writer said:

'I still have the doll you gave me. It was the first really new doll or toy of any kind I had ever possessed. I am happily married now and my husband has a good position in the south. Each Christmas, I always bring out the doll and show it to my two daughters, as a reminder of our own good fortune, and they go *to our local hospitals to take some things for the children who will be forced to spend their Christmas there. It is our way of trying to say thank you for so much.'*

It is I who have to give thanks so often, too. As I did the year I was in Cyprus at the height of the troubles, dispatched on yet another reporting assignment. On Christmas Eve, I was invited to have a drink in the sergeants' mess of the Durham Light Infantry, and a fellow came up to me with a blinding smile and a strong Geordie accent, calling out, 'I want to shake your hand mon'. After which he went on to tell me why. 'There's a picture of you with my mam, and me a wee nipper, cut out of the paper and framed in our front room. It was taken when you came to Jarrow, the week-end my Dad marched to London. Anyone would get a bashing from me who said anything against you in our home. Mind, we've got a fine place noo, and Jarrow's a fine town, and doing as well as any town in the land,' he ended up, with a kind of glory shining in his face.

For a moment, I felt isolated, despite the overwhelming warmth of that gregarious din which surrounded me, as my thoughts went back once again to that other Christmas. In a way, it had been a sad one for us all, as we had so recently lost the king who was never crowned, and who, in his own final tour of those other special areas in South Wales, had come back to London declaring, 'Something must be done.'

What was done was to send him into exile, because nothing would change his determination to marry the only woman in whose presence he felt really fulfilled. I had seen him at the Opening of Parliament that autumn, seated on his throne in the House of Lords, a slight, still-boyish figure, borne down by his royal insignia. Yet, for all the usual panoply, the jewels glittering under the lights, the peeresses in their coronets curtsying to their monarch, I was left at the end with one consuming impression above all; the trapped look in his eyes. Some people may still consider that he bought his freedom to live his own life at too great a price. Be that as it may, among all the notes that I have made of conversations which I had with the man who did so much to shape my own career as a writer, there is one concerning a summer's evening at the Villa Mauresque, when its owner and the Duke of Windsor had walked, after dinner, on the terrace in the shadow of the tall cypresses. Whereupon, moved perhaps by a sudden awareness of the beauty of the southern night, Maugham's royal guest had confided, 'Every day I feel more privileged and grateful that the Duchess consented to marry me.'

That Christmas of 1936, which so closely followed the Abdication, with Mrs Simpson herself marooned at Cannes, she received an invitation to spend the not so festive season at Cap Ferrat, and accepted gratefully. This she told me herself last summer; I had the special pleasure of spending the Saturday of the final of the World Football Cup in the company of the Duke, watching the match on Television at the old mill they have transformed and turned into their welcoming summer home, outside Paris.

When I asked my hostess whom she considered was the most interesting person she had ever met in the course of a not unvaried life, she answered instantly. 'Somerset Maugham. He was what the French call *très sérieux*. He could talk on any subject. He was so wise and such a philosopher, too. What many people did not understand, only reading his brilliant books, was that Willie was at heart a very kind man. That Christmas I felt in the wilderness, and I have never forgotten his sympathetic understanding in those especially difficult, lonely days.'

Earlier, in the long and utterly candid talk we had together, the Duchess made a comment that surely deserves to be put on record.

'Somehow we have made our own private happiness. We have come through, despite all that our critics said at the time. But it has not been easy for either of us. And every day of my life, I can't help remembering, however hard I try to forget, all that he gave up for me.'

To watch them together, living peaceably in their own home, thirty years after the Abdication, is the final vindication of the choice that they both made. For his eyes never leave her when she is in the room, and the atmosphere surrounding her is such that not even the most cynical of human beings, or the most violently disapproving at the time of his surrender of his throne, could deny the strength of the contentment of the Duke and Duchess today. They have come through the storms, and there have been many storms, into the harbour.

Fortunately, there were no storms, since I am a poor sailor even in the most luxurious conditions, except minor squalls at the bridge table, during the voyage I took to South America at the start of that new year heralding a fresh era with the reluctant accession of King George VI to the throne. My newspaper had generously offered me a month's leave to escape the worst of the winter, and on my suggestion had, to fill in during my absence, put the name of an old friend of mine at the head of the page.

Pamela Frankau had, for a short time, been a member of our Ebury Street club, in that she had occupied furnished rooms further down the street from me, opposite the house belonging to Merton Hodge. There Merton wrote *The Wind and the Rain*, which provided for this young New Zealand doctor, who came to London hoping to win fame as a playwright, the one concrete achievement of a frustrated career destined to end in tragic circumstances. J. L. Garvin, one of the really great ones of Fleet Street, once remarked to me that in life everything makes either for happiness or experience. It is a concept in which Merton could not find enduring comfort, but Pam, like myself, did. In those early days, she and I had been delighted to collaborate in debating discussions in magazines, for the fee of a tenner a piece. However, it was not difficult to surmise, as one gazed appreciatively at that dark, chiselled head, that beneath the witty, self-deprecating mask, there was a far richer talent not yet fully come to fruition. Which, indeed, was the case. For later, Pamela Frankau became rightly acclaimed on both sides of the Atlantic as one of the major novelists of the post-war scene.

I made the trip to Rio de Janeiro in a German cruise ship called the *Cap Arcona,* commended to me by my fellow voyager, Jack Lysaght, because, in the advertisements, he had read that there was a full-size tennis court on the top deck. In our mutual enthusiasm, we had reckoned without the wind that invariably blows at sea, however calm the waters themselves may appear to be; thus any hope of serious practice-games was out of the question. Still, it was exercise, and even in these unpromising playing conditions, it was clear that Jack felt more at home, more at ease than, for all his wealth, his abundant charm and instinctive good manners, which brought him a wide and varied circle of acquaintances, he did in life itself, where increasingly he was finding himself out of step through a physiological defect in his make-up, a fatal inability to espouse any serious project. A voyage like this was for me a temporary escape, a breathing space; for him, the most delightful and considerate of companions, it was an ideal way of killing time. Tennis of a sort in the mornings, bridge, sometimes with dramatic overtones, in the afternoons.

In the bridge four in which we found ourselves was someone who, appearing in a succession of striking dresses, had clearly in her day been a considerable beauty. Her manner was extremely regal. During the time her husband, Colonel Keppel, took his daily exercise walking round and round the deck, his wife dominated our table. One afternoon when Mrs Keppel was my opponent, she announced triumphantly, 'Two Clubs'; a bridge convention meaning that you have been dealt a hand of aces and kings, a royal flush. The response from one's partner, if possessed of no matching court cards, is 'Two Diamonds'; if, on the other hand, you have some support, you declare it. Perhaps due to the heat, Mrs Keppel's partner had a sudden blackout, and said nothing; no bid came from her lips. 'No bid,' echoed her partner, in an incredulous booming voice, 'There is no such bid as 'no bid' when I called Two Clubs.'

An ominous silence enveloped the table. As I stared down uneasily at my own hand, I remembered that it was she who, when King Edward VII lay dying, was sent for by Queen Alexandra. The two companions who had meant so much to him had taken turns by the side of his bed. What would it be like in another thirty years time for the man with the very fair hair and the very blue eyes and the woman for whom he had surrendered his throne? As almost inevitably the comparison passed through my mind, I found myself recalling the macabre scene in the third act of Somerset Maugham's *The Circle*. Here Lady Kitty, who had flouted the rules of Society by running away openly with someone else's husband (who because of the scandal had had to surrender his chance of becoming Prime Minister) turns over the pages of a scrap-book of photographs of house parties of her youth. Instinctively she hides her face in her hands when she comes upon a picture of herself, once upon a time so beautiful, so confident, so secure.

'No, I seldom play bridge,' the Duchess of Windsor said to me when she received me at her home outside Paris, thirty years after the Abdication. 'You see, there is so little time. Oh, I know that some people talk as though I spend all my time on choosing clothes, but that in fact is absolute nonsense. I spend far more time on my housekeeping. And although the Duke and I see each other all day long, there is never enough time for us to be together.'

As I listened and gazed at her, so unravaged by the passing of the years, I found it rather reassuring that for once the cynics had been proved wrong; were utterly confounded.

The *Cap Arcona* sailed on through the burnished, stormless seas. Mrs Keppel fanned herself in the increasing heat, and forgave her partner, while I decided, not for the first time, that it is a graceful warmth of manner and strength of character, and above all, the gift for building a man into something bigger than himself, that enslaves us, rather than beauty in its own right, however spectacular it may be.

* * *

The beauty and the impact of the Christos Redemptor was, of course, another matter, in another world. As we anchored in Rio's bay after dusk, the light from the plateau high up on the side of Mount Corcovado caught and held one's eye far more than the dim outline of the Sugar Loaf itself; while, on land, it proved an unforgettable pilgrimage to climb the road to the spot where rests that stone figure of Christ, a hundred feet high, with arms outstretched to bless. At night, it is an everlasting beacon for all the sailors of varying nationalities who enter and leave the harbour, the first and last landmark they see; by day, as one lingers in the statue's shadow, one is reminded of the parable behind that other great sacred symbol, the Christ of the Andes, which itself is placed on the borders of Chile and Argentina, as a guardian of perpetual peace.

Sometime in the middle of the last century, this symbolic landmark was built with a percentage of the money that the two countries had set aside to spend on armaments.

The day came when the church leaders concerned had put their heads together to suggest this accusing challenge to the perpetually increasing menace of war. And rather surprisingly, the Governments themselves were sufficiently enlightened to accept the proposal. Moreover, there had been peace between Argentina and Chile ever since. With those arms spread wide above one's head, it seemed at once so obvious and so sensible a solution. Why could not a similar plan be adopted to ease Europe's own tensions? The corollary, the inevitable question-mark came into my mind, and then vanished again. It was too soporific, too sybaritic an atmosphere in which to worry about such problems; we were on holiday and Europe anyhow, was far away.

Meanwhile, there was so much to revel in and enjoy. The mile upon mile of white sands, so hot that one could scarcely walk upon them; tennis out of doors in the cool of the night, the courts lit by flood-lighting; the rows and rows of candy-striped skyscrapers, the first that I had ever seen, climaxing in the fantastic luxury of the Copacabana Hotel. Again, there was the pleasure of taking the road out of the city to Petropolis, to lunch with our ambassador, and finding the forest trees festooned with wild orchids, like mistletoe branches, and everywhere butterflies, the span of a man's hands, glittering and iridescent in the perpetual sunshine, exactly matching the carnival mood, when all work completely ceased for four days and nights and everyone danced through the streets and the acacia avenues, whose trees were lit with beckoning, flowered lights. Strangers embraced each other; all doors were open; all class-barriers down. How could there ever be another war, anywhere?

However, on the return journey in the *Cap Arcona,* that had gone on to Buenos Aires and returned to pick us up, I was jolted out of my mood of complacent, wishful thinking. Very early one morning, unable to sleep because of the stuffiness of my cabin, I put on my dressing-gown and made my way for air to the top deck. Here, to my astonishment, I found the tennis court filled to overflowing with a concourse of the crew being drilled with dummy rifles, while another spectator, not hidden as I was behind a funnel, looked on with obvious approval. This was the captain – Captain Niejahn – at whose table I sat during the voyage, and about whom I had cabled an enthusiastic piece, from Rio, to my paper. I had described how he had stood up at dinner on the first night out of Southampton, welcoming the British passengers on board, expressing his pleasure that there were so many of us, and avowing at some length the desire of his country to remain on friendly terms with all Europe, but especially with ourselves. He was so convincing, so disarming, that I even found myself thinking how much my own seafaring grandfather would have enjoyed meeting his fellow-captain. That was until I watched Captain Niejahn give and receive the Nazi salute at the end of the parade.

I only slipped away just in time before the command for 'troops dismiss' thus avoiding detection. Yet when I recounted my disturbing experience to my travelling companion, he pooh-pooh'd my fears, strongly urging me neither to print or pass on to my fellow-passengers what I had seen, as it would only do 'more harm than good'. I do not blame him for his reaction, for we all wanted to continue to live in a fools' paradise, to pretend to ourselves, as long as it was possible, that the lights were not beginning to go out once again, over Europe. Later in the day, when my steward came into my cabin with some shirts he had had washed for me, he was so polite, so smiling, I could not believe that only a few hours before I had seen him with a gun in his hand. In fact, I almost began to wonder if I had not dreamt the whole episode, had never left my bed that morning, in the dawn, but instead that menacing phantasm was the result of something I had eaten at dinner the previous evening.

On my return, however, I did recount in every detail the incident to one person, a far abler commentator on international crime than myself, who was destined in due course to attend the Nüremburg trials as a literary observer. Rebecca West. She listened gravely to all I had to tell her, and then gave her verdict. 'The trouble with the Germans is that they have always been taught to stand to attention, never at ease.'

Her prescient comment came back to me when I learnt of the *Cap Arcona*'s sinking as an enemy raider in the war. For once, I had no pity, no regret, that a fine ship should have found such a grave. Its tennis court had become the landing ground for its reconnaissance planes; it had been built to a special plan, one more pawn in the master strategy. The cruises to South America, the lulling to sleep of the English passengers on board, like myself, not yet conditioned to accept the inevitability of the struggle for world domination that lay ahead, was all part of a conjuring act on a fantastic scale, and which so very nearly succeeded.

I was soon to have another warning, though from a very different angle.

On my return to England that February, I knew that I must suspend all plans for further holidays until I had produced another fifty weeks of *Personality Parade* pages. On the other hand, Hugh Cudlipp generously agreed that I should no longer have to write a page for Saturdays. This meant that I would get away occasionally on a Thursday, and not return till the following Monday, provided that I wrote Monday's column in advance. I took advantage of this concession that July when Jack Lysaght again invited me to accompany him, this time to share his invitation to play in an unofficial match against a Hungarian tennis team in Budapest. I leapt at this chance to explore the Regent's palace, where in the white marble ballroom, under the huge chandeliers and with the silver sconces on the wall, the Hapsburgs once upon a time, legend said, would entertain a thousand guests at a time. I was equally eager to discover if the Danube was really as blue as recorded in song, or, as it turned out, like so many legends, in reality, a muddy grey.

In actual fact, I very nearly did not see Budapest at all, or hear the serenading zigeuner violins in the cafés on the hillside beyond the city, or admire the herds of white horses grazing amid the plantations of mulberry trees with the golden strips of sunflowers, whose seeds could later be pulped into oil, dividing the plain like the boundaries of so many allotments. I imagine the glories of the Hapsburg palace no longer exist; certainly nothing would ever induce me to return to Budapest now that Hungary is one more subsidiary police state. All the same whenever the name crops up nostalgically in the songs of yesteryear, I find myself re-living once more the moment when a page boy came to our luncheon table, on the terrace of our hotel an hour after our arrival, to announce that my secretary was calling me from London.

I had left my second secretary to hold the fort and given 'Joan' the week-end off, like myself. Ena Restall was a much younger woman with a head of close curls, whose charming femininity concealed a clockwork brain and immense driving power. Although she had only been with the column for a short time, she was to become the loyalest supporter any man could wish for as an 'office wife'. All the same, I am afraid I was cursing her, as I left the melon I hadn't had time to eat, to return inside the hotel. Was I never to have any escape from my working shackles? Who wanted what, now?

After all, we had had a very early start that morning, having left London by eight and flown to Rotterdam where we had changed planes. The one that had brought us from Croydon was routed to Amsterdam, and we found that we were the only two passengers proceeding to Prague, Vienna and Budapest. On the first plane there was a small boy opposite us in the aisle, whom Jack had fed with chocolate. Our attachment eagerly kept on accepting more and more. So that it was not really surprising if in the middle of the exodus at Rotterdam, the youngest passenger chose this moment to gorge up over the gangway a brown, gelatinous mess. The expression on the faces of those who had to step over it convulsed us. In the transit lounge a few moments later, our new young friend, who with the resilience of his age had swiftly recovered his spirits, came sidling up like a puppy, begging again for more as we drank our coffee. The call for our plane came, with Jack emptying his pockets into those eager hands, and for the rest of our journey we both kept on bursting into laughter at the conjured spectacle of the stomach of that chocolate addict revolting for a second time, and the horrified reaction once more of his fellow passengers. Elaborating the tableau with gruesome details was an amusing way of passing the time as our plane sailed on as serenely through the cerulean sky, as the *Cap Arcona* had carried us across the South Atlantic Ocean, to Rio.

Absurdly, the joke had attached such proportions, as part of our holiday mood, that its recurring memory now dispersed my feeling of irritation at the moment that I picked up the receiver and heard Miss Restall's voice at the other end, asking on a note of anxiety, 'Are you all right, Mr Winn?'

'All right?' I echoed. 'Of course I am all right. We had a perfectly splendid flight and arrived absolutely on time. I am just having lunch. I hope everything is all right your end,' I added, wondering what was coming next. Though what did follow was the very last thing in the world that I had expected or could have imagined.

'Your mother is up in Town for the day, shopping, and she has just rung up. She has seen the midday posters for the evening papers which announce a terrible air crash over Holland. Apparently it was a plane that crashed soon after leaving Rotterdam. There was an explosion and then it burst into flames. And I knew, of course, that you were changing planes at Rotterdam,' she went on. 'I said I was sure you were safe, but your mother insisted that I rang up. You see, there are no survivors from the other plane, which had come this morning from London at about the same time you left.'

Our plane. No survivors. I was too stunned, too astonished to answer. I had always believed that this kind of situation only happened in a film, not in real life. Not to oneself. 'Are you there?' Miss Restall kept on reiterating. At last I found my voice again. 'Tell Mother that all is fine as far as we are concerned, and please ring up Mrs Lysaght at Chapel Cleeve, in case she has heard the news. Just to reassure her.' Then I rang off, and slowly walked through the dark, shadowy lounge, back into the sunshine of the terrace, where my tennis partner in his sports shirt, sunburnt and in his athletic prime, was sitting drinking beer.

'What was it? They're not going to make you work out here, after all?'

'No, nothing like that.' I told him the news and we were both silent, with the same picture in our mind of our last glimpse of that small boy, his face full of joy as Jack pressed a final Cadbury's bar into his greedy palm. It seemed incredible, impossible to believe that fragments of his charred body were now scattered over the Dutch landscape, while we sat here, untouched, in the Budapest sunshine, with the river flowing by a few yards away. It was not a question of no more chocolate, but of no more anything. Oblivion. Why should it have happened to him, almost before his life had commenced, while we, the only two, should be allowed to escape?

It is a question that is being asked every minute of every day, and even the hills from whence all help is supposed to come have been unable to give any answer except an echoing sigh. However, when my companion announced. 'We'd better cancel our return tickets and go back by train,' I did provide an answer to that.

'Nonsense,' I retorted. 'Don't you realize it wasn't *our* appointment in Samarra?' So why should it be on our return journey, either? We just don't know, ever. Anyway,' I went on, 'the narrowness of our escape this time should make you more confident about flying in the future. Not less so.'

In the end, Jack accepted the pragmatic logic of my reasoning, though I suspect the final impression was not so compulsive for him as it was for me. In that it transformed my whole attitude towards the inevitable hazards of our time on earth, an attitude as obdurate today as at that initial moment of impact and subsequent decision. I had been made suddenly, overwhelmingly conscious how every human being goes to his fate, and must accept that premise with philosophical calmness of spirit.

Of course, I do not mean by that that one can afford to take idiotic risks, such as driving a car too fast after having had too many drinks at a party. Such conduct is tempting our personal fate too far. But leaving that kind of arrogant and foolish behaviour aside, it is surely fear of life and living which breeds fear, together with all the ensuing cancers of the mind and body. I realize now that it was on the day when my secretary reached me with her terrible tidings, sounding as though she was at the other end of a long tunnel, she in the darkness, I in the light, that I cast out physical fear for ever. I would go to my destiny, accept it how and when it came, and meanwhile enjoy, with an added awareness, every moment of my brief stay in Budapest.

This I did; playing in the tennis matches, bathing in the warm waters of the Dunopolata pool with its cascading fountains, which matched the mood of the lovers strolling in the dusk on the Corso, and watching the dancing out of doors at some of the czardas. Here I fell unexpectedly into the arms of Hermione Gingold, who was having a second honeymoon with her second husband. Alas, their second thought about their marriage partnership did not prevail. In sophisticated contrast to the bucolic revels of the czardas was the only night-club I have ever visited in my life. Not only were the walls composed of sliding panels of glass, but the dance floor was glass, too, with changing lights beneath it, and some kind of gimmick machinery which possessed the power to raise you and your partner isolated above the rest of the throng, inducing exactly the kind of floating sensation to suit the early hours of the morning. The same sensation of euphoria as I was to have on our return flight. Glancing up from the book I was reading between Vienna and Prague, I beheld, like a pointed reminder of how hauntingly beautiful the world can be, vast cumulus clouds of glory in the sky, heralding yet another sunset. Pale pink turning to saffron, merging into shades of mauve and green, and finally spreading over the horizon into one united expanse of scarlet, as though the Almighty had just emptied a colossal bottle of red ink across the heavens.

Just before this ultimate climax, we seemed to be floating through a petrified sea. The clouds below were the waves that did not break against our prow, or shiver against the surrounding landscape. Instead, they allowed us to pass serenely on our way. Now they were assuming the shape of icebergs, now they became as smooth as layers of cotton wool, changing once more into the turrets of a medieval castle with spiral staircases leading up and up into Infinity. My own imagination soared, I was filled with extra-sensory impressions, I was blazingly aware, as I had never been before or since, of the embracing splendour of the universe. Indeed, of all the hundreds and hundreds of journeys by air that I have since made, never has any vision of the skies (not even the experience of flying over the North Pole and the wastes of the Arctic, that assume all the colours of the kaleidoscope under the midnight sun) made me so abundantly conscious of my good fortune in being a human creature, instead of some sort of vegetation, than that return journey from Budapest in the summer of 1937. Equally, how important it is to give thanks each day of one's life, just for being alive.

*   *   *

The next week-end after my return from Budapest, my feet were very firmly on the ground again. I had been invited to stay on the banks of the Thames near Henley in a Queen Anne house, where my host until that moment had been a shadowy figure, an *éminence grise* in the corridors of the *Mirror* buildings. Very tall, with a deceptively quiet manner and soft flaxen hair brushed smoothly across his neat head, Cecil King, then in his early thirties, already bore a striking physical resemblance to the portrait of his uncle, Lord Northcliffe, which hung above the fireplace in his office. If I had met him at a party, an extremely unlikely supposition since he deplored such social gatherings as a waste of time and energy, I would have erroneously taken him at sight for a university don. He had the same precise, dry voice, the same pursed lips, of someone who has chosen to be a spectator rather than a participant in the hurly-burly. Whereas in actual fact, this Wykehamist with the ice-cold mind, who was driven from the start by an implacable ambition to surpass his uncle's achievements, was already the inspiration and the force behind the palace revolution. Mr Bartholomew and Hugh Cudlipp supplied the actual fuel that made the flames burst into each successive conflagration, but the third member of the trio, who preferred at that period to remain behind the scenes, could be just as intransigent in pruning the dead wood off the branches.

These recurring week-end visits that I spent, strolling in the gardens overlooking the river, seemed at first like any other house-party. Small boys were running around (later to make their own mark in their father's wake), dogs to be petted, my host in grey flannels and a Leander-pink shirt, the *ambiance* was unexpectedly peaceful on the surface. But gradually I began to sense, in a way that I had not been able to do in our brief exchanges in the office, where I was always fighting against the clock, how privileged I was to be listening to the thoughts and the ideas of someone who so clearly, so thrillingly, knew exactly where he was bound. Although even in the relaxed atmosphere of his own home, his innate instinct for taciturnity remained, still, almost unconsciously, unobtrusively, the map of the future was unrolled. Though it never occurred to me, I could scarcely envisage that the evening would come when my host would give a dinner in my honour, taking over the River Room at the *Savoy,* so that in addition to the members of my family, like my brother and sister-in-law, and my editorial colleagues, and old family friends, such as Sir Robert Blundell, the Chief Metropolitan Magistrate, he would invite many leaders in their respective fields. No gesture could have given me more pleasure as a seal upon my career, and equally, in his speech of congratulation because I had succeeded in writing every week for a quarter of a century for one or other of the magazines that he now controlled, he said something which made all the grinding solitary hours of concentration worth while.

'The diverse men and women who are gathered here to pay this tribute have, it seems to me, two qualities in common. The obvious one is success. The other, much rarer, is a deep understanding of human nature.

I think the writer with whom Godfrey has the greatest affinity is Samuel Pepys. Both have written with infinite labour and infinite enjoyment of the small doings of everyday life. Both on occasions explore the secret places of the heart.'

Of far greater general interest is another quotation which to my mind exactly sums up the authority of this remote, mysterious yet outstanding figure in English public life today. In answer recently to a note of congratulation from myself for the outspoken way, at the possible cost of offending many of the *Mirror's* millions of readers, he had bluntly deplored in a speech the blind weaknesses both on the side of the Government and the workers, and exactly what harsh measures must be taken to restore the country's economy, he wrote laconically: '*I wish the PM had paid more attention to what I told him in private, and then this public pronouncement would not have been necessary.*'

No two people could be more contrasting in temperament and in attitudes of behaviour than Hugh Cudlipp and Cecil King. The former when I first met him was – and still is – a confessed extrovert, who nevertheless chooses to hide his heart; the latter insists on remaining the power behind his own throne, psychologically incapable of repeating any of the flamboyant campaigns of the uncle whose success was paradoxically such a spur and incentive to him in his own youth. It so happens that I have had the urge even lately to seek out both these men in their respective sanctums in that striking futuristic block of chromium steel in High Holborn that has replaced those dingy, out-of-date buildings in Fetter Lane, at a time when I have been in a mood of some perplexity and my spirits at a low ebb, and both have shown me a degree of gentle understanding that one would be more inclined to expect from a priest or a doctor. Thus when I hear speculation as to how this partnership should have survived so triumphantly across the years, when superficially the two participants seem to have so little in common, I am able to explain exactly why I believe that the alchemy has succeeded.

After all, I saw it all from the beginning, the sorties, the coups, and then the more cautious pause for regrouping and replanning, so that it came as no surprise when Hugh – who was clearly bound for higher things than being the architect of our page and the paper's other features – announced that he was to take over the editorship of *The Sunday Pictorial.* Even as I congratulated him on being the youngest editor of a National newspaper, ever, and tried to thank him, however inadequately, for all that he had done to turn me into a professional even half as expert as himself, I was filled with dismay as to who his substitute in my working

life would be, and how much I would miss his daily dose of
adrenalin in my veins. My doubts were to prove well-founded. A
succession of new faces seemed to come in and out of my room,
but with none of them was I able to achieve the rapport and
mutual stimulation that I had done with Hugh. In consequence,
I began to count the weeks till my next annual leave was due after
Christmas. But before that happened I received an invitation to
lunch with John Gordon at the *Savoy*. I accepted happily, since
he had been the first to give me an occasional by-line in his
own paper, and I imagined, if I thought about it at all, that there
was no more significance to the lunch than that. But I was wrong.
By the time we reached our coffee, I was being made an offer.
The offer of a whole page to myself in *The Sunday Express*.
I would not be taking over from anyone; instead, this feature
would be an innovation and act as an antidote to the sparkling
social comment made each week by Lord Castlerosse, who has
never been equalled, in his own line of country. I would be given
complete freedom and choice of subject. It was an exciting prospect, indeed.

All the same I asked cautiously, 'Does Lord Beaverbrook know
and approve?'

'Lord Beaverbrook knows everything and entirely approves,'
replied my luncheon companion in his decisive, Dundee accent.

As proof of his organization's sincerity, which in our long
association I never had cause to doubt, he offered there and then
to write down the exact terms, and what he was prepared to offer.
A three-year contract that would permit me, unlike the majority
of feature writers for the Beaverbrook papers, to deliver also a
weekly piece for the Fleetway magazine to which I was committed. Together, the united fees would undoubtedly constitute
a freelance record for Fleet Street at that time. Was this really
happening to me? I looked round at the expensive, cosseting
setting of the Savoy Grill Room. So much money represented
at the tables scattered all round us at just the right distance so
that no one could eavesdrop; so many other deals being projected
over a helping of roast beef from the trolley. Wonderingly, I
thought of the thirty shillings for each sports paragraph that I
had been so ready to accept such a short while back, as I heard
the man with the best news flair in the Street, and who was to
be my editor for the next five years, suggest :

'If you will come with me now, I will write it all down as we have discussed it.'

My heart was pounding against my chest as I followed his commanding figure through the room, past the entrance to the American Bar, into the front hall of the hotel itself. There was the usual slow-motion ballet of arriving and departing guests against a backcloth of smart pages in grey uniforms, and a frieze of hot-house flowers for sale. Without more to-do, my companion sat down at a writing table next to an American tourist despatching postcards home, and proceeded to arrange the details for the proposed transfer of my body from the *Mirror* offices to those of the *Express,* in short, sharp paragraphs such as he employs in the John Gordon column that still flourishes so mightily today, and signed his name at the bottom of the sheet of *Savoy* stationery. As though sensing what was passing through my mind, that if I burned my boats there was no return, he concluded crisply, 'This constitutes a contract. We would never go back on it. You need nothing more in writing from us.'

And I never did; just that original scrap of paper, still in my possession as other people cling to their old love-letters. But, in my case, it was more like a bomb in my pocket as I walked back up Fetter Lane, to clear my desk for the morning. One thought was uppermost in my mind; as though directed by a benevolent providence in my direction, the offer had come at a crucial moment, in that my existing contract was up in the spring, soon after my planned trip to go on a Swedish boat this time, to Nassau, with the whole Lysaght family. How could I return to the same desk to survive another year without the daily presence and topical improvisations of the man who had set me up in business?

A solution had been handed to me, unexpectedly, on a plate at the *Savoy*. I must make up my mind now, now without dithering or over-counting the consequences. I knocked on the door of Mr Bartholomew's office, took a deep breath and told him the truth about my lunch engagement. The ten minutes that followed were not among the more pleasant ones in my recollection, though in retrospect I admired the manner in which he handled the kind of situation that is always embarrassing for everyone concerned. The *Mirror*'s editorial director was clearly torn between an immediate feeling of relief that this could mean that he would never have to endure my one-track monologues any more, and a wary appraisal of what this switch-over could mean in circulation to his paper itself. In actual fact, it didn't make a single copy's difference.

'Come and see me at the same time tomorrow afternoon, Winn,' he said. This gave both of us the chance to sleep on it. The next morning I dictated my page in a daze, wondering what three o'clock would bring. Like John Gordon, Bart came to the point at once.

'We are prepared to reduce your output to three pages a week, and increase your salary to four thousand pounds, with expenses in addition, for another year at the end of your present contract.'

The offer was a surprise, and very tempting. I should be relieved of a considerable pressure, have time to write more slowly, to plan ahead; moreover, it would mean staying with the readers who had become my friends, rather than risking a completely new atmosphere and background. On the other hand, the Sunday page would be a challenge, and equally, would be regarded professionally as an advancement. And if I could not work any longer as a team with my existing column's originator?

The arguments, for and against, chased themselves round my mind as I drove down the Kingston by-pass in my Renault roadster, to consult the woman to whom I always instinctively turned in imperative moments of decision.

She poured me out a cup of tea from the same silver pot as she had used in the days when I had walked back across the fields from Bromsgrove station, with my school books swinging from a strap. The half-hour's respite before I went once again to my room to tackle my 'prep'.

Mother listened carefully to everything I had to tell her, and then with the extraordinary gift she possessed for pin-pointing the crux of any crisis that concerned her own flesh and blood, summed up like this:

'This is a compromise for them, forced upon them, but it gives them a breathing space in which to find your ultimate replacement; for you, it can only be a cowardly, retrogressive step. You *must* take the plunge. Because remember, those who read you will have no knowledge that your salary has been increased; they will simply infer that your powers are waning, and your popularity, too, because you are writing less. Whereas in the

Sybil Thorndike in *St Joan*.
Photograph by Jane Plotz

'Quag' christens my third
novel. In the picture, with me
are, on the right, Eddie Marsh
behind Louis Golding, then
Mary Kate Bruce, niece of
Somerset Maugham, Lady
Patricia Moore, Ethel
Mannin and Viscountess
Tredegar. *Photo: The Tatler*

Somerset Maugham after his victorious tennis match against Michael Arlen. *Photo: Ulay Lyon*

Somerset Maugham playing bridge with Godfrey Winn in his London home: also Kenneth Konstam and Edward Mayer. *Photo: Daily Express*

Sunday Express, you can only write once a week, and that is quite enough for you with all your other commitments. I have always told you that you do too much, take on too much, but you never listen to me . . .'

On the contrary, I did listen. Mr King himself could not have given me more shrewdly balanced advice, though not surprisingly I kept out of his way. I wrote to John Gordon that evening, from Esher, and was thankful when the day came that my leave was due. I was still supposed nominally to report back in March for a final couple of months, but I had little doubt that I was seeing for the last time my small dark cell, for which I had acquired a certain affection. It was a different matter saying good-bye to 'Joan,' who had taken me and the page on as a temporary engagement, never expecting that any of us would survive for a year and a half, and now was anxious to return to her home ties. She had given me so much of herself in patient loyalty. I am full of gratitude still. As I am to her successor, Miss Restall, who it was arranged should cross the Street with me, where in the great glass *Express* building I had been allotted a room, with wide sunny windows, next to the Managing Director's office. Miss Restall was left to clear up while I sailed for the West Indies. Perhaps as a punishment for deserting the other ship, we encountered the most appalling weather the whole way across the Atlantic. Thus, by the time we finally berthed I felt as though I was being released from serving a life sentence. I had scarcely left my cabin the whole voyage, and could hardly stagger down the gangway. I had lost a stone in weight during the last year, from unceasing working pressures, and strongly suspected that I had lost another, *en route* from England.

Nor did I have what could be described as a comfortable dinner that evening, though with what eagerness I had been looking forward to my first meal on shore, at an un-rocking table, and the promised bottle of champagne from Jack's father. Instead, scarcely had I had time to unpack, when the telephone in my room rang, and an unknown but authoritative voice said, 'Is that Godfrey Winn?'

'Yes.'

'Well, this is Lord Beaverbrook speaking. I have been informed of your arrival, and I would like you to come and dine tonight. Eight o'clock at the Colonial Hotel. And no

M

need to change. Good-bye to you now.'

He had rung off before I could say 'Yes' again, or 'No.' Clearly he did not believe that the latter word existed where he was concerned. Indeed, when I explained to Jack's parents why I should have to be out that night, Mrs L.'s more than ample bosom heaved, and she clutched at her three ropes of pearls for reassurance, as someone who was used to getting her own way herself, at all times. 'I hope,' she remarked piously, 'that this doesn't mean your holiday is going to be spoilt.'

I devoutly hoped so, too. On my embarkation for Nassau, that paradise of coral reefs seemed as remote from the street in which I now worked as the moon itself. No one had warned me that my future lord and master was already installed there for the winter, having previously found the climate efficacious in keeping his tendency to asthma at bay.

Punctually at eight I presented myself at the door of his suite, comforting myself with the thought that, at least, we were staying in different hotels. I was both curious and apprehensive, for I was very much aware that a great deal hung on this first encounter. He was going to make up his mind about his new boy. Would I pass the test?

To my relief, I found that we were not to be alone. Lord Beaverbrook had two house-guests staying with him, a dazzlingly good-looking pair, Henry* and Daphne Weymouth. I prayed that they would help me out. But they knew and accepted their rôle. During the meal that followed they made no effort to enter the conversation, which consisted entirely of a succession of machine-like questions from my host, followed by longer and more elaborate answers from myself. If he really wanted to know everything, he should be told everything. Where was I born? How much money had my parents had? Why were they divorced? What had my father's job been? When did I start writing? Why had I left the stage? Why had I given up writing books? What had the *Mirror* paid me? Why was I not married? What did I want to do with my life? Had I saved any money? What did I mean to write about in the *Sunday Express*?

That was the only question I did not have to answer, since my interrogator replied for me. 'I want you to go out and speak for the inarticulate and the submerged.'

* Now the Marquess of Bath.

He spoke with passion, though on a softer note now. It was like listening to the chief speaker at a revivalist meeting. I was carried away by his fervour, and surprised by his warmth and simplicity. He was not in the least what I had expected, and not at all frightening, in that I had the impression, right from the start, that if I always spoke the truth to him and shirked nothing as regards the intricacies of my job, I had nothing to fear from him, ever.

Several years later, when I encountered Daphne Bath, as she had become, at a party, I asked her if Lord Beaverbrook had given any verdict to her and her husband after I had left that evening, completely dehydrated by the most intensive cross-questioning of my career.

'I'll tell you exactly what Max said. Henry and I were both curious to know why he was proposing to pay you more than any other writer on his staff. To which Max replied, "Y'see, he shakes hands with people's hearts." '

Coming from such a source, it was naturally a verdict which gave me considerable pleasure. Though I could not help feeling that rather it was he who possessed this power, since in his instinctive response to life, he was the common man himself. I am sure that he could have discarded all the rich panoply that surrounded him and lived quite contentedly in a spartan room in a lodging-house.

Indeed, the portraits that have been drawn, by those whose incompetence or treachery he had laid bare, of a megalomaniac with a rasping voice and a bullying manner, who terrified his executives by threatening as well as exhorting them on the telephone at all hours of the day and night, dismissing instantly anyone who had the courage to answer back, are not only grossly exaggerated but give a completely false picture in that they only show one profile – and that out of focus – of his public and his private image.

It is true – and fair enough – that he had no patience with the incompetent and complacent, and no use for those who took his money and tried to cover up their own shortcomings by being disloyal to him behind his back. I worked for him, on and off, for twelve whole years myself. During that time I received dozens of telephone calls and telegrams from him, always constructive, never carping, sat with him alone at Cherkley or at

Arlington House on many occasions, listening in wonder to his amazingly catholic knowledge of the affairs of the world, and never once did I receive anything but consideration and affectionate encouragement that I would have sought, had it been possible, in the presence of my own father. Even when I finally decided, for personal reasons, to cross the Street once again, he wrote me the most laudatory and generous letter, wishing me good fortune in the future; while after my mother's death, one of the most moving expressions of sympathy that I received came from the man whose own memorial service at St Paul's was filled to overflowing with those who like myself had not come to pay lip service alone, but really felt that day they had lost both a good counsellor and the staunchest of friends.

After I had been enrolled under his banner for about a year, I was staying the week-end with one of his high executives. During Sunday lunch, the telephone rang and it transpired that it was Lord Beaverbrook himself at the other end of the line. At which the head of the household disappeared with some alacrity out of the room. Immediately his wife turned to me and in a bitter voice exclaimed, 'You do not know, Godfrey, what it is like to be married to someone who is married to Lord Beaverbrook.'

Startled, I half-repeated the words aloud. Why had they such a familiar ring? A cold finger touched my spine, as I was forced to remember. The beams of that Hampshire farmhouse vanished, and instead I saw once again the pastiches by Marie Laurencin in their tarnished silver frames on the walls of that other dining-room in the south, and that desperate, stuttering voice crying out: 'You do not know what it is like to be married to someone who is married to . . . drink.'

How lucky *you* are, in comparison, I decided, but, of course, did not say so aloud. There are many office 'widows' in a multitude of other organizations beside the newspaper world. The exigencies of high office, in any sphere, tend to make all personal relationships in private life hazardous and frustrated. Whether the price is worth it must remain an individual decision. But as far as Lord Beaverbrook was concerned, all of us who worked for him were more than amply rewarded for our services, in that we profited enormously from his unfailing knowledge as to what the ordinary man-in-the-street was prepared to believe and accept, and what the average reader would condemn and discard as being of no lasting import. I have often felt that this particular press lord could have been the best reporter in the business, so tenacious was he in finding out all the facts for himself.

Mrs Webb, though now gone from the scene like Lord Beaverbrook himself, would have borne witness to that. She was an elderly woman in a shabby grey cardigan, who presided, before the war and the coming of the Welfare State, over the tea urn in the out-patients' department of St Mary's Hospital, at Paddington. She saw the patients come and go, and offered them a cup of 'hot char' for a penny, and if they had the appetite and the money, a bun for another penny. One day a little man in a shiny blue suit that had seen better days, came and sat down on one of the benches. Patients round him were called to their appointments, but no one took any notice of him and he did not seem to be taking any notice of anything, until Mrs Webb went up to him and asked, in her kindly way, if he would like a cup of tea. 'How much is it?' he asked. She told him, and he shook his head. So she went away, but twenty minutes later he was still there, and this worried her. Having an invalid son herself, she had a special sympathy for the sick and lame. So she went over to him again and this time he explained that he had no money in his pockets. 'Never mind,' she whispered, 'you can still have a cup of tea, and a bun, too, if you like.'

At that moment, one of the House Governors of the hospital happened to pass through the room, and recognizing the gnome-like figure on the bench went over to him with outstretched hand. 'Good heavens, Max, what are you doing here?' Mrs Webb retreated, astonished, to her urn. The matron was sent for, a posse of doctors closed in, and a little procession was formed for a tour of the hospital. The visitor was shown all the wards, and statistics were pumped into his ears, as to how many yards of bandages were used in the course of a week, how much it cost to feed each patient, all the latest scientific equipment was produced, until at the end of an hour the procession reached its starting point again. Whereupon a very agitated Mrs Webb clutched at the House Governor's arm. 'What shall I do? Shall I apologize now, or write to him? I offered him a free cup of tea, because you can never tell, however they are dressed, whether they can afford to pay for one, and he said he had no money in his pockets. I suppose that's because he is a millionaire. Oh dear, I am so sorry.'

'Sorry, Mrs Webb! You have nothing to be sorry about. On the contrary. You have got us our money.'

And indeed she had. Because of her spontaneous gesture towards a fellow human being, Lord Beaverbrook gave the hospital the eighty thousand pounds to build a badly-needed new Nurses Home, for which they had been pleading. Like a good reporter, he was just checking the background to the story. Actually, this was only one of many such gifts that he preferred not to talk about at the time. But he never forgot Mrs Webb, and after visiting the out-patients' department, and hearing the story from her own lips, neither did I.

During my stay in Nassau, Lord Beaverbrook invited me to accompany him on several expeditions in his flying boat, for picnics on the beaches of the surrounding islands. Equally he liked me to walk beside him when he explored some of the side streets and the unbeaten tracks of Nassau itself. He would knock at random on any door, and ask whoever opened it all about their family and themselves. How many lived there? How much came into the house each week? How did they spend it? What did they do about water? The kind of questions that a social visitor or a census employee might ask, but somehow, because he spoke in such a straightforward, sympathetic way, everyone seemed to unbend to him at sight. You could sense that they felt he was truly interested in their way of life, and wanted to discover what could be done to improve their lot. Because of his Scottish ancestry, there was not an ounce of class-consciousness in his make-up. He really believed that 'Jock's as guid as his master,' always provided that Jock, or Jack, whatever his trade, worked as hard.

The trouble about the Jack who had become my closest friend during the last eight years, was that despite all the entreaties of his family and his well-wishers – and everyone with whom he came in contact liked him – he could not make himself settle down in a worth-while occupation. In the winters, he roamed the world, in search of the sun, seeking escape from himself; in the summer he played tennis, trying to believe, as a beauty does about her looks, that his prowess would last for ever. It couldn't. He had already passed the thirty mark.

One morning, when he was in my room playing his portable

gramophone, another of the drugs he used to sustain his fantasy existence, the telephone rang and it was Lord Beaverbrook's voice once again, giving me my marching orders for the day. 'We are taking off in the plane for the islands in half an hour.'

Putting my hand over the receiver, I explained about the command I had just received. Jack shook his head in violent protest. 'You can't go. You know that we are both lunching with Lord Iliffe on his yacht, and I have arranged a tennis four for the old boy this afternoon. The least I could do, after all the times I have played on his covered court at week-ends.'

I was between the devil and the deep sea. An old friendship, a new allegiance.

Pleadingly, I explained my predicament over the telephone. There was a snort and the voice the other end retorted, scornfully, 'Anyone can play tennis with Lord Iliffe. Tell your friend to fill your place.'

'I'm sorry, sir, but I have promised,' I repeated as firmly as I dared. This time it was I who rang off, unpleasantly aware that it might be a case of *hara-kiri* as well. In consequence, I wasn't in my best form that afternoon. Lord Iliffe, surprisingly spry and determined on the baseline, seemed to enjoy his game, supporting Jack valiantly, who it was clear felt that he had scored a victory, not so much on the courts as in releasing me from bondage. More and more a kind of absurd jealousy was creeping into our relationship, because of my increasing absorption in my work. Even on holiday I wasn't free, and that irked him twice over because of the contrast with his own life, which was too free, too empty. However, that evening he was in high spirits, insisting after dinner on our going to the club, over the hill in the native quarter.

I agreed, provided that we didn't stay too late, because we had another far more important match scheduled for the next day. The American Davis Cup players were in Nassau for a few days, and Bobby Riggs, who was to win Wimbledon that year, had offered to partner me against Jack and the Colonial Hotel professional. For me to play in such company, and in front of a large crowd of spectators, was both a thrilling and a nerve-racking prospect.

As we sat at the club with the tom-toms beating, watching the hula-hula girls, Jack chose to ask: 'Will your job with the

Sunday Express give you more free time than you had with the *Mirror*? I do hope so.'

Exasperated, because I had been anxious all day about Lord Beaverbrook's reactions. I exclaimed: 'You shouldn't be worrying about my free time, but about your own. You don't even do any work for charity.'

When he didn't answer I went on desperately. 'I am one of the few of your friends who has the sense to tell you this to your face. Most of the others just ride along with you. You are so easy-going, but you could be someone in your own right, not just a rich play-boy. And what's to happen afterwards? I mean, after you get bored with tennis?'

'You mean, when I can't win tournaments any more? But you said yourself today that you thought I was serving better than ever.'

'I know I did. I long to be able to serve aces like you, but I can't. But at least, in twenty years time, with any luck, I shall still be able to hold a pen in my hand.'

Jack flicked his hand at the waiter and ordered more drinks. The heat was stifling. I felt the sweat running down the back of my silk shirt. When the drinks had come, and Jack raised his and said 'Here's to tomorrow's match,' I didn't answer his smile for once. I refused to be side-tracked.

'Even if you went once a week to help at your Old Etonian club in the East End, that would be *something*. Or nursed a constituency for the next election. You told me how you have been approached in your own county. You always say you couldn't do it, but how do you *know* till you *try*?' I added desperately.

'I just know I wouldn't be any good,' he answered, with a different kind of desperation in his voice.

'But everyone can be good at *something*. I mean, apart from games. If you weren't rich, you would have *had* to have a job.'

'And I suppose you mean, I would have been much happier?'

'Yes, I suppose I do mean that. It's been my salvation that I never had a penny and had to work for everything I've got. In a way, I've been much luckier than you, but it's still not too late for you, though it soon will be.'

When I rose to go back to our hotel, he refused to come with me. Our conversation had been like an old cracked gramophone record, and the only effect of all the effort I had expended once

Lord Beaverbrook in his garden at Cherkley. *Photo: Daily Express*

Painting by Paul
Tanqueray

With my mother in
the garden at Esher

again was to bring back his melancholy, his accursed mood, the hour of the *cafard*, when he could no longer blot out the knowledge that all his former Oxford crowd, his fellow blues, like Freddie Birkenhead, had one by one settled down, were married now with children, as their personal stakes in immortality, and had achieved, in addition, a satisfying, creative background. He was the poor rich boy, born an only son to doting parents late in their life, doomed. However hard I tried to rally him out of this mood, reminding him of the amount of affection he engendered wherever he went, and how he could find a dozen solutions, but first he must come to terms with himself, the cloud of depression would return again like a sour stomach-ache, and he would fall back on another dose of brandy and then another.

'Come back to the hotel, Jack. Remember our match tomorrow,' I entreated him in the adolescent language he understood best, remembering myself at the same time, with a sense of horror, how when we had first met he had refused anything stronger than cider so as to maintain his unsullied fitness.

But he would not budge and I could only leave him, full of forebodings, myself defeated.

In the morning, Jack's mother came into my room, still in her *peignoir* covered with lace, at once agitated and evasive. All the same, I sensed what was coming before she spoke. 'Jack has had one of his attacks. You know how delicate he is. He must have eaten something last night. What did you have at the club?' she asked accusingly, as though it was all my fault. 'I came home at midnight,' I said, and left it at that.

Later it transpired that Jack had been brought back to the hotel when the first breakfasts were being served, and the sun already high over the sea, by one of the coloured cab-drivers. He had ended up drinking hooch whiskey in their cabin on the shore. All morning he stayed in bed, with that matriarchal figure fluttering over him. I could not reproach him; my disgust and anger were for myself, that however hard I tried, however many times I returned to the theme, I seemed absolutely powerless, despite the strength of our own relationship, to prevent these bouts of self-degradation occurring more and more frequently. That afternoon when the Somerset champion threw up the ball to serve one of the cannon balls for which he was justly renowned, he missed the ball altogether, and after a set that became a nightmare, left the court.

It was at that moment that I had an awful premonition of what the end would be. He was to die miserably, before his time, within a week of my own mother's passing. I did not go to the second funeral. The ashes were already in my mouth. I could only lament the terrible waste of a human being who had not an ounce of cruelty in his make-up. The only person he was cruel to was himself. Although he did in the end find a suitable marriage partner for himself he had already gone too far along the road to turn back. At the post-war Wimbledons, hobbling from a war-time injury to his leg, he would be seen, like a remittance man, hovering round the outside courts, too shy and bemused to talk much to his old partners and friends of those earlier enchanting summers.

*　　　*　　　*

In all of us are planted at birth the seeds of self-destruction, and equally those of self-preservation. Which crop we nurture is for us to decide. In my own case, because of the choice my father made, an acute instinct for self-preservation has influenced and coloured the whole of my adult life. An example of this was to occur only a couple of months after I had started to write my page in the *Sunday Express*.

There had been teething troubles from the start. My appointed space was so much larger in actual physical size than the previous page I had had to fill. In consequence, the make-up, the arrangement and choice of pictures, the type in which the headings were set, became of even more paramount importance. At least, they did to me. Unfortunately, there was no one with a flair even approaching that of my previous partner to assist me in planning the weekly lay-out, and when in desperation I took my problem to the Editor himself, his reaction was, being a disciple of hard news, that if the writing on any page in the paper was sufficiently arresting from the start, the readers would continue until the end, without noticing or needing any embellishments.

His own column, as an apostle of wrath, has certainly rigorously eschewed any adornments in the way of presentation. The more austere it looks, the more strongly it seems to read. In contrast, what I had been engaged to do – or was under the impression that I had been – was to bring a greater degree of warmth to the feature side of the paper, at that time. I tried to do this, but found myself out of step, as one does in a new school. The embrace and welcome of the initial publicity campaign had worn off; inevitable reaction had set in, on all sides. Not for the first time I was to appreciate how utterly alone a writer, or for that matter any creative artist, is; unlike a director of some large business, or member of any governing board, one had to make one's own decisions, in the end, and above all, be one's own most ruthless critic. There is no dodging the issue, hiding behind a blanket ruling.

I could sense a puzzled uneasiness mounting each Friday morning when I presented my copy at the Features' desk, making at the same time suggestions about the possible illustrations for my copy. Nor were my own fears allayed when someone from the circulation department would put his head round the door of my office, interrupting my flow of dictation to enquire, 'What's your story this week, for the bills?' I seldom had a story, in the concrete shape to suit a news placard. My own technique, such as it was, was to take a theme, often a very simple one, and expand it. But I only aroused a look of bewilderment, mirrored again in my editor's eyes, when I tried in a few sentences to explain the full purport of this week's discussion that I was planning with the paper's readers.

The show-down came the week that I decided to give up all my space to a play that had just been produced, in which the central character, a young girl who was a university student in a mid-European town, believed that she saw visions, as Joan of Arc once upon a time had done. Was that credible? Did ordinary people still have visions in our workaday world? Or were such traumatic experiences exclusively reserved for latter-day saints? And were there such in our midst?

An hour after I had delivered my views on what I believed many would find an intriguing subject, I was sent for to the editor's own office, who told me, without preamble, that he could make no sense out of what I had written. Had I any other ideas for a page that I could substitute? Dumbfounded, my mind was a hopeless blank. Staring bewildered across the desk, I could not believe that this was the same person who had been so persuasive about my joining his team that day at lunch at the *Savoy*.

N*

What had gone wrong? Where did our failure in communication lie? Surely I could not have changed so greatly in a few weeks myself? Surely I was the same writer whom he had considered worth buying at such a price? Now, in a moment, my confidence had been hopelessly eroded. Yet without confidence, a writer can achieve nothing. Despatched to the Tattoo at Aldershot that evening, to write, instead, a description of that conventional parade pageantry, I squeezed out of myself two thousand words the next morning, with the presses impatiently waiting, such as any average reporter could have equally well produced. My copy was no better, no worse.

That Sunday was one of the most miserable days of my life. I simply did not recognize my own handwriting. I was in a state of shock as though I had been caught out committing a crime and was about to come up for judgment. The crime I had committed was against myself. I read and re-read the pages of typescript that had been cast aside, and compared them with what had been printed, instead. But there was no comparison.

That night I did not sleep at all; at least, it seemed as though I did not; and at breakfast the next morning I consulted, or rather I told my mother what I intended to do. For my mind was made up. Monday was the day-off for the Sunday's staff. There would be no one in the Glass House, as far as *The Sunday Express* was concerned. So I would ring up Lord Beaverbrook at his country house at Cherkley – only a few miles from Esher – and ask if he could spare time to see me. I would explain to him exactly what had happened, and put myself in his hands. We had not met since the day that I had been compelled to refuse his invitation to picnic with him on the islands. Nor had I received any communication from him. For all I knew, I was badly out of favour, and my column in its present form was equally a disappointment to him. If it was, I would be made abundantly aware of the fact, and then there would be nothing left for me to do except to resign, and start afresh, somehow, somewhere. At least, there would be an end to this diminishing uncertainty.

I had rather expected my mother to counsel caution; to remind me that I had, after all, a three-year contract, that it was foolish of me in a mood of pique to throw away security. Surprisingly, she didn't. On the contrary, she urged me to telephone Cherkley as soon as breakfast was over. 'I heard you tossing and turning overhead last night. I knew, of course, what was worrying you and I wished that there was something I could do to help you, my dear.'

I bent and kissed her forehead, as I passed her, on my way to the telephone in my work-room. It was like a talisman.

Yes, Lord Beaverbrook would see me at 10.30. Not a moment later, as His Lordship was going riding. As I drove over, I was so nervous I could hardly control the wheel of my car, but as I turned in at the gate, and started down the long approach to the house that in the end I was to come to know so well, but which I was seeing for the first time, suddenly I remembered the advice that Marie Tempest had given me, and started once again to breathe in and out deeply. I don't know whether it was this remedy for nerves, or the kindly welcome I received when I was brought to his study, but the moment I was in my patron's presence all my doubts, all my fears, left me. Whatever the outcome, I was certain now that I had taken the right step when he announced, 'I didn't care at all for what you wrote yesterday, Godfrey. I couldn't understand what had made you do it. Have you got your other piece with you?'

I handed over the sheets of typescript. Taking them he looked at me, standing beside him, with a piercing glance of appraisal, as though deciding whether I was the same young man whom he had invited to dinner in Nassau, and about whom, afterwards, he had given such a generous judgment.

Now all he said in a brusque voice was, 'Of course, I cannot make any decision until I have read your piece.'

'Of course not, sir,' I agreed, and went away. It was a long day. I visualized him out riding in the park, with an amanuensis beside him on another horse, in case any instructions to be taken down came into his mind, and then on his return, the continuous, overriding telephone calls now London and his editors, after their midday conferences; now Prague, the current centre of surmise, now New York, now Canada – and the notes and memos to be dictated after each conversation, interrupting over and over again his reading of my account of the girl who believed that she saw visions. This was his daily routine, his constant fare. Where did I come in, what chance had I got, I decided gloomily as I ate my own lunch in silence.

After we got up from the table, and I had helped clear away, my mother, only too aware of the vacuum in which I found myself, made a quiet suggestion. 'I am going to do some weeding of the herbaceous border. Why don't you get another mat, darling, and start the other end?'

I agreed, thankfully, and we worked in unity all the afternoon. At tea, on the lawn, she broke the armistice silence, to ask abruptly, in a voice that was full, not of reproach or sadness, only of concern. 'What will you do?'

'Do? You mean if the verdict goes against me?'

'Yes,' she did mean that, and she also meant that as I had heard nothing, she believed it already had.

'I have been thinking about that all afternoon. I imagine they are bound to give me something, probably six months pay, even though I have resigned. I shall use that to go round the world, stopping where I feel like it. You know, a slow boat to China. I shall take a year over it, and hope in the process to pick up sufficient plots for half a dozen books.'

Mother went back to her weeding. I could sense that she suspected I was only talking like that to try and sustain my own spirits. Too restless now to kneel down again on a mat, and pray, I started to walk up and down the grass quarter-deck, as Hugh Cudlipp and I had done on another such summer's day. Was it really only two short years ago? The golden refracted light, so different from the hour before the sunset in those countries situated on the other side of the Equator, and for which achingly one longs when far away from England, gave to the terraces of roses such a burnished sheen of loveliness that I almost stopped worrying about my own problems, a minute speck on the face of the universe. Then suddenly the telephone buzzer in my writing-room broke the stillness of the early evening. Whereupon Mr Sponge started to bark furiously as though he guessed that this wasn't just another incoming call, this was a question either of a reprieve for life, or a long, long exile.

As I raised the receiver, he gazed up at me on his haunches, with the dark alchemy of a dog's eyes. Absurdly, it was reassuring to have him beside me at this moment. At least he believes in me, I told myself, as once again that now familiar voice which I had first heard in my Nassau bedroom came to me as clearly, as persuasively, as though its owner was standing at my side. No secretarial link, no preliminaries.

'Are you there, Godfrey?'

Yes I was there, waiting.

'Well, I have read your page that should have gone in last Sunday. And it's capital, capital. It is exactly the kind of writing I intended you to do for us. So it will go in next Sunday, and you can stop worrying. I am telling Robertson in the morning. Good-bye to yer.'

He had rung off before I could speak one word of gratitude, of overflowing relief, that I should have been vindicated. E. J. Robertson was the head of the managerial side of the organization, the most powerful figure under Lord Beaverbrook; a good and just man, in whose presence I had felt completely at ease from the start, as I did with Tom Blackburn, who was in due course to take his place, and who at that time was the manager in charge of *The Sunday Express*. Consequently, we came into frequent contact but never conflict. A north-countryman, by upbringing so much less inhibited than most of those who are born in the south of England, Tom Blackburn, with his air of a lay preacher, right from the start seemed to understand what I was trying to do; like 'Young Max' – as he was affectionately known, though today he has taken over his father's status and authority – and my regard for them both has only increased with the years. As it has, too, when I count up the many imaginative kindnesses that I received from 'Robby' himself – E. J. Robertson – who has provided a now legendary example of unwavering, unquestioning loyalty to the boss such as has never been surpassed.

That I was safe now if Mr Robertson's aid had been invoked, was the uppermost thought in my mind as I dashed out into the garden to tell my mother my news. Slowly she straightened her back, pushing back a strand of silky hair from her forehead, her face pink and smudged from her exertions. As I bent excitedly over her, it came back to me how I had once heard her remark to someone to whom she was showing her roses, 'I have always been the garden boy, and though my hair has grown white, I have never been given promotion.'

'You did the right thing,' she said quietly, though there was no answering note of triumph in her voice. For she recognized that this was not a triumph but simply a breathing space, another chance to prove myself. 'Things will not be easy for you in the office,' she could not help reminding me.

I tried not to contemplate that side of the sequel. I could so easily have found myself entirely in the wilderness, and I hadn't. Instead, I had received this strong and authoritative encouragement to continue writing on the kind of subjects that lit my own imagination. Such as a visit I paid soon afterwards to the studio of Dora Gordine, the sculptress who lived in a red-brick house with an unfruitful air from the outside, on Kingston Hill.

The atmosphere was transformed the moment one was inside and entered the embracing studio with one wall of windows looking out on to Richmond Park. I spent an enchanted afternoon, and at the end of my tour I found myself returning again and again to the head of a Chinese girl raised on a plinth, an exquisite creation, her eyes gazing downwards, with veiled lashes, as though she was dreaming away eternity.

After a silence of contemplation, I turned to my hostess beside me and exclaimed: 'If I could afford an example of your work, that is the head that I would love to possess.'

'I am afraid this is only a cast, the original has gone to a museum,' its creator replied. However, she did not move on, for she had something to tell me which was to irradiate my consciousness for a long time afterwards.

One Saturday morning, Dora Gordine had been shopping in Selfridge's. When she gave her name and address for her purchases to be delivered, the girl behind the counter, in a sudden rush of recognition, looked up from her account book, her own face glowing.

'Are you *really* Dora Gordine? Oh, how wonderful to meet you. I have seen your work in the Tate, and have admired it so much. I often go there on a Saturday afternoon.'

They were no longer customer and shop-assistant, but two fellow creatures sharing a common interest. Touched by her enthusiasm, the sculptress, whose name is renowned in art circles all over the world, suggested that it would please her very much if one Saturday afternoon, for a change, her admirer would come and see all her own current work in her studio on Kingston Hill.

So her other guest had done exactly what I had done; climbed the long hill and turned in at the gate of that uncompromisingly modern building; walked slowly round the lofty colourful room with its backcloth frame of the oaks and beeches of the park, until again, as in my case, she came to a final stop in front of the head of the unknown Chinese girl.

But from this visitor's lips came no expressed longing to possess it; no easy, gushing words of admiration; instead, she simply stood there, without speaking for a long time, and then having quietly thanked her hostess, went away.

Miss Gordine did not hear from her admirer for a year. In fact she had forgotten all about that chance encounter until one morning a registered letter arrived and out of the envelope poured on to the table a hundred pound notes. These the recipient counted with wonder and in bewilderment, after reading the enclosed note, which said:

'If that head of the Chinese girl has not been sold, would the enclosed be sufficient for it? I have been unable to get it out of my mind.'

As she read this, the creator of that work of art had exactly the same reactions as my own; a clear picture of what that hundred pounds represented; all the sacrifices and privations that must have been starkly adhered to to achieve the saving of such a sum from her inevitably modest weekly pay packet. Going without all treats, all theatre and concert tickets, cutting down on make-up, on visits to the hairdresser, on the buying of new clothes. A summer holiday had, doubtless, been surrendered, too. All in pursuit of a vision, and equally, in order to keep faith with herself. Because here was someone who believed that there was more to the meaning of life than being compelled to get up in her bed-sitting room each morning, as soon as her alarm clock woke her, strap-hanging in the Tube to work, coping all day as best she could with fractious customers, and then the return journey in the rush hour, wearing the protective armour of a robot, her individuality and her youth slowly, inexorably, crushed out of her.

At once, Dora Gordine wrote back, returning the hundred pounds, explaining that the original of the head had now gone to a museum and that she only had casts of it left in her possession. 'But I will gladly send you a cast, if you will accept it, as a present,' she ended up.

Once again came back the hundred pound notes, which represented in the sender's creed not what she had had to give up, but instead, what she had achieved; freedom for her imagination, a glimpse of all the beauty there is in the world, to be epitomized hereafter for her by that particular example of the sculptor's art. She herself expressed her inmost feelings like this:

'Thank you very much. The cast will mean just as much to me. You see, I wasn't buying the head. I had earned it.'

When he read this modern parable on my page, Lord Beaverbrook sent me one of his congratulatory telegrams. On the other hand, I never was to learn what my editor's reaction to this particular contribution was since I had been virtually 'sent to Coventry' inside the office, on the editorial side, for having sneaked to the Headmaster. I am not complaining about that now. On the contrary, gazing back today through the right end of the telescope at that plateau in my development as a writer, I am far more sympathetic towards John Gordon's dilemma than my own. After all, every editor carries the final responsibility concerning the complete contents of his paper or magazine. It can be a very hard and frightening burden. In consequence, between the majority of editors and their contributors, seeking the same right of expression as one has in a book, there comes into being an almost inevitable love-hate relationship which is in a constant state of flux. Therefore, it was with special pleasure that I received an invitation to sit at the high table at the dinner given to celebrate the seventy-fifth birthday of surely one of the most successful Scots ever to spend his days south of the Border. In the Stationers' Hall that December evening, there were many other fellow editors standing to their feet as the guest of honour was piped to his own seat, and when at the end of the party I was, to my complete surprise, called upon to add my own memories of the days when I had been a member of John Gordon's team, I was glad to have this chance at last to thank him, publicly, for the influence he was to have little by little, during those five years, on my emerging craftsmanship. I was persuaded to cut down on the frills, to adhere more rigorously to the story line.

This training, if absorbed at first almost against my will, was to be of enormous benefit to me at a later date, when I became a war correspondent. Now at last both editor and contributor spoke and wrote the same language, and there was mutual respect and understanding between us; indeed, on my side, lasting admiration. For I appreciate that my editor at that time, with his tremendously developed news sense, saw further ahead than I did, and more clearly. Thus his attitude as to what was sufficiently important to go into his paper was subconsciously coloured by his increasing awareness that war was inevitable. Whereas I, like so many others, still shied away from even such direct warnings as I had received on the return journey from South America.

By a curious chance the week that Hitler succeeded in annexing the Sudetenland, while the rest of Europe stood impotently by, wondering who the next victim would be, I was the member of a large house party at Eaton, the Cheshire home of Bendor Westminster. A tennis tournament among the thirty guests had been arranged, and all our battles, all our rivalry, were contained within the perimeter of the covered court. In the end, I carried off second prize in partnership with that indefatigable retriever, Phyllis Satterthwaite, and was presented by my host with a silver cigarette box. It was the last tennis prize I was ever to win. Time was running out, though I tried not to admit it. Surrendering myself instead to a kind of Lucullan state of luxury that scarcely exists any longer in England, I sought reassurance from the setting at dinner each night, where the polished table, reflecting the magnificent gold and silver ornaments, with the orchids from the Eaton hot-houses as decoration in the centre, matched the splendour and poise of the women guests like Doreen Linlithgow*, later to take her place in the long line of India's Vicereines, and Serena James† one of Ursie's childhood friends, and herself radiantly possessed of the same traditional English skin and romantic, heart-shaped face.

It was to Serena's own home, in the other Richmond from my childhood, this one set amid the Yorkshire Dales, that I was gratefully to turn for refuge five summers later, when I was discharged from the Meanskirk Hospital. Undisturbed by conscience or command, idle at last, I spent long, delicious, recuperative hours lazing in the gardens of St Nicholas, whose green lawns and yew hedges became for me a kind of sanctuary, so blessed a contrast to the baleful waters of the Arctic.

Already that autumn of 1938, at the moment when others were standing to attention on Armistice Sunday at the Cenotaph, I had my own preview of what happens after the marching to the band and the waving of the flags is over. I accompanied an

* Doreen, Marchioness of Linlithgow.
† Lady Serena James.

elderly couple, whose home was in Greenhow Street, Walkley, outside Sheffield, on a pilgrimage arranged by the Salvation Army, to their son's grave in Flanders. Mr Shillito had been an upholsterer in his day, and told me proudly how he had had a hand in the making of the memorial chair that had been presented by his city to King Edward VII. Now he and his wife had one deep longing left, to see with their own eyes the permanent slab of stone that had been set up in place of the original wooden cross. Although they were existing on their old age pension, plus the seven-and-twopence they received each week as a pension for their son who had been killed at the age of twenty-two, some-how they had managed to save threepence-halfpenny, sixty-five times over, for the number of letters that could be inscribed on the new headstone. They had chosen:

He passed out of our sight by the path of duty and self-sacrifice. From all at home.

This was in the June of 1918. Afterwards, their son's special mate came to see the Shillitos, on his next leave, and tried to comfort them in his own fashion. Len had had a proper military funeral, with four shining black horses to carry him. When, not knowing what to say, I asked the mother if she had a picture of her boy to show me, and she took the one she always carried out of her bag, I saw that the photograph had been tinted. At the same moment, she explained, almost apologetically, 'I am afraid the colour has faded a little.' What struck me most, the observer, who had himself been a small boy with a bellyache, in bed at his preparatory school, on the day the First Armistice had been declared, was how unscarred by life the face in the faded picture seemed to be. As though there had not been time for anything to happen to him except death.

The chaplain and the boy's lieutenant also wrote to the mother, and both used almost identical words. 'Len was a very willing and able fellow, and such men are hard to replace. Indeed, we can't replace them.' Except with other corpses, spreadeagled against the barbed wire, I found myself thinking, as the mother repeated, one felt for the thousandth time, 'You couldn't have nicer words than that, could you?'

Passing from cemetery to cemetery, I seemed to age until I was as bowed down as the two elderly people at my side. Each hour I became increasingly aware of just how many other letters of condolence must have been written, and the utter futility of it all. My horror and hatred of war that had found protesting expression in such passionate phrases as 'It is surely better to live for one's country than to die for her,' came back to mock me. 'The pen is mightier than the sword.' Was it? Was it? Not only were past events closing in on me but equally I was menaced by the threats of what lay ahead.

After we had visited the small cemetery at Couen, where Len Shillito himself is buried, in the company of 58 soldiers of the Lancashire Regiment, 342 from the United Kingdom, 2 from Canada, 4 from New Zealand, and one Marine, we passed, in contrast, an enormous German burial ground. Thirty-five thousand black crosses, two bodies lying head to head for each cross, and the crosses themselves pitch-scarred as though at some moment there had been a great cleansing fire. It was then that Len's mother made her only reference to those on the other side of the barbed wire. 'I don't believe that they were as black as they are painted. I didn't believe it even at the time,' she said.

I could only marvel at her forbearance and her natural dignity, in the same way as I had done when she had knelt and placed the wreath that she had brought on her son's grave, and Mr Shillito had added a piece of spa stone to prevent the wreath blowing away in the timeless wind. 'I do hope they will let it be,' she said, in her soft and gentle voice. Gazing up from her knees at the inscription itself, she added, 'It's only in small type, but I'm sure the dear boy would understand.'

A few paces away there was another stone inscribed 'J. Donoghue.' Len's mother gave a little cry when she read it, for the name had a kind of poignant coincidence for her. That had been the name of Len's girl. No, they were not actually engaged, but she knew and approved that Len was courting, and on the evening that she first heard of her son's death, and the dreaded telegram came from the War Office, she had sent for her at once. Then the two women had sat together, watching the fire die down in the grate.

'Len's girl is happily married now, I'm glad to say,' Mrs Shillito told me, 'and we have been to stay with her. On her dresser she has the same picture of Len as I always carry with me. The one that I showed you, Mr Winn.'

On the journey back to Arras, the mother kept her hands

tightly closed on her knees. I touched one and it was so cold, I had to break the silence to say: Would she not put on her gloves? She shook her head. Then, after a little while, she spoke her thoughts aloud.

'I don't think I should have minded so much if Len had been married, because then the chief part of him would have belonged to his wife. But my dear boy was all mine, though no doubt if he had come back he would have had children of his own now, like his brother. Billy has two boys, both fair like their uncle. Isn't that strange, considering their father is so dark? When my own two boys were kiddies, all the neighbours used to stop me in the street and compliment me on my two beautiful sons.'

Drogo Montagu, then married to Lord Beaverbrook's daughter Janet, had come with me to take the pictures for my page. I was very grateful to him. For the results, in their evocation of the father with his white hair and the mien of a good craftsman, and his wife in her dark coat and felt hat, and rubbed fur tippet around her throat, exactly matched the simplicity of the text. I had rightly left it to the father and the mother to speak for such a multitude of other parents of their generation beside themselves. Drogo, himself, already enrolled as a week-end flyer in the Auxiliary Air Force, was destined to be one of the early casualties, in the next war to end all wars, even before the Battle of Britain had fully commenced. When I sadly heard the news of his death in the skies, I saw again our little group, with the Salvation Army major, the only one in uniform, standing on Vimy Ridge. Beside the Canadian Memorial of the mourning mother, gazing down at what was once the trenches where month after month the Germans and ourselves and our allies checkmated each other, in grim attrition, and at such a cost. It was then that the spirit of the living mother, so small and frail beside the huge counterpart in stone, cried out in protesting wonder:

'Why, they were so close, they could have talked to each other.'

*   *   *

The talking went on and on. Pro-Munich talk, anti-Munich talk, desperate fears only half-expressed countered by foolish waves of escapist optimism, without firm foundation, straws of hope clutched at in the fading daylight of that final winter. After

Mr Chamberlain returned from Berchtesgaden with his umbrella still unfurled, the sandbags were removed once more from Hyde Park, and we continued with the pretence, the charade, as best we could. I remember one early December day, lunching at Gwen Melchett's* Palladian house in Smith Square, with its marble hall and superb collection of modern pictures, reminding me of the days when I had my first introduction to that kind of life, in the Portman Square home of the Courtaulds. Among the party of *chic* scented women and MP's on their way to the afternoon sitting at the House, there was an elder statesman with a leonine head set on his wide shoulders, who, at the coffee stage, suddenly cut across the cackle of Christmas plans, and theatres, and winter sports, to embark upon a prophetic speech of warning. There was no accommodation that could be made with Hitler, no compromise that would provide any lasting security, with honour or without. It was only a question of a few months before the ultimatum that would swallow up all ultimatums.

Winston Churchill's fellow guests shifted uneasily in their chairs. They glanced at their wrist-watches. They made excuses. Fittings for clothes, an appointment with the hairdresser, or the dentist, Christmas presents to be bought, a committee meeting in the House at three. One by one they stole away, there was a general, guilty exodus, until only I and my hostess were left with that brooding, prophetic figure, his hand round the stem of his empty brandy glass.

I was to see Winston Churchill again that winter when, early in the New Year, still pursuing the false image of the phoney peace, I went to Monte Carlo and had beginner's luck at the tables. Dining one night on board Bendor Westminster's yacht, which had its accustomed berth in the harbour, all his party were presented with a thousand-franc note with which to have a flutter, while our host stalked majestically to the highest baccarat table to take on once again, for the entertainment of the spectators, as much as for his own, the reigning members of the Greek Syndicate.

In contrast, I cautiously took a seat at the most modest of the chemmy tables. Here to my delighted astonishment, my first bank ran three times before I passed it, and soon the pile of chips stacked in front of me began to multiply to such an extent that

* Gwen, Lady Melchett.

I was recklessly calling out 'Banco', like an old-timer. At midnight I got up winning a hundred pounds, and have never chanced my luck at any form of gambling since. In the morning, as soon as the shops on the terrace outside the Hôtel de Paris, where I was staying, were open, I celebrated my victory by spending most of my windfall on a pair of ruby and gold cuff-links from Van Cleef, which I still wear occasionally as a reminder that to challenge Fate once is usually enough. Or so I chose to tell myself whenever during the rest of my stay I visited the Rooms for an hour before dinner. Often I would come across that same isolated figure, in the dark serge suit and blue spotted bow tie, playing for the kind of small stakes such as I had done, with the usual crowd of the hangers-on at the Sporting Club milling indifferently round his table.

Winston Churchill was killing time, a prophet in the wilderness, at that moment; yet he was to be acclaimed scarcely more than a year later as Champion of Civilization, the saviour of the free peoples of the world. Surely the most fantastic *volte-face* in the whole of History. His parliamentary colleagues had mostly crossed him off as a spent force, now they eagerly took each their own ration of courage and hope from his hands, while we all alike marvelled at his magnanimity. Even today, looking back on our collective indifference, I feel a sense of personal shame that we could have been so blind and so unheedful. Though, at least, I had the sense to ignore the soundings that came to me through the German Embassy in London in regard to an exclusive interview with the Fuehrer, aware at once that I was simply being wooed and flattered into becoming one more instrument for Nazi propaganda.

For the same reason, I refused instinctively an invitation to the Nuremberg Games that summer, choosing to visit instead the two Butlin Camps then in existence, at Skegness and Clacton. Although still foolishly derided by those who have never taken the trouble to examine at close hand this unique kind of provision for mass holiday accommodation and entertainment, I had no doubts in proclaiming in print my own initial approval. Moreover, my reactions were completely endorsed by someone who was destined to achieve a new stature herself through the challenge of war. Then when it was over at last and we were all out of uniform again – standing at ease, instead of marching in step – at her own

With Mr Sponge the
First, outside the
writing room at Esher.
Photo: Alfred Furness

Dictating to my
secretary, Miss Ena
Restall. *Photo:
Sport and General*

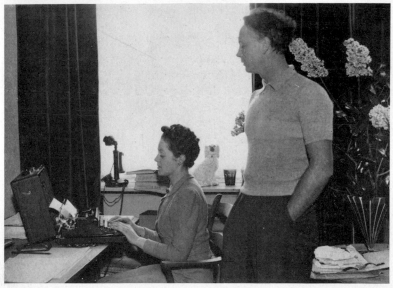

The last picture of my mother in her flat in Eaton Square. *Photo: Keystone Press Agency*

request I took Edwina Mountbatten* to the latest addition to the Butlin empire at Filey. After immersing herself for two long days, including visits to the kitchens and crèches, in every branch of this form of co-existence where six thousand people at a time are able to spend their holidays in unruffled if gregarious harmony, this woman who had begun her own life with the handicap of inheriting her grandfather's millions, wrote both to me and to the man who had started his own career with one stall, on the front at Skegness, to express her unqualified enthusiasm, emphasizing that she considered that what had originally been a pioneer experiment had consolidated itself into one of the most satisfying social services of the age.

I was so intrigued after my own first visit that I returned a second time during that August of 1939, and on this occasion was persuaded by my host, Billy Butlin, to address a vast concourse of the campers, in the open, beside the swimming pool at Skegness. Inevitably, many of my audience who had booked for a fortnight, and paid their deposits much earlier in the year, were now wondering with increasing alarm whether they would be allowed to have their money's-worth, in peace. I tried, foolishly, to allay their fears, and to stifle any undercurrents of panic, induced by each morning's fresh headlines, by employing at one moment what seemed an encouraging simile from Nature. It had been a louring afternoon, with the threat of rain never far distant, but as I warmed towards my peroration, suddenly, as though in confirmation, a glimpse of blue sky, the size of a tablecloth, appeared. It wasn't much, but just sufficient for me to point dramatically upwards. 'Look at that patch of blue,' I cried. 'Let us take heart from that, let us regard it as a symbol that the clouds *are* going to clear for us all.'

My comparison was received with a spontaneous outburst of applause. However in the months ahead, especially when the camp itself was taken over as a training depot for naval recruits, and re-named *HMS Royal Arthur,* I sometimes found myself wondering how many of my audience that afternoon were now upbraiding me for having engendered a mood of false optimism. If it is not too late to apologize, I do so now. At any rate, it was almost my last effort to keep up my own spirits as well as those of my listeners. The next Sunday I had been booked to appear by Jack

* Countess Mountbatten of Burma.

Hylton in a *Youth Takes a Bow* concert, at Felixstowe. But on this occasion I left it to the extremely professional compère of the show, Bryan Michie, to allay, somehow, the inevitable anxieties of those who were on the other side of the footlights, by giving such a build-up to his discoveries in turn, that these youngsters would really believe in themselves and perform like the stars of tomorrow. Which one of them, Ernie Wise, a diminutive lad with fair hair, was in due course to become. For today, the clowning of Morecambe and Wise is a sell-out at any box office.

Nevertheless, the best performance that evening was given by Bryan himself, whose outsize, beaming figure and disarming manner somehow succeeded in coaxing the audience into a mood of euphoria. He even triumphed in making the young soprano who sang *One Fine Day* off-key, sound in his introduction like a budding Galli Curci. It was only on our return journey to London, after midnight, that we both began to wilt. Any temporary elation we had felt at the success of the show against considerable odds now swiftly evaporated as we became uneasy spectators of an utterly different kind of parade.

As we left the coast behind, there came towards us what seemed to be an endless succession of army vehicles, trucks and vans, crudely and hastily camouflaged. Sometimes the lorries were so large, so menacing, that our own car had to draw in to one side of the road to allow the implacable procession to rumble past us. Where were they bound in the small hours of this Monday morning? To planned vantage points for a speedy transference across the Channel? If, if. All was dim surmise. We were too tired, too depressed to talk much. The show, all the make-believe, was over. Moreover, I think we both were finally aware in our hearts, as though we had unexpectedly been presented with a secret password, that here, in the darkness, was the exact reverse of my unwise references to patches of blue sky, that this first of so many ensuing cavalcades represented the inexorable march of events, from which there was no turning back, no escape for any of us now.

The ultimate week of watching for portents and omens was upon us, so that after an increasing crop of rumours and counter-rumours, it was almost a relief, like two pains counteracting each other, to have to accept that all our secret fears had come to a climax of realization. At that moment, on the next Sunday morning, when almost immediately after the Prime Minister's radio speech the sirens sounded throughout the metropolis, I was in Brixton, of all places, trying out a second-hand motor-cycle. It was a fruitful moment for such gambits. Everyone had their own. This was mine, this way I would save petrol, I would stay mobile, I had decided, ignoring the fact that I had never used this form of locomotion in my life before. In consequence, at the first sound of that wailing of the banshee, soon to become only too familiar, I looked up, startled and nervous, at the sky that I half-expected to be black with enemy bombers, and promptly fell off into the gutter. In the long silence that followed, I was ignominiously picked up and dusted down by the would-be vendor. But now my impulse seemed silly and impractical, and I shook my head, thankful to climb into my comfortable car and drive back through the portentously deserted streets. I should have gone home to Esher for my Sunday lunch, but I felt I could not face the meal seated opposite my mother, with my mind in a jumble as to what was my best way of trying to serve my country. So that it was late afternoon before my car turned the corner into Broom Close, where for once I hardly acknowledged the sentinel figure of Mr Sponge, waiting patiently on the grassy verge for his master's return.

I did not have to ask him where I should find his mistress. At the low sill of my mother's sitting-room, I paused instinctively before stepping over it into the garden, not so much to brace myself for what was to come as to capture for ever after in my mind the scene that was framed between the wide windows.

Perhaps to point the folly of mankind, it had turned into a golden afternoon. Slowly I walked towards her up the grass path beside the herbaceous border that we had weeded together the day that I had awaited the verdict of my boss. How unimportant that seemed now beside the overriding crisis in all our fortunes. All the same, my mind went on automatically recording the details, the small pleasures belonging to yesterday. The delphiniums that had made a particularly good show were over, together with the madonna lilies, and the high clumps of anchusa that were the very blue of heaven. Now it was the turn of the dahlias, with their faint emanation of autumnal decay, and the michaelmas daisies, and then another summer's pageant would once again pass by. And next spring? In a movement that was at once dear to me, and yet at this moment too cruelly familiar, my mother got up slowly from what had become as much a praying mat as a weeding mat during the long summer afternoon, and pushed back the hair out of her eyes. She was wearing a pink cotton dress that was the colour of the one that she had chosen that day when my school chum had arrived in his family chariot, with his own mother shrouded in a motoring veil, to carry me off. Mine had seemed that morning so undefeatable, so eternally young, as she had stood with the bunch of freshly-picked roses in her arms; whereas now, with a shock as though seeing her again after a long time, I could not help noticing that she had suddenly sagged, looking her age, a widow in her sixties with the privations and the dangers of a very different kind of war this time, ahead of her. I wanted to touch her cheek, but she did not give it to me to kiss. At first, we were like strangers, in our own garden.

'So it was a false alarm,' she said.

'Yes, I was at Brixton when it happened.' Desperately seeking to break down the barriers of self-protection raised between us, I started to tell her about the episode of the motor-bike. Alas it didn't seem either funny or real any longer, and even to myself my voice took on the too bright, too brittle note of a small-time comedian trying to make contact with a first house on a Monday night.

Her family news had so much more meaning than mine.

'Joyce rang me as soon as the All Clear sounded, telling me that I wasn't to worry. I assured her I was quite all right. I was in church when it happened. Rodger was at the Admiralty.'

'At the Admiralty?' I echoed.

'He enrolled there on Friday. He offered his services a year ago, at the time of Munich. He always said that war was inevitable. And he was right.'

'What is he going to do at the Admiralty?' I asked.

'Oh, I would never question him, any more than I would about one of his cases. I am afraid it will mean a big financial difference, though, to him and Joyce, and with his leg he would never have been called up, but all that matters to him is that he will be in the company of naval men at last. You know how he always wanted that, and now it has come true. I am so thankful for his sake.'

Her voice soared on a note of pure joy. She was remembering the days when she had brought him his Latin and his history books in bed, and had had to explain that he would not now be able to follow in his grandfather's footsteps at sea. This was the next best thing, though it had taken a long time to happen. Later, so successful was my brother to be at his chosen war work that soon he was to discard his civilian clothes and be given naval rank, first that of Commander, then promoted to be a four-ringed Captain, a unique privilege in the RNVR; ending up by being made a Commander of the Order of the British Empire, Military Division, for his services, especially in tracking down the U-boats, the implacable deductions of a supremely logical brain, in the secret underground room, where the progress of every ship, every convoy, was plotted on the wall. Including the ill-fated one* I found myself by chance in on my way to Russia in the summer of 1942.

The last moment I was able to communicate with home was in a hurried note scribbled from the dockside of Belfast, before *HMS Pozarica* sailed for an unknown destination. For my mother, a three-months' silence followed, broken one day by a call from a Fleet Street Photographic Agency. Could they come down and take some pictures of the garden?

'But my son, Godfrey, is away at sea,' my mother explained.

'Yes, we know, but it is pictures of you yourself that we would like to have in stock.'

It only transpired why when, not realizing how remote my mother's life was from the one that her son had led, the photographer made a sympathetic reference to the strong rumour that was current in the street where once I had worked in peacetime, that I was missing, believed lost, at sea.

Even then my mother's stockade of stoicism did not crumble; she told no one till long afterwards, because she refused to believe it. All the same, she could not bring herself to ask her other son whether he could reassure her as to what had happened to *HMS Pozarica*. While he, in his turn with the double reticence of the lawyer turned naval intelligence officer, would never have considered volunteering the information that my ship had at last reached temporary asylum against a wharf outside Archangel.

All this had still to happen, was a long way off, hidden from

* See the author's *P.Q.17.*

us both by the far horizon. What mattered now, what only mattered now, was the immediate future.

'Rodger said he imagined you would be going to the Ministry of Information,' my mother said, with a note of interrogation in her voice.

A desk job at the Ministry of Information. It was unthinkable. 'No, no,' I burst out, only conscious of the full fury of my reactions when I started to walk away towards the house. She did not call after me, she did not follow me, so that I found temporary asylum in my writing-room, where the Epstein watercolour of scarlet peonies on the white wall, one of the first pictures I had acquired in my growing collection, reminded me like the garden outside of that other life, which would never, at least for a long time, be quite the same again.

If not the Ministry of Information, or some other pen-pushing occupation, churning out propaganda bumf, what was I to do? I had no illusions about myself as a gallant soldier, or even an umprotesting footslogger, since when I had been an enforced member of the Hereford School OTC I was the boob of the platoon, my puttees always coming down, unable to acquire sufficient military sense even to 'present arms' properly. One, two, three, crash bang. So that on numerous occasions I was shame-facedly hauled out in front of the rest of the platoon, for a dressing-down from our OTC commander, so immaculate himself, with his natty cane.

Again, I was for ever turning left, perhaps because I was so hopelessly left-handed, when the bawled order was 'Right.' And now how I longed to take the right course, to be of some positive use but my mind was a blank as to where to turn for help for guidance. Offer my services, join up, in what? All my life I had been aware of the gulf, in intellect, in achievement, between my brother and myself, but never more so than at this moment. Despite his early infirmities everything had fallen into place for him while I only became more conscious of my physiological handicaps, my inherent weaknesses, as the years went by. Would it always be so?

I have no idea how long I sat there in the winged armchair that my mother had given me on my twenty-first birthday, gazing out at the great beech tree in the field beyond the lawns that always gave me the spurious though pleasant sensation of being

right in the country. Wasn't that where my mother should transfer herself for the Duration? To some small village, say, in
Worcestershire, immune from the bombing of London and its
surrounding corridors when it came as at any moment it surely
would.

At once, the shifting of the load of my thoughts, to my anxiety
for her rather than for myself, brought me comfort, even a sort
of strength. Thus, when the door opened at last, it was my first
question, not an attack mounted as a counter-defence, but simply
because she mattered more to me than all the rest of the world
put together.

'What are you going to do yourself?' I asked.

She had changed from her cotton working garb into a silk
dress. I could smell the *Numéro Cinq* Molyneux perfume I
always gave her for her birthday. She stood there, in the doorway, with the decanter of sherry on the silver tray that had
belonged to Granny Rodgers, and a single glass. For her it was
the ultimate capitulation to offer me an alcoholic drink, and I
was stirred in my belly.

'What are you going to do?' I repeated.

'I am going to stay here, of course.'

'You hadn't thought of shutting up the house, and evacuating
yourself?'

'This is my home,' I noticed that she no longer said 'our home',
as though she had already accepted in her mind that from now
on I would only be a transient visitor, on a week-end's pass from
who knew where.

'I could not bear to sleep for any length of time in any other
bed than my own,' she added firmly. Despite the fact that it had
been cut in half? How she must be thinking of Dad today, I
told myself, longing for his reassuring presence instead of my
own in this room. My sense of inadequacy returned with a rush,
as she continued.

'I have talked it over with Auntie Ethel. She is staying
at Mortlake and that is bang next door to the river, for as you
know, Uncle Ernest's brewery overlooks the finishing post of the
Oxford and Cambridge Race, and they say that enemy aircraft
will use the river as their guide. But where else could we go?
Ethel cannot leave Uncle Ernest or Mollie, and Uncle Ernest
won't leave his beloved brewery. And they are right. After all,

it would be different if we were all small children, to be evacuated like parcels, labelled to some such village as Winchcombe, where Auntie Violet used to have her lodgings.'

And I asked her to send you the ten shillings, instead of keeping it myself, I thought, because you were on a number 3 tour, existing in the cheapest possible digs, with an outside lavatory and no bathroom. All the past welled up in me, all that she had survived, that we had both, in a way, survived. Perhaps what was coming would not be any worse. My mood changed, for the first time I felt at ease that afternoon, as I took the glass of sherry she had poured out for me, like a tribal libation.

'I have joined the WVS,' she told me, looking almost young again, 'and there will be lots for me to do, I am sure. To keep busy, that's the best thing. I have told my bank manager, who's in Civil Defence, that they can have the field for allotments, if they like. In the last war there was a very popular slogan, "Dig for Victory." Ethel and I were reminding each other – she rang me up, too, after the All Clear – of the night we saw Doris Keane in *Romance,* such a thrilling evening it was, because it was the night the zeppelin came over London and we weren't allowed to leave the theatre at the end of the performance, for ages.'

When I did not answer, thinking how at least I was lucky in that respect, I would not have to struggle through this war, comparing it all the time with the other one, she came to what had been uppermost in her mind.

'I would like to keep my borders, if at all possible, and it is not considered unpatriotic. I always think the second crop of the roses is even more beautiful than the first. They seem to have all the sunshine of the summer in their petals.'

Had she read that somewhere? Did it come from her heart?

Yes, it came from her heart, like the gesture that she would not make until we were in the hall and she knew that I was not going to stay for supper. Instead, I was collecting a mass of unnecessary things, as though I was going on a long journey, instead of simply returning to my flat, filled with other question marks, in Ebury Street.

'Have you got your gas mask?'

It was the first time she had ever asked that; usually it was, Had I got all the books I needed, my notes, my scribblings, my

typewriter, my brief case. Not my gas mask. 'Yes, it's in the car,'
I said, getting rid of as much irritation as I could in my voice
for my futile civilian gas mask that I hadn't the least idea how
to use.

'You'll let me know where you are, and what you are doing,'
she said, almost pleadingly, and before I could explain that I
wasn't going anywhere, doing anything, she had put up both
hands to my shoulders, as though to keep me there with her a
little longer. In turn, I bent and did something I had not done
since I was a small boy, leaning up to say good night from my
bed in the nursery at Cherrycroft. I kissed her on the lips, leaning down towards her, wrapping my arms about her like a cloak,
whispering over and over again, 'I'll try not to let you down, I
promise. I'll try to march in step, somehow.' Though I doubt if
she heard what I was saying, because my voice must have been
muffled above her head.

Later, I could not understand, since it was a brilliant evening,
why there should be a blur on the windscreen of my car, as I
turned out of the Close, not daring to look back at that waving
figure, with the small white blob at her feet. Automatically, as
I joined the returning Sunday procession of cars in Esher High
Street, I switched on my windscreen wiper. Still the view ahead
remained obstinately clouded, until it came to me at last how
stupid I was, since I should have been reaching in my pocket for
a handkerchief, instead.

I could not bear the accusing silence of my flat, but I did not
like to ring up any of my friends, feeling an intruder at that
moment when everyone else's ordered existence was equally being
disrupted. Even Jack was on duty at the Foreign Office, roped
in as an extra telegram decoder, a useful asset he had acquired
during a brief spell as an honorary attaché at the British Embassy
in Lisbon. How strange that at last he should be busier, more
usefully employed, than I was, and that stabbing knowledge made
it unbearable for me to sit there any longer, listening to a continuous series of bulletins, of one sort and another, on the radio,
read out in the self-important voices of the announcers who had
over-night come into their own.

In the end, I found myself making for Hyde Park, and the
magnet of Marble Arch, where I joined the fringe of the eddying
pools round the usual incongruous assortment of speakers who

were having a field day. The first banner raised aloft that caught my eye had the warning words in large capitals, 'PREPARE FOR THE END'. It was a relief, after a few moments, to discover that the orator, an old regular with a straggling grey beard, was referring yet once again to the end of the world. In consequence, his fiery denunciation of our sins sounded almost cheerful and humorous beside the other far more convincing trumpet of doom which had sounded in our ears that morning.

After a time, bored by the interruptions from a persistent heckler, who was more concerned with settling ' 'Itler's little old 'ash before Christmas' – this had an ominously familiar ring – I extricated myself from my vicarious attachment to the crowds and moved away to find a quiet seat. As though by instinct, impelled perhaps by some motivation from my sub-consciousness, I discovered with a shock of surprise that my feet had led me to that same bench on which I had sat the first Sunday evening of my baptism in London; a barn-storming youth of sixteen, dumped in a nearby hostel, longing for just one companion on the same wave-length as myself.

Nearly fifteen years had passed. I had seen so much, listened and recorded many stories that were, indeed, far stranger than fiction. I had encountered the famous and the infamous, the noble ones and the unknown. On my own part, I had achieved much by material standards, and yet, in other ways, so little. How brief, how infirm for me had been the glory. The sense of isolation that is with us all from the moment we are born could not be banished, especially at this moment, although surely if the much-quoted phrase about the greater fellowship of man meant anything at all, I would encounter many examples of such communion in the months and years ahead. To that I must cling, for that I must hope, in whatever way came to hand, to warrant my own entry into that fellowship, to earn in time, perhaps, an utterly different kind of recognition.

Meanwhile, I must never allow myself to whine, now that I was back at the beginning again.

The Mill House
Falmer
Sussex
Jan:–Dec: 1966

INDEX

References in **bold** type are to illustrations